# SEÁN MO...
# IN HIS OWN WORDS

His Memoir of the
Irish War of Independence
with a selection of speeches and poems

Manuscript typeset by Joe Keenan

Cover Design: Timothy Lane

Aubane Historical Society
Aubane
Millstreet
Co. Cork

| | |
|---|---|
| Capture / Prison / Trial | 130 |
| Cork Detention Barracks / Spike Island | 137 |
| The Truce | 142 |
| **Annex 1** *"A fhile chirt ghéir"* by Eoghan Ruadh Ó Súilleabháin | 146 |
| **Annex 2** "Can anybody tell me where did General Lucas go?" (Anonymous) | 148 |
| **Annex 3** Moylan's contribution to debates in the 2nd Dáil | 149 |
| **Annex 4** A poetic exchange with a Blueshirt - Ned Buckley of Knocknagree | 153 |
| **Annex 5** Irish America (Speech at the Mansion House, 12 February 1946, *The Capuchin Annual* 1946) | 158 |
| **Annex 6** Updated Index of Contributors to Bureau of Military History | 172 |
| **Index to Moylan's Statement** | 190 |
| **Epilogue**: Brendan Clifford | 195 |
| **Postscript to Second Edition**: Brendan Clifford | 224 |

# Introduction

This book consists of the statement made by Seán Moylan to the Bureau of Military History (BMH) on 6th May 1953. The Bureau was set up by the de Valera Government in 1947 with the aim of getting participants in the War of Independence to record their own accounts of involvement in that war. In the course of about 10 years written accounts were taken from nearly 1,800 people, along with other material. It was originally to be opened after 25 years when it was assumed all concerned would be dead but the opening was put off a number of times and finally opened by the Taoiseach on 11 March 2003.

Moylan's contribution seems to have been made available to others besides the Bureau and has been used by a number of historians in recent years. It is a great pity that this account has not already been made available to the general public and this is an effort to rectify that situation. It is also a great pity that there is no full biography of him available that would do justice to his many talents, achievements and personality.

In letting people describe events as they experienced them the Bureau used a most useful format that is both very readable and gives a very good insight into what motivated the people who made the events—and nothing is more important than that when it comes to understanding history.

It is to be hoped that other Societies such as ours will use the Bureau's material to make the contributions from their own areas available and we hope that they will follow our approach and make the contributions available *in toto*. (To help in this we have included an index of all those who made contributions to the Bureau at Annex 6). Otherwise, there is a danger that the contributions will be selectively used, and abused, by the revisionist-dominated professional historians of the present time to serve their own agenda.

Full and convenient availability of the material to the public would be in the spirit of the original idea behind the setting up of the Bureau and it would also be a most appropriate way of showing due appreciation to some, at least, of the people who made our independence possible.

**Jack Lane**
jacklaneaubane@hotmail.com
*Aubane Historical Society*
July 2003

# Seán Moylan: Milestones In His Life

Born, Kilmallock, 19th November, 1889.
Joined Gaelic League and GAA, 1904.
Carpenter's apprentice, 1905.
Worked as carpenter in Dublin, 1905-1913.
Joined Volunteers, April 1914.
Captain, Newmarket Company, May 1914.
Building Contractor, 1915.
Mobilised, Easter Sunday, 1916.
Captain, Newmarket Company, September 1917.
Imprisoned and escaped, 1918.
Commandant, Cork No. 2 Battalion, 1920.
Led ASU, North Cork, 1920-1921.
OC, Cork No. 2 Brigade, April 1921.
Captured, Interned on Spike Island, May 1921.
Sinn Féin TD, North Cork, May 1921.
Released to attend Dáil, August 1921.
Opposed the 'Treaty', December 1921.
Presided over IRA Convention, March 1922.
Married Miss Nora Murphy (Kiskeam), 1922.
Active Service, from June 1922.
Sent on three IRA missions to US, between November 1922 and November 1924.
Re-elected TD, 1922. Did not go forward in 1923.
Chairman, Sinn Féin, North Cork, 1924.
Joined Fianna Fáil, 1926.
Re-started business as building contractor, 1926.
Fianna Fáil TD, North Cork, 1932.
Parliamentary Secretary to the Minister for Industry and Commerce, 1937 – 1943.

Parliamentary Secretary to the Minister for Defence and Director of ARP, September 1939 – 1943.
Parliamentary Secretary to the Ministers for Defence and Finance, 1943
Minister for Lands, 1943 – 1948.
Minister for Education, 1951 – 1954.
Minister for Agriculture, 1957.
Died, 16th November, 1957.

**STATEMENT BY SEÁN MOYLAN, T.D.,
Minister for Education**

132, St. Lawrence Road, Clontarf, Dublin.

*Officer Commanding, Cork II Brigade, 1921
Officer Commanding, Cork IV Brigade, 1921*

I

# [Kilmallock / Newmarket / 1916]

When I was a small boy a bearded stranger arrived one Summer's evening in my home. He was greeted with a silent handgrip by my grandfather, with tears of welcome by the womenfolk of the family. He was Patrick Pickett, my grandmother's brother. He had taken part in the Fenian Rising at Kilmallock in March 1867, had served a prison sentence afterwards and shortly after his release had emigrated. This was his first visit home. He picked me up in his arms and enquired who I was. I was shy and fearful of his bearded countenance, reassured by the kindness of his eyes. I was consumed with curiosity and questioned everybody. I was told he had been a Fenian, had been in jail and in America. From an outside source I later got a story which disclosed his character. On the morning of the Rising he had been ordered to intercept a police despatch rider who travelled between Bruff and Kilmallock. He did his work successfully, disarming the rider and taking his horse and despatches which he handed over to Captain Dunn, the Irish American officer in charge at Kilmallock. After the Rising he, with a number of others, was interned in Limerick Jail. While he was in prison another man was convicted of the attack on the policeman and given a five years' sentence, which meant transportation to Australia. On Pickett's release when the amnesty came, he reported to the R.I.C. sergeant at Kilmallock and stated that he and not the sentenced man was responsible for the attack on the policeman and the capture of his equipment and despatches. Enquiries made confirmed the truth of his statement. The man in Australia was released and brought home, receiving £300 as compensation for his imprisonment. It was decided, in view of the amnesty, that a new trial was inadvisable and Pickett was again released. He emigrated shortly afterwards. I recall the story because it etches sharply the character of the Fenians. Of their deeds they were neither repentant nor ashamed and they were too proud and honourable to permit any resultant punishment to be borne by others.

Kilmallock, where I was born, is situated amidst the finest lands in the country. It was, therefore, the happy hunting ground of the ascendancy. A walled town, its strategic value ensured the existence there of an English garrison. The annals of the mere Irish existing in the locality were short and simple—poverty, oppression and that contempt which only the Mississippi Negro knows. But in a manhood denied its natural rights, resentment of that denial always smoulders. Lecky calculates that there were one hundred thousand United Irishmen in Munster and the organisation must have had some existence in Kilmallock. At any rate, there is a tradition there of a visit by Lord Edward Fitzgerald. This visit to a family named Green, who were tenants of the Duke of Leinster, lasted two weeks and one of the men with whom Lord Edward discussed the question of organisation was named Fleming. Fleming lived at Deebert beside the town. *'Dibirt'* is an ominous name. It means "banishment, persecution". Fleming was afterwards banished from the country by Richard Oliver and his yeomen. This is the Oliver who got £15,000 for voting for the Union. An old Fenian, Nicholas Gaffney, born in 1840, recalled how, as a boy of twelve, he read *The Nation*. This was probably a file of the newspaper kept by some ardent admirer of the Young Irelanders. But the fact goes to show that the teachings of Davis and his comrades were known and appreciated in the district.

About 1861 a branch of a society called The National Brotherhood of St. Patrick was formed in the town. Ostensibly a literary society, it was in actual fact a cover for Fenianism. The society, like all such gatherings at the time, became suspect by the English authorities and came under such unfavourable notice by the R.I.C. that all the members other than the Fenians severed their connection with it. Those men who remained became definitely suspect in 1862 when they paraded at the railway station when the train carrying the body of T. B. McManus on its journey from San Francisco to Dublin passed by.

The meetings in the rooms of the Literary Society were discontinued and the hurling field was afterwards used as the Fenian meeting place. Hurling was at that time not the game as now played but a cross-country affair which made it possible to elude police supervision. The only arms the Fenians had were pikes made by local blacksmiths and carpenters. Arms were promised from America and in 1864 the Fenian movement developed a more military type of organisation than theretofore based on somewhat the same model as that of the I.R.A. of 1920. Then the date for the Rising was fixed—March 25th, 1865. The Fenians were under the ban of the Church but there was a Nationalist priest in Milford, Co. Cork, prepared to disregard that ban. To him the Kilmallock Fenians made a night march in the week before the appointed day and received from him the consolation of their religion. But the Rising was postponed and, alas! there were further postponements. The realisation of the aims the Fenians set before them was to be postponed. But the story of Fenianism has been written by Stephen O'Leary and others. I refer to it only for the purpose of depicting the tradition and the background of the environment in which I grew up. There is a further memory of my boyhood days that remains with me: the memory of another Fenian, Batt Raleigh, my grandfather's brother. Small and insignificant in looks, shy, retiring and deeply religious in character, one could not, from his looks and manner, regard him as one possessed of a soldierly spirit and a disregard for danger. Yet he was deeply involved in the Fenian movement. He evaded capture after the Rising but was on the run until the amnesty when it became possible for him to return home. My memory is of his love and admiration for Robert Emmet who was for him the greatest Irishman. Whoever had any doubt in 1916 of the wisdom of Easter Week he had none and Pearse was placed by him on a pedestal beside Emmet. When some years ago I was discussing political movements with a man who was not only well off in his own right but also was a member of a family which for many generations had been comfortably circumstanced, he said to me, *"Why was it that there was so little respect for the Fenians? In my youth"*, he said, *"I remember that those of them who lived in my district were regarded by my people as more or less as a joke"*.

The memory of Patrick Pickett and of Batt Raleigh flashed into my mind and I cast my thoughts back to the Fenians I had known in my own youth. They were all workingmen, and, as far as I remember, employed in poorly paid occupations. On the spur of the moment I conceived what I think was a reasonable answer. I said: *"They were all poor men and they were beaten"*. It is a difficult matter for a rich man to appreciate the courage and selflessness of a seemingly ineffectual effort by poor men, and so the Fenians were misunderstood by the well-intentioned but thoughtless, and despised in the homes of those whose only criterion of effort is success, whose only standard of success is material advancement.

But the Fenian organisation, the Fenian effort, the Fenian sacrifice was the humus forming the rich soil out of which burgeoned the red bloom of 1916 and the fruit, sweet and bitter, but finally wholesome, of 1921, 1922 and 1923.

Because it has become the fashion in many quarters nowadays to question the wisdom of the men who served Ireland under arms from April 1916 to April 1923; because not only their wisdom but their motives, their courage, their selflessness, are, too, often impugned, I think it may be of some interest if I set out on a voyage of discovery of the motives that brought me, who had neither physique nor courage, nor soldierly flair, nor capacity, into a movement where guns alone talked, where force was the only arbitrament; into a fight in which, the odds counted, it was unwise to expect success; that set my feet on a road on which those who walked to Journey's End frequently found only a jail or a gibbet.

Irish History was not taught in the schools of my youth nor were there many books available to me. But such as there were I read avidly. On the five foot shelf Dickens and Thackeray paraded beside Mitchel and Kickham and in my imaginings I placed Becky Sharp in the background of Knocknagow and wondered if Pip's Convict was familiar with the Tasmanian scene depicted by Mitchel. *"A boy's will is the wind's will"* and his mind is not curbed by the shackles of reality. Carleton too was there and I did not then deeply appreciate him. I made many attempts to read Butler's *Lives Of The Saints* but my unregenerate mind rejected Hagiology. I was a grown man before an opportunity was given me of studying my country's past. But my youthful ears were filled with stories of the Fenians. I followed the processions on the 6th March and on the 23rd November. I listened to the speeches on those nights. I saw the attitude of the R.I.C. to the crowds. I looked in awe and respect on old toil worn men marching, because I knew that they, unarmed and untrained, had faced the rifles of the police in '67, that they had gone to jail, that they had suffered, and I, who loved Ireland also, felt in my craven soul that much as I would desire to serve her I could not face the dangers that these men faced.

They were strangely humble, strangely quiet, strangely reticent. One or two of them were British soldiers who had been in the Crimean War and, as I had not then heard of John Devoy and *'Pagan'* O'Leary, I was puzzled to reconcile membership of the Fenians with the taking of the Queen's shilling. Yes, humility, quiet and reticence were attributes of the Fenians I knew. Many of them were men of high intelligence, none was possessed of any book-learning. Most of them had lived as boys through the grim famine years. Mitchel was one of their heroes, perhaps because his was the name of note likely to be heard by boys when their interest is first captured by a discussion between their elders. Meagher, too, they admired; knowing of his distinction in the American Civil War, but Captain Mackey was the man they most loved. Most of these men, conditions being as they were in the Ireland of their boyhood, must have known poverty and privation. Government was to them a thing hateful and indestructible. In their boyhood there was a population of eight millions in a country where the land was the property of the few, where craftsmanship languished. Except for the fact that men, under pressure of circumstances, adjust themselves to almost any sort of living conditions we must regard the Ireland of the Fenians' boyhood as a vast concentration camp where manhood was maimed, spiritual development stunted and the only gateway of hope was the port of call of the emigrant ship.

Young Ireland was a movement with a leadership of intellect and a mass support made possible by the work of O'Connell. The coming of the famine, practically coincident with the appearance of Lalor and Mitchel, foredoomed the revolution they preached to failure. The leaders, one by one, disappeared. The followers were decimated by plague and famine, scattered by emigration. *"The Celt was gone"* with a vengeance. Ireland was a "corpse on the dissecting table". To quote John O'Leary: "It was a proud and not undeserved boast of the Young Irelanders that they brought a soul back into Eire", but before Fenianism had arisen that soul had fled. Fenianism had "brought it back again". It is to the credit of the Fenians that the blood of regeneration flowed again through the veins of this corpse-like nation.

The politics of my boyhood years I did not associate in any way with my ideals of Irish Nationhood. I heard no word of political approval or condemnation in my home or from those who frequented it. Parnell and Davitt, O'Brien, Healy and Redmond were names I heard occasionally in men's mouths at the street corners. I sensed the tragedy of Parnell but my questionings in its regard were discouraged and remained unanswered.

Those who would serve a nation are confronted with many difficulties, not the least of which is a mental outlook created by past conditions and continuing unchanged when those conditions have disappeared. But that mental condition—the Fenian distrust of political action—is understandable. They had seen the formation of the Catholic Defence Associations; the

infamous conduct of the unspeakable Sadlier, had been lectured on the iniquity of rebellion by the renegade, John Keogh. Knew that—
> "the aspiring national member during those years, as he stood upon the hustings and asked the people's votes was glib of tongue and prodigal of promises as a man could be...".

Had seen that
> "when the candidate entered parliament he at once forgot his promises, scoffed at independent opposition, attached himself to the Government party whip". That "his reward came in due course...".

And if some indignant supporter charged him with his pledge-breaking and treachery, he coolly admitted his offence, chuckled at having made so good a bargain with the Government and even thanked God he had a country to sell. Looking back now on the many elderly men whom I knew, I can understand that they were disillusioned, bewildered, hopeless; depressed because of failure, subdued because they had had their fill of victimisation, reticent because of training and distrustful of politics because of their experience and because of their experience and because they realised the futility of words.

The '98 Centenary brought my first vivid lessons in Irish history. At the fireside gatherings I listened while the schoolmaster read the history of '98 as published then weekly in the newspapers—Ballinahinch to New Ross, Killala to Ballinamuck. In my mind's eye I saw the Wexford pikemen and the swift fierce onslaught of the French; went breathless with Dwyer from Wicklow to slip down Marshalsea Lane; sorrowed at Downpatrick for the man from Dromahane, while only subconsciously I heard the fierce comments of men who relived the scenes of their youth and in whose hearts the fiery Fenian sap had risen again. English injustice was something of which each of them had personal experience and men of such an experience are not prone to be philosophical about it. I learned thus early a hatred of British rule in Ireland.

There is no objectivity in a child's viewpoint. I saw the pitchcap, the cat-o'-nine-tails, the gallows, the Hessians, the burned homes and churches, Father John Murphy, Hempenstall. In bed I cowered shivering in the darkness. I leaped and twisted in frightful dreams, yet no one connected my terror with the nightly readings and thus I continued to sit open-eyed, tense, entranced, absorbing the story through every pore. Occasionally the reading was taken over by a young girl who read with beautiful rhythms and intonation, and the school master sat between a man with the goatee of an American Civil War Veteran and a huge bearded man who was a survivor of the Crimea.

My next memory was that of the Boer War—Oom Paul, Joubert, Cronje, De Wett, Colenso, Ladysmith, Modder River and Mafeking were names jubilantly associated in my mind with disaster to the England that had hanged Allen, Larkin and O'Brien, and I followed the fortunes of the South African Republic through their years of agony.

Then death brought changes and I went to live in Newmarket, Co. Cork, where no tradition of Fenianism seemed to exist, where the people seemed entirely absorbed in their own affairs and where politics was a bitterly vocal, immediate and partisan affair with no apparent thought or knowledge of a historic past and no concern for the national future, no pre-occupation except with minor and local affairs. There was a grovelling outlook on the part of the so-called Nationalist population quite different to that of the Unionist population. To be a Unionist was to be a superior being who owned of right the fruits of the earth and the fullness thereof. A substantial intelligent Nationalist farmer was *"Mickeen Murphy"*. His dull-witted Unionist neighbour was *"Master William Brown"*. The local bank manager and his assistants were Unionists; so also were the local station master, the petty sessions clerk, the postmaster. There were no other white-collar jobs. All of these people were possessed by a perfervid loyalty to England. The Nationalists seemed to have no loyalties. Once or twice a year we had a concert to raise funds for the support of the local foxhounds. They were poor performances and invariably finished with the singing of *"God save the King"*.

The ascendancy occupying the front seats stood bareheaded. A few respectable shopkeepers then arose shamefacedly, but, like the rest of the audience, with an unquiet feeling that they were not entitled to participate in the ceremony. The last of these concerts was a riotous affair. The usual programme was carried out. The Colonel spoke a few words of thanks to the audience and at length on the benefits bestowed on the locality by the foxhunters. Then we had *"God save the King"*. As it went on its quivering way a small boy, my brother Joe, at the back of the hall, started to *sing "God save Ireland"* and the King and his minions had to make way for the nation. The gallery shouted the song and immediately we were all singing. As we surged into the street there were cheers and laughter and a general feeling of elation. It was the last of the Foxhound Concerts and also the first sign of dissatisfaction with the hitherto accepted scheme of things.

To a boy who had lived with and listened to Fenians, current politics had no appeal; for several years I was in the doldrums. It was not until a branch of the Gaelic League was started that I found myself again in a congenial atmosphere. Here was something real. I worked hard to learn Irish. Always the first to arrive when the Gaelic League classes started at the beginning of the Winter; always the last of the straggling few when the coming of Spring brought opportunity for outdoor activity.

Dan Galvin of Glashakinleen was our first teacher. He cycled into town twice weekly to take charge of the class. He got no recompense other than the satisfaction it gave him to promulgate the Irish Ireland ideas on which his character was based. In the years to come he was to become one of my greatest friends, to make many a personal sacrifice and to be regarded as the most stalwart supporter of the I.R.A. in his own district.

His successor was Seán Kavanagh, Seán na Cóta, from Dunquin, later to prove himself an authority on the Irish language. In the few years I spent under the tuition of these men I got a reasonably good grip of the language and when I returned to Kilmallock to be apprenticed as a carpenter I was abreast of all the students in the Gaelic League classes there. Here in Kilmallock, I remember in the late Spring of one year there came the last evening of the session. The half dozen students present prepared to depart, I lingered, loath to go, and heard a discussion on politics between the teacher and the only grown man who attended class. This was a quiet scholarly man who was in the years before us to face the death sentence of a British court-martial. They discussed Home Rule and the work of the Irish Parliamentary

Party. They expressed the hope that the Irish Party's effort would be successful and spoke of the need there was to avoid saying or doing anything that might adversely affect the work of the Parliamentarians. They spoke of Griffith and Sinn Féin. I had heard of Sinn Féin but knew nothing of it. Here, then, was light. I listened and asked questions, grasping the fact that Sinn Féin was something other than Devolution, and that Arthur Griffith was closer kin to me than the noble Lord, its advocate.*

In all these years I had never seen behind the talk and discussion the lightning flash of gunfire. I accepted the view that the days of armed revolution were over, that the grip of England, England the rich, the powerful, the invincible, was too firmly fixed on Ireland ever to be broken in the field of battle. That concessions might be won by persuasion I believed, yet doubted; that the nation's freedom might be fought for I could not realise; war was a far off thing, of long ago or of distant country. It could not concern me and I was ashamedly glad. I owed no loyalty to England and was pleased and yet not pleased that my loyalty to Ireland would not be tested in combat for her rights. Perhaps I had lived too long with old men, beaten men, and had absorbed their philosophy, and so when 1913 came I found it difficult to realise that either the Irish or the Ulster Volunteers were in earnest. Yet I joined the Volunteers and was not impressed. In my district the great majority of the members looked upon the movement as an adjunct of the Irish Party. At the inaugural meeting the principal speaker was Larry Roche, later a commissioned officer in the British Army. Roche was one of my boyhood heroes, a man of magnificent physique. A great all-round athlete, he had been a member of Limerick's victorious All-Ireland football team. He had thus all the qualities that appeal to youth. I knew, too, the G.A.A was deeply impregnated with Fenianism. The football club meetings at which when a small boy I was occasionally present with my grandfather were also attended by all the old Fenians I knew. Roche was then Chairman and there was the regular weekly ritual of payment of subscription. The Fenians knew that the purposes of Cusack went far beyond the question of athletics development and maintained their interest in the organisation. Thus, at this later date I was very much predisposed in favour of Roche. Yet he did not impress me. His and all the other speeches were of a tinpike flamboyance. There was no reality about them. The exception was that of the man whom I had heard speaking with the Gaelic League teacher about Sinn Féin. This man was Joe Gaffney, son of the old Fenian, Nicholas Gaffney, who was to serve his country so selflessly and so effectively from 1916 to the end.

My association with the Kilmallock Volunteers was short lived. My apprenticeship finished, I left Kilmallock in April 1914, to start business for myself in Newmarket. Here in June 1914, a Volunteer Company was formed. It was composed of over two hundred men. The great majority of the Volunteers in this 1914 Company had no conception of or concern for soldiering. They were a gay irresponsible crowd of young men attracted for the moment by the drilling, marching and shouted orders. That they were first class raw

---

* [*the noble Lord* : This is probably a reference to Lord Dunraven who was a well-known advocate of Devolution at the time. J.L.]

material for military purposes was proved afterwards by those who joined in large numbers the I.R.A. in the early days of 1920. Their nightly drills in the weeks before the outbreak of war were honoured by the presence of the Unionists. Like the British politician of a few months later these saw Ireland as the one bright spot in the Empire where the continuance of their ascendancy would be guaranteed by the physical protection of an Irish manhood which they controlled. It was a vision that was to be swiftly dispelled. England declared war on Germany in the first week of August 1914, and the Company that a week before had filled the village street with marching men had dwindled to eight. Of these eight men, one was killed in action in 1921, one was sentenced to death in the same year, two died prematurely of wounds and disease.

Sometime that year after Mr. Redmond's Woodenbridge speech a Volunteer organiser, Tom McCarthy, arrived from Dublin and stayed a few months. He worked hard but he had the difficult task of convincing a people who, like myself, had never dreamt of fight, of the need, reality or use of a Volunteer organisation, and his success was not great. People talk nowadays of the conflicting orders of 1916 and the might have beens. Had the orders agreed, been clear and explicit, there would have been here and there throughout the country an attempt at fighting, but little more, for there was not a countrywide organisation, very little arms and no general will to fight. Roger Casement, for example, was taken by two R.I.C. men in Kerry. And so through 1914 and 1915 the few Volunteers in Newmarket met secretly and drilled half-heartedly. Living in an isolated district, their only contact with the world was through the daily newspapers and these were filled with the war news and contained neither information nor comment on the Volunteer Movement.

Then came our mobilisation orders for Easter, 1916. For the first time we met Companies from adjoining areas. The mobilisation point was Barley Hill, near Newmarket. The officer sent to take charge of the Volunteers was the late Captain David Barry, recently Secretary of the Irish Tourist Association. In the evening of Easter Sunday we were ordered to return to our homes and we were not again called upon.

Many of those who paraded in 1916 emigrated in the following years, some played minor parts in the movement, some disappeared from it; a few were faithful to the end. Where only a *"few are faithful found, they must be more faithful because they are few"*.

Again I venture an opinion. The faith of the few was rooted in a refusal to disbelieve. Irishmen, they could not accept the view that they were of a lesser breed, that their country was fated to remain a Province. Blindly, instinctively, they held to this refusal; out of it, because they were blindly, intuitively right, came light and guidance and strength to achieve. 1916 proved one thing—that Irishmen could fight and die for their country. It proved, too, that, the first breath-taking shock past, Irishmen's allegiance was still to their own land; that they were proud of the men who made manifest that allegiance. The spell of national inanition was broken. Ireland would never again be quiescent under foreign rule.

The gravel was raked over the prison graves of the dead; the fighting men were tucked securely away in English prisons. Sir John Maxwell could report that quiet was restored, rebellion quelled and that the King's Irish subjects repudiated and abhorred the action of the rebels. But the gravel smooth over quicklime graves was deceptive; for the replacement of each man in prison there were two others, fiercely earnest and now clear of purpose; the quiet was ominous. In this quiet the prison gates were opened and the prisoners streamed back to an enthusiastic welcome. An insurrection was to become a revolution and I was to become one of its organisers. I was never again to follow my humdrum occupation, to live my quiet uneventful life. I was to travel many a weary mile, to make good friends and bitter enemies, to develop endless patience and tolerance, to know wounds and hunger and weariness of spirit, to learn how fear is conquered and to stand at last in the shadows of the gallows tree.

## II
## [Volunteer Training / Sinn Féin Courts]

As far as military knowledge was concerned the brain of the Volunteer organiser of 1917 was a vacuum. Such a man had everything to learn and no one to teach. He had to absorb knowledge of drill, tactics, arms and explosives from *An t-Óglach* and from text books. He had to develop the power and confidence of command. He had to create for himself a simple, forthright, clarifying speech, adapted to local idiom. He who thinks that a standard English is spoken in Ireland has never known the oft-time need of casting rural Munster speech into Irish before one understands it. Local prejudices had to be avoided and it was essential to act with a healing, judicious calm in closing the wound of ancient altercation. It was a grand training in character development. The physical side was just as strenuous and trying, long distance cycling on bad roads in all weathers, hard lying and oftentimes short commons, marching, drilling, training. Those who imagine that commando tactics and training are a new discovery know nothing of the work done by the I.R.A. organisers in the years that preceded the real clash of arms.

I truly said on one occasion: *"The one supreme quality of the I.R.A. was its suitability to its purpose"*. Critics of every effort and every accomplishment are manifold, and the Irish army, its effort and accomplishment has not escaped criticism and odious comparisons. But it had a particular piece of work to do in circumstances unique and extraordinary. It cannot be argued that it was created as a result of clearly conceived plans, that its campaign was related to a considered strategy, that it was directed and controlled by a clearly recognised Headquarters Staff, or had its needs supplied by a well-organised quartermaster's department. I consider it to have been, it was indeed, the spearpoint of an uprising of a people. It had its roots in the age long tradition of resistance. It was shaped and conditioned by the long continued underground organisation forced on a subject people who would not accept subjection.

It was brought into effective being by the insurrection of Easter Week and, lucidly escaping the direction of professional soldiers, reverted to the traditional guerrilla tactics of the locally organised clans.

That is not to say that there was no control and direction by Headquarters; there certainly was, but it was a general rather than a specific direction. Headquarters was a co-ordinating body which left each Brigade to its own resources, to take the most of the opportunities offered, which kept brigades informed as to the general situation and of any development of enemy tactics.

The looseness of organisation was a source of strength during the whole period of the fight against the British, as the fact that one area was inactive or had suffered a setback did not affect the activities or morale in other districts.

The military effort was so mingled with the development of the political side, the work of the soldier so gradually shaded into the work of politics, there was such a complete fusion of thought and action that it was difficult to say where the ever-widening circle of activity ceased to absorb the community. It was a concentrated effort in which each citizen subordinated his private interests to the welfare of the nation, and the I.R.A. was adequate and wholly suitable to this background. A phrase I often heard used in those days was: *"You must think militarily";* which meant that I.R.A. officers should divorce themselves completely from any concern of the public and think only in terms of guns and fighting. There was reason in this precept if it was addressed to men who tended to base their hopes on peaceful parliamentary action but given as an instruction to men who had come to despise parliamentarianism it was not wisely conceived. War is politics on another plane. And those who make war most successfully are those who weld the nation into a single-minded political unit directed to a clear objective. Apart, therefore, from the actual work of creating and training a military force, a vital part of the organiser's work was to align the minds of the people with the mind of the I.R.A.; to create sympathy; to foster a belief in the soundness of policy and its ultimate success; to build up behind the fighting men a governmental system on which the people in their ordinary avocations could depend for justice and protection.

The army thus loosely organised developed along the lines most suitable to the task before it. It was not an implement for war in the hands of the nation. It was the nation; and because the ideas, prejudices, training and background of so many men, working independently of any immediate central control, contributed to its creation, development and effort, it followed, of course, that the development, effort and results in the various districts were unequal and its activities open to criticism if judged in accordance with theories that are discarded by all nations in time of war.

But, in considering the evil a man does and the mistakes he makes, one's judgement is less liable to err when the man is placed against the background of his time and country. The intransigent who, when his country was invaded and overrun during the latest great war, took up arms against the invader and in secret, and in civilian guise, killed, burned and destroyed the forces and equipment of the invader is lauded as a hero—in Poland *tuigeann tú*—but here in Ireland every man who took up a gun, who, with the dice completely loaded against him, went out to fight for his country's liberty in the only fashion possible, was deemed a murderer by those who controlled all the organs of publicity.

This demand for a recognition of their manhood and for their rights as men has been the real source of revolt in Ireland. It is in complete opposition to the dialectics of the Marxist Materialists and even though the demand for economic rights has been interlocked with it, always the driving force has been wrested from the things of the spirit.

But a physical subsistence must precede cultural and spiritual development, and during the long years of English domination of Ireland the struggle on the part of Irishmen for the most meagre livelihood in their own land was an all absorbing one. Burke, in his description of the penal laws, said:

"A machine of wise and elaborate contrivance and as well fitted for the oppression, impoverishment and degradation of a people, and the debasement in them of human nature itself, as ever proceeded from the perverted ingenuity of men".

And the results of the penal laws with their cycle of oppression, famine and revolt continued into the twentieth century. The evil was attributed by the British Government to the recalcitrant, even criminal character of the Irish people; its real root was unsought and when it obtruded itself through the dark cloud of governmental unwisdom it was deliberately ignored. The force that in 1917 brought into the Volunteer ranks the best type of soldier was emulation. Young men who had been boys when the '98 Commemoration was celebrated, who had lived in ordinary Irish homes, who had read the publications of Sinn Féin and of the Volunteers, who had been members of the Gaelic League or Gaelic Athletic Association, all to a greater or lesser extent had had their characters profoundly influenced by the national tradition. The Volunteer organisation since 1913 had by its work and propaganda *"created men of a more intensely Irish character and outlook"*. Many of them had stood to in Easter Week, probably not wholly believing that there would be a fight, had listened eagerly, though confusedly, to conflicting rumour during that week and had heard in bitter stony silence of the subsequent executions.

The I.R.A. organisation, reconstituted in 1917, became as widespread and effective to a remarkable degree and in a remarkably short time as anything of its nature, anywhere. Without financial resources or equipment it was created by men of selfless purpose and indomitable energy. When I say without financial resources, I may be asked were not funds subscribed generously for the purpose? Were there not huge sums subscribed for the Irish Republican Dependants' Fund? What about the Dáil Loan and the generous subscription from U.S.A.? I can only say that, as far as my knowledge goes, not a cent of any of those funds was devoted to the organisation of the Irish Republican Army. Up to the time of the *"German Plot"*\* I lived at home. All my spare time was devoted to I.R.A. organisation. Now and again, as occasion demanded, I for weeks gave up the work which I did for a livelihood to devote myself wholly to the I.R.A. After May 1918, it was no longer possible for me

---

\* [*German Plot*: On 15th May 1918, during the Conscription Crisis, the British Government arrested the leaders of Sinn Fein on the pretext that it had discovered evidence that Sinn Fein was engaged in a treasonable conspiracy with Germany. J.L.]

to live at home; no longer possible to undertake any work that might bring a financial return. I was on the run. Generous friends gave me food and shelter. I needed nothing more. I didn't smoke, I drank only when wearied muscle had to be flogged to meet unexpected demands or as a remedy for complaints caught from soaking rain and chilling winds. An occasional pound and an odd parcel of underclothing came from home. If there is virtue in poverty and ascetic living, then I have experienced it. I doubt, however, that I would have had the approval of the unco guid.*

Let me say now that while the Active Service Units were to live off the country those who carried out the work of organisation in the years from 1917 to 1920 lived on the generosity of a very narrow circle, of a relatively small group of people who knew they had a country and a duty to it and who were the yeast wherewith eventually the whole mass was leavened. Among the multitude of voices claiming a record of work done or service given theirs have not been heard. They have employed no public relations officer. They have no desire for publicity. Content they are in a knowledge of duty done. Of such is created the national barrier against derision and despair, the springboard of each new national advance.

I have already referred to the close association of Sinn Féin and the Volunteers, of the fact that the leadership of each organisation was often embodied in the same persons. There was a much closer affiliation of these bodies than there was between either and their respective headquarters. Ireland had been federalised. Brigades and Constituencies were a loose Confederacy, giving allegiance to a central authority and driving towards a common purpose, but subsisting entirely free inside their own areas. Side by side with the intensive reorganisation, training and recruiting Volunteers went a determined effort to expand the influence of Sinn Féin and to augment its members. Night after night the organiser went from Parish to Parish reviving dormant clubs, setting up new ones where none existed, weekly club delegates met to report progress, to discuss ways and means to bring information in regard to all matters affecting the people of their various localities. At periods, not greater than a few months, a general convention of delegates from all over the constituency was held when these matters reported from every parish in the constituency were discussed and where reports from headquarters were read. Thus men in the most remote parishes were fully informed of the general situation and developed a feeling of strength and cohesion. Men got to know each other, passed judgement on each other, were welded into a coherent political unit. Political parties in settled conditions tend to become mere collection agencies. They collect votes, gather money and leave policy and planning to their leaders.

The Sinn Féin organisation escaped this condition of political decadence. Its members were too enthusiastic, too energetic, too full of a desire to serve, to permit their thinking to be done for them. Leadership had to prove itself and the ideas of any man aspiring to leadership had to stand the fire of

---

* [*unco guid* : see *Address To The Unco Guid* by Robbie Burns, J.L.]

criticism and be judged by the standard of comparison. Theory was subject to the assay of practice.

And there was room for practical effort. The retreat of the R.I.C. to central barracks, the fact that the King's Writ ran only within the extremely limited circle of their influence round the large towns had left the countryside open to the creation of a state of lawlessness. Land trouble, the ever suppurating sore affecting a rural community; rights of way, of water, of turbary, became major sources of irritation; trespass, an ever recurring trouble. The Petty Sessions Court, with its background of authority, had disappeared from the countryside with the R.I.C. Right was might. Bullying, burglary, riotous behaviour, the uncontrolled and unregulated sale of drink and the poteen still made their appearance. Such a condition tended not merely to disrupt the life of the community but to destroy any possibility of keeping either Volunteers or Sinn Féin in existence. It was a time for decision and for definite action. Leadership could not evade responsibility and it did not do so. The remedy for the evil appeared as spontaneously as the evil itself and long before Republican Courts were set up, Arbitration Courts to deal with ordinary civil disputes were created by the local Sinn Féin organisation. Courts of summary jurisdiction to deal with crime came into being under the aegis of the Volunteers.

No Court can be so effective as that whose members are fully acquainted with the full history and details of the matter in dispute. Such a Court, too, has the support of a fully informed public opinion. These were the Courts set up by Sinn Féin and such the conditions in which they operated. They had behind them again the dread power of armed men uncurbed by statute or precedent, the roughness of whose justice was a healthy deterrent to the non-acceptance of any litigant of the Courts' decisions. There was no settled procedure and decisions were often made on evidence that could not be accepted by any regular tribunal. But evil existed and had to be combated and the Volunteer organisation was now so widespread; its intelligence system had proceeded so far towards perfection that the perpetrators of crime or disturbers of the peace could not escape discovery. In most cases it was sufficient to warn the culprits; certain cases were adjusted by payment of compensation to the injured person, in a few cases sentences of deportation were given. That these Courts were a success was proven by the resultant crimelessness of the countryside. The prestige of the Volunteers and Sinn Féin was immensely increased, there was an ever developing membership and the work became easier.

At first these Courts were ignored by lawyers, for the Law is conservative. No difficulty was created by their absence. These were Courts of Justice, not Law Courts. An intimate knowledge of the conditions out of which the litigation arose was possessed by the Judges, the ignorant and dull-witted were treated with endless patience and broad understanding. The background of each case was known to the Volunteers of the locality from which it emanated and the reputation of the litigants and the rights and wrongs of the matter in dispute easily discoverable by shrewd observant men. Business with the legal practitioner in rural areas began to shrivel and here and there laymen sent circulars round to the units of the Sinn Féin organisation advertising themselves as Sinn Féin advocates. The lawyers came in. Some were from the start definitely helpful and sympathetic, others were inclined to be critical and patronising. But the edge of criticism is turned by the armour of righteousness and those who created and composed the Courts were men with a mission, who believed intensely in themselves and in the value of the work they were doing. And it is difficult to patronise men who are the leaders of an all-powerful organisation whose power is recognised and whose judgement is respected by the general public. Those who *"came to scoff remained to pray"*, some at least to recognise the selflessness and capacity of the men who had created a revolution. Again the influence of the revolutionaries was strengthened, their prestige increased, their ranks augmented.

Many lawyers came with the belief that only partisan judgements would be delivered and found to their surprise that an entirely different condition of things obtained. What they had regarded as an ill-advised and sans-cullotte political party disclosed itself as a de jure government acting with complete objectivity towards all citizens.

Some few cases may be cited as an example of the work of the Courts. The influx of British troops had been so great and constant that the housing accommodation for these must have been a difficult problem for the British Authorities. At any rate, married quarters attached to barracks were in the ordinary way quite sufficient to provide housing for the families of married members of the garrison. But under the new conditions soldiers' wives had to seek housing accommodation in the garrison towns. At the beginning many householders were pleased to have these as tenants but as the pressure became greater there was a boom in rents and some owners sought to dispossess those to whom they had let houses at comparatively low rents so that they might avail themselves of the new conditions. It so happened that a British soldier's wife who had rented a house at the beginning of 1920 was served with notice demanding possession and, unable to find alternative accommodation, refused to leave. She was taken to the British Courts and a decree for possession secured. No curb was placed on old father antic, the law.

Somehow or other the woman heard of the Sinn Féin Court and, women having more commonsense than logic, made her appeal thereto. The leaders of the organisation recognised all the implications and difficulties of dealing with the case, but, after discussion decided on handling it. Notice of Appeal was served on the house owner and all precautions taken to deal with the repercussions. It was only too obvious that it might have been a trap. We were aware of British astuteness. We were also aware of their muddling through or their *"try anything once"* attitude. They might be hoping that the very simplicity of the trick, if it was a trick, would reassure us. The Court day came, the Court sat and the case was listed for hearing. But during the previous night scouts were posted over the countryside, ready to pass the alarm if they discovered any sign of British military activity; the Court was held within a few miles of a major garrison town. Nothing untoward happened and the case came up for decision. The landlord was indignant. The case had been heard by a Law Court and a decision given in his favour. He was an Irishman, he didn't see that it was the business of Irish Republicans to interfere on behalf of a British soldier's wife; the property was his, he could do what he liked with it. He was torn between two opposing desires. He believed that an expression of his anti-British attitude would influence the Court in his favour and wanted to impress on everybody his unqualified allegiance to the Irish Republic. At the same time he did not wish to slip the anchorage of the British Court's decision, with the result that he antagonised all his hearers. The Englishwoman was called; middle-aged, rotund, good-humoured, fussily loquacious. There was something familiar to me in her appearance as she sat in the witness chair stating her case. Yet recognition eluded me and then suddenly I reached it. She waved her umbrella to emphasise some particular point and I remembered an old Cruikshank drawing in Martin Chuzzlewitt. Here was Sairey Gamp, younger certainly, with no appearance of an indulgence in the beverage favoured by her prototype and Betsy Prig, but without doubt a midwife. She told the tale of her fruitless search for a house, of her numerous children, of efforts to make ends meet on a private soldier's pay and allowances. She had eager listeners, though sometimes her Lancashire speech rendered her meaning obscure to them. But she was a stranger in our midst; she was a woman, poor and in difficulties. With the air of a practised public speaker she included the audience as well as the Court in the sweep of her oratory. The crowd was with her and the verdict in her favour was entirely popular. She came to me when the case was over and asked if there were costs to pay. I said: *"There are no costs"*, and then, taking a chance, said: *"Nurse"*. She beamed and said: *"How did you know I was a nurse?"* *"We know everything"*, I said, and then she turned the joke on me. *"Young man"*, said she, *"when you need a midwife you know my address"*.

A case in which both litigants lived under the shadow of the British military barracks, in which one litigant was the wife of a soldier in those barracks, was decided by a Republican Court and the decision enforced. The British influence in Ireland was being confined in an ever narrowing circle.

Another case was that of a dispute between two gangs of poachers about a salmon net. The Blackwater passing through the brigade area was a noted stream for salmon, and anglers had good sport. The fishing was reasonably well protected by a number of bailiffs with the help of the R.I.C. Here again the effects of police concentration were felt. Long reaches of the river were entirely unprotected and nets were freely used. The poacher remains a figure of romance, he always was a nuisance, he has ceased to be a sportsman, but poachers will exist until the antediluvian fishery laws are revised, until weirs are properly controlled, special privilege abolished and a proper licensing system introduced. At any rate, here are two groups of men indulging in an illegal and anti-social activity bringing a dispute, arising out of that activity, for settlement before a Court. The case was heard and a verdict promptly given. Both sides were heavily fined and the net confiscated. Another illusion was shattered, the illusion that since Republicans refused to recognise British authority they were against the law; they could, therefore, be regarded as having no objection when the law was broken by others. What form of logic it was that expected a Court to protect lawbreakers in pursuit of their illegalities passeth all understanding. But an appreciation of the Court's attitude to this and cognate matters developed among the people. Not only the probity of the

Courts but the wisdom of their decisions affected the attitude of the public towards them. Truly. *"Righteous men can make their land a nation once again"*.

Another nuisance that disappeared during the regime of the Court was that confounded one—the sempiternal litigant. There is in every community some discordant human element, crank or trouble maker, who has a genius for the manufacture of grievance and an insatiable desire for litigation. He discovered in the Courts a fresh field for his activity, but it was a disastrous field for him. The obsession of the most notorious of these litigants in the district was his claim to a farm occupied by another man. He had on one pretext or another hauled this man through all the British Courts in an effort to dispossess him. His effort was a complete failure everywhere. The coming of the Sinn Féin Courts gave him a new opening of which he availed himself, and his case, which had no merits, was decided against him. When the verdict was given he rose in Court and proclaimed his intention of having it again tried before the British Courts. This, naturally, could not be permitted and he was at once placed under arrest by the Volunteers. His case was discussed by the battalion officers who decided he was suffering from some form of monomania which might be cured by shock. A mock court-martial was arranged and he was sentenced to death. He was still defiant, but when he faced the firing party his nerves gave way, he begged for mercy and promised to refrain from litigation in future. At last his neighbours lay down at night in peace. Nor has he since had recourse to law courts. Critics, who may readily accept the view that democracy entails the right of fifty one per cent. of the voters to coerce the other forty nine per cent. may say that this was not democracy. Democracy is the will of the people, embodies the right of the people to live, move and have their being in peace and security. If under the conditions that existed in Ireland from 1918 to 1921 these Courts were not truly democratic institutions, then democracy awaits a clarifying definition.

Apart from the work of the Sinn Féin Courts the Volunteers within their own special jurisdiction made short work of developing lawlessness. There was nothing that might be styled major crime; all law-breakers were swiftly dealt with. The countryside was tranquil apart from the activities of the R.I.C. and British military, who searched and raided constantly, interfered with fairs, markets, football matches, or any other form of known gathering.

I remember one case, however, in which all the efforts of the Volunteers failed to secure evidence against one individual whom they believed to be constantly engaged in stealing from his neighbours. He had little means but possessed a poor holding and four or five cows. There was no hay in his haggard, no roots other than a small pit of potatoes. Yet all through a hard winter his cows flourished, looking better fed than any others in the locality. And all through the winter complaints were being made by farmers of stolen hay and roots. The Volunteers were constantly on the watch and this man was included amongst the suspects. A process of elimination finally directed the finger of suspicion directly at him and a constant watch was kept on him, without result. Finally, before dawn one morning, his house was surrounded by half a dozen Volunteers. They hid in positions in the fences from where his house could be seen and from where he was under constant survey all day;

and all day nothing happened. Just as dusk began to envelop the countryside he emerged from the house with a rope slung over his shoulders and crossed the fields in front of the house. Each silent watcher hugged himself and as the dark descended they closed in on the house and waited. An hour or more sped by and then the light sound of his approach was heard. He crossed the last fence and landed on the road. He was immediately collared and charged with stealing the heavy bundle of hay with which he was laden. He protested, alleged that he had bought the hay, gave the name of the seller and was dragged back, laden with the hay, two miles across the country to what the Volunteers believed would be his discomfiture. Arriving at the house the Volunteers asked the farmer: *"Did this man buy hay from you tonight?"* The farmer went across to the dresser, took some silver from a shelf, held out his hand with the money in it and said: *"Indeed he did, two cwt. at 4/- a cwt."* The discomfited Volunteers freed the purchaser who, before he left, gave a vivid description of their seed, breed, generation and final destination.

Information was never secured as to how he discovered he was being watched. I have always believed his escape was due to a few Volunteers, practical jokers, who were in the farmer's house when the prisoner was brought back and who laughed loud and long at the dismayed countenances of their comrades when the pieces of silver were produced.

# III
## [The Brigade Council / The R.I.C.]

There was only one Brigade in Cork City and County and when it was reorganised in 1917 I was at the first meeting. There was less than a score of men present, among them Tomás MacCurtain, Terence MacSwiney, Seán Hegarty and Tom Hales. The meeting opened in stormy fashion, Tom Hales charging the Brigade Staff with neglect of duty during Easter Week, 1916, with a lack of initiative and a desire to avoid fighting. Those against whom his recriminations were directed were Tomás MacCurtain and Terence MacSwiney. Their reputations need now no defence, nor are there any doubts of their courage or selflessness. This, however, is not to condemn Tom Hales. His attitude was rooted in the sincerity of a man disappointed in a great purpose. The storm blew itself quickly out and then we got down to a discussion on organisation. One of the instructions issued at the end of the meeting directed each one of us to make contact in each area adjoining his own, to try to pull together whatever strength of organisation was left and to ensure that representative Volunteers from each district would be present at the next meeting to be convened.

Now, may I say that, in comparison with his contemporaries, a biographer of a public man is always prone to make his subject a whale among minnows and seems to ignore the fact that without the aid of a multiplicity of his fellows no public man can wisely plan or effectively execute. The central figures of each Irish National movement are remembered and honoured. The memory of the many men of capacity and patriotic outlook who worked so selflessly for the benefit of their fellows in the background of each such movement is dim and clouded and unappreciated. It is significant that the grave of the first unknown soldier is in Ireland.

The gift of leadership is a priceless one. Men possess it in varying degrees, and in different men it is adapted to different purposes. Its value is qualified by such things as the range of vision of its possessor, by his capacity to see his objective clearly, to realise the nature of his difficulties and the strength and suitability of the instruments at his disposal.

The Battalion Commandants and Company Captains were the local leaders without whose efforts whatever success we achieved would not have been possible. One of these local leaders I met at the second meeting of Brigade Council. He was a nervous and highly strung type but the only one who had any doubt of the quality of his courage was himself and his only failing was that of taking foolhardy chances, apparently to disprove to himself those doubts of his. We worked in close co-operation from 1917 onwards. And he was thus one of the pioneers of the Volunteer organisation in the brigade area. Now and again he asked my advice and I suppose all men are flattered by any apparent deference to their judgement.

I had not seen him since some time before Easter, 1916, and it was then September or October 1917, when I met him at the second Brigade Council Meeting. He gave me the name of the hotel in which he was staying. I asked him if he had a latch key. He said *"No, but there is a porter on duty until midnight"*. I knew from previous experience that we were not likely to be finished until 2 a.m. Since I had previously stayed in the same hotel and had to spend the hours after 2 a.m. on the street, I had on this occasion made arrangements to stay in a quiet street in a house recommended by a friend. As I left the house that evening I informed my landlady that I could not be indoors before 2.30 a.m. and asked for a latchkey. I was informed that there were no latchkeys but that a cord was attached to the door, that all I needed to do was to insert my hand in the letter box, pull the cord and the door opened. I did not impart my knowledge of his probable difficulties to my friend.

At the meeting place were men whose names are now familiar in every Irish household, who gave brilliant and effective national service and who in battle or before the firing party in the jail yard gave the final guarantee of their sincere patriotism. Meetings such as this were run on severely business lines. There was no oratory but each item on the long agenda was discussed at length and each man leaving the meeting had a clear conception of the condition of the organisation, was completely informed in regard to any change of policy or conditions and had explicit directions as to future activities. This meeting ended as usual about 2 a.m. and together my friend and I started for his hotel. Arriving there we loitered, ringing and knocking for a considerable time until the continuous racket attracted the attention of the patrolling police. On their approach we decided that our meeting them would involve too many explanations so we moved away and directed our steps towards the house where I was to sleep. The bed was large and I could offer him shelter. Approaching the house it suddenly dawned on me that I wasn't sure of its number. It was either number eight or number nine. However, I cheered up when I remembered the instructions about the cord. I marched up the steps of number nine, pawed through the letter box for the cord, found it and pulled it; the door opened. I struck a match and we proceeded upstairs to the bedroom. We met nobody, but the sound of splashing in an adjoining bathroom indicated that we were not the only folk who kept late hours. Everything looked quite normal to me except that I couldn't find my bag. But it was too late to worry and we both got to bed quickly. Lying in bed we were discussing various matters raised at the meeting when the door opened and a lady, candle in hand, and in extreme déshabillé appeared. Immediately she caught sight of us she proceeded to prove that Galli-Curci could not reach a higher note and disappeared like Kai Lung's Maiden *"uttering loud and continuous cries of apprehension to conceal the direction of her flight"*.

Automatically, we jumped to the correct solution. We were in the right room but in the wrong house. The opening of the doors in all the houses in the street was performed in the same simple manner. It should have been a paradise for burglars. Under the particular conditions we felt that explanations would be useless. We slipped on our trousers, gathered together the rest of our belongings and raced for the street. We halted round the corner into a church doorway, got on the rest of our clothes, cursed our luck and then the humour of the situation striking us, laughed ourselves back into a philosophic acceptance of it. We were taking no further chances with cords and letter boxes; we spent the night on the street.

The organisation developing from these Brigade Council meetings was more closely integrated as a result of a Volunteer Convention at Croke Part in October, 1917. Most of the delegates were, like myself, I assume, in Dublin for the Sinn Féin Árd Fheis and were notified verbally of the time and place of the Convention. Time has denied for me much of the memory of that meeting but while there were some heroics, some recriminations, it was from the viewpoint of organisation building eminently businesslike. Reports were made, a central council appointed and decisions reached as to future activities. The use to which the organisation was to be put when fully developed, its actual military methods and objective, may have been clear in the minds of some of the leaders. I was, however, thinking in terms of a nation wide military effort along the lines of Easter Week and from discussions I afterwards had with other Volunteers it seems to me that the same idea was widely held. In the months to come, with conscription regarded as an imminent possibility, preparations for such methods of fighting were actually being made. The fact that conscription was averted permitted the development of an altogether different and more effective method of fighting. I have often thought that if it had been possible to get guns and ammunition a more orthodox text-book type of fighting would have taken place, with disastrous results for the I.R.A. But it was impossible to purchase the material for war. The weapons to be used against the British had first to be taken from them. In the country districts the only rifles were in the hands of the R.I.C. and from the attempts to secure these rifles by the swift sudden attack of unarmed men developed the ambush and the guerrilla tactics.

The concentration of R.I.C. at places of popular assembly, fairs, sports fixtures, etc., was continued down to 1918. On a fair day in the towns and villages the local gendarmerie were always reinforced from the surrounding stations. According to the strength of the station to which they were attached, groups of two, three or four men came in the early morning to the town in which the fair was being held. They were armed with carbine, revolver and baton and travelled by outside car or bicycle, generally the latter. Time and again in the winter of 1917 and the spring of 1918 I attempted to stage a hold-up of these groups, so as to secure the rifles and revolvers, and failed. They travelled by different roads to those expected. They travelled without arms; the men set to watch their movements failed in their assignments; the men mobilised to take part in their disarming failed to turn up. There were many reasons for the failures. One was the lack as yet of a really disciplined and aggressive force; another was the prestige and physique of the R.I.C.; a third that the police were well informed of our movements and intentions. It would be incorrect to say that in the years immediately before 1916 the R.I.C. were unpopular. They were of the people, were inter-married among the people, they were generally men of exemplary lives, and of a high level of intelligence. They did their oftimes unpleasant duty without rancour and oftimes with a maximum of tact, therefore they had friends everywhere who sought the avoidance of trouble for them. But the constant attempts at ambush were the best of training methods; the constant failure weeded out form our ranks all but the most earnest and determined and eventually we achieved success.

Success is oftimes the combined effect of many failures and seldom is it entirely clear cut and satisfactory. So it was with us in our first effective venture. The long wait, the endless planning, the hard work did not end as we expected in a general haul of arms. The rifles we got were few. But a beginning had been made, an example set that was widely followed. Also a schism had been created between the police and their friends. Men who heretofore would not scruple to give a quiet hint to a policeman now felt that such a hint might mean a term of imprisonment for a neighbour and kept a shut mouth. In Ireland the name *'informer'* is one of most evil import and because of the resultant raids, searches and arrests, men who had been on friendly terms with the police now avoided them lest any suspicion should arise that police activities were helped by any speech that passed between them and members of the R.I.C. The police position, always delicate and difficult, tended to become more and more impossible as the months sped by. Before July 1921 they had become, as a weapon in the hands of the British, entirely useless.

I was in the audience at a meeting in September 1917, which Seán Milroy addressed. His opening words were: *"People of Ireland and policemen of England"*. Two R.I.C. men standing near me growled *"We are as good Irishmen as you are"*. That explained the root cause of their final incapacity against the I.R.A. They were Irishmen, and, to quote Liam Mellows, *"Blood is thicker than water and Irish blood is the thickest in the world"*.

The R.I.C. was created by Sir Robert Peel and in his book *Ireland from 98 to 98,* pages 89-90, O'Connor Morris describes its originator and its purpose:

"Peel was associated, however, with the narrow Toryism which was the faith of the Liverpool Ministry; he went to Ireland, as to an unknown land, with the prejudices of a Tory, of the great commercial class of England. He became a formidable opponent, we have seen, of the Catholic claims; and though he was far too able a man not to discountenance Orangeism and its lawless spirit, he was true to the Protestant Ascendancy which he found supreme. He considered Ireland, too, from a purely English point of view, without sympathy with Irish feeling, with no real knowledge of Irish needs or wants; and he carried out a policy in many respects unfortunate. Like his predecessors, he made a free use of repression and extended it to social mischiefs which it could not remedy; he steadily upheld the rights of landlords, even when these were morally unjust, he gave his sanction to a cheap law of ejectment, the source of manifold and most crying evils. He had no insight at this time into the ills of Ireland, and dealt with them according to a bad system of routine, and he quarrelled with O'Connell and denounced the Catholic Board as a mere nest of sedition. Peel, however, gave proof of his great capacity as an administrator at the Castle in these years. He tried, and not without success, to put a check on the scandalous jobbing of the Irish public services; from this time forward we hear less of Irish corruption. The reform in Ireland, however, then chiefly connected with his name, was the institution, in disturbed districts, of a central police force, under paid magistrates, replacing an ineffective local police and the bodies of troops often engaged in this service. This was the origin of the Irish Constabulary and of its present system, one of the most admirable instruments that could be formed to maintain order and law and a powerful agency in Irish social progress".

Law and order for writers like O'Connor Morris meant the preservation of the status quo and had nothing at all to do with social progress. Professor Curtis in his *History Of Ireland*, page 364, says:

"The new police force called the Royal Irish Constabulary, whose ranks were filled with native Irishmen, became a force of high efficiency for keeping order, though, indeed, it was more like an army, and later was used for eviction purposes and as the first line for suppressing rebellion".

Here we have its true purpose, the preservation of landlord right and of English control in Ireland. In *Dublin Castle And The Irish People,* pages 126-127, R. Barry O'Brien quotes a secret R.I.C. circular:

"Furnish without delay a list of persons in your sub-district now alive who in the past five years have taken a prominent part in the Irish National movement either as Fenians or Nationalists. The list is to include:
1. All Fenians or members of the I.R.B. to rank of county centre or whose influence is worth noting.
2. Prominent secret society men of considerable local influence, who have taken, or are likely to take, a leading part in the commission of outrages.
3. Active influential Fenians who travel about the country organising and promoting the interests of secret organisations.
4. Roman Catholic clergymen, and other persons of note, who take a leading part in the National Movement, and from their position and status have

influence over the people.

Persons of prominence who move about between Ireland and Great Britain, or who are in the habit of visiting Ireland from America; also persons of note who have recently returned from America to settle in Ireland. In the list, opposite each man's name, his antecedents, character, opinion (where extreme or moderate), in fact, everything known about him in connection with Fenian or Nationalist movements should be given. The list is to be in the following form...".

The carrying out of the order embodied therein would leave little time for ordinary police work or for the promotion of social progress. In *The Fall Of Feudalism in Ireland,* page 443, Michael Davitt quotes a cipher message from Dublin Castle to Captain Plunkett, R.M. This message was naturally circularised to all Resident Magistrates:

"Do not interfere with Gaelic meetings at present. Get athletic men in the police (Royal Irish Constabulary) to mix as much as possible with the (Gaelic) athletes in the country, so as to try and get the Gaelic Association antagonistic to the National League. Croke (Archbishop of Cashel) has gone against the crowd".

Those who today criticise the continuance by the Gaelic Athletic Association of the ban on foreign games do not realise how closely integrated were the G.A.A. and the Fenian organisation; do not understand the conditions that made the imposition of the ban a national necessity; have no word of condemnation for the ban imposed at Imperial instigation on athletic teams to represent Ireland in international competitions.

Rule 1268 of the R.I.C. code says:

"It is the duty of the District Inspector to see that each man under his command becomes personally acquainted with the inhabitants of the sub-districts in which he is stationed in the shortest possible time".

The police were to insinuate themselves everywhere into the lives of the people.

The concern for social progress might be exemplified by Rule 1274—

"When men thus proceed into the country upon patrol at night one half of the party are to be armed with carbine and revolver and the remainder to have the sword bayonet only",

which sounds more like an order to the patrols in no man's land described by Crozier in *The Men I Killed* than an instruction to a police force in their native country. Rule 938 gave instruction as to the methods to be pursued to prevent ballad singing, again probably in the interests of social progress. *"They think they have purchased one half of us"*, said Pearse, *"and cowed the other half"*. Dublin Castle believed that there could be no Irish thought, word or act that was not covered and controlled by a rule in the R.I.C. code. It contained 1,993 rules. They were inadequate and futile against the love of country that no matter how deeply buried has never been found wanting in the hearts of Irishmen.

When the danger of conscription became acute many of the younger members of the R.I.C. resigned. There has never yet been a generous action for which an ulterior motive has not been found by the ungenerous. It was sometimes said that these men resigned in fear. I have never believed it and the fact that many of them were afterwards found in the ranks of or co-operating in some fashion with Sinn Féin and the I.R.A. is proof sufficient that they were impelled by no unworthy motive. Many of them in 1918 had long service for which a pension was assured; they had families and dependants. Even if they understood and sympathised with the motives of the I.R.A. it would have been most difficult for them to realise that any success would attend the efforts of the handful of men putting their puny strength against the might of Empire. It was expecting too much of them to expect that they would resign en masse. Looking back now, I begin to believe that it was a providential thing for the country that these older men remained at their posts. They were a moderating influence that kept within some bounds the irresponsibilities and criminalities of the Black and Tans and doubtless men of their character were found everywhere among them. I have known many who believed that the Republican effort was madness, indefensible, bound to result in evil, but I believe that the opinion of the majority of them found expression in the words of those brave men at Listowel who spurned Colonel Smith's invitation to become charter members of Murder Incorporated. In appraising the facts that made for success in 1920-21, the resignation of a substantial number of the R.I.C., the passivity of the greater majority of the remainder has not so far received due attention. Like the Condottieri*, they were loyal to their paymasters until their own country was attacked.

# IV

## [Finances / Bands / Rockchapel / Kiskeam / Kanturk]

There is an economic side to the least selfish and [most] idealistic movement and very often the touchstone of sincerity is a willingness to pay in terms of cash. Those who hold the purse strings of an organisation should not only be quite clear on the aims of the organisation but should also be capable of accumulating funds sufficient for the forwarding of these aims and the securing of adequate value for any expenditure of such moneys. The capacity for generous service is not always associated with financial acumen and a sense of thrift, and one important facet of developed leadership is the ability to spend wisely and with the maximum of profit. Niggardliness is fatal in any man dealing with money voluntarily subscribed for an altruistic purpose and often what looks to the uninformed eye as reckless prodigality may be in actual fact true economic wisdom. Finance Ministers, treasurers, quartermasters may be born, but not often. The control and direction of finance is

---

* [*Condottieri*: mercenary bands of military adventurers in Italy in the 14th and 15th centuries. J.L.]

developed only as a result of training and experience and the less grounded in materialism a national movement is the less likely it is to have everywhere business-like custodians of its finances.

The proper control and handling of the organisation funds was one of the many headaches that affected the organisers of the Irish Volunteers in 1917. Little money was needed, all were voluntary workers. Each unit of the organisation provided its own funds and those funds were secured with reasonable ease. In those early years the line between the politically and militarily minded was not rigidly drawn. In rural areas Volunteers were members of Sinn Féin Clubs and all but the older members of Sinn Féin Clubs were Volunteers, and irrespective of the nature of the work, all without distinction were participants.

There was often a common war chest. The Sinn Féin Club Treasurer was frequently the quartermaster of the Volunteer company and the manner in which he disposed of this common war chest was a constant cause for criticism by those men who made both organisations possible.

In the temple of nationality there are always the money changers and in 1917 the purveyors of the ingredients of the froth of sentimentality were rampant. They pushed their wares beneath the gibbet and rooted their profits in the graves of the dead. Picture postcards, belts and badges, ballads and banners were extolled as the weapons wherewith a nation's freedom might be bought. The constant urging of organisers that books on history and economics, Gaelic League publications, military manuals might be purchased; that funds might be conserved for the purchase of arms, for the fighting of elections was in great measure ignored. It was only the patient, tolerant, persevering and never ending work of the organisers that replaced a satisfied emotionalism and implanted the understanding that this new national movement demanded a personal effort and an acceptance of responsibility from each single supporter. Emotion within reason is not to be decried. It may be used to create enthusiasm which, tempered by resolution, can work wonders in an organisation; left to run its natural course, it saps all strength and the end is decadence.

The desire for music and pageantry was the chief obstacle of a serious and sound organisation and he who said *"Music is the only noise which one must pay to hear"* must have had in mind the bands from which I suffered. In the western side of the constituency every Sinn Féin Club and Volunteer unit desired to have a band, a pipers' band for preference, by way of second choice, a fife and drum band, and God! what bands!

My antipathy to bands was well known. I had preached at Battalion Council meetings the inequity of spending money on flags and fifes and drums and paraffin for torches and among the more earnest workers a reaction had set in. These had found that constant band practice and parade did not make for progress and efficiency and I had at this time created a healthy spirit of rivalry between the various companies. One of the keenest men with whom I had to deal was Dan Martin Murphy of Glounakeel. I had appealed to him at a Battalion Council meeting to prevent the funds accumulated in the Rockchapel Company area from being dissipated. I had heard that negotiations for the purchase of drums from a Dublin firm were going on and

I hoped to prevent a further addition to the grand total of bands in the locality. There seemed to be one in every townland, the organisation extended to the accompaniment of drumbeats. If the vibration of the drums could have disintegrated an Empire, imperialism as a political theory would be now defunct. Dan and I discussed what I had now come to regard as the possible tragedy of the Rockchapel Company—the purchase of a band. He urged that only my presence in his area, a serious talk from me to the members of the company and an insistence on my part on the aims and objects of the organisation would divert the minds of his associates from their preoccupation with music. I had not had for some time an opportunity of visiting his district and made arrangements for a visit there within the ensuing ten days. He argued earnestly the advisability of an earlier visit but my engagements were such that I was unable to agree. We made the final arrangements as to the place and hour of my next visit and parted, he to return to his home, I to continue my trek through the Brigade area.

One afternoon a week later I turned my face to the west and pedalled thirty miles of rough and muddy road. I had to avoid the direct route through Kanturk and Newmarket and went to Boherbue, about fifteen miles from my destination. Arriving there I decided to have a meal and was lucky to meet an old lady who seemed more concerned with my hungry, undernourished looks than with any desire to profit financially from my visit. She was inquisitive and plied me with questions. I was keen enough at this time to refrain from parrying them. Experience had taught me the necessity for a *"full and frank"* answer to all such queries. The *"veracity"* of my answers troubled neither of us and I soon had her in the anecdotal stage where in an hour's conversation I gleaned a valuable knowledge of local affairs that I could not have acquired if I on my side had shown the least reticence. We parted with mutual expressions of goodwill and with her *"God protect you, boy"*, I faced the darkness and Rockchapel.

It was cold and a heavy mist filled the valley. The road was rough and the patches of stone laid to repair the worst ravages of traffic and weather were scattered and lay buried in the oozy surface, as if placed specially to damage tyres or to accentuate the danger of skids. It was necessary to trundle the bicycle; until one got used to the darkness it was impossible to see a hand's breadth ahead. After a while grey took the place of black; it was possible to see the road surface, to avoid the roadside hedges and to steer clear of the occasional straying animal. The sudden flame of a torch by the river bank betokened that the spawning salmon were arriving and marked the spot where that day a scouting poacher had noted a *"scour"*.

The mist became a drizzle, driven obliquely across the valley by a south west wind. Water seemed to pour down my neck, it hammered on pistoning thighs. I turned north at a bridge where two streams joined and entered another glen. The wind was now behind me but the road was uphill and it was with aching muscle and a glorious sense of relief that I reached the top and faced the three mile descent to Glounakeel. I did not reach the boundary of the company area until I crossed the streamlet at the bottom of the hill. But once across it I ran into a group of men on their way to the mobilisation point. I dismounted, they greeted me quietly and we proceeded together. I made conversation and received monosyllabic answers. These men of Rockchapel were not subject to any swift enthusiasm for strangers. They would be helpful and hospitable to them, but they would keep their own counsel. Their confidence was not readily given to anybody other than their intimates. And I was a stranger in great measure, known only to the officers whom I had met at Battalion Council. The rain and the darkness seemed to be non-existent for these men. None of them wore an overcoat. One took my bicycle and went off in the darkness. Half a mile further on a lamp burning brightly and the flame of a huge turf fire made a pathway of light from an open door, a dog thrust a cold nose inquisitively into my hand and retreated satisfied to the fire where in a few moments, divested of my overcoat, with a huge steaming mug of strong sweet tea in front of me, I too was seated. The bean-na-tighe, quiet, soft-spoken, yet matriarchal, gave her orders, *"a fire in the room and candles"*. I'd stop the night. *"Take out the tick and let it be airing before the fire"*. A word to one of the girls, a nod to another and without fuss all preparations were made for my comfort and entertainment.

In the meantime the house was gradually filling. The settle was first occupied, then the chairs and stools and finally the rooms were robbed of their scant furnishings to provide accommodation. And still the Company came. The walls of the kitchen were now lined three deep. There was a low animated murmur of conversation. I was under a constant if covert survey. There was a watchful solemnity about the whole affair which reminded me that it might have been a wake and I the corpse but for the fact that no prayers were offered, at least publicly, on my behalf. The change from the penetrating cold and dampness of the outside world to the now steaming atmosphere of the kitchen was becoming oppressive and I was about to suggest that the conference with the officers in the upper room might begin when the matriarch spoke again, *"Danny"*, says she, *"wouldn't ye play the band for the organiser"*. Danny frowned and looked sheepishly at me as there was a rattle of hobnailed boots on the floor behind me, shrugged his shoulders and smiled. I turned round. Two large men had a smaller man on their shoulders. He was handing down bright, new, gaily painted drums from the collars where they were resting to the reaching hands of the others. I counted a big drum and four side drums. A space was cleared in the centre of the floor, the big drum was braced, the smaller drums were screwed up and the drummers stood to line. Then it seemed as if all the others present buried their left hands in inner pockets and produced fifes. The big drummer gave a preliminary and encouraging tap and then while thirty fifes shrilled forth the *"Wearing of the Green"* all the drummers, like demented semaphores whirled their sticks as if their lives depended on their drowning all sound other than that of their own production. The windows rattled, cups danced on the dresser, the lamp flame jumped agitatedly; the sheep dog lifted his pointed nose in the chimney corner and howled mournfully. In sympathy and approval I scratched him between the ears. He expressed my viewpoint.

But all the bands were not of mushroom growth. Away to the south across the hills in Kiskeam was another Company centre where there was one with a long and chequered career and a fighting tradition. Organised in the seventies as a temperance band, it evolved into an instrument of Land League organisation. Now and again through the years it disappeared but in time of public turmoil or rejoicing it sprang forth again. Its continued existence was due to the real love of music and the restless excitement and loving character of the Kiely family. The Volunteer movement provided an outlet for their explosive energy and the band was reorganised and sedulously trained.

*The Soldier's Song* was new and was not included in the repertoire of the village band. Old Tim Kiely was, however, able to give a very creditable rendering of the piece of music that was so soon to be heard in every parish in Ireland; he had heard it sung by a man recently home from prison and his unforgetting ear retained its melody.

I remember my first introduction to it, in November, 1917. The Clare Election was over and Eamon de Valera and other prominent members of Sinn Féin touring the country were due that day in my district. It was my duty as organiser of the meeting to have the Volunteers and Sinn Féin Clubs in full strength there. During the preceding weeks I had cycled and tramped over road and boreen for forty miles around. The work of organisation was easy; there was no need to arouse enthusiasm, everywhere was the excitement of preparation. In one parish the awkward squad was being taught to form fours; in another the fife and drum band, equipped, to paraphrase Billy Heffernan, *"with Matt Delaney's bellows in its stomach"* was practising its tunes, the fifes shrilling vainly against the overpowering thunder of the drums; in a third the main preoccupation was with the collection of saddles for those who would participate in the cavalry parade.

Rising before dawn in the memorable day, I arrived in Kiskeam to be greeted by the resonant reveille of Tim's cornet blaring forth in the notes of *The Soldier's Song* his belief in a resurgent nationality. I still see him marching from the corner of the lane, towel on shoulder, his huge hairy chest thrusting through his unbuttoned shirt, placing particular emphasis on *"the despot and the slave"* as he passed the doorway of a crony, John Daly, who had dared to argue the merits of constitutionalism.

Soon the village was awake and astir. The sweet smell of bog deal burning, the cloud of turf smoke and the rattle of the fan bellows betokened that breakfast was on the way. Cattle weaved through the village on their way to the drinking pool or fields. Infants cherubic in cutty sarks appeared at doorways or on the street. The crowd gathered. Volunteers in their various conceptions of what constituted military equipment—belt, badge and buckle,—as soon to be discarded for the barest and most effective essentials of violence by the grandsons of the men against whose sardonic and cynical humour Davis was warned in 1842 when he wrote to Barry of ceremonial uniforms*; the pipe smoking elders of the Sinn Féin Club, later the efficient judges, the commissariat, the intelligence, the impenetrable wall of silence behind which the I.R.A. operated.

Then the band, and an argument as to who should have the drums and cymbals. These were the consolation prizes to the non musical. John Daly, the constitutionalist, is awarded the big drum. Even though his faith is not as yet

---

* [*ceremonial uniforms*: see *Thomas Davis* by Charles Gavan Duffy—pages 171 and 214 of Aubane Historical Society edition. J.L.]

ours, he's a neighbour, a fellow craftsman, a congenial or better say a convivial spirit who will ask no awkward questions about the time of adjournment of any festivities; and this was to be a great day, unaffected by any puritanical inhibitions. *"Lá d'ár Saoghal" mar a dubhairt an t-Oileánach.* These men who were to be so grim and fierce and unbending were out for the day and Davis knew them when he wrote of their neighbours:

*"You'd swear they knew no other mood but mirth and love in Tipperary".**

The cars assembled, every sort of vehicle and animal, bicycles of every vintage year. The procession is ready to move, but first we must parade through the village. The women and children who are to be left expect the parade. A banner, reminiscent of Knocknagoshel, is hoisted.**

The band falls in behind it. The Company Captain parades his men—smart, slovenly, self-conscious or awkward, they come to attention and swing into line. The general public comes too, women last and children everywhere.

What'll we play? What would we play but *God Save Ireland*! And so we started the march and knew it not, that among us were those who were to stand where Allen, Larkin and O'Brien stood and for the same undying cause.

At last we're ready. We mount cars and bicycles. The cavalry closes in behind. We cheer ironically as we pass the R.I.C. Barracks, and *The Soldier's Song,* as a cornet solo, once again assails our ears. As we progress the procession swells, each mountain and bog road yields its quota. Each new contingent is greeted with the brazen *Soldier's Song* and finally we arrived in Kanturk, the meeting place. The roads are thronged. Because we have the only brass band we are given pride of place on entering the town; also, because we are reputedly a hard tough crowd and one never knows what the police will do. We know nothing of police law except that 'tis agin us.

And the police are present. What manner of man is this, what force does he represent that this grim battalion of giants is needed to overawe his hearers? It stretches along the street in endless lines with carbines slung; cloaked, helmeted, silent, in marked contrast to the exuberant mass that marches past towards the meeting place. The paymasters of the R.I.C. have as yet no conception of the fact that out of this amorphous purposeless mass will be hammered the finely tempered weapon of a disciplined people, and they have not realised that ties of blood and kinship will make the R.I.C. ineffective for their purpose and that a great body of these men will not ignore the call.

How to describe the meeting, the parade and inspection of Volunteers, the discussion on organisation, the speeches? Strand Street was filled with people. It looked like Croke Park when the whistle goes after the hurling final; but this crowd was silent and expectant. A local singer got on the platform and opened the proceedings with *The Soldier's Song.* There was a rustle in the crowd betokening the uneasiness felt by rural folk when one of the

---

* [*in Tipperary*: from *The Men Of Tipperary* by Thomas Davis. J.L.]
** [The Knocknagoshel Land League Banner carried the slogan *"Arise Knocknagoshel and take your place among the Nations of the earth".* J.L.]

number makes a public exhibition of himself. Then Tim Kiely, emerging from an inn, a giant refreshed, chimed in with his cornet, his notes echoed off the walls of the houses; the singer faltered and went on, and then, drowning the music, came a defiant joyous full-throated roar from the crowd.

No longer could there be any doubt of the success and enthusiasm of the meeting. The speeches did not really matter that day. Instinctively the people knew the terms of the message. They were concerned merely with the sincerity of those who brought it; accepted as a guarantee of that sincerity the story of their participation in the Easter Week Rising; knew now the lesson of Easter Week that a country unfree must be a nation in arms and that there was a place for each one in the Bearna Baoighill.

The meeting closed, darkness and a cold drizzle of rain emptied the streets. It is never easy to marshal such a home-going crowd but eventually we got under way. The rain driving from the west beat in our faces. We passed a farmhouse. A dog barked. He was joined by the dog in the next house and the chorus of sound echoed across the countryside, became intermittent, died out. No other sound but the rattle of hoof and wheel; rain, cold and hunger had damped enthusiasm. It was a tired, silent crowd that dismounted in the village. But the band had to play, otherwise the people of the village would think that something untoward had happened. Mothers, who on days like this always waited in anxiety, would be uneasy. Therefore the band played. It was not a concentrated effort but it sufficed.

A final wallop of the drum, a cheer, and so, with *O'Donnell Abú* and *The West's Awake* strangely mingling in our ears, to bed.

My organisation work started again the following day. I called to the village and on my friend Tim Kiely when on my way to another district. He was cleaning his cornet. I made a certain suggestion to him. We moved to the nearest hostelry and on my invitation he laid the cornet on the counter and buried his face in the healing brew. I examined the cornet, the bell of which was bent and crumpled, and remarked, *"What happened this; was it damaged yesterday?"* He finished the pint, looked reflectively and, perhaps, hopefully at the empty pot and said *"No, I bent that on the sergeant's head at a Land League Meeting in Millstreet in '98".* Davis might not have wholly approved of him. I felt that Tone and Mitchel, Fintan Lalor and Rossa would have understood him. I put my last shilling on the counter and nodded at the man behind the bar. He did his stuff and we had one on the house.

The destruction of this band by R.I.C. and military was one of those incidents that tended to accentuate the dislike for British authority in the district. On June 21st, 1918, there was a by-election in Cavan. Arthur Griffith was elected. Against my opposition it was decided to hold a victory parade in Newmarket. In April, 1918, the threat of conscription brought a great influx of men into the Volunteer movement and this imposed a heavy burden of work on organisers and training officers. These men had to be trained, disciplined, lessoned to an appreciation of the national position and to an understanding of the objective of the Volunteer movement. This could not be simply accomplished. Most of these men had not the same ideals or tradition of the original Volunteers. Into the Sinn Féin Movement came older men perturbed about conscription and its possible effect on their sons. These had memories of Land League agitation, of old time political efforts. They believed in the effectiveness of demonstration, mass meetings, oratory and torchlight processions. They did not understand that an entirely different situation had arisen. They could not realise that an Empire fighting for the retention of its control was a different proposition to a class fighting for the retention of its special privilege. It was men of this type who urged the desirability of the parade. It was to be an anti-conscription demonstration as much as a political victory celebration. My opposition was based on the desire to avoid bringing prominent members of the organisation to the notice of the R.I.C.; on the need for an understanding of the fact that gasconnade was not a substitute for steel-like purpose. There was nothing wrong or illegal about the holding of such a parade. But Law in Ireland, as it related to politics, was under British Control, not a matter of legal enactment but one of the personal opinion of those responsible for the administration of Law and Order. The parade, headed by the band, marched round the town. All went merry as a marriage bell until the police barracks was reached. Here the marchers were met by an unprovoked baton charge. A struggle ensued and into the mass charged a party of about one hundred soldiers bringing the rifle butt to the reinforcement of the baton. The police concentrated on the smashing of the band while the soldiers used their rifle butts indiscriminately on the crowd. An indescribable scene of confusion resulted and soon the streets were cleared of all but the wounded. Scattered about the roadway were broken drums and battered instruments. Most of the police behaved decently. Afterwards it transpired that the District Inspector, a neurotic individual, was solely responsible for the attack.

The affair had a sequel three years later. On July 12th 1921, men on the run arrived home. On the same day this Police Inspector had gone on a holiday to the city. Some bright genius decided that an opportunity for the rehabilitation of the band had presented itself. A list of broken instruments was made, a few cars procured and a few hefty service men proceeded to the city. Their first call was on a dealer in musical instruments from whom they got an estimate of cost of the replacement of the instruments destroyed. They then proceeded to the Unionist Club where they found the District Inspector at lunch. Having barred all exits from the Club they presented their bill for damage. The unfortunate man, whose misjudgement or misdeeds had overtaken him, produced a cheque book. The cheque was refused and he was compelled to find, by borrowing from fellow members and the staff, enough money to foot the bill. A week later the parade that started three years before to celebrate the Cavan election victory was resumed in honour of the greater victory won by the efforts and sacrifices of the intervening years. The band in all its glory of new and shiny brass instruments and gaily painted drums paraded past the R.I.C. Barracks. There was, to the disappointment of some who had felt the weight of baton and rifle butt, no repetition of the charge of 1918. A week later the British Inspector resigned and left the country. The wheel had come full circle.

# V

## [Elections / Donegal / Prison / Hunger Strike / Arms Raids]

I was awakened about 5 a.m. on the morning after the attack on the band by the owner of the house in which I was sleeping. *"The soldiers are all round the house"*, he said, *"I'm afraid you're caught"*. I dressed hurriedly and went swiftly to the front window. There was an array of soldiers in the street. I looked out the back. They had already gone over the wall into the yard. Then came a thunderous knock at the front door. I raced up to the attic and went through a skylight on to the roof and dropped twenty feet into the yard of the adjoining house. Luckily I was unhurt. I climbed over a number of walls and fences and then reached the open country. I ran towards the West for two miles without a stop, then feeling the pursuit, if any, could not reach me I turned north and arrived at the house of a farmer I knew. I arrived in time to participate in a substantial breakfast. I also arrived at the decision that the district would in future be honoured by my presence only during my waking hours.

All the effective political leaders were again in prison. Some of the prominent Volunteer leaders and organisers were also in prison. The great tide of 1918 recruitment to the Volunteers had begun to ebb and the need for intensive organisation of Sinn Féin and the Volunteers was more imperative than ever. I travelled through the district, holding meetings of Sinn Féin, instructing Volunteer Companies, trying to inspire men, to arouse flagging interest, to devise ever new methods for retaining the organisation in being. I kept in touch with the Brigade O.C., Tomás MacCurtain, who had escaped capture, meeting him in the Boggeragh Hills when he was in my district.

Then disaster struck us. The influenza epidemic of 1918 struck the country like a plague, and numbered among its victims were some of the most promising men in our organisation. I fell a victim and for a month lay lifeless, dead in body and mind. Even when I recovered my energy had completely disappeared and it was another month before I was back in fighting trim again.

My first duty on recovery was to organise a convention for the selection of a candidate to contest the coming General Election. My organising work of the previous years had made me a well known figure all over the constituency and as a result my name was put in nomination. I had no desire to be nominated. I believed that the position of public representative needed a man of much more knowledge and experience than I possessed. My viewpoint also was that the purpose and earnestness of our policy would be more effectively emphasised if a man who had taken part in the actual fighting of Easter Week was selected. This viewpoint was accepted by my friends and an Easter Week man, Páidín O'Keeffe, was given the nomination.

It looked for a while as if there would be a contest in the constituency and all preparations for a fight were made. A week before the date of nomination for candidate came, our only opponent, John Guiney, M.P., signified his withdrawal and our man was returned unopposed.

I was sent to North Donegal where a contest was to take place. I utilised the opportunity to try to build up the Sinn Féin and Volunteer organisation there. I also made speeches at public meetings, but am afraid that their content and delivery had nothing to do with the success of our candidate, Joe Doherty. Those who accompanied me from North Cork were Michael McAuliffe, Seán Breen, now in the Army Medical Service, and Charlie O'Reilly, killed in March, 1921.

It was a new experience for me. I was in a constituency where elections were always bitterly fought, where there were very clear and distinct differences of opinion and where every class in the community took an intense interest in politics. In my own district the political wing of the organisation was comprised of and controlled by the Volunteers. All young men, none of whom had little [sic], if any, previous experience of political effort, none of whom had that inestimable quality of which we have often heard so much, *"a stake in the country"*. Here my daily contacts were with experienced politicians, business and professional men, clergy and farmers. It was a most valuable experience. I learned much of the ways of politics, of many sidelights of political history which I had read and the meaning of which I only now fully grasped. My chief mentor was John McLoughlin, afterwards a Senator. It was, too, I learned later, an experience for those men to meet me, entirely unwise in the ways of politics, selfless, untiring, without personal ambition, convinced that political effort, though essential, was yet a mere adjunct to and background for a more deadly struggle. None of these older men had any faith in a military struggle. I think they believed that the years would wean us, of the Volunteer Movement, away from the idea. It is to their credit that when the struggle came they stood fast and did not waver and though in the years to come I was to part with some of them politically I have always retained a pleasant memory of our association and a respect for them as men who loved and served our common country.

Home again to my own district, the land of abandoned and destroyed police barracks. *"Tombstones of British Supremacy in Ireland"* as the London *"Times"* styled them. But as yet British supremacy in Ireland did not need a tombstone. The Great War was over, the Peace Conference in Paris was engaged in laying the foundation for another Armageddon. The danger of conscription was past and many of those who rushed into the Volunteers in the Spring of 1918 had departed, almost disrupting the organisation. The weary work of rebuilding it had to begin all over again. It was a never ending task and indeed the labourers were few. They worked under harassing conditions and their efforts often at the most vital stages likely to be terminated by capture and imprisonment. And this was my fate. I was arrested and given a prison sentence. It was the penalty of achievement, the guinea stamp of accomplishment. But I felt it as a personal disaster.

Prison is an excellent test of conviction, a glacial immersion of enthusiasm. The cold, narrow, stone-floored cell was like a vault. The light from the small window, high on one wall, served only to emphasise the presence of the bars. In one corner was a shelf on which were a bible, a small wooden box of salt and a comb, broken and not overclean. Against one wall was a narrow wooden platform standing on edge; on this, neatly piled, were several rough blankets. A slop-pail completed the furnishings. At 4 p.m. supper was served. This consisted of a piece of soggy black bread and a tin of some kind of cocoa without milk or sugar, nauseous and bitter. With the delivery of this meal business closed down for the night. Silence more profound descended on the prison, broken occasionally by the footstep of a warder on the stone floor of the corridor. I repeated to myself Lovelace's poem *To Althea, From Prison:*—

"Minds innocent and quiet
Take that for a Hermitage".

My mind was neither innocent nor quiet. I was fed up. I got tired of walking four paces back and forth. I did physical jerks, tired of these too, made my bed and lay down. The bed was hard and lumpy but to such beds I was not unaccustomed. The blankets were thin and comfortless yet I slept almost immediately. I woke in the darkness, sat up wondering where I was, then remembered and lay down again. I found it difficult to go to sleep again but eventually did so. The noisy opening of the door and a gruff voice from a warder brought me back to consciousness. I got up and dressed. I was ordered to fold my blankets, place the bedboard on its side against the wall and lay the blankets neatly on its upper edge. I did so but not to the warder's satisfaction. I tried again and my second effort, while it produced no applause, passed muster. In the meantime another prisoner left a bucket of water at my door. The warder handed me a piece of soap, a scrubbing brush and a small towel. He instructed me to wash first and then scrub out my cell. My personal ablutions performed I directed my attention to the floor, starting at the inner wall. I worked towards the door, moving crabwise on my knees. As I reached the corridor I raised my head, looked left and right, and saw, in extended order, the posteriors of my fellows emerging from their laundered igloos. I got on my feet and placed bucket and scrubbing brush by the door, awaiting instruction for their disposition. The prisoner on my right spoke, *"Can you sleep on that damn bed?"* he asked. *"Yes"*, I replied. *"I'm here three days"*, he said, *"and I can't sleep, my back is broken from the boards"*. I slipped into his cell and examined the bed and found nothing wrong. Then he explained. He had been placing the boards face down on the floor and lying on the frame to which they were nailed. An Eastern hermit might have reached Nirvana under such conditions but it was not surprising that my questioner failed to find rest. *"What are you in for?"*, I asked. *"For stealing thirteen pounds"*, he replied. *"Did you steal it?"*, I asked. *"I did not"*, was the reply. Perhaps he told the truth. I found it difficult to believe that a man so utterly incapable of looking after himself could have got away with the property of another.

Breakfast came at eight. Half a pint of cold and lumpy porridge and a few ounces of black bread. Then in their turns the doctor and the Governor. Any complaints? None: but others must have complained. From my cell door I saw a line forming in the corridor. At the head of the line was a huge Negro, obviously a sailor. The doctor passed down the line, questioned each man shortly and the parade was dismissed. All cell doors were then closed and each prisoner was left to his own devices for a further two hours. Then those of us who were political prisoners were ordered into a small yard for exercise—*"With slouch and swing around the ring"*— we followed each other at intervals, bunched together, until the warders got tired of ordering us apart.*

We got to know each other. We were prisoners from Kerry, Tipperary and Cork. Two were mere boys from Cork City. One of these, Michael Kenny, was small, eager and hungry. He gladly ate the bread I found uneatable. He confided in me that he had two ambitions, one was to fight for an Irish Republic, two, the first accomplished, to go to Texas and become a cowboy. In the years afterwards I heard of him as a keen soldier. Recently I met him. One of his ambitions was not achieved. He had never gone to Texas and since he now has family responsibilities it is unlikely that he'll go there. My own memory of my trial is that of the prosecuting officer, a small Welshman, a Lieutenant. I argued with him over the precise meaning of certain words used by the witnesses, not indeed in the hope of any mitigation of my certain sentence but just from sheer cussedness. I was satisfied when he lost his temper. I was sentenced to a year's imprisonment.

I was escorted back to my cell for my few belongings and then transferred to No. 10 Wing, a portion of the prison that had not been in use for many years, in which political prisoners were now placed. The change from constant movement, ever fresh contacts, friendly faces, to the dreariness of solitary confinement of the narrow cell and to the dour outlook of warders was indeed depressing. I shall always hate jails and sympathise with prisoners. The food was uneatable; the bullying tones of the warders unbearable; the harsh routine of prison life a constant insult. I went on hunger strike. Then began the struggle for freedom. Day after day I found my mind preoccupied with the devising of menus. Elaborate and often incongruous combinations of food—flesh, fruit, vegetables—passed on the assembly belt of imagination before my eyes leaving the craving that encompassed me more insistent as the days went by. At no time, however, did this delicious dream of food tend to weaken my determination to continue the strike. Spirit triumphed over matter. *"Not by bread alone does a man live"* would at any time probably have expressed my viewpoint. Since then I have now and again considered the phrase and it seems to me that *"bread"* is the operative word. It makes clear the point that before a man can live spiritually he must have a physical being; the measure of man's spiritual development is the extent of his control over the body's demand. Where the struggle for existence is unduly harsh, man's concern for the things of the spirit is atrophied.

It is with nations as it is with men. A down-trodden, impoverished, enslaved nation must, somehow, anyhow, live. Denied freedom, unable to loose its shackles, its weaker or more worldly-minded citizens make compromise. A birthright is sold for a mess of pottage. But when the mess is eaten, when the pangs of hunger are assuaged, comes again the desire to regain the birthright.

The abstract principle that freedom is the birthright of a nation is generally conceded, but the putting into operation of abstract principles is not highly regarded in this workaday world and so powerful nations with a lust for conquest have enslaved weaker ones. Ireland has been the victim of English

---

* [*With slouch and swing*: quoted from *The Ballad Of Reading Jail* by Oscar Wilde. J.L.]

conquest but that conquest has never been accepted by the Irish people. Time and again that non-acceptance has been emphasised in revolt. Always there has been the minority who preached that submission was slavish and a majority who consciously or subconsciously believed in the doctrine preached but were awed to silence and inaction. It was a doctrine that gave no thought to economics. It was the expression of a psychological need; the need that men felt for a recognition of their manhood; the acceptance of the fact that man being endowed with an immortal soul is, in the one fundamental essential, the equal of his fellows and, therefore, not to be exploited, derided or enslaved.

Wearisome, interminable, the days of my hunger-strike dragged out the slow length. Threatened, abused, ridiculed at first, later I was wooed and tempted with specially prepared delicacies. I refused to break. I was taken to the prison hospital and here I found the instrument for my swift release. I was weak, emaciated, with a ragged beard when taken to hospital. The warders placed me by the fire while they made up a bed for me. As I crouched over the fire another prisoner came to speak to me. In after years I was to know him well as an incorrigible practical joker. He was Martin Beckett of Kilgarvan. He asked my name and address, which I gave him. He then asked what was wrong. I told him of my intention to hunger strike until released. He gathered the other prisoners in the ward around him, issued swift instructions and then facing the warders said, *"We're not going to stop in this damn place, we know what this chap is and what's wrong with him. He's dangerous"*, said the humourist, whose long solemn face was a perfect portrayal of earnest alarm, *"He's a lunatic and every relation of his died in a lunatic asylum"*. The warders pooh-poohed the statement, and while they finished their work of bed-making and tucking me in, my new found friend collected tongs, poker and every movable article in the room which might conceivably be converted into a weapon of destruction by a homicidal maniac and insisted that the warders on their departure should remove the results of his collection. He was strenuously supported by the other prisoners and the warders left more than half convinced of the truth of his argument.

We had immediate results. The prison Governor and doctor arrived hot foot, questioned and examined me. I refused to talk and snarled when touched. I had the greatest difficulty in refraining from laughter at the inspired performance of the practical joker. Compared with him Munchausen was a tyro and Ananias a novice. He gave a family history of paranoiac performance equalling the combined stories of Landru and Jack the Ripper. Under his leadership and direction the whole cast put on an excellent show. The visitors left. I felt we had won the second round. An eavesdropping warder was placed outside the door but we had now fully entered into the spirit of the joke and everything he heard merely tended to confirm the fact of my insanity.

The evening meal arrived for the other prisoners. I leaped frenziedly out of bed, grabbed the tray from the table where the warder laid it, hurled it at the window and yelled *"Poison, Poison"*. I was bustled back to bed and while two warders were left on guard the other prisoners were taken out and given a meal outside. They returned with apparent reluctance. The rumour had by then spread through the prison that the hunger striker had gone mad. Excited faces appeared at all cell windows. Men yelled for information and received it in returning yells. The Pélion of conjecture was piled on the Ossa of rumour. Prison discipline went by the board. Doors were kicked, windows broken, pandemonium reigned. The unfortunate prison Governor and doctor were far nearer to mental derangement than I even pretended to be. The prisoners in the hospital divided the night into two watches. While one half slept the other kept guard lest I should during the night develop homicidal tendencies. Warders visited us at short intervals, while I sat in bed brooding like a character of Dostoevsky. Early in the morning came the Governor, the doctor and a mental specialist. I maintained my position and my silence. They departed, an hour passed, and then came four warders. They dressed me while I lay passive on the bed, hauled me downstairs in their arms, put me in a cab and delivered me at a city hospital. Here I spent a day still speechless, still refusing food. Early the following day Tomás MacCurtain, the Brigade O.C., came to see me, looked at me without speaking. There was no need for speech, we understood each other. A few days later the hospital had a number of visitors. They took up positions quietly at doorways and in the hospital corridors. Ten minutes later I was speeding to the mountains in the company of my comrades. My sanity had returned. But my ordeal had taken more out of me than I realised. Never very robust, the hunger strike superimposed on the gastric flu, from which I had not fully recovered, had reduced me to a shadow. It was some time before I had sufficiently recuperated to continue the work interrupted by my imprisonment.

During my absence conditions had worsened. The dreary round began again and then again I remembered the discussions I heard in my youth between the Fenians, of the delays and heartbreaking postponement of the date of the Rising; of the hope deferred that maketh the heart sick. It struck me that Stephens had perhaps spent too much time at routine organisation work, tried to create too perfect a machine. He failed to realise that he was not dealing with stable conditions and material, that the minds of men are generally in a state of flux and that it is the exceptional individual who, accepting an idea, is inspired by perpetual faith in it and ready always at a moment's notice to make sacrifice for it. I decided that effective preparation might occupy so much time as to bring forgetfulness of purpose, and remembered Fintan Lalor's *"Every beginning is premature"*. I believed that action should be substituted for preparation and considered how this belief could be made effective. The serviceable arms in Volunteer hands were so few as to be negligible; there could be no attacks on the existing R.I.C. barracks where the members of that force were now concentrated. Successful attacks on military patrols were out of the question.

These patrols, designed probably to replace the abandoned R.I.C. barracks as indication of British power and control, cycled about the countryside, attended public functions, such as race meetings, feiseanna, hurling matches, sometimes were used to prevent these being held, always bringing a feeling of unease among the people. The rudiments of an intelligence system was created. These patrols were watched, their movements known or anticipated and such simple expedient as a glass strewn hillside down which the cycling soldiers were coasting swiftly, a line of wire across the road in the dusk brought at first disaster, then rage, finally discontinuance of the patrol. This was work with the element of danger which appealed to the Volunteers and made them more keen. The ill-temper of the soldiers vented on the people of village and countryside aroused the dormant dislike which our people ever have for the dominance of a foreign soldiery in their own land. The activities of the red coats was a keen and personal memory with the older folk who had seen and suffered from evictions and who had commented sardonically on *"the war for the Freedom of Small Nations"*. We were thus accomplishing our purpose of creating a keener Volunteer spirit and building a background of popular support for our activities. A few safe people naturally pointed out that all the trouble might have been avoided if the Volunteers were quiescent, but old traditions die hard and Ireland is eternally rebel against the idea that foreign domination is admissible; and the wise ones were quickly silenced. The rudimentary intelligence service which I have mentioned developed into greater effectiveness. No move of R.I.C. or military went unnoticed. *"As a result of information received"*, to quote an old police cliché, an opportunity came to strike a more serious blow to the British than had hitherto been given us.

I was not to know of or to participate in this action. I.R.A. intelligence officers in the Fermoy Company had watched, among other things, the Church Parade of British troops and noticed that a group of between twenty and thirty attended the Wesleyan Chapel each Sunday morning. Liam Lynch, the Company Captain, and Lar Condon, later Battalion Commandant, conceived the idea of getting the rifles with which these men paraded. Such small arms as were available to them, and they were pitifully few, were gathered, a party of resolute men selected and then, with some assistance from the Mallow Company, one morning they struck hard, simply and successfully—result two dozen rifles and the realisation that these military automata, perfectly drilled, moving with such beautiful precision, appearing so formidable, were only men who could be smashed into a helpless mob by a sudden fierce onslaught from determined men with no regard for personal consequences. The attackers quickly dispersed, the alarm was sounded and without delay thousands of soldiers and hundreds of R.I.C. were holding up roads, ruthlessly raiding the countryside, breaking and destroying property, bullying and assaulting the civilian population.

Now came the test for the organisation we had been at such pains to create. We had the rifles, could we hold them in spite of this activity? And the organisation stood the test. The rifles were spirited away across the countryside by pre-arranged relays of men to a remote district outside the immediate limit of serious search. It was an action in which hundreds of men were deliberately employed. It was successful. No word or rumour was whispered of the destination of the rifles or of the manner in which they reached it. Volunteers everywhere who had had the least participation in the effort formed a new estimate of their capacity and responsibility. We had the nucleus of an army. How were we to use it? Opportunities for attack were not again to be readily found. But the rifles were not to be laid by for use in the yet unconceived future of the Active Service Units. Combat troops are not made quickly or to order. They must be made above all familiar with the weapons they are to use and here the rifles were a Godsend. Here and there was a resigned R.I.C. man or ex-soldier familiar with the mechanism, care and use of the rifle. Selected men in each battalion were trained by these when they were available. These men were given military manuals and sent round to all the Companies and a new era of military organisation evolved. It is amazing now to look back on the change these rifles made on the mind of the Volunteers. Hard sinewy hands gripped them and grasped reality. Keen eyes looked over their sights and saw a vision of battle, a dream of success, a realisation of this hope for freedom which remained immortal while generation after generation sacrificed and died. We were on our way.

British military precautions were redoubled, vigilance increased and with it always came this feeling of insecurity, the nervous strain imposed on men faced with an unseen enemy and operating on hostile ground. Opportunities for action by the I.R.A. now became limited. Enemy activity broadened but became less effective. We concentrated on the building up of our forces. The day of band and flags, torches and processions departed. The loud voiced patriot disappeared. A man's safety and that of his comrades lay in his ability to keep a shut mouth, to be circumspect in his movements, to remain a law abiding citizen while consumed with the deadly intent of smashing that authority which passed for law.

## VI

## [Carpenter Again / 1920 / Monitoring The Mails / The Imperialist Mentality / Capture Of A General]

I was at this time in Ring College in Co. Waterford where I spent several months. It was the most satisfactory holiday I ever had in my lifetime, before or since. The peaceful beauty of sea and mountain; the sympathetic atmosphere; the enthusiasm of the students for all things Irish, all had their appeal. Yet my physical condition did not improve. I suffered from constant haemorrhages from stomach ulcers. I decided to go to Dublin to seek treatment for these. I knew nobody in Dublin but Páidín O'Keeffe, then T.D. for North Cork and General Secretary of the Sinn Féin organisation. I made contact with Páidín, told him my story and suggested to him that if I could get work anywhere as a carpenter I'd manage to look after myself. The first remark Páidín the realist made was, *"Take down that adjectival Fáinne. Do you want to go back to jail again and maybe take better men with you?"* I saw the point and put the Fáinne in cold storage. Páidín then gave me a letter to Tom Foran, President of the Irish Transport and General Workers' Union. I presented this letter to Tom Foran at his office on the following morning. Tom 'phoned Michael Somerville, Secretary of the Carpenters' Union. He first gave me the name of a horse that he thought should do well at the Curragh that day. Then he told me of my difficulties. The result was that I attended a meeting of the Society that night in Aungier Street and was enrolled a member. When the meeting was over it was arranged that Louis Byrne, a builder's foreman who was present, would put me to work the following morning. The kindness of all these men is a unforgettable memory with me. Tom Foran remains my very good friend. Mick Somerville, a most loveable and humourous character, died some years ago. I have not seen or heard of Louis Byrne for many years. Starting work again was a strange experience. My hands had lost their former skill and for several weeks I and the materials I worked with were at odds. My physical weakness too was a handicap, yet I was consumed by a nervous energy. I had a regular wage, had money, purchased books and after my hardest day's work was able to study far into the night. The medical treatment which I was receiving failed to overcome my ailment and on Christmas Eve, 1919, I returned home. I took the train from Kingsbridge to Millstreet, walked from there to Newmarket, arriving after nightfall in a state of collapse. It was the last I was to see of the outer world for four months.

Christmas, 1919, came in fog and mist. Throughout Ireland it was not the season of peace and goodwill. A week before Lord French, King's Viceroy in Ireland, and his heavily armed escort had been attacked near Dublin. Raiding activity by R.I.C. and military, already intense, became more widespread and ruthless and the I.R.A., the homeless ones, found little rest. For a number of my comrades, full of life, high with hope, ardently planning for the future, it was to be the last Christmas. In 1920 men who had borne the burden and heat of the day, creators of a revolution that was to change utterly the character and outlook of the Irish people, were to die, some in fair fight, as far as a fight in which the numbers and armaments were so unequal, with arms in the hands; some murdered in fields and on roadside; some to face in the cold dawn the rifles of the firing party in the barrack square. All of them in their lives and deaths setting an example which a Young Ireland, risen to unprecedented spiritual heights, were prepared and willing to follow.

The bells that ushered in the New Year of 1920 rang out not merely over an Ireland in travail but over a world in turmoil. Woodrow Wilson had gone back to America; the Democratic Party had been defeated; the inept and unfortunate Harding was the President Elect. The eighteenth Amendment had added two new and little known words to the world's vocabulary—bootlegger and hi-jacker. Their connotations of utter lawlessness, merciless and moral degeneration were as yet but little understood. In the first month of the year Wilson was writing to the Democratic Party leaders assembled at their Annual Jackson Day Dinner urging support for the Treaty of Versailles and the Covenant of the League of Nations, ratification of which two months later was to be rejected by the Senate.

Voroshilov and Budenny were marching on Rostov and on to the final destruction of Denikin and his White Russians. Hitler was as yet unknown but Schusnigg had returned from a prisoner of war camp to complete his legal studies at Innsbruck in an impoverished Austria. The Turks were attacking the French in Cilicia and a Kemalist Chamber of Deputies met in Constantinople.

Trade Unionism in France had adopted the slogan, *"The War is dead,*

*Long live the War"*. Strikes, run often in opposition to the wishes of Trade Union leaders, were widespread. The Russian Revolution had gone to the heads of the French workmen. Clemenceau was defeated in the election for President by Deschanel and retired from public life. Another chapter of French history was closed.

Disorder reigned everywhere in Spain. Soldiers had mutinied in Saragossa; there were outbreaks in Valencia and Santander and a militarist outburst was soon to drive the Cabinet out of office. Truly Mr. Dooley interpreted Sherman right when he said, *"War is hell when 'tis over"*.

Leaders are often harshly criticised for permitting their hands to be forced, for adopting a course of action which is premature, for not standing rock-firm against any deviation from considered policy and planning. But the actions of men organised to fight, drilled and in some sort armed, are apt to outstrip the conceptions of their leaders. They wait impatiently the word for action which leadership, weighing all the chances, with its wider and more intimate knowledge of conditions, hesitates to give. Then an opportunity, too inviting to be resisted, presents itself to a forceful individual, he grasps it, and willy-nilly all the hesitant forces are set in motion. Leadership must accept the situation, take control or for good or ill be swept aside. It is easy to plan for inanimate things, only when the human factor is involved do complications obtrude themselves. Those who followed the seemingly logical development of the Irish revolutionary effort might conceivably think that it was the outcome of a well considered strategy, of an inspired plan calculated to meet all eventualities. There is no basis for such a belief and the manner of its development was as unexpected by the leaders of revolutionary Ireland as it was inconceivable to the British.

Some, I think, saw an Irish army in the field fighting its battles in orthodox fashion or what the civilian mind is taught to regard as orthodox fashion. These men were not afraid to die. They were willing to be sacrificed but what they hoped to achieve thereby is not easily understood. It is difficult for a new idea to gain acceptance and revolution to these men meant a repetition of Easter Week. Easter Week had achieved its purpose. It had awakened in the mind of Young Ireland a consciousness of its manhood, an understanding of the fact that a denial of freedom meant a stultification of that manhood, an appreciation of the idea that the race that will not seek that freedom as a plant seeks the sunlight will wither from the earth. It is clear now that a repetition of Easter Week was impossible and even if possible wholly undesirable.

Others there were who thought that Easter Week was enough, who had come to believe that with the background created the political strategy of Sinn Féin was bound to be successful. They were wrong. They had builded better than they knew. They had shaped circumstance but they had not kept pace with change nor understood the upsurge of men who made no fetish of formalities, who believed that a soldier's work was to kill, not to be killed, and who went back, it seemed inevitably, to the guerrilla tradition of their saffron-shirted forebears. The sporadic outbreaks of 1919 rendered inevitable the countryside activity of 1920. Ireland was at war.

I, too, had a grim fight on my hands—with death. The effects of the influenza which had struck me down in 1918 I had never finally overcome. My imprisonment, though short, my hunger strike, my strenuous work and the conditions under which it was carried out had undermined my resistance. For months I lay in pain and utmost weariness. The unsparing efforts of Dr. Algie Verling and his wide experience of the disease from which I suffered (he had served for four years with the British Army in France and was quite familiar with the dire aftermath of gastric 'flu) pulled me through. During my illness I was visited by many of my comrades. While I was not aware of the fact, nobody expected me to recover and these were farewell visits. But I never thought that the bended sickle was so close to the thread of my existence. After the first few weeks my interest in national affairs was made all the keener because of my incapacity to participate in them. My mind was clear and eventually it became a habit with the local leaders to come and consult with me. Police Barracks were being attacked in other districts. There had been no such attack on ours. The local Volunteers felt the urge to keep pace with their comrades. An attack was planned. It was discussed in all its details in my bedroom. It was carried out unsuccessfully. Again another action was planned and again without success; worse still, several Volunteers were wounded.

There was still another bedchamber conference and I decided on this occasion that there would be no further attempt at distance control. I was going to take part. Everybody vetoed the idea. The doctor was called and argued against what he called my suicidal tendencies. I was adamant; I struggled out of bed and into my clothes, which hung woefully about me. I got outside and mounting the waiting car was driven to the point of mobilisation and when all was ready marched a further four miles to the point of attack. It was a weary march for me. A dozen times I lay flat on the road in sheer weariness, but I arrived, and while the work we had in hand that night, the arrest of a gang of robbers whose reputation as desperate fighting men was exploded on that occasion, was, compared with that we had later to face, of very minor proportions, the point is that it was done and successfully done.

I do not wish to obtrude too often the perpendicular pronoun. I do not want to claim in anything I write that my ideas or efforts or example were the decisive factors in any of our undertakings. It would be a ridiculous claim. It was just the luck of the game that I happened to be present when the tide turned; when the effects of previous failures, countered with determination, created success.

The effect on myself was well nigh miraculous. After that first night's march my recovery was assured. I was back in harness again and grew daily stronger.

The Brigade Commandant, Liam Lynch, hearing of my recovery, arrived to visit me. He insisted on putting me back in charge of the organisation again. I demurred. I pleaded my poor physique and ill health. My real reason was for the fact that there might be disgruntlement and disruption if men down the line were demoted because I was again on top. I need have had no fear. There was no dissatisfaction. There was perfect loyalty and co-operation and the man I immediately displaced, Charlie O'Reilly, served with me in perfect amity until he was killed in action a year later. I decided after much discussion and consideration that one reason for the failures I have mentioned was indiscreet speech and a consequent leakage of information. The cure adopted was to keep the knowledge of proposed future activity within a very narrow circle and to carry out certain raids on the mails so as to discover if the channel of leakage was through the post office.

We believed that the raid would be prolific of information. It was more so even than we expected. It resulted in several deportations, a number of warnings and an almost complete drying up of enemy intelligence.

The raid took place on the night before the initial meeting of the newly elected County Council. A dozen men under my direction skimmed through the letters, laying aside for my perusal any of which they had a doubt. It was a long night's work; we finished at 6 a.m. and had breakfast. Among the group were two members of the County Council and as we finished breakfast they prepared to set off to the nearest railway station on their way to the Council Meeting. They washed and shaved and then one drew attention to the condition of their shirts and collars. These were dirty and crumpled after a night spent in hauling mailbags across the country. I got a brainwave. I remembered seeing among the various parcels which were set aside unopened one with the label of a well-known laundry on it and addressed to a police barracks in Portmagee, Co. Kerry. With all the water of the Atlantic Ocean at his doorstep, this fellow must needs send his laundry to Cork. I opened the parcel. If to clothe a friend an enemy must be despoiled, then there was nothing unjustifiable in the action. Inside the parcel were several shirts and collars. In these we dressed our representatives and sent them off to their first public session resplendent in their borrowed finery. I was afterwards to regret that many more laundered shirts had not fallen into my hands or that I had not had the prescience to provide them; for the first unforeseen difficulty arose for us almost immediately in an outbreak of scabies. Improper hygiene, lack of underclothing, irregular hours, food and sleep, were probably the causes of this irritating disease which affected men in different ways. I have, in fact, seen strong athletic youths completely incapacitated by it. Séamus Brislane was the first man to fall a victim. Everywhere he went he left a trail of infection behind and when it was finally discovered that he was the carrier the curses that were poured on him were varied, eloquent and all inclusive. Nevertheless, we all laughed at each other's misfortunes and in our laughter he escaped annihilation.

The British decided that the mails from the town near the railway station where the raid took place should be escorted each night to the railway station, the soldiers getting to the station before the arrival of the train and remaining till its departure. We got wind of grumblings among the Tommies about the extra duties imposed on them and decided the trick was too good to miss. We raided the mails at another railway junction further South and saw as a result further escorts provided and heard the reports of grumblings by British soldiers. This raiding of mails was continued for about a month until we had forced the British to guard every movement of mails and terrified the gossip writers to discretion. The last raid was productive of much laughter among the I.R.A. The mail bags arrived at Newmarket in the early morning accompanied by their retinue of cycling troops. The bags were delivered to the Post Office, the Tommies waited in the street outside for their own letters. Two or three Volunteers arrived into the office by a back door, held up the staff and disappeared with the bags. The sulphurous eloquence of the Tommies when they discovered the trick is still a treasured memory with the ungodly in the district.

The Rural District Council, too, had its initial meeting at this time. I was a member of the Council. The new members received a very flattering welcome from all its officials and employees but the reason for it swiftly appeared in what was practically an all round demand for an increase in salaries and wages. The most efficient and helpful official clerk, William Murphy, made no demands; there was no mention of some women who performed the most menial tasks around the hospital for starvation wages; many of the demands were justified but the loudest voiced were those who had inherited the sinecures. All found that the new inexperienced members were not soft fibred. They would pay for service but they intended that the service should be rendered.

My association with the Council was quickly terminated. Raids by the military on the Council Chamber for wanted men put an end to my attendance and to my work as a local legislator.

Releases after a hunger strike at Wormwood Scrubs prison, London, the escape of Paddy McCarthy from Strangeways prison, Manchester, had brought a number of us, pioneer Volunteers, together again. The fact that the number of men now on the run and not distracted by any other occupation had increased considerably had made the work of organisation easier, had brought about a strengthening of Brigade and Battalion Staffs and made available for swift and decisive action the necessary force. The force of circumstance had brought an Active Service Unit into being. And if these men had been welded into a cohesive force, the Irish people were matching them step by step in effort and sacrifice. The railway men about this time were refusing to handle trains on which British troops were travelling. This meant, of course, the dismissal of engine drivers and guards. I spoke one Sunday afternoon to the Constituency Committee of Sinn Féin and asked them to collect one thousand pounds for a fund in support of the railwaymen. It was subscribed and lodged with the officials of the men's union within a week. This was not a forced contribution. It was a spontaneous gift from a people who realised they had a country and were determined to do their duty to it.

A meeting of the Brigade Staff was held in June. During a discussion on the number and movements of British troops in the district, a Battalion Commandant mentioned that it was customary for the General and senior officers of the troops in barracks in his area to spend their leisure hours fishing on the Blackwater near Conna. We discussed the matter of their capture, principally from the viewpoint that it was more than possible they carried arms and were attended by an armed escort. We were anxious to add to our store of weapons. Later we decided that the capture of senior officers of the British Army, whether armed or otherwise, would have a good effect on the morale of the I.R.A.

To the minds of the imperialists the mere Irish were a subordinate race, morally and intellectually inferior, not regarded as fellow creatures of a less well-endowed class but as the slaves in ancient Athens were regarded. These officers were of the class that created and controlled an Empire, were, in excelsis, the Imperial Ascendancy. And they were accepted by men who had not known freedom at their face value. Why not pull them down and see what made them tick? Why not prove to the Volunteers that they were mere men not endowed with any qualities denied to the rest of the human race? The affair was planned. It was discovered that Saturday afternoon was the most suitable time to make the attempt. I provided a car and with another Volunteer, my particular friend, Paddy Clancy, Deputy Brigadier Commandant, who was killed in action six weeks later, proceeded by a roundabout route to Brigade Headquarters where we picked up the Brigade Commandant and his assistant, George Power. After a few hours drive we arrived at the scene of operations, were met by Lar Condon, from whom the information emanated, and a section of men whom we had on the spot to watch developments and to take part in the capture. All the men were well under cover and were called together for discussion and instruction. The centre of the immediate operation was a small fishing lodge surrounded by a low stone wall and occupied, we were informed by the scouts, by a number of British soldiers, the officers' escort. The Brigade Commandant decided that the first step should be to capture this escort and Clancy and I were detailed to lead the charge on the house. My men and I crept through a shrubbery and took cover outside the boundary wall at the front. My comrade with his section carried out the same manoeuvre at the back. At the whistle both sections charged for the front and back doors, burst them in and swept through the house. There was nobody in possession but an old lady, the cook and housekeeper, and a young girl. We searched the house for arms but found nothing. We reported back to the Brigade Commandant, who instructed us to take cover and await developments. We lay in the shrubbery for about an hour and then three men approached the house, coming from the river. Two were tall, athletic men, one was smaller and lighter. The bigger men disappeared from my sight round an angle of the house. The smaller man came in my direction and I took him in charge. He proved to be a batman. Driving him before me, I came to where the others were. Here those others had been held up by the Brigade Commandant and those with him. The first part of the operation was over.

We knew that there was still another officer on the river bank and after waiting awhile the Brigade Commandant said to me, *"We can't wait too long, we'll go and get him"*. He had given up fishing when we reached him on the river bank and was on his way back. We accompanied him. We permitted the batman to prepare a meal for the prisoners and then started on our way. We had now two cars; the car I had brought out and that of the British Officers. It was decided that the Assistant Brigade Commandant, George Power, would sit beside the driver of the leading car. He was familiar with the area and knew all the bye-roads we had to travel. I sat in the back with one of the prisoners. The Brigade Commandant sat with the driver of the next car and Clancy sat between the two remaining prisoners at the back. We started.

George Power kept an eye not merely on the road we were travelling but backwards also to assure himself that the second car was following. Having travelled several miles we rounded a bend. Power looked back but the car that was to follow did not appear. We turned at once and a quarter mile from our turning point we came upon a dog fight on the road. The second car was ditched. The driver had just extricated himself from behind the wheel and there was a life and death struggle between two pairs of men on the roadway. I could not help in the struggle. I drove my prisoner out of the car and kept him covered. The little driver dived like a terrier on to the back of the big British officer who was on top of Clancy on the road, both struggling for possession of a gun. At that moment a shot rang out and the struggle between the Brigade Commandant and his opponent was over. The British officer lay wounded on the road. The second combatant, seeing the game was up, threw in his hand.

We decided at once to release my prisoner to attend to his wounded comrade. We handcuffed the remaining prisoner, the General. We decided to put the Britishers' car out of action and to abandon it. We all crowded then into my car bringing with us the driver, who had proved to be such a determined little fighter, to the nearest village. Here we dropped him with instructions to despatch the local doctor at once to the wounded man.

The rest of the journey was uneventful but the delay prevented us from travelling as far as we had hoped to go. Towards midnight we decided to lodge our prisoner in the house of a farmer (McCarthy of Creggone) whom we knew and whose sons were Volunteers. When we arrived at the house we found it already in use as a temporary prison for yet another captive. This was a railway official who had been very much concerned with the dismissal of railwaymen who refused to co-operate in the transport of British soldiers. Unceremoniously we got rid of him and his captors and took over the house for our own prisoner.

We then discussed our position and decided that if we were to hold our prisoner his removal to a distant place in another Brigade area was needful. Clancy and I set off, made the needful arrangements with the West Limerick Brigade and returned the following night with Tom Malone (Seán Ford), the Crowleys of Ballylanders and some other Limerick men to escort him to his destination. The morning after the capture the police everywhere were busy pursuing enquiries. The first house visited in my own town was that of Denis B. Curtin who had lent his car for the adventure. In the early dawn a police posse knocked him up and made enquiries about his car and its movements. He arose, came down to his garage, opened the door and, sure enough, there was the car. He laid his hand on the radiator and almost yelled. It was red hot. Driven with speed through the night, it was only a few minutes since we had left it in the garage. He leant on the radiator for fear any of the policemen would touch it and asked what the reason for the enquiries was. He got no information but a thorough search of the car was made, yet nowhere was there any clue found to the night's adventure. Denis Curtin was an elderly man who had built up a magnificent and lucrative business, who was, as the situation developed, to clothe and feed the Active Service Unit, to find money for political purposes when we needed it, to be carried as a hostage through the

53

country on British military lorries, who never failed us, who was to live long enough to get the thrill of a lifetime in watching from behind the man he most admired, on the Saluting Base at Cork, the seemingly endless ranks of an Irish Army, the foundation of which he worked so effectively to lay, marching past in 1942.

The Curfew Order came into operation about this time and nightly in the garrisoned towns and villages curfew patrols were established to ensure that no civilian remained out of doors. It can be readily understood how harshly the imposition of this order bore on the people. Those working indoors during the day had no opportunity for outdoor recreation, the children's play was stilled and the ordinary friendly intercourse of the village street brought to a complete cessation. The curfew patrols in Newmarket sometimes came direct in single file and extended order from their barracks. Sometimes they came by scheduled and roundabout ways into the streets in the hope of catching some persons disobedient to the order. The Volunteers watched them, noted their movements, and on half a dozen occasions descended on the town in the hope of getting an opportunity to attack. Strangely enough, none of their missions ever bore fruit. The British never left their barracks on any such occasion. Somewhere there was a grape vine. It showed, however, that the British had a healthy respect for the Volunteers and indeed they need not have allowed themselves to be obsessed with any such feeling, as, apart from the Active Service Unit, the Volunteers were pitifully armed and could only have hoped to be successful against well armed patrols by way of sudden rush and swift surprise. But these ambushes laid for the British troops had a salutary effect, they set the British nerves on edge and confined both police and military inside a very circumscribed area of control. They also developed that self confidence in the Volunteers which is the first step towards creating an effective fighting force. So self confident did they become that when an order came from Headquarters in July to cut the police and military telephone wires without damage to the ordinary telephone communications, two Volunteers, interpreting the order in most rigid fashion, barefoot and with a padded ladder, got on the roof of the Police Barrack and cut the telephone wires at the chimney shaft and got clean away.

# VII

## [An Arms Purchase / Death Of Paddy Clancy / Flying Column / Battalion Training Camp / Mallow Barrack / Ernie O'Malley's Mistakes]

In early July I got some money from a few personal friends and received an unexpected windfall from a relative in the United States. I decided to utilise the cash to augment our rather sparse supply of arms and ammunition.

I consulted with the Brigade Commandant and, as a result, paid a visit to Dublin. I registered in a hotel and slept in the actual room where, four months later, a Limerick man, Jack Lynch, a member of the Sinn Féin organisation, was murdered by Black and Tans. Next day I called round to another hotel where an appointment had been arranged for me. Here I found three members of the Headquarters Staff, Liam Tobin, Tom Cullen and Fintan Murphy calmly sitting down to lunch as if they had not a care in the world. This amazed me. I knew that a constant effort was being made by the British to capture them, yet they sat there unabashed in a gathering of which one-half at least were their sworn enemies. I discussed my needs with them and they pointed out that the stuff I asked for did not grow on blackberry bushes. Finally, we got down to a specification of what they could supply and its price. I got six *'Peter the Painters'*, two parabellums, with ten rounds of ammunition for each, one dozen percussion bombs, a rifle and 50 rounds of .303 ammunition. The stuff was delivered at my hotel that evening by Chris. Harding. I paid one hundred and twenty pounds for it. While I knew of all the risks that had to be taken to get those guns and of the difficulty and danger it involved, I felt I was paying through the nose for them, but I had no option. I made, as a matter of fact, a far worse bargain than I realised. The bombs were useless. I found that the only way to explode them, and I gave them a fair trial, was to put them into a fire, cover them carefully and wait until the casing got red hot. There was then a light explosion, enough to crack the bomb casing and cast the burning turf in the air in a pretty fire works display. The pistols were good but when the few rounds of ammunition supplied with them were exhausted it could not be replenished. The rifle was the only valuable article I got for my money. The stuff had, however, a psychological value. The interest aroused among the Volunteers by the automatic pistols, of which they had heard but never seen, had a good effect. Instruction in their use, in taking them asunder and reassembling them was eagerly anticipated and made men keener in their work. The delivery of these guns was also, it seemed to them, a promise that all men would, without delay, be effectively armed.

The Brigade Council, i.e., the Brigade Staff, and the Battalion Commandants, met a few weeks later. Among the business to be done was the distribution of a small quantity of revolvers. To my amazement, these were divided among the Battalion Commandants and none was allotted to me. I protested, fuming. But my rage was unavailing. The Brigade Commandant pointed out that I had been to Dublin and had been enabled to buy guns. In vain I pointed out that I had taken the risk of going to Dublin and of bringing home the guns, that I had with my own money paid for them, that the revolvers now being distributed were the property of the Brigade and, therefore, that my quota was included. All my protests were useless. I subsided. But I wasn't finished. I intended to get my share somehow or other. The table was cleared, the revolvers parcelled up and put away into a room beside that where we sat and the business of the meeting continued.

After a while I went outside and with a table knife I picked up in the kitchen slipped from the outside the catch in the window of the room where the guns were. It was my intention to take a gun from each parcel but there was no time. I grabbed one parcel, opened it, removed two guns, leaving but one and substituting pieces of firewood and a stone for the guns I'd taken, retied the parcel and went back to the meeting.

Strangely enough, the robbery was never discovered. The man whose parcel I raided was captured the following day asleep in a farmhouse and the British military, after a search, found the parcel hidden in a hay rick near the house. What they must have thought of a parcel containing one revolver, a stone and some kindling I've never heard. Another parcel of those guns was also lost. The loss was a minor one compared to the tragic one which accompanied it. Paddy Clancy and I travelled back to our own district together. As we went along, I began to have misgivings about my action in stealing the guns. I could picture the rage and disappointment of the man whom I had deprived of them. I told the story to Clancy. He laughed uproariously and refused to be serious about the matter. We then for the first time examined the guns we had secured. They were rough, badly finished weapons, proved eventually to be almost useless. They were, of course, the rubbish that is produced in certain European ports for sale to revolutionaries.

We were now more convinced than ever that the British opponents were to be our only source of effective supply. It was Sunday, a beautiful summer morning. We went to Mass in Kanturk, listened to a discourse from Father Bowler that was more deeply tinged with rebellion than would have been approved of by his Bishop, and we continued on our way to the house which was then Clancy's headquarters. During the week I found it necessary to go into another brigade area for a discussion on a proposed co-operative effort. I was delayed over the weekend. When I opened the newspaper on Monday morning I read of his death and the manner of it.

On Saturday a British aeroplane had made a forced landing in the district. A company of British soldiers were dispatched to protect it until needed repairs were made. During the night Volunteers in the local battalion, poorly armed, without any real plan or information, attacked the British soldiers. The experienced, better armed, professional soldiers drove off the Volunteers after several hours' fighting in which a number of Volunteers were wounded. The fight brought the British military in force into the district.

We had made arrangements to meet the following week, both of us having a good deal of work to do in our districts in the meantime. I never saw him alive again. Clancy and Jack O'Connell, the Battalion Commandant, were surrounded in a farmhouse by British military. They defended themselves and the guns they had until they had expended all the ammunition. They ran out of the house on the offchance of escape. They were both shot dead; one a good courageous officer, the other outstanding in courage, character and capacity, the possessor of all those manly graces which endeared him to all who knew him and which keep his memory still fragrant in our hearts. The sun shone brightly, there was a scent of hay from the meadows, the Irish countryside was beautiful; but for me the world was empty that day as I carried his body over hill and dale and murmuring stream to bury him beneath the haunted mountain on which his eyes first opened.

I returned from the funeral by way of unfrequented by-roads. The general body of those who attended drove back along the main roads, all of these were held up, searched and questioned by British military and all the young men among them were savagely beaten. The effect of this action was to intensify more than ever the support given to Volunteers and to add to their increasing numbers.

I visited the Brigade Commandant on the following day to discuss the situation and the difficulty created for us by the death of Paddy Clancy. We had already arrived at the conclusion that the methods heretofore utilised would no longer be effective. The logic of events had forced on us the view that there could be no success if we were to continue to depend on ordinary Volunteers, poorly armed, hurriedly mobilised, not sufficiently trained and disciplined, to act as a coherent unit under a responsible leader.

The British were now moving in much greater strength; if they were to be attacked with success it could not be done by men who at a sudden call left the plough to grasp and use a shotgun for a few hours before returning again to the plough. The most suitable men in the brigade should be called together, given the best arms we had at our disposal, and trained to act as regular soldiers. The Brigade O/C conveyed this decision to the battalions and asked for volunteers. A quota for each battalion and a date for mobilisation was fixed. The quota for all battalions would have been filled in any one of them. Volunteers came tumbling over each other for a chance to join the Flying Column, as it was then called. Clancy, as Deputy Brigade O/C, was to have had charge of the Active Service Unit. Now Lynch was anxious that I should take his place and yet felt that the general work of organisation would suffer if I did.

I attended a Convention of Sinn Féin for the Constituency, made an appeal there for financial support, was voted a very substantial sum which was paid to me in cash the following day. I placed this money in the hands of the Brigade Commandant at once. We now had some arms, all the money we needed for our immediate needs and many more men than we, at this stage, could use. The troops went immediately into training.

To obviate disgruntlement and to provide for replacements and development, I decided to establish a Battalion Training Camp. And from that time until the end this and other training camps were in operation. It was moved from Company Area to Company Area so that the burden of billeting would not bear too heavily on any locality and so that the normal occupation of Volunteers would not be too harshly disturbed during their period of training. The result was most satisfactory, men responded more intelligently and energetically to demands. An esprit de corps was created and each company sought to outshine its fellows in soldierly flair and effort.

The training started with close order drill without arms and went from that to the handling of the rifle. Next came physical training—jerks, running, jumping, wrestling, route marches on roads, where possible, cross-country marching. Mechanism and care of rifle and revolver. Bomb-throwing and the mechanism and manufacture of bombs and mines. Assembly of electric batteries. Sentry and outpost duties. Simple signalling. Special services, engineering, signalling, first aid, got advanced course in these. At the end of April

1921, courses in street fighting were developed, including revolver practice and bomb throwing, and in silent movement at night.

The British were constantly watched and it became evident that, despite apparently conflicting reports, there was a regular schedule of movement in certain cases. It was certain that two lorries of Black and Tans travelled between Cork and Mallow weekly and that the hours of their travelling varied but slightly. The Flying Column was to have its first assignment.

A meeting of the Brigade Council was held on Sunday to make final arrangements. The attack, if nothing untoward happened, was due to take place on Tuesday forenoon. I was a little late for the meeting; I had to detour round a party of British soldiers who were engaged in searching houses. They were holding up all traffic, questioning passers-by and had, when I sighted them, a number of prisoners in their lorries. I arrived at the house where the meeting was held to find that it had been burned to the ground. The blackened walls were crumbling and a chimney stood gaunt against the sky. Crouching behind a fence was a Volunteer who was waiting to direct me to the new meeting place. We watched the British, they watched us. But their information in this case was just short of accuracy. Raiding the houses in the hope of capturing us, their timing wasn't perfect so they did what to them seemed the next best thing, they burned the place down.

Three hundred yards away round a bend of a by-road the Council had assembled and the work was going on as if these men were unaware of the fact that hundreds of their enemies were at that moment scouring the countryside for them. But it was an unusual meeting. Instead of the usual friendly informal discussion with which I was familiar, I found a group of men sitting solemnly round a table being questioned by a stranger who sat beside the Brigade Commandant. Red hair standing on end, blue eyes, with a scar on his keen face, he seemed to be clad in guns and fountain pens and surrounded by maps and notebooks.

He was a Staff Captain from Headquarters, apparently, on a tour of inspection. I had a horror of notebooks and fountain pens and typewriters; they were a combination that had too often disastrous results for our organisation. My one experience of G.H.Q. was not a too happy one. So I was prepared to dislike this fellow even before he barked a reference to unpunctuality at me. However, my comrades seemed to have accepted him and he had, apparently, the authority and approval of the Brigade Commandant. I sat at the table and listened to the questioning. It seemed to me that Headquarters must have been intent on spinning a huge hempen rope with which to encircle all our necks. After all these years I still cannot see what Headquarters wanted with all the information that was written so neatly in those smart field books. Maybe they had a number of Civil Servants on their staff.

When my turn came I answered all the questions with perfect inaccuracy. The Brigade Commandant knew I was lying. I knew he knew it and disapproved but he expressed neither commendation nor disapproval. We both kept straight faces but the glint in the eye of Moss Twomey, the Brigade Adjutant, showed that he was enjoying the situation.

The Staff Captain was a very serious young man with a sense of his own dignity and importance. Such an individual always rouses in me the spirit which actuated Trabb's boy when he fainted at the appearance of Pip's sartorial grandeur. But appearances are deceitful. This fellow had tons of courage and ability of a high order, even though he had allowed himself to be inveigled into asking endless and foolish questions by some confounded statistician in Dublin. He had already seen a good deal of fighting and during his short stay with us we developed a respect and regard for him as a man who could take it rough, smooth or anyhow. He was Ernie O'Malley, author of *On Another Man's Wound*.

The inquisition over and the routine business of the Council completed, everybody present was anxious to discuss the arrangements for the fight which we expected on the following Tuesday and much disappointment was felt when the Brigade Commandant informed us that it would not take place. He proposed, he said, to discuss an entirely different activity. Information had been brought by a young Volunteer, Dick Willis, who was working on a building contract in a British Cavalry Barrack that the arrangements for exercising the horses was such as reduced in the morning hours the strength of the garrison to such an extent as to bring within the bounds of possibility the capture of the barrack. He had carefully noted the methods of mounting guard, the disposition of sentries and the manner in which visitors to the barracks were received. His idea was that he and Jack Bolster, his comrade, should be given revolvers, that they should introduce a third man, also armed, ostensibly a foreman, come to check on the work done and that at a given signal they should hold up the guard and sentries to allow the A.S.U. an opportunity of rushing the gates from outside. The question of getting the gate open was a ticklish one and the proposal was made that a member of the A.S.U., armed with a letter for the officer in charge of the garrison, would appear there holding it open for the charge of the A.S.U., who would, under cover of darkness, have crept to positions as near as possible to the gate which was to be their objective. The selection of men for the key positions was then discussed. There was no lack of Volunteers; every man present seemed to be confident that he had special qualifications which entitled him to a spearpoint position.

O'Malley arrogated to himself the part of the visitor with the letter. This was really the most important post as even if the men inside were not wholly successful, a cool, determined man could hold the gate sufficiently long to permit the rushing troops from outside to charge through any opposition and to possession of the buildings. The builders' foreman was then to be selected. I pressed my claim to this post. In private life I had been a builder. I knew the trade from the ground up and felt that nobody could handle the job as effectively as I could.

The Brigade Commandant put his foot down. He paid me a compliment with which I was not at all pleased. He said that I was too valuable an officer to permit him risking my loss in an attempt where the chances of success were entirely out of proportion to the risk involved. I pointed out that officers of a fighting force, if they were to be of any value, should not be kept in cotton wool, should not merely share the risks which their men joyfully undertook but should be continually setting a standard for their men to follow. My arguments were unavailing. Another man was selected. The selection was wholly admirable. The foreman was to be a man who had been one of my closest companions in all activities since his escape from Strangeways Prison almost a year before, Paddy McCarthy, who was my first selection for membership of the A.S.U. He was one of that sparse but richly endowed brotherhood, the men who know no fear. Yeats must have had him in mind when he described his *"affable irregular cracking jokes as though to die by gunshot were the finest play under the sun"*. I became his technical mentor. For an hour we worked over a draft of a repair specification which I had made. I explained to him the meaning of the terms, the methods by which he could at least minimise the danger of showing his complete ignorance of the building trade and felt at the end that he was at least sufficiently lessoned to pass muster among a group of men who were doubtless no better informed than he was.

My cup of disappointment and humiliation was not yet full. I had no doubt that being denied the post I sought I was to be a member of the storming party. The Brigade Commandant called me and ordered me to proceed to a district about twenty miles from the scene of the proposed operations, there to undertake another activity which we had previously discussed and in the carrying out of which he was keenly interested. And this wasn't the last straw. In expectation of the ambush which we were to prepare for and expected on the following Tuesday, I had brought with me a few first class Volunteers who had not yet had their baptism of fire. I had hoped to give them an opportunity of being shot over; to utilise the ambush as the finishing touch to the training they had undergone. The Brigade Commandant ordered them to hand over their rifles. He had more than enough experienced and tried men. He needed all the arms he could gather.

We were a disconsolate crew as we cycled away into the darkness. Curses deep and sincere were poured by my Volunteers on the head of the Brigade Commandant and on the men who with callous joy had pounced on the rifles of which they had been deprived.

There was little conversation on the homeward journey. We followed each other at intervals of one hundred yards. At the end of each mile the leading cyclist halted to allow the others to pass and thus ensure that the whole party continued present and correct. This slowed our progress somewhat but there was need for care. The British, following our example, were perfecting the tactics of the ambush and round any corner the cry of *"Halt"* and the simultaneous crack of the rifle might send one or all of us on a longer journey. Before the dawn I arrived at the house I left in the morning. The Kerry Blue, a fierce watchdog, raised a momentary clamour; then his canine instinct recognised a friend. A window opened and a voice said: *"Who's there?"* I identified myself. The window closed, there was a patter of feet on the stairs and the door opened. *"I knew 'twas one of you when the dog barked only once"*, said the man of the house, Dan Galvin. He and his wife knew the purport of my morning's journey and did not expect me back for several days. His wife came downstairs, anxious because of my swift return, fearful that something had gone wrong. The embers were gathered together. I turned the wheel of the bellows, soon the kettle was singing over a glowing fire.

Both had earned the right to be informed of all happenings. They were completely in my confidence and their advice and comments were always valuable. I told them of the happenings of the day, my disappointment with the outcome of my journey was apparent in my speech. The man's comment was typical of his wisdom and experience; *"Such is life"*, he said, *"When I left college I thought I might eventually be engaged in teaching philosophy in a university. Now, after thirty years I am still in a one room dilapidated school engaged in the futile pursuit of trying to drill into the heads of Tadhg Vik Flurry's children the fact that there are no 'fs' in enough"*.

I slept long and as I ate breakfast in the late forenoon, my companions, the victims of yesterday's disappointment, gathered from the houses where they had spent the night. They were still affected by a deep sense of grievance. If they could that morning have transferred to another brigade, nothing on earth would have held them. And I could not blame them. I had had too much experience of disappointment, had too long practised self discipline to be for long aggrieved by any order, no matter how distasteful. But these were young men who had proved themselves sufficiently to be entrusted with the only rifles in the battalion's armoury. They had gone out full of enthusiasm to their first fight and instead of being allowed to play their part were disarmed at the order of their Brigade Commandant and their guns given to men whom they did not accept as having qualities superior to their own.

But work is a great healer. We proceeded to an unoccupied house where we were to make our first experiment in the making of explosives and in devising land mines. I was exceptionally keen on the latter project. I felt it was one effective way of stopping the swift system of motor transport which gave the British such an advantage over us. We knew nothing of chemicals but we had set a local chemist's apprentice to study the subject and from his notes we made our first tentative trials.

From this unoccupied farmhouse and from our first crude attempts to create munitions of war evolved a well-equipped factory and a staff of skilled craftsmen which enabled the brigade to face the British on the morning of July 11th, 1921, with a feeling of disappointment that a truce had been declared.

While we worked our minds were occupied with speculation as to the activities in Mallow district. The attack was timed for Tuesday morning and the news did not come until the night had fallen. Then I got a brief note from the Brigade O/C. Amidst all his preoccupations he remembered that I'd be on tenterhooks and dispatched a Volunteer with a message. I didn't need to read the message when I saw the dispatch rider's face. Unlike Tony Weller he was *"A Bear"* of good news. He radiated importance and success. The note said briefly *"Complete success, fifty rifles, two machine guns, ammunition to burn, no casualties"*. Our grievances were forgotten. My companions exploded into a roar of triumph. I returned to the Schoolmaster, not to sleep but to await wakefully the morning newspaper and its splash headline.

The headlines certainly appeared and the news I had received was confirmed in detail. But there was additional grave and unexpected news. The town had been burned and sacked by the British.

Later I got an "eyewitness" account of the venture from those who participated in it. All day long on Monday the plans for the attack were discussed. A large scale map of Mallow was procured and the ways of approach decided on. Volunteers of the Mallow Company were detailed as guides to the various sections and during the day all the sections were prepared and instructed in their roles. The Column had mobilised at Burnford and Looney's house was Headquarters (Tadhg Looney was Vice Commandant of the Mallow Battalion). Here on Monday night came Dick Willis and his companion, Jack Bolster. Bolster was a stripling of nineteen, shrewd, cocky and full of confidence. He confirmed the news expressed previously by Willis who brought a piece of news. This was that the British officer in change at Mallow who had been worrying about the inadequacy of the water supply to the barrack had spoken to Willis about it. Willis had promised him that he'd speak to the Town Clerk and arrange that the water inspector should call to the barrack on the following morning to see if a better supply could be arranged. Willis also had informed the sergeant that the stand pipe should be put into position in the morning so as to be ready for the inspector's visit. This arrangement fitted in perfectly with the I.R.A. plans. Arrangements had been made for a fifth column of three men inside the barracks. The visitor who was to get the gates open was to be a water inspector and as I have already said this part had been assigned to O'Malley.

Some time in the morning Willis and Bolster arrived home to Mallow and having seen some of the local Volunteers to convey to them final instructions they donned their overalls and reported for work. Soon after Paddy McCarthy arrived. He and Willis proceeded ostensibly to discuss the work being done but they did not allow their inspection and discussion to lead them far from the guardroom door at any time. Bolster, meanwhile, was working outside the window of a room where a number of soldiers off duty were engaged in various ways. O'Malley, Urban Council official, appeared at the gate, was admitted, grabbed the sentry's rifle. This was the signal for the others to move. Bolster threw up the window where he was working, drew his revolver and yelled at the troops inside who were moving out when they heard the noise of the struggle. Willis and McCarthy rushed to the guardroom door. McCarthy with a blood-curdling yell and with two guns drawn jumped between the soldiers and the rack where the rifles were stacked. Willis stood at the door to cover any attack that might be made on McCarthy. The British sergeant, a brave man, charged Willis who had no option but to shoot him. Simultaneously, a number of the A.S.U. poured into the barrack, rushed through it, expecting at all points a fierce resistance. But the inside men had done their work too well, had been able to prevent the British soldiers from gaining access to the arms, had dispelled any idea the Tommies might have had about the usefulness of a counter attack.

There is an account of this action and of its consequences contained in the book *On Another Man's Wound* and while the writer was a first class soldier who took a leading part in the attack and who should, therefore, have had first hand knowledge, yet his story, which I have carefully read, casts, unwittingly, I believe, a reflection on the reputation of the men who planned and carried out the attack. I may claim from my association with the planning of the attack, my close comradeship with the Brigade Commandant and my intimate acquaintance with the whole background of the matter, to be able to speak with certain authority. I am not, however, depending on my own knowledge and memory of events. I have discussed with and questioned the men who formed the storming party that covered the barracks. They are all in agreement that every weapon and round of ammunition in the barrack was seized by them, that the whole place was painstakingly searched and that none of the men left the barracks until the cars containing the material captured had got away. Then the storming party, the covering party on the R.I.C. Barracks, the outposts covering the points of possible enemy approach, were withdrawn, the whole party marching away only when every detail of the operation had been completed.

Further, there was no anticipation of the fact that reprisal action of the extent and nature of that taken would be indulged in by the British. It was believed that there might be sporadic outbursts by unruly troops of the type which had occurred in Fermoy after the affair of General Lucas* and arrangements had been made to combat this. But that a reprisal, deliberately planned, with official approval and carried out by a large body of regular troops, under the command of their officers, would be undertaken was unexpected and unbelievable. We had been taught to believe that regular soldiers do not make war on civilians. We were to learn a new lesson and to profit thereby in the months to come.

# VIII

## [Black & Tans And British Regulars / A False Alarm / Ernie O'Malley / An Ambush]

The success at Mallow, the capture of a relatively large amount of arms made possible at this stage the creation of a well equipped Active Service Unit, no longer as theretofore dependant for its strength on the mobilisation of rifles from the various battalions. It was a self sufficient body, and strangely enough this self sufficiency swiftly showed a major defect. Several weeks were devoted to intensive training and afterwards for a few further weeks the Active Service Unit lay in position on various roads along which the British troops would naturally be expected to travel; yet no opportunity for action presented itself. In the meanwhile, members of the 3rd Charleville, a most aggressive battalion, had brought off two engagements with the British, both

---

* [See Annex 2 for a version of a popular song about the capture of General Lucas. J.L.]

of which were reasonably successful. In one of these engagements Commandant P. O'Brien of Liscarroll was wounded. He was shot in the face at point blank range with a .45 bullet. The wound should have been fatal but luck, that sometimes seems to clothe in armour plate the exceptionally courageous man, was with him, for after a few weeks he was back again in harness, his only loss a number of teeth extracted from the fractured upper jaw. The explanation of his escape from death was probably a defective cartridge.

Those who have written of the history of the period lay much stress on the indiscipline and sadism of the Black and Tans, under which general term the R.I.C. were often included, and compared it with the magnificent discipline and forbearance of the regular British troops. Other than combat contact and as prisoners in my hands I have not known or had experience of Black and Tans. And while there is overwhelming evidence of evil sadistic conduct by many of the members of this body, I have no personal knowledge of any brutal or criminal conduct on their part within the limits of my brigade area. Nor have I or mine suffered in any way at the hands of the R.I.C. Every act of terrorism and murder of which I have known was carried out by the so-called disciplined regular troops of the British army.

As a result of one of these engagements successfully carried out under the command of Commandant O'Brien, the British troops stationed at Liscarroll burned a quantity of newly-saved hay, the property of the farmers in the district. One of the farmers concerned was a man named Noonan whose sons were active Volunteers. A few nights after this occurrence Noonan's house was raided by British military. The father and one son, Paddy, were in the house. Another son, John, and a Volunteer named Morrissey were coming towards the house when they saw the troops approaching and moved away. Mr. Noonan and his son were questioned and beaten. Finally, the son, a boy of nineteen, was brought out, placed against the wall and riddled with bullets. As he lay on the ground, the officer in charge put a bullet through his face, smashing his jaw and teeth and almost severing his tongue. Leaving him for dead the British marched away. It was a glorious victory. Father Barry and Dr. Corbett of Buttevant came swiftly to attend the wounded boy. Strange to relate, even though he got ten bullets fired at point blank range, he eventually recovered. He is now the father of ten children. This would seem to indicate that England's problem in Ireland cannot be solved in her munitions factories.

I had made several unsuccessful attempts at this time to engage British troops and in the meantime had been closely scrutinising the weekly reports of the Company Intelligence Officers. The report form was of the nature illustrated on the facing page.

These routine reports of line of movement, dates and times enabled the A.S.U. to act with greater effect.

In regard to (2) a report of this nature resulted in a successful ambush at Ballydracane, Kanturk, in October, 1920. (4) Resulted in the capture and disarming of twelve British soldiers at Kilbrin, Kanturk, in April 1921.

The reports of Jack O'Connell, the Newmarket Intelligence officer, were always most reliable and for several weeks he had recorded certain movements of British troops in his district. It was clear from these reports that two

## ENEMY MOVEMENTS (N.B. Dates illustrative only)

| Group | Numbers | How armed | Transport | Where seen | Moving from | Towards | Date. Time. |
|---|---|---|---|---|---|---|---|
| (1) R.I.C. | 6 | Rifles | Bicycles | Castlemagner | Kanturk | Buttevant | 2.1.21 11.30 a.m. |
| (2) Military | 60 | Rifles Machine gun | Lorries. One armoured car | Allensbridge | Kanturk | Newmarket | 15.1.21 9.15 a.m. |
| (3) do. | do. | do. | do. | do. | Newmarket | Kanturk | 15.1.21 12.30 p.m. |
| (4) do. | do. | do. | do. | Castlemagner. **Note:** Twenty soldiers dropped at Castlemagner. Houses in locality searched by these. | Buttevant | Kanturk | 26.1.21 10.0 a.m. |
| (5) do. | do. | do. | do. | Castlemagner. **Note:** Lorries picked up searching soldiers at Castlemagner Cross at 3.30 p.m. | Kanturk | Buttevant | 26.1.21 3.30 p.m. |

lorries of military passed to and fro between Kanturk and Newmarket at least once weekly. It seemed reasonable to expect that an ambush party well hidden on this road for a day or two would be almost certain to get action. I decided to visit the Brigade O/C. who was with the Active Service Unit near Freemount. When I arrived all the men were in a field practising bomb throwing with dummy bombs in front of the house where he was. Three weeks had passed since the barrack was taken and there had been no further action. I commented on the fact and he informed me that the Unit had almost constantly lain in positions covering the roads along which British troops were likely to pass. I gave it as my opinion that it was useless for the Active Service Unit to lie in ambush without being reasonably assured of the possibility of action and expressed the view that the system of utilising the unit without close co-operation with the battalion was definitely defective. I gave him a summary of the Intelligence Officer's reports and convinced him that there was a clear possibility of engaging the enemy on ground of our own selection and with the odds in our favour. He decided that he and Ernie O'Malley would accompany me on the following day to look over the ground and select the position.

When our discussion ended evening had come, the Active Service Unit which had been engaged in their various exercises under the supervision of O'Malley had completed the day's chore, sentries had been posted and all those not on duty adjourned to Freemount where there was a travelling circus.

The village was crowded and the carnival spirit so apparent that a foreigner visiting the place that evening would have no suspicion that there was a state of unrest in the country; no idea that the village was under the protection of groups of armed men posted at all vantage points, no conception of the fact that there was a price on the head of many of the athletic men who strolled unconcernedly about the village street, nor that within half an hour's ride was stationed one of the major groups of the British garrison in Ireland.

The circus over, the people dispersed to their homes and with them went the members of the A.S.U. to their various billets.

We got back from the village at midnight and quickly retired to bed. Quiet descended on the countryside. I slept the deep sleep of one to whom that commodity had become severely rationed. I was roughly awakened by an excited scout. *"Get up, the British are surrounding the place. They're using cavalry".* I jumped out of bed and quickly slipped into my clothes, grabbed my gun and hurried into the yard. Outside I met groups of others hurrying from the neighbouring houses to a prearranged position. I lay on a fence facing the main road, seeing nothing in the darkness, but listening to the sound of horses trotting on the road below. A number of dogs barked on the road and the horses started to gallop wildly. The man beside me breathed deeply and shivered. I leaned towards him and after a moment recognised him. It was Paddy McCarthy of Meelin. Just then a scout arrived laughing. It was a false alarm. The cavalry we heard were the circus horses that had been driven along the road by the village dogs. Paddy McCarthy swore audibly and as we reached the house I understood why he shivered. He was clad only in a shirt and a cartridge belt. He and three others were sleeping in one room. In the dark and with the rush and excitement he couldn't lay hands on his clothes so decided to move without them. I am sure that he never had heard of Cremona but I am also sure that on the night Prince Eugene broke through there was no better soldier than he among O'Mahony's Sans-Culottes. We took it up again with Morpheus.

The Brigade O/C. and O'Malley set off with me on the following afternoon to ascertain for themselves the value of the information I had given them. We travelled along the byroads in a pony trap and as we went discussed events and the situation generally. Some remark of mine found favour with O'Malley for he turned to the Brigade Commandant and said, *"Do you know, these country fellows are coming on amazingly"*. This remark was enlightening. It showed that he regarded the Brigade O/C. in intellect or experience as being on his own plane. But the country fellows, *"untaught knaves unmannerly"*, they could never hope to breathe the rarefied atmosphere of G.H.Q., but by sticking round they might eventually win free of the deeper mists of outer darkness. *"Ah, well! 'tis but in vain for soldiers to complain"*. We marched the last mile across the fields to the spot on the main road which I had selected as the most suitable for our purpose. It was not by any means an ideal position, but I was able to assure the others that nothing better offered. I was then questioned about the accuracy of troop movements and as the reports indicated that this was one of the days on which those took place I suggested that we should wait for a few hours and test the worth of the reports. We had not so long to wait. As we lay on the fence peeping through the thick hedge we heard the sound of the lorries and within fifteen minutes of our getting into position two lorries of British soldiers, about twenty-four men, passed along the road. The I.O. had proved his reliability. Referring again to the reports, we decided that the ambush could, in all likelihood, be carried out early in the following week. We then parted, they to return to prepare the Active Service Unit, I to prepare the local companies for road blocking, outpost duty, etc.

The next few days for me were busy ones. The most reliable men had to be selected, their duties explained to them. Transport had to be arranged; saws and axes for tree felling provided; the Section Leaders taken over the ground at night so that they might be familiar with the positions they were to occupy. All these precautions were necessary as the two towns were only four miles apart and both had strong garrisons of military, Tans and R.I.C. If a force larger than we anticipated arrived the fight might be prolonged and so the necessity might arise of defending both flanks against enemy reinforcements. The ambush position was a straight piece of road leading out of a sharp curve. Midway in the straight was a gate. It was our intention to let the lorries well into the position and then to block the roadway by rushing a farm cart through the gateway on to the road. For this piece of work four strong active men were selected—Joe Keeffe, Jerh. O'Leary, Tom Herlihy and another. They did their work perfectly even though it eventually proved to be unnecessary.

The night before the ambush arrived and with it came unexpectedly the Active Service Unit to my Headquarters at Drominarigle. I expected to meet them in the morning at the ambush position and had made no arrangements for their reception. I had, therefore, at a moment's notice to provide food and billets for about thirty men in an area already occupied by a number of men from the battalion who had arrived during the evening and who were to act as outposts on the following day. I have already paid tribute to the generosity of those on whom we who organised the Volunteers had to depend in the early days of the movement. Never was that kindly hospitality so effectively displayed as on that night. Corney Lenihan's was our Headquarters then as always when we were in the district. The Lenihan family took every risk and spent a fortune in providing for the I.R.A. during all these troubled times. But in all the houses round that night the women folk set about preparing a meal and in making provision for another in the morning; the men stood on guard while those who were to fight on the morrow snatched a few hours sleep.

At 3 a.m. we were on our way. Courage and enthusiasm are at a low ebb in the hours before the dawn. It was bitterly cold and we trudged along in grim silence across the sodden fields to our destination. Ninety minutes later we were in position and here and there as necessity arose men were engaged in cutting holes in the thick hedges with billhooks which we had provided for the purpose. When this work was done there was nothing to do but wait. Waiting in a cold muddy ditch is not the ideal way of spending a morning and the hours seemed endless. Eventually the early morning workers passed on their way unsuspectingly, later came children on their way to school. At eleven o'clock we were still crouching beneath the fence and still there was no sign of the British. Suddenly we heard the sound of a lorry and the order went down the line: *"Let the first one well in before you fire"*. On it came. We waited for the second lorry. Out through the gate swung the farm cart; those who propelled it scuttled back. We opened fire. In five minutes the fight was over. By some mischance there was only one lorry on the road that morning. All our elaborate preparations were needless. Those English boys showed grit but they were outnumbered and caught in a trap. After a few volleys we held our fire and they surrendered. All of them were wounded; their driver was killed. We collected their rifles, equipment and ammunition. I looked at the young driver as he lay dead across the wheel. I am no soldier. I hate killing and violence. The thought ran through my mind:-*"God help his mother"*.

Our plans were made to deal with a particular problem or any reasonable development of it. We expected two lorries. We could have dealt with four at least. But our experience as soldiers was not sufficient to enable us to realise that we could have dealt a severe blow to the reinforcing troops from Kanturk. However, the work we had set out to do was done and our natural instinct was to retreat. As we crossed the Dalua we could hear the rattle of a Lewis gun from the Kanturk direction. Since there could be no possible target, all our men having retreated, it seemed to me that the mental outlook of the British troops was rather disturbed.

The Active Service Unit retreated to Drominarigle; the men of the various companies moved off to their own districts. But the day's work was not over by any means. We had learned a lesson at Mallow where on the night after the capture of the barracks a raid was made on the town by strong forces of British military and houses and property to the value of at least £150,000 burned and destroyed. We did not intend that the same thing should be permitted to occur in Kanturk town or district. When night fell the Active

Service Unit took possession of the town of Kanturk which had been closely watched during the day by members of the local company. All Creameries in the district were covered by the strongest forces we could muster—the British seemed to make a special point of destroying Creameries—a day had come again before the guard was withdrawn. There were no reprisals attempted. The Active Service Unit marched back to its old billets at Freemount and I changed my headquarters from Drominarigle to Kiskeam. Life goes on when great men die and battles for a cause must still be fought when comrades or even leaders have paid it their last full measure of devotion. During that week the funeral procession of Terence MacSwiney had marched through his native city and Kevin Barry had been hanged in Dublin. If the British thought that by encompassing the deaths of tried man or gallant boy they had found a method of solving the British problem in Ireland, then they had not plumbed the depths of that fierce Irish resolve to tread the path of freedom even if, strait and narrow, it led each Volunteer into the valley of the shadow of death.

# IX

## [Dispatch Rider Taaffe's Adventures]

It was essential that each unit of the organisation should be kept in close contact with the others. Several orders, information and instruction had to be conveyed swiftly. Our intelligence system had ramifications everywhere and its discoveries had to find their way swiftly to a central point and to be distributed from there. The despatch riders were generally young men, cyclists or horsemen, knowing the topography of their district well, with a courage that enabled them to take constant risks and an initiative and adroitness that enabled them to carry through difficult assignments and find their way out of tight corners. Since their name was legion and the stories of their activities unending I shall have to be content with recounting a short history as my association with one of them and permit my readers, if any, to conceive for themselves the sterling character, the gay courage and the unending efforts of those who must be numbered among the nameless.

*"WHEN WE WERE BOYS"*.

I was awakened early one morning in the beginning of September 1920 by the sound of an unfamiliar boyish voice. I got up and went to the window. A number of loads had been brought into the yard during the previous day and now Jim Riordan and his workman were engaged in building a rick, and a short sturdy boy was pitching the sods on to it. He worked swiftly and his tongue kept pace with swinging arms. Whatever was the subject of his conversation it was in full spate and the boy was in possession, short interjection or query from the others forming the punctuation marks.

I dressed, shaved and came out into the yard. On my appearance he came to attention smartly and saluting came towards me, producing as he came a letter from his pocket which he handed to me. It was a note from the Brigade O/C. informing me that the bearer had been selected as my dispatch rider and general utility man, that he was thoroughly reliable and that he was not known to the R.I.C. I had been looking for a man with these qualifications, believed I'd get one of the men attached to the Brigade Staff whom I knew and was quite disappointed at having a new boy thrust on me. He was not more than seventeen, quite short but with wide muscular shoulders, a broad good-natured face, bright and merry brown eyes and white teeth flashing in a confident smile.

I was to discover that the broad shoulders were only a minor indication of his inexhaustible energy, his pleasant face that of an imperturbable temper and the merry eyes and confident bearing were the outward signs of a courage and impudent daring I have not seen surpassed. I questioned him. He had been a Volunteer for a year, before that he had worked on his father's farm. He had been for three months a Company Despatch Carrier and had done relief work for the brigade. He had never used a gun but his ambition was to graduate from despatch carrying to membership of the Active Service Unit. His father knew where he was and had voiced no objections; there were enough others at home to do all that was required on the farm. I accepted him with misgivings. I was later to oppose with profanity a proposal to transfer him to the Brigade Staff.

From that day until the end he was my companion in my peripatetic wanderings. Everywhere he became a general favourite. In his off moments he tackled all jobs that had to be done, from milking cows to rocking cradles, in the farmers' houses where I stayed. He had a gift for lying which transcended mere truth. His imagination was such that no story he told but was embellished and expanded. The perfection of his detail so impressed that among his listeners there was no question of unbelief. He built a character for me that I found impossible to live up to. I had the fighting capacity of Cúchulain, the military knowledge of a Clausewitz. Had I but one tenth the qualities which he attributed to me in his tales of wonder, I'd still be a superman. And he did not merely shine in the reflected glory of my fictional prowess. He was part of it. At a psychological moment in all our reported adventures when unforeseen circumstances tended to bring about a failure for our enterprise he stood like Horatius, or charged like Sergeant Custume, to change what might have been a defeat into a glorious success.* As a folklorist he had no equal.

While he was as yet unknown to the R.I.C. he was questioned on several occasions and his answering was so satisfactory that for a while no further notice was taken of his comings and goings. But his trouble was imminent. He was delayed at Brigade Headquarters one evening by the presence in the locality of a British search party and it was rather late when he started the return journey of about twenty-five miles. All went well until about midnight

---

* [*Sergeant Custume*: the hero of a famous incident in the Jacobite resistance to the Williamite conquest. The incident is the subject of the poem, *The Bridge Of Athlone, Or, How They Broke Down The Bridge*, by Aubrey De Vere. This poem appears to have been forgotten recently for no good reason. J.L.]

when he cycled into a byroad to get round a town. At this time of night all non-participants in the international disagreement were safe indoors. Night prowlers were definite objects of suspicion. As he rounded a bend there was a shout of "Halt" and two policemen stepped from the shadow of the fence. He swerved round them and increased his pace, but, alas, there was another pair and as he repeated the manoeuvre one of them thrust a walking stick through the bicycle spokes and spilled him on the roadway. As he hit the road he rolled over a few times into the long grass and briars by the fence. Lying on his face he thrust the dispatches into the briars and lay still until hauled to his feet by the R.I.C. men.

They questioned him roughly and for a moment he acted as if stunned by the fall, then recovering he made a violent protest at their action, demanding why he in pursuit of his legitimate business should be held up and assaulted. The questioning opened up a field for his inventive faculties. Saul was sent to look only for his father's asses. The animal of which he was in search was much more dangerous—a strayed bull—and his concern was to find the bull before he had done any damage rather than for any loss that might be otherwise sustained.

The R.I.C., while doubtful, could not pick any holes in his story. They searched him thoroughly, found nothing, and dismissed him with a warning to halt when called on in future, or, better still, to remain indoors at night. He departed, trundling the damaged bicycle and still protesting at his treatment. When he got out of sight he dumped the bicycle and returned across the fields to the place of his misadventure. The smell of tobacco enabled him to locate his men and he waited inside the fence until they finally moved away. He then recovered the package of letters, collected his cycle, which he managed to put into some sort of running condition, and finally arrived to me at three in the morning fully satisfied with his adventure and delighted to have a new basis for another wonder tale for the delectation of his ever growing group of listeners.

But he was caught at last. The small police patrols had been discontinued. As the I.R.A. became more confident and aggressive, these patrols became mere sources of supply of arms and ammunition. They were surprised, overpowered, and disarmed. Their utility had disappeared and they were withdrawn. Raiding and search parties were now tenfold strong, composed of military using R.I.C. men only as guides. Ambushes had become pitched battles and the shotgun of the earlier days had been displaced by the captured rifle in the hands of the I.R.A. It was at this time my despatch rider again came a cropper and again his magnificent impudence pulled him through. The Brigade O/C. was in an adjoining county attending a conference. A despatch from Michael Collins had come for him. The Brigade Adjutant forwarded it to me with instructions to have it delivered at once as it was urgent and important. I handed the despatch to my familiar, told him where he was to go and repeated the warning I had had about its importance and the need for speedy delivery.

He put it away carefully, got his bicycle and departed. I did not expect to see him again for several days and was surprised with his return again early that evening; more surprised to see the woebegone look on his invariably cheerful countenance. He told his story. He had run into a column of British military and Black and Tans; had been taken to the garrison town and thrown into a police cell. He intended to eat the despatch but wasn't given his opportunity. The cell door, opening into the guard room, was not closed and he was ordered to strip to the pelt and hand over all his clothes. He did so but managed to extract the despatch and throw it under the plank bed in the cell. It was a slender chance but there was no alternative. The clothes were searched, linings ripped out, each square inch closely examined and without result. He dressed again under close supervision and was then released. He took the precaution of returning to me by a devious route and here he was, an entirely deflated, self-condemnatory object.

Here was a problem which demanded considered action yet also demanded that the action should be immediate. I assume that when one is at one's wits end the brain reacts swiftly to the problem. I got a brain wave. I called the farmer in whose house I was, told him to ride to town, get in touch with a friend of mine there, find out who the woman was who cooked for the police or the name of anyone who had access to the barrack. Finally to give that information to a tobacconist in town whom I knew could be trusted. He left at once and I knew that his part of the contract would be completed.

I left the house and cycled to another three miles away. In this house there was a dump and among the various properties there was a British officer's uniform. I donned this. At that time I could not otherwise enter the town and avoid capture, and cycled to the town ten miles off. I arrived in the vicinity as dusk was falling. Dropping the cycle I crossed some fields, got in at the back of the houses in the Main Street and knocked at a door. The woman who opened the door put her hand swiftly to her mouth as if to stifle a scream, but made no outcry. The raiding British soldier had become so familiar that it was accepted as a normal routine. Without speaking I passed through the house and found myself on the Main Street and almost beside the tobacconist's shop which was my destination. I turned into the shop and asked for cigarettes. The tobacconist took a packet from the shelf, then for the first time looked at me, replaced the packet and handed me another from beneath the counter. I opened it; overlaid on the cigarettes was a note with the name and address of the woman who cooked for the police. I gasped when I looked at it. There are times when one can't go wrong and the tide of luck was now definitely in my favour.

I knew the woman. Her husband joined the Irish Guards and was killed in France early in 1916. She had a number of small children and I, sorry for her plight, tried to help her and the children on a number of occasions. Maybe the bread cast upon the waters would return. I walked into the street just as two Tommies passed by; they saluted and I waved my gloves nonchalantly in return. I stood for a few moments lighting a cigarette while they moved on up the street. I then followed them and having walked for a short way slipped into a side street and made my way to the house of the woman I sought. I told her my story. *"There was a packet beneath the plank bed in the barrack cell, I needed it and desired her to get it for me".* She promised to do so. I went to a house outside the town where I knew I'd be welcome and slept there that night. I spent a day on tenterhooks. The following night I recovered the packet. She had fished it out with her broom from beneath the plank, thrust into her blouse and brought it safely away.

I arrived back in the early morning to my headquarters, handed over the packet casually to my despatch rider with instructions to deliver it immediately. For once he was nonplussed. In the local idiom *"his eyes shtud in his head"* and he departed speechless.

His family name, Taaffe, was Norman and was borne by many a rough fighting buccaneer of whom we read in 16th and 17th century history, and certainly his nature did not deny his fighting forbears. He had a not unsoldierly dislike of police and even the Irish Republican Police he looked upon with disfavour. It was then with a tremendous distaste and under protest he became associated with them. The Brigade Police Officer had his headquarters in the battalion area, which was my usual stamping ground. He came to me one day and suggested that my despatch rider should carry his letters as well as mine. I consented, with the stipulation that they should be carried along the same routes as mine and should in no way interfere with the delivery of mine or place any added burdens on the bearer. We reached agreement but in a short time there was a sequel to the arrangement which in the month later resulted in a return to the status quo ante and the story of which I didn't hear for almost a year, when I was in a house in that district.

I got into this house in the evening wearied from sleepless nights and endless marching and, having a meal, went to bed. The despatch rider and another chap came later in the night and went to bed in a room adjoining mine. The partition between the rooms was a half inch board, warped and shrunken here and there through which every sound was audible. The sound of voices aroused me and I was about to curse their owners into silence when I recognised one voice and lay still.

It was my familiar with a new victim. He was telling the story of the police despatches, and this is what I heard:

"From that day my legs were torn down carrying despatches. The Boss hardly ever wrote one. He was always saying: 'The bloody typewriters will get us all hung', but the police despatches were going and coming all hours of the day. I was persecuted and then one day a despatch came in a creamery car marked 'Urgent and Important'. 'Urgent and Important' says I, in a creamery car? I took it into the house and put down the kettle and I censored it with the steam of the kettle and opened it. What was it but a letter from a girl asking him to meet her at Moll Carthy's bridge on Sunday at twelve o'clock. I closed the letter again and put it in my pocket. Saturday night I went across the fields to him and gave him the letter. He opened and read it. 'When did this come?' he said. I told him it came about an hour ago. 'I'm going to enquire about this', he said, 'this is an important matter and the letter has been delayed for at least three days'. I told him that giving letters to farmers going to the creamery was not the way to get them delivered quickly and then I left".

"I got up early the following morning and had my breakfast; then I went to the house where he was staying and hid in the haybarn where I could see everything about the house and yard. After a while he came out, shaved and shirted, with his rifle. He made straight for the haybarn, dumped his rifle and ammunition, got on his bicycle and went off. I came down off the hay and got the rifle. I couldn't touch the ammunition. I knew he counted every cartridge but I had a few three-o-threes of my own. I made off across the mountain, Moll McCarthy's bridge was only two miles away and I knew, since he started so early, that he had some other jobs to do before he went to meet the lady. An hour later I was lying between the bushes on a fence two hundred yards from the bridge. At twelve o'clock I saw him cycling from the west towards the bridge. The Angelus was ringing in the chapel a mile away when they met on the bridge. He leaped off the bicycle and put his arms around her. With that I hit the parapet of the bridge about five yards away from him with my first bullet. She gave a screech and the two of them flopped down on the road behind the parapet. I ran like hell till I came to the stepping stones and before I left cover I fired again so as to keep his head down while I was crossing the river. I ran like blazes across the mountain to the house. I pulled the rifle through and put it back where I got it. I was sitting down to a fine dinner of bacon and cabbage when he arrived. He brought his rifle and ammunition into the house. He examined the rifle and counted the ammunition. He said nothing but I knew he had a doubt on me. At any rate that finished me with the police. I got no more despatches."

"Did the Boss ever hear about it?" asked the listener. *"He did not"*, was the answer, *"if he heard about it he'd know what happened and he'd choke me"*. The bed creaked, there was a yawn and then silence. The Boss turned over in his own bed, untroubled by thought of mayhem. He, too, had a sense of humour.

# X

## [A Diary / Seán Nunan / A Court Case]

It has been borne on me on many occasions during my lifetime that one may be intensely and earnestly busy and yet accomplish nothing because one has permitted detail to obscure objective. It is easier to discipline and direct others than it is to discipline oneself or to keep one's own eye fixed on the desired goal. I was busy on the numberless and never ending tasks of the man who has charge of an ever developing organisation in ever changing circumstances. The Active Service Unit had been formed. It was now strong in numbers, effectively armed, properly led. I was anxious to join it if the Brigade O/C. gave permission. In the meanwhile it was my responsibility to create a background against which it could successfully operate. My direct commitments to it were to provide intelligence, billets, transport, replacements, stores. The perfecting of organisation, the keenness of the Volunteers, the courageous generosity of the people made possible the carrying out of the commitment but it was no easy task. The work went endlessly on. Yet I was not satisfied with myself.

I was able to keep the battalion's nose to the grindstone. There was nobody to perform a like office for me. I had a hatred of notebooks and memoranda, knowing the danger there was of their falling into enemy hands. Yet I deliberately decided to keep a diary of activities. I wanted to assure myself that each day something definite was accomplished. The diary was to be my overseer and as I looked over it from day to day I realised how a little more attention, a little more energy would have made it possible for me to overcome many difficulties and deal more efficiently with the work in hands. I don't know how the idea would work with other people or under different conditions but with me it acted as a tonic which made me tireless in tackling and solving all my problems. So much so that I insisted that every Company Captain should keep a diary. These diaries were produced at Battalion Council meetings and formed a day to day report of all company activities. After each such meeting they were destroyed.

I produced one month's record of my own activities for *An t-Óglach* under the caption *"A Fighting Commandant's Diary"*. It was never published, being captured with a number of other documents during a raid on one of G.H.Q's many Dublin hide-outs. Its capture resulted in the drafting of extra military into my district and redoubled enemy activity therein. I retired from literary composition.

I had, however, by this time provided myself with a much more effective spur to action. Paddy McCarthy had been detailed to the Active Service Unit and the Battalion Quartermaster's post, which he held, became vacant. I did not immediately fill it and now I selected Seán Nunan for the post. A post may be held to the general satisfaction by a line of men in succession, and then another man comes into possession and by his energy, initiative and capacity makes of it an entirely new and more important one, broadens its ambit and sets a man-killing pace for all who are associated with him. Of this type was Seán Nunan. He made an immediate survey of all the companies, checked arms and ammunition of all kinds, sharply reprimanded any laxity, arranged for the building of well-concealed waterproof dumps for all equipment and brought the Volunteers everywhere on their toes. Apart from his other qualities, his knowledge of men, his business experience and his fine intellect marked him out as a leader. He had no use for slackness of any kind and I found that if I was to keep pace with him I needed still further to increase my efforts. Men such as he were an inspiration, the backbone and real driving force of the I.R.A. He was wholly sincere, sought no advancement for himself. He could make allowance for folly but was harshly severe with the careless or negligent. I have not in my experience met any man of clearer intellect; never a more loyal or generous friend.

Actually a fine soldier, he hated soldiering and only a sheer sense of duty brought him into the Volunteers. Once a member, he dismissed all thought of home and of personal ambition and set out thoroughly and painstakingly to perfect himself and those he led for the work they had to do. A tremendous worker, he refused to tolerate any slackness. A strict disciplinarian, he had developed an esprit de corps among his men that was far more effective than any rigid regulation. For him no day was too long, no task too arduous, no hardship too great to be borne, yet he felt that soldiers were entitled to grouse while he could be harsh. He loved his men and sought their comfort in every way. The shining example of his courage, earnestness and energy was an inspiration to all his associates. His code of self-discipline was the basis of his success.

He was exceptionally keen on the development of the Sinn Féin organisation side by side with the Volunteers. He was particularly desirous of having a well-organised system of justice and helped everywhere with the creation of Republican courts. He used to say:

"The people and all their needs and concerns must always be matters for keen consideration by us. If they know that their real interests are ours, if they appreciate the fact that in each area where we are in power strict and absolute justice will be done, we shall have the goodwill and co-operation essential to success".

He did not believe in cheap law. Where the poor circumstances of disputants rendered it inequitable to impose ordinary costs, he advocated the appointment of arbitrators and for the arbitration there was no charge. Where people brought their cases to Court, however, he always urged the view that they'd respect law only when they paid for it. He insisted, also, that litigants and all involved in Court cases should not be unduly inconvenienced. If a case was listed for a Court on a certain date, Judges sat and that case was heard. I remember, on one occasion Judges sat in relays until all cases were cleared. I recall only one case in which an adjournment took place and its humorous sequel.

In May or June 1920, there was a row at a fair in an outlying district in the battalion area. Starting probably in a mere ebullition of youthful spirits, it would be classed as nothing more than violent horseplay if the R.I.C. had been on hand to check and control it. But the R.I.C. no longer functioned as police. They were now definitely absorbed into the army of occupation. And a row of this nature they would regard as an I.R.A. trick directed towards depriving them of their arms and so a simple rough joust developed into a serious faction fight. I have seen a few such rows in my boyhood, the instruments of attack are the knuckle and the ashplant. Both were wielded with effect that day.

Almost coincident with the row, a Parish Court had been set up and both sides, having soundly beaten each other, decided to have further satisfaction by summoning each other to the Parish Court. The Court sat in due course. The new Justices, sound men who would be admirable if involved in the intricacies of matchmaking or arbitration on a turbary dispute, were taken aback when faced by two truculent hostile groups of muscular young men both convinced of the righteousness of their cause and of the iniquity of their opponents. The Justices fought a delaying action. They heard all the other cases that came before the Court. They accompanied their decision in each case by long obiterdicta and managed to delay the business until nightfall when they adjourned Court without hearing the assault cases.

Nobody was deceived; the Volunteer Company Captain, at least, was under no illusion. He arrived that night at Battalion H.Q. where I happened to be with Nunan. We heard the Company Captain's story, agreed that the adjournment of the case was a sign of weakness that would tend to bring the Court into disrepute and agreed to the proposal of the Company Captain that Seán would attend the adjourned Court and, ex officio, act as Chairman. Eventually the day of the adjourned hearing came round. The countryside was agog with excitement. The *"Courthouse"* was not capable of holding one tenth of the crowd of spectators, and the litigants came reinforced by their relatives from other parishes. There was already present the material for a truly magnificent and widespread row when the Court opened. The Justices sighed with relief when Nunan moved through the crowd and took his place as Chairman. Without preliminaries the case was called, charge and counter charge, long protestations and irrelevancies from the women witnesses, accusations wild, fierce and dogmatic from men who now felt that honour and prestige depended on a favourable verdict. Finally a hot angry exchange between two of the litigants. It looked at this stage as if a fierce row was unavoidable when, crash, down came barrel and cylinder of a Webley 45 on the Justice's table. The Chairman was bringing the Court to order. All eyes turned on him as he sat there quietly, the gun held loosely in his hand, resting on the table.

*"Let it be clearly understood now by everyone here that whatever fighting is to be done in this locality in future the I.R.A. will do it, and maybe"*, he added with uncanny prescience, *"you'll all have quite enough before they're finished. I have listened carefully to all the accusations and arguments today. I believe that there were faults on both sides, faults for which each offender here will now have a penalty imposed on him. I fine each man concerned in this trouble one pound and bind him to the peace for twelve months. The money will be paid now".*

When he had finished speaking, only among the litigants did there remain any tensity of feeling. The general body of the people knew or had heard of Seán's reputation and appreciated the fact that a decision once made by him would be enforced. But among the litigants there were scowling faces and there was some murmuring.

No member of the local Volunteer Company was present. It had been so arranged, as we wanted to avoid the creation of local difficulties and ill feeling. A Volunteer from an adjoining company stood in the doorway. Seán nodded to him; the Volunteer turned and nodded to some unseen person outside. This by-play was unnoticed by the general body of those present. A sharp word of command outside and a crash of rifle butts startled everybody. A Volunteer officer appeared in the doorway, saluted and disappeared. *"The fines will now be paid to the Clerk of the Court"*, said Seán quietly. All present realised that this was not the voice of the farmer's son, the Creamery Manager whom they all knew, but the voice of the people; it represented the authority of Dáil Éireann; and the arms of the State were ready to enforce its dictates. A few men smiled, the smile broadened, developed into laughter and in a few minutes peace and good humour reigned in Court.

Every unbiassed man who was present knew there could not be in equity any other judgement. Those who appreciated order were vastly relieved. The

British Authority had abdicated; there was a vacuum; here was Irish authority stepping in and speaking with no uncertain voice. The prestige of the Court was immediately established; during its period of office none of its decisions was ever questioned and it remained an important factor of reassurance to the minds of the people in the difficult times that then lay before them.

The Court decision had an amusing sequel. Early in 1921 the Active Service Unit, strong, well trained, hardened and experienced, was striking everywhere. According to the nature of the work and its conditions, its strength varied. It never had a greater number than fifty except when several units combined, as happened occasionally, sometimes as small a number as ten was styled the A.S.U. But at its major strength or otherwise, its effectiveness depended on the swift mobilisation and ready co-operation of the Volunteer Companies in the areas where it operated. Practically every man wanted a rifle and urged his claim to a place in the A.S.U. It was possible to provide rifles for a small number only. Each gun and round of ammunition had first to be captured from the British. Even had the rifles been available it would have been entirely inadvisable to develop an A.S.U. beyond a certain strength. The question of cover was all important. A small body of well trained determined men might feint, strike and disappear, strike again and again dissolve into thin air in a most tantalising and irritating fashion. With a large body such tactics would be impossible. And so the great majority of the Volunteers pursued their ordinary vocation side by side with their Volunteer activities. They carried dispatches, broke roads and railways, did protection duty and intelligence and participated with any available weapons when the A.S.U. pulled off a fight in their own area. For some fights a few local companies were organised; for others all companies in a battalion, for some again the whole Brigade was in some manner involved.

A fight took place about six months after the Court proceedings which I have recorded. The number of members of the A.S.U. participating was the minimum and two local companies were mobilised to help.

It became known by accident that a number of Black and Tans and a high ranking officer were in an adjoining county collecting evidence wherewith to support charges against prisoners confined in the Military Detention Barracks. I decided that, their inquiries concluded, they'd return at once to their headquarters. An examination of the map showed me three possible return routes, the shortest and best through my own area. I decided to lay an ambush at a particular point. Mobilisation and preparation went on during the night and early in the evening a horseman went to east and west carrying detailed information to the commandants of the adjoining battalions of my plans and detailing my views as to what should be done to hold the other routes. Perfect organisation and fighting spirit were displayed in the fact that on the three routes ambushes were laid at vital points at dawn on the day following and the men were not withdrawn until two days later when dispatch riders carried the news that the work had been successfully carried out. And it had been. From dawn to dawn on a weary day of drenching fog and mist, from dawn to noon on the second day, when the sun struggled through the mist, the men lay in cold discomfort by the roadside, the heather their only cover. As the sun came out I focused my glasses on the road; then, slowly searching along its length, picked up the cars travelling at speed and still four miles distant. That momentary sunbeam was unlucky for those ill-fated Tans. I barked sharp orders, everybody got into position, each man knew his job thoroughly. I got my rifle into position, snuggled down amid the withered ferns and lay still. A disturbance in the heath and ferns in the little glen beside me distracted my attention. Somebody was moving towards me under cover. Suddenly a head appeared, then a hand holding a shotgun. It was one of the litigants of last year's Court case, Con Finucane of Glounalougha. With a mocking grin he looked at me and said: *"What will I do, Sir? Sure I'm bound to the peace"*. I spat a vile word, turned with a grim smile to face the road, cheered and confident that men who could joke in the face of battle and sudden death were unbeatable. I shall at a later stage relate the story of this fight and some of its results.

## XI

## [Spies / Bomb-makers / Death Of Paddy McCarthy / Attack On Tans In Millstreet / Insurrection And Revolution]

The inspection of arms and equipment carried out by Seán Nunan and me was associated with a general survey of the conditions of each company. There were company parades and drills, discussions on the various activities to be undertaken and of difficulties which had to be met. This entailed a tour of the battalion area and occupied us for several weeks. Our inspection finished at Freemount. Here we met a group of the members of the A.S.U. They had had a number of adventures since we parted with them at Drominarigle. Ernie O'Malley had left. The Brigade O/C. had returned to his headquarters at Lombardstown and Commandant P. O'Brien was in charge of the group. The inspection of the arms and of arms dumps was carried out during the day, in the evening we had a general parade of the company and took the opportunity that the presence of the A.S.U. presented us to give the company special instruction in the use of rifle and revolver. We then adjourned to a house in the village where we discussed the details of work and organisation with the company officers and section leaders. Before the discussion had quite ended a number of Volunteers arrived with two British soldiers. These men they had found prowling round the roads. British soldiers had been picked up on previous occasions by the Volunteers and had given the same explanations of their movements that these men gave. They claimed that they were deserters. But their release after questioning had always been the prelude to an intense raid by the British in the area where they were captured. I questioned these men and, I think, succeeded in thoroughly frightening them. I got certain information from them which, associated with further information received later, was to bear fruit in the months to come. Their story might have been true but in view of our previous experience that was unlikely and death is the penalty for spying. An army has to protect itself. The shooting of unarmed men was not, however, an action that commended itself to me and I had no desire to go to extremes in the matter. I decided to hold the prisoners during the night and to release them in the morning. Before their release the following morning I spoke to them again, told them I believed them to be spies who deserved shooting and warned them when they returned to barracks to inform the Intelligence Officer who sent them and their comrades that any British soldier captured again in like circumstances would pay the extreme penalty. They were then escorted out of the village and put on the road to Buttevant. That afternoon they again arrived but this time they were accompanied by at least one half of the garrison at Buttevant. They searched, raided and questioned but their errand was fruitless. We had by this time left for the great open spaces.

We had been experimenting for some time with the making of land mines and bombs. Our knowledge of explosives was so meagre that it was only by a continuing miracle that we escaped disintegration. Our tour had also disclosed the fact that the greater portion of the shotguns in possession of the Volunteers were defective and in need of repair. We decided that we'd have to get somebody familiar with gun repair to overhaul these dangerous weapons and as it would be impossible to have this work done in the ordinary farmhouse we further decided that we'd have to set up a workhouse somewhere. If we were to have bombs and mines we needed iron and other metals. Seán and I discussed the matter as we journeyed towards Meelin, where we parted. He went to Tullylease. I proceeded to Drominarigle. The following day I sent a note to all companies with instructions about the collection of scrap iron. I arranged for a raid on the home of a British official where I knew there was a lighting system. I needed the engine and dynamo. I decided on the site and nature of the workshop and arranged with Con Flynn of Newmarket for the delivery of the material on the site.

For some time reports from Millstreet indicated that the Black and Tans stationed there were behaving in a more and more obnoxious manner to the people and acting as if the I.R.A. were non-existent. The local Volunteers had decided that such a situation could not continue and arranged that the A.S.U., a number of whose members were from Millstreet Battalion, should tackle the problem. The Active Service Unit moved into Millstreet district during the week. At this time I had constantly in my company a young lad, my cousin, Liam Moylan. He was most anxious to join the Active Service Unit but I considered him too young for the arduous tasks its members had to perform and further I needed somebody on whom I could rely to carry out the various odd jobs arising for me out of the Volunteers. This companionship was now to end. He had been with me since the day that the police first searched for him. He was only seventeen and I kept an eye on him and kept him close to me until he developed experience and a capacity for taking care of himself. This was a source of never ending grievance to him; he felt he was as good a soldier as any of the older men and the fact of my refusal to permit him to participate in certain activities irked him. I was now to yield to his importunities. Paddy McCarthy arrived from the Millstreet district. The A.S.U. intended to go into Millstreet town that evening to shoot it out with the Tans. He wanted any revolver ammunition I could spare. I gave him some and then he asked for permission to carry the youngster with him. I knew that the time had arrived for decision. I had either to release him or retain on my hands a disgruntled and therefore useless helpmate. The pair went off in high delight.

On the night of this attack I was engaged in another venture elsewhere and during the night I had misgivings about the wisdom of sending the boy into a fight which was bound to be fierce and perhaps bloody. Maybe it was a premonition of evil. When I arrived back to my headquarters in the early dawn he was already there. Paddy McCarthy, into whose charge I had given him, was killed beside him by a revolver bullet in the close fighting entailed in a street attack. It was plain that he had got a shock. Until then war, to his youthful seeming, was a game. Now he realised its grim reality. Though my heart was sore for the gay, gallant man that was gone I treated the matter casually and I think he was disturbed at the apparently callous manner in which I received the news. Theretofore I wanted him to realise that my refusal to attach him to a combat unit was not merely my concern for his personal safety but fundamentally my desire to utilise only trained effectives in the fighting ranks for their own and their comrades safety and so to ensure that all precautions had been taken to secure success. I wanted to impress on him then that the loss of men was inevitable and no matter how close our comradeship the grim shadow of death was in these circumstances closer to us all. That the occurrence which to the civilian mind meant tragedy must be accepted by soldiers as the routine of their trade. His generous boyish mind was revolted at my attitude but he was too intelligent to misunderstand me for long and his reaction from his first nervous shock was swift. He had been under fire in fierce hand to hand fighting, had been bespattered by his comrade's blood. No longer would his mind be troubled by the heroics of the uninitiated. He was now a soldier.

I had a coffin made in Kiskeam and proceeded to Millstreet to bring home the body of my comrade for burial. I found the A.S.U. in the hills west of Millstreet. The Brigade O/C. had arrived to ensure that they entered the town again on that and following nights. This was wise policy as otherwise their comrade's death would have had a bad effect on their morale. He had so much of dare-deviltry, was so infectiously gay and good humoured that he was an all-round favourite and his death was the sorest blow that could be given to them. It was an eerie experience, following a coffin at midnight along lonely byroads from Millstreet to Kilcorcoran. And in spite of the secrecy with which the proceedings had to be veiled, the funeral cortege at Kilcorcoran had reached immense proportions. Men seemed to come from everywhere to pay their last tribute of respect to the dead soldier, and our loyal friend, Father Leonard from Freemount, came to say the last prayers at the graveside.

Paddy McCarthy had been arrested after a battalion parade in March or April 1918. He was sentenced to eighteen months in Belfast prison. He participated in the strike there under Austin Stack. Afterwards he was transferred to Strangeways prison, Manchester, from which he escaped about September 1919. From the date of his arrival home in Ireland until August 1920, when he was selected as a member of the newly organised A.S.U., he had been associated with me in all activities. Now I was no more to see his friendly face, to hear his merry laughter, to have my spirits renewed by the impact of his unbreakable courage. At Kilcorcoran I met Charlie O'Reilly who had been acting as Battalion Commandant during my illness. In the destruction of a police barrack in the early part of the year he had, with others, been injured and badly burned when a petrol tin exploded. He now claimed to be completely recovered and asked to be permitted to take Paddy McCarthy's place in the A.S.U. I acceded to his demand and another fine young fellow marched away to keep an early appointment with death.

Two days later I sent a group of men to collect the engine and dynamo. Con Moylan, Liam's brother, was in charge of these. He was a forceful individual and an expert mechanic. He had, therefore, the essential qualities for the post. The material was delivered and carefully stored before the sun rose. Con Moylan was not as yet suspect. He was still able to live at home and while his continuing to do so placed him in a most dangerous position he was so useful to us there that I insisted on his remaining. How he escaped and lived I know not. All his nights were occupied with work for the I.R.A. Yet he never failed to be at home and in bed when the British raiding parties visited his home. He took charge of the erection of the workshop and purchased a lathe, vice, fitters' tools, all the equipment needed, and at the same time kept me fully informed of all matters relating to the military and police in Newmarket. The scrap iron collection was an embarrassing success. We soon had so much of it delivered to Kiskeam that we found a difficulty in storing and concealing it.

We had other difficulties, too, at this period. Various well-intentioned people had been negotiating for a truce and had given Lloyd George the impression that *"he had got murder by the throat"*. Roger Sweetman, a Deputy of Dáil Éireann, explaining in the Dáil on 21.1.1921, a letter he had written to the press on November 30th, 1920, said that *"he considered the Volunteers were in the process of disruption"*.

Other deputies seemed to favour this view but our own deputy, Pádraig O'Keeffe, knew his own people when he replied that he'd be disowned by North Cork if he expressed that viewpoint. I have already said that the activities of the I.R.A. were not related to a considered strategy nor was it under the close control and direction of a clearly recognised headquarters staff. Many people have even expressed the view that its efforts were not directed to a clearly defined end.

The I.R.A. fought for a Republic, for complete political freedom and severance from the British Empire. True enough! But did those who served the ideal of complete independence appreciate the implications which the efforts towards the achievement of their ideal entailed? They knew the might of Empire; too well they should have realised and did realise the military weakness of Ireland. What then were they fighting for? What did they hope to achieve? Towards what particular goal were their activities directed? Was the

I.R.A. composed of insurrectionists or were its members revolutionaries?

An insurrection is a protest, staged not so much in the hope of the immediate adoption of the ideas on which it is based as in the belief that the sacrificial promulgation of these ideas will eventually bear fruit, will propagate the doctrine of the insurrectionists. Revolutionaries seek a more immediate effect, expect that their efforts will result in radical change! It is my view that what began as an insurrection swiftly evolved into a revolution. Everywhere in Ireland was the old leaven of the Fenian tradition. Deep in the hearts of all Irishmen was the sense of racial solidarity. Those who looked with dismay on Easter Week were proud of the courage of their compatriots; bitterly resentful of the execution of prisoners. The British had made insurrection inevitable, the utilisation of the background so created had produced the revolution. The revolutionaries set out to make British Government impossible in Ireland and prepared to take over governmental control wherever the British had been ousted or where the allegiance of the people had been weaned therefrom. Sinn Féin would not have had the ghost of a chance of success but for the activities of the I.R.A. I.R.A. success would have been pointless but for the consolidation of the effects of these successes on the people.

Every man was called upon to do his part, big or little; none dared refuse and few were who had any objection to co-operate. Some have expressed surprise that the I.R.A. campaign was not made more spectacular. By this they meant, of course, a concentration of forces and bigger battles. Such people had no conception of conditions or of the grand strategy that directed the campaign. We visualised the fight as a long one in which British ruthlessness would be the more intensified the longer it continued. It was essential to keep an army in the field, its liquidation could not be contemplated, but more essential it was that forceful men of the fighting service should more and more concern themselves with the development and maintenance of the spirit of civilian resistance, for many peacetime war mongers became war time pacifists as the situation developed and many of the Lord's anointed, the elected representatives of the people, had developed the coldest of cold feet.

The British had placed Munster under Martial Law. Cork City was burned and the Black and Tans and Auxiliaries set out on an unprecedented campaign of murder and destruction. The Active Service Unit was harried from pillar to post without getting any real opportunity for striking and the continuing raids on the houses of those from whom I had hitherto found shelter seemed to indicate that the net was irrevocably closing on those of us who were regarded as the hard core of the resistance. It was now the magnificent spirit of the people manifested itself. Capture of a wanted man in any house meant imprisonment or worse for all the male members of the household. It meant the destruction of home and property, the unbridled licence of undisciplined gangsterdom. Yet in every household were the wanted men made welcome. What the people had was theirs. This attitude was finely expressed by Mrs. Nora Galvin of Glashakinleen when on one occasion I apologised for my too frequent visits to her home. *"This"*, she said, *"is my country as well as yours"*. She and her husband were teachers. They stood to lose everything by a continuance of their efforts on our behalf, yet, unassumingly, with quiet determination, they took that risk. There are various kinds of courage, but theirs, it seems to me, may be numbered amongst its highest forms.

At a Brigade Council we reviewed the situation and decided that the best use could no longer be made of the Brigade A.S.U. in its existing formation. It was too large for its purpose. The new proposal was to disband it, to reform it as Battalion A.S.U.s and to allot one of our two Hotchkiss guns to the western and eastern sides of the Brigade. Dick Willis and Seán Healy tossed for choice of guns. Willis, Bolster and the men from the eastern battalions departed. We were not to see them again until the Truce. The Brigade area, officially divided into two just before the truce, had actually been divided by the force of circumstance in November 1920. The result of this division proved its wisdom. The British instead of being able to concentrate on one fighting force were confronted with the problem of dealing with such a force in each of the seven battalion areas, smaller certainly but more easily hidden, more elusive and capable of a swift combination into and co-operation in a large force when the need arose.

We had immediate results in the eastern side. The British were successfully ambushed at Leary's Cross on December 10th and on the 19th another successful ambush was brought off at Glenacurrane. In this fight the East Limerick Column was associated with the Cork troops.

In spite of all the activity of the British, training camps had been created in the 5th Battalion and were in operation in every company area and now a group of the best men from each company was brought into the two Battalion Training Camps at Ballinguilla and Tureen for a special course covering a period of two weeks. Not only did these men get an intensive training in rifle, revolver and machine gun practice, but what we styled the special services were also catered for. These services were engineering, signalling, first aid and intelligence. The articles in *An t-Óglach,* military text books and particularly the results of our own experience formed the basis of the courses. When the course was finished on Christmas Eve these men went back to their companies hard and fit, with a higher morale and a more soldierly spirit than could have been by any other means developed. As the men paraded on Christmas Eve for dismissal, a scout arrived with the information that the British were approaching.

The men formed into their allotted sections and took cover awaiting further information. Most of them were armed only with shotguns and could, therefore, fight only at close quarters. I proceeded with the scout to the position from which he saw the British and with my glasses picked up half a dozen lorries on a road a mile to the west across the Kerry border. They came slowly along but when they came to the cross roads leading up to our position they continued on towards Killarney. I found out later that they had been raiding about Gneeveguilla and had picked up a middle aged man named Moynihan. They took him some distance then shot him and threw him off the lorry to die on the roadside. Two days before Mr. Lloyd George had introduced his *"Better Government of Ireland"* Bill in the House of Commons.

I had an appointment that night in Newmarket. I needed to see both Con Moylan and Con Flynn in regard to the workshop. Liam Moylan accompanied me. We met a large body of British soldiers between Kingwilliamstown and Kiskeam. We luckily sighted them first and avoided contact. Newmarket when we arrived in the darkness was a dead town. No Christmas candles were alight, not a soul on the streets. The cheerful Christmas bustle of former years was notably absent. Yet the imposition curbed nobody associated with the I.R.A. My friends were waiting and we discussed our business to a conclusion. All doors and windows were carefully shrouded to comply with curfew regulations. We talked by the light of a single candle. Liam's mother, calm, competent, imperturbable, put together a parcel of underclothes for her son, recounted local news. His father produced a bottle and he and I drank his usual toast *"Success"*.

We were ready to leave when Con Flynn said to me *"Are these the only clothes you have?"* I looked down at my clothes and saw them for the first time in six months. I hadn't realised how bedraggled I'd become. I looked like a scarecrow without portfolio. I laughed without answering and we took our departure. That night in Newmarket an old man, John Murphy, took his Christmas candle from his kitchen to his bedroom where there were no curtains. A military patrol in the streets seeing the light knocked at his door and called to the old man. He came to the window and the officer in charge shot him through the throat. Law and order was being enforced. Two days later Con Flynn sent me a beautiful suit of Irish tweed.

The extreme pressure brought to bear on us then made communications extremely difficult. On several occasions Brigade Council meetings had to be abandoned owing to raids by the British. I had never cared to put in writing any proposals for future action, always preferring vocal to literary efforts. It was essential, however, that the battalions should keep in touch with each other and as the third battalion was that with which I worked most closely I decided to visit its commandant, Séamus Brislane. It was getting on for Christmas when I directed my steps towards Dromina. It had been a hard year and while we had not escaped unscathed we had punished our enemies severely and now the countryside was so overrun with enemy forces that movement was possible only over little known roads or by field, glen and mountainside. But, however difficult, it was necessary to keep in touch and a visit to Séamus was overdue. The use of cycle or horse was ruled out. I had to walk. It was a thirty mile march that I had undertaken. I set out early in the afternoon and had not proceeded far when rain began to fall. All that day I walked and all that day it rained unceasingly. I arrived at my destination before midnight, chilled, hungry, exhausted. Immediately Séamus was all fuss and excitement. His immediate reaction was to haul me to the fire, to rush across to the kitchen cupboard and to produce a bottle of whiskey. He brought the bottle towards me, holding it to the light, expatiating on its purity, on the business rectitude of the man who supplied it and on the fact that it was held specially against my coming. I stood before the fire, my clothes steaming, my body numb with cold. I swore at him, advising him to cut the cackle and get a corkscrew. He got the corkscrew, put the bottle between his knees and pulled. *"Will you have it hot or cold?"* he asked. *"I'll have a drink"*, I replied, *"while you're making the punch"*. He held the bottle to the light and again held forth on the superior quality of the whiskey. With profanity I demanded action. He reached to the table for a glass and as he did so the bottle slipped from his hand and broke with a crash on the flagstone before the fire. There was a groan of anguish from all those present. He stood petrified and then moved towards me chattering apologies. I was gazing at the fragments of the bottle on the flagstone at my feet. I put my left hand towards him and said: *"Don't move"*. I bent down, carefully removed some of the broken pieces of glass. There was a depression in the flagstone worn by the feet of many generations who had lived in the house. It was now full of whiskey. Hygienists and teetotallers may raise their hands in holy horror, I was no Philip Sidney*, and my need was greater than theirs is ever likely to be. I went on my knees on the flagstone and drained the depression dry.

## XII

## [Meelin / Human Shields Used By British / Tureengarriffe Ambush / Informers]

My memory of January 1921, is one of incessant rain, intensifying sometimes into sleet and snow. I don't remember ever wearing a dry garment during the month. On a few occasions, sleeping in the shelter of a fence, I woke covered with snow yet I never caught cold nor did I ever regard the conditions under which I lived as abnormal. Truly is human nature adaptable.

On New Year's Eve Mick Sullivan of Meelin visited me at John O'Leary's, Killoseragh, a house where I had always been made welcome. Mick was a quiet, reserved and intensely earnest Volunteer who was later to develop into the brilliant leader of an Active Service Unit and to earn among his not easily impressed comrades a reputation for the most reckless daring. We both felt that we had sufficient men now trained as far as it was possible to train them without bringing them under fire, and considered that even if we accomplished nothing other than the provision of this final lesson for them our attempt would be justified.

The cramped quarters of the British in Newmarket, the fact that they had to live inside barbed wire and sandbag emplacements necessitated that the men should now and again get some exercise. This object was secured by marching them out of Newmarket a few evenings every week. They had used the Meelin road on a few occasions and we decided to get a group of Volunteers together and wait for them on this road. I arrived in Meelin in the early hours of New Year's Day. I left for Tullylease and Freemount on the following day for the purpose of selecting men for the group who were to take part in the project. I arrived back on the 3rd and early on the 4th got into position about one mile south of Meelin. We lay inside a low fence on the roadside. We had half a dozen rifles, the rest of the men were armed with shotguns. It was, therefore, necessary that the fight should be at close quarters. Scouts were stationed in positions where an early view of the approach

[* *Philip Sidney*: probably a reference to Sir Philip Sidney (1554-1586), the ultimate courtier and sophisticate of Elizabethan England. J.L.]

of the British could be obtained. There was nothing to do but wait and we waited well into the afternoon without result. We then got word of their approach, not from the south as expected but from the west, not a marching patrol but a strong raiding party in lorries. They had, in fact, already that day raided the houses of some of the Volunteers who were members of our party.

The position we occupied was exposed, without any real cover by way of retreat and quite unsuitable to this new problem. I decided that if we had time to get to the turn of the road at Michael K. Barry's at Meenkeragh that we'd reach a position that would be reasonably satisfactory. On our way we got a further message that they were coming too swiftly towards us to enable us to reach the desired position. We had perforce to turn off the road when we had passed through the village and take the cover that immediately offered itself. Scarcely had we done this when the lorries arrived. Our position was, from the point of view of success, rather hopeless. Nevertheless, we opened fire with the rifles and succeeded in stopping the lorries. The British dismounted quickly and there began a duel that lasted till dawn and then the arrival of British reinforcements. Unluckily we had chosen the day on which the garrison at Newmarket was relieved and there was available for reinforcements more than double the usual number of men with adequate motor transport. There was nothing to do but retire. This we did unhurriedly but with downcast spirits. At least my spirits were downcast. We had engaged the British with a number of men who had not hitherto been shot over but we had nothing to show for our efforts. I made two decisions: one was that in future there would be only a single command. The disruption caused by the swift change from the plan of dealing with a certain anticipated problem to that of dealing with a new and entirely unforeseen one had upset the men, they were excited and, instead of obeying orders, Section Leaders were shouting contradictory commands and suggesting contradictory methods. This was fatal to any success we might have achieved and I grimly decided it was never to occur again. My second decision was to use a lesser and more carefully selected group. There were too many men, some quite unsuitable, and the weakest link is always the measure of the breaking stress. We retired a few miles and that night went to Kingwilliamstown with Johnnie Jones of Glencollins. While he was only a boy in years, he had been with me in several fights and was a cool and most placid individual even in the most difficult circumstances.

The following day a punitive party of British military arrived in Meelin, looted and burned half a dozen houses, rounded up all the men they could find and in general behaved in a bullying and brutal manner. We spent the day thawing out gelignite which had been frozen. We had brought the gelignite from Sixmilebridge in Co. Clare in May or June 1920. Its effect on us was to make us very ill for several days.

Jack O'Connell's reports now showed no regular movements of troops or R.I.C. and showed that when they did move their numbers were larger than theretofore. They did indicate, however, that the British had visited a few villages and posted up a proclamation. I don't remember what the purport of the particular proclamation was nor was I then concerned but it might be possible that they'd visit each village in turn and, therefore, we kept strict watch everywhere, lay in ambush between Newmarket and the unvisited villages but nothing came of our visits.

At this time the holding of the established fairs and markets was prohibited and fairs were held in outlying districts so as to permit farmers to carry on their usual sale and purchase. The reports indicated that the British had gone out in force to prevent the holding of several of these temporary fairs. Such a fair was to be held in Rockchapel on the 15th. I believed that the British would surely visit Rockchapel on that date and made preparations accordingly. I got together a specially selected group and collected every available rifle. I secured about twenty and then proceeded to select a spot for the ambush. The difficulty always was to stop all the lorries, to prevent them from spreading out and permitting the British to outflank our position. This time the problem was solved swiftly enough. Somebody, the owner of a Humber car, had an accident about two miles west of Newmarket. The car had remained on the roadside for several days. I felt sure that when the British came upon the car they'd halt to examine it and arranged my ambush accordingly.

I left Kiskeam after dark on the 14th. I had a number of calls to make during the night and finally arrived at the ambush position about 4 a.m. It had been raining heavily. The rain had now ceased but it was bitter cold. I crept under a hedge and went to sleep for a few hours. When I woke there was a slight drift of snow. It was not yet daylight and the boys had begun to gather. Inside an hour we were all in position. During the next few hours nobody would suspect that a group of men of deadly purpose were concealed behind the bare hedge that lined the road. A messenger cycling furiously from Newmarket brought the news that four lorries of soldiers had arrived in the town. They were at the military barracks as he left. This was the number we had expected and prepared for so there was no need to make any alteration in the arranged position. The wait had been tedious but everybody was satisfied now at the prospect of action and each man, ready and alert, settled himself into his position. Then another breathless cyclist arrive with a hurriedly written note from Con Moylan. The British had a number of hostages in their lorries and were then engaged in gathering a number of others in Newmarket. Among those already seated in a lorry was our most prominent and effective supporter, Denis D. Curtin. I was in a quandary. I had made every effort and taken all care to make a success of this fight. Now, if I fought, it meant certain death for a number of non-combatants. It certainly meant *"lights out"* for Denis Curtin, my very good friend and a man we could ill spare. I still hoped against hope that an opportunity would present itself for attack which would at the same time embody a sporting chance for the hostages. I explained the position to my comrades and ordered that except my whistle went there was to be no attack. I got back to my own position beside the fence outside which the car lay.

We soon heard the sound of approaching lorries, immediately they were in sight. They were crowded with men in civilian dress and these seemed to outnumber the soldiers they carried. My anticipation was sound. When the British sighted the car they slowed, their rifles were pointed outward. Two lorries moved past it. One pulled up in line with it. The last lorry twenty yards to the rear of this. Had there been no hostages there would have been slaughter. Each lorry was in perfect position for our purpose. An officer and some men dismounted to examine the car. The others remained in the lorries with the hostages, all of whom were handcuffed. Where I lay half a dozen British Tommies were five yards away, no member of the group more than fifty yards from an I.R.A. rifle. Yet I could not blow my whistle. I could not condemn those unarmed, handcuffed men to the death that would be surely theirs if the fight started. The British remounted their lorries and drove away, never suspecting how close they had been to death. We waited all day in the hope that on their return the position might have altered. But their return through the ambush was a repeat performance. They again halted, some dismounted and again examined the car while the majority stood guard over their prisoners. Had these prisoners been young I might have taken a chance, but some of them were old and most were middle-aged, breadwinners, with dependent families, I couldn't do it. And so again we marched away disgruntled. We had worked hard for success but success evaded us.

The 3rd Battalion, still most aggressive, was having slightly better luck. At midnight on the same day they lay in ambush at Shinanagh. They had discovered that a number of British cars passed weekly in the early hours of the morning between Limerick and Buttevant. They decided to dig a trench across the road at a selected position. Digging operations couldn't start until the people of the countryside had gone to bed and the trench was not completed when the one British carload only arrived a few hours before their usual time. Séamus Brislane, who was in charge had only a few rifles but he at once opened fire. Give the devil his due, the driver of the car was a bold man. He was under fire. He saw the twelve feet wide trench yawning before him. He trod on the accelerator, charged it and almost got away. But the car was too heavily laden, its back wheels struck the face of the trench on the far side and it toppled back into the trench almost on top of the men who had been digging and who hadn't had time to get out. The good soldier he was, the British driver shut off the lights of the car. There was an interchange of shots in the pitchlike darkness. They were only a few miles from their barracks and intimately familiar with the ground. But if they got away, an important capture was made. They left some guns and ammunition in the car, but, more important still, a bag containing files and dispatches from the British I.O. in Limerick to the I.O. in Buttevant. Before morning these were in the hands of the Brigade O/C. and as the mail train left Mallow that evening the guard carried a bulky package Dublinwards. Mick Collins had the gift of language. He should have been worth hearing that night.

It was no longer possible to attack a police barracks by the methods that were successful in 1920. Now the garrisons were strongly reinforced by Black and Tans, there were sandbag emplacements, steel shutters, barbed wire and machine guns, while we sadly lacked explosives. In the centres where the police still remained, military posts were set up garrisoned by from sixty to one hundred men. While we were able to keep both military and police closely confined within a narrow circle we had no equipment with which to drive them from the positions they occupied.

I began to consider the possibility of using an old seventeenth century cannon. We got one of these from Killarney. I think it came from Ross Castle. We cleaned it up, built a frame for it and one night Dan Vaughan, Tom McNamara and I went into Newmarket Railway Station and collected two wheels from a railway truck which we attached to the frame. We tried it early one morning. We set it up one hundred yards from a disused limekiln, loaded it with a quantity of black powder and a ten pound sash weight, set off the charge with a short piece of fuse. It worked perfectly. We hit the face of the kiln dead centre and burst a hole through it.

We were elated. When the British travelled over our district they were sheltered behind a screen of hostages. Now we had a solution for the problem. We could attack them inside their own barracks. We made preparations for such an attack. In the meantime we lay daily on the roads without seeing hair or hide of the British.

As I have before mentioned, the weather of January 1921, was cold and wet. This endless waiting on the roadside entailed much hardship. I told those who lived in country districts that they could take a few days off to visit their homes. I retained only the men for whom it would be too dangerous to make such a visit. This was the condition of things when on an afternoon in the last days of January Dan Vaughan and I left Jones of Glencollins to visit Con Murphy, the Kiskeam Company Captain. It poured rain and the road was deserted. Suddenly Vaughan pointed to the road surface. There in a patch of mud was a wet tyre track, that of a heavy wide type. We leaped for the fence and over it; the middle of the road might quickly become unhealthy. Inside the fence we discussed the matter. We were sure the track was left by a British military car. We decided that the British had gone to Kingwilliamstown to post their latest proclamation and we both cursed the decision that had dispersed our group. We waited an hour for their return and then decided to proceed to Kiskeam to make inquiries about the matter.

The rain came down in sheets. Kiskeam was a deserted village. Con Murphy had no knowledge of the passing of any cars, nor could we elicit any information anywhere in regard to such an occurrence. We returned to Glencollins. On our way we met a man loading rushes into a cart. As a last hope we questioned him. Yes, he had seen the cars, two of them, loaded with Black and Tans; they had a cannon. He described the cannon. I diagnosed a Lewis gun. We proceeded to Kingwilliamstown and made inquiries. A few people had seen the cars passing; they had gone through the village toward Castleisland. It was natural for us to think that they had gone to Tralee, which was British Headquarters in Kerry, and we considered that owing to the lateness of the hour they were unlikely to return particularly in view of their experience at Shinanagh a few days before.

I returned to Jones, Glencollins, decided to ambush the cars on their return, if they did return, at Tureengarriffe, two miles to the west of the village. I sent a note to the Commandant of the Kanturk Battalion, explaining to him what I intended to do and suggesting that, as there was a possibility that the return route would be by Killarney and Rathmore, he should lay an ambush at Clonbanin. Another message I sent to the Kerry Brigade O/C.

Jones' kitchen that night was a scene of tremendous activity. Men came and went, guns and ammunition were examined, the attacking party selected.

We got to bed for a few hours in the early morning and at 5 a.m. were again astir. We marched off an hour later and having reached the selected position began to dig a trench across the road. It was a vile day, fog so thick that one could see only a few yards, and so wet that it seemed to penetrate to the bone. All day long we waited and well into the night there was no sign of our quarry. A number of men were left on guard, the majority of us snatched a few hours sleep. At six the following morning the whole party was in position again. The fog had disappeared, it was a clear dry day. At noon I decided to let half the men go so that they might try to get a cup of tea in the nearest house but before I issued the order the sun shone out and I focused the glasses on the road at Scartag schoolhouse which was a bright yellow colour and easily identifiable. Just as my glasses rested on the patch of road two cars swung in. I shouted to the others and told them what I'd seen. I had determined at this time that nothing was going to stop the attack.

For this fight we had ten rifles. Our position approximated to a semi-circle, with the road cutting it in half. Tom McNamara, Dan Vaughan, Johnny Jones were on its northern end. Denis Galvin, Seán Healy, Liam Moylan, Con Morley, Tom Herlihy, the local Company Captain, David McAuliffe and Con Finucane on the south side. I lay in the centre armed with a parabellum. From the viewpoint of observation we had perfect cover, from that of protection, none. The fight had to be fought to a finish. There was, too, no retreat for the Tans. If they came into the position their retreat was cut off by the men of the local companies armed with shotguns. The cars came swiftly around the bend, the leading car skidded to a halt when the driver saw the trench, the second car came to a halt in the same fashion. We opened fire. The Tans leaped wildly out, took cover behind their cars and in a loop in the fence. They fought gallantly. I blew a whistle and we ceased fire. I called on them to surrender. Their reply was a volley from their guns. We again opened fire and again at my whistle our fire ceased. I called again to them and this time they dropped their rifles. We found that practically every man was wounded; two of them, one the leader of the party, General Holmes, were killed.

The fight was over. A fine haul was made, rifles, automatic shotguns, grenades, revolvers, ammunition. Everything portable on the cars was loaded into one, which was driven off by the I.R.A. The Tans were searched and their personal property returned. One car was set aside to permit them to carry off their wounded and the I.R.A. marched away to a previously designated rendezvous about a mile from the ambush position. A bush heavily weighted with stones tied into bags was attached to the captured car. This effectively wiped out the tyre tracks in the mud; the car was never traced, nor did the huge search party which turned out even consider the road along which it travelled. Instead, the party feverishly pursued the I.R.A. along a road leading in quite another direction and on which the I.R.A. had taken the precaution of felling several trees to lend colour to the idea that they had taken this particular road and were endeavouring to delay their pursuers.

The car was dumped, the arms distributed, some ammunition distributed too, some placed to reserve. Among the captured material was a number of waterproof overcoats and they were shared according to the need and suitability of size. (The wearing of these had almost a tragic ending for two members of the A.S.U. that night). The boys marched across the hills, tired, hungry but jubilant. For some men of the local companies this was their first time under fire and their first experience of the fierce excitement of battle and they felt like walking on air. In the evening we arrived at the district where we had proposed to halt for a few hours, bleak, cold, bare, unfruitful land; ugly, small and ill-kept houses.

Here was the submerged tenth of the Irish farming community. Here for one who loved his fellow man was one incentive to revolution. These were the people to whom Kickham's sympathy went out. They sheltered Doheny and the Fenians. They were those for whom Davitt planned and worked and suffered; for them, too, as for the town labourer Connolly died. *"To hell or Connaught",* but not the whole Gaelic race crossed the Shannon. Within the limits of their poor resources they fed and cared for the fighting men. Under cover of darkness they went back with them for the hidden car and by secret and devious ways guided them the many miles that they marched to ensure as far as possible their being outside the ring of the search parties that they knew must now be on their way from the H.Q. of the British Division and from the Black and Tan and R.I.C. Barracks everywhere in the vicinity.

I have read somewhere that the word *"Ironside",* accepted now as an indication of the invincibility of the Cromwellians, was originally a term of contempt applied to them by the Cavaliers. The cognomen *"Bogtrotter",* generally accepted as contemptuous, must have originated as an expression of exasperation with heavily armed troops bewildered by the will o' the wisp tactics of the elusive Irish guerrillas.

This intimate yard by yard knowledge of the country enabled them to guide the A.S.U., bringing with them the captured car, across seeming trackless and impassable country. The billeting area was finally reached. The A.S.U. parted from its guides who returned knowing that they would on the morrow have to steel themselves to meet the questioning search parties, knowing, too, that an inadvertent word, the slightest accident, might bring disaster, a blazing homestead, cattle destroyed, prison, perhaps a bullet, for some of these Black and Tans were maniacal and sadistic.*"Ask the local man",* was a phrase that was used so often in those days that it eventually became a general utility slogan. The local man was the encyclopaedia of conditions in his own district. Man, woman and child he knew, their opinions, their capacity, their weaknesses, their outside associations. He knew the amount and nature of the property and equipment possessed by each householder, their availability and suitability for Volunteer use when needed; he knew the capacity of each household for billeting purposes and the last was the knowledge the A.S.U. needed now.

The I.R.A. intelligence had informed the Company Captain of the district of the movements of the A.S.U. and he was on the spot to meet them on their arrival. He had with him a few men from every townland and in a very short time the party of weary men was split into small units and, under guide, departed to their assigned billets. Eager were the questions of the guides, the fight had to be refought for them and naturally for their delectation the results were exaggerated by the *garcon* [sic, Gascon?] of each party.

The Company Captain then proceeded to place guards on each line of approach to the district and while the A.S.U. slept the men of the local company stood on guard nor relaxed their watchfulness until the A.S.U. had departed.

On this night there was an incident that ended in laughter that might have been tragedy. Two tall powerful members of the A.S.U., Con Morley and Denis Galvin, were taken to a farmhouse by a guide who, knowing the sympathies of the household with the I.R.A. and in a hurry to report for guard duty left them at the door of the house. They entered, found the household by the fire, where room was made for them. One of the women filled the kettle and hung it on the crane over the fire, another laid the table, while the man of the house, twisting the bellows, blew the fire into flames. The visitors removed their overcoats, hung their slings of ammunition on the end of the dresser, removed the magazines from the rifles and proceeded to clean, dry and oil them.

So much had the importance of a clean gun and the necessity for the use of the pull-through been impressed on the men that the use of the latter had become as automatic with them as eating. The gun cleaning and the preparation for supper proceeded. Conversation centred round fair and market, anything other than I.R.A. activities. All was amity. The lady of the house, however, sharp eyed, naturally watchful, had surreptitiously examined the men's discarded overcoats, recognised them as police coats, slipped out and gave the alarm. Ten minutes later, as the men sat at the table, front and back doors opened suddenly and two groups of Volunteers, revolvers drawn, surged into the kitchen. Luckily, at the head of each group was a member of the A.S.U. who recognised their comrades, otherwise there might have been that night a bloody tale.

The ambush and its results were the links in a chain of events which, strung together, form an interesting sequence. In May 1920, the R.I.C. Barracks at Kilmallock was attacked by the Volunteers. This barracks had also been attacked by the Fenians in 1867. It was a detached building standing back thirty feet from the street, strongly built with barred windows and steel shutters. The Volunteers attacked it with rifle fire and eventually, by smashing the slates with stones, saturating the roof timbers with oil thrown in bottles, and finally by dropping burning torches on the roof, succeeded in setting it alight.

With the roof blazing like an inferno over their heads, the R.I.C. refused to surrender. As each room became untenable they moved into another. Day broke and the barrack was still held. Finally, when no ammunition was left, the Volunteers retreated. Almost coincident with their withdrawal, out marched the survivors of the garrison, charred, wounded and weary but still defiant, and with bayonets fixed. The enterprise and daring of the Volunteers must be recognised. They kept up a night long attack with inadequate weapons on a strong post encircled at a few miles distant by a group of posts just as strong and from which reinforcements might at any time be expected; with the huge British garrisons at Limerick and Buttevant only one hour's journey from Kilmallock. But one cannot withhold admiration from the determined men who grimly refused to surrender even when the building which they held was consumed and in ruins around them.

The man in charge of the barrack at Kilmallock was a Sergeant Sullivan. He was immediately promoted and transferred to Listowel. His experiences of that fierce night in May seemed to develop in him a mania for vengeance. Shortly afterwards he appeared in Kilmallock with a group of police and soldiers, burned a number of houses and ill-treated a number of townspeople. It was reported to me that he passed between Cork and Limerick with a military party on a number of occasions and many times I lay on that road awaiting him and his party. Luckily for him, or for me, we never met.

About this time Colonel Smyth was appointed Police Commissioner for Munster. He appeared in Listowel where his incitement of the R.I.C. to murder resulted in a police mutiny there. To this town Sergeant, now Inspector, Sullivan was sent. He was shot there at the end of 1920. Colonel Smyth was shot in Cork in July 1920. About November 1920, Colonel Smyth's brother arrived in Ireland to take his place; this man was also a Colonel. His first assignment was an attack on Dan Breen and Seán Treacy at a house in Drumcondra. Here he lost his life. To replace the second Colonel Smyth came General Holmes as Police Commissioner. This was the leader of the party who had been killed at Tureengarriffe. As well as the fine haul of arms that was captured we also got in our search all the papers carried by Holmes. Incidentally, I found in his breast pocket a sum of two hundred pounds in notes. I replaced the money but obviously it was not being carried as travelling expenses.

The papers I got were illuminating. As a result of the shooting of Inspector Sullivan, a number of Kerry men were prisoners in Cork Barracks. General Holmes' chief mission to Kerry was to collect the evidence that would condemn these men. He got it but it never reached the official files and the lives of those around whose necks might have tied a noose were saved. Those who gave the information were unfortunately unable to repeat their story. They met a fate intended for the prisoners.

# XIII

## [William Casey, J.P. / History / 'The Three Musketeers']

That night a group of us went with the captured Crossley car to Caherbarnagh. We stayed at Horan's and in the morning hid the car as well as we were able among the rocks at the mountain foot. We then moved back to Cullen. Here we were greeted with the news that Kingwilliamstown had been burned in reprisal for the ambushes. Barbed wire, steel shutters, armoured cars, hostages, reprisals, the British had all the advantages. There was nothing we could do about Kingwilliamstown for the moment. I had a slight wound in my leg. We decided to stay in Cullen that night. We slept at Casey's of Ardnageeha. William Casey was a J.P., a former member of the County Council and a great supporter of the Irish Parliamentary Party. He and I talked far into the night and as I parted from him in the small hours I had developed the idea that his views in regard to Irish Nationality and mine were not entirely poles apart. He was not a deeply thoughtful man and had accepted such leadership as offered in his time. But the veneer of divergent opinion that overlays the common love of country that possesses Irishmen swiftly disappears in time of actual emergency. Irishmen may differ widely in their political views and be none the less good Irishmen and the most unfair charge that has been levelled against the men of my generation who took up arms against the British was that they had no realisation of this fact.

Often it is said of us that the history of Ireland began for us in 1916. This is true only in the narrowest sense. It would be more correct to say that we learned our most important history lesson from 1916, that national history is a continuing process and that its last chapter will be written only when the world disintegrates and dissolves into nothingness. The result of the thoughts, the efforts and the sacrifices of each generation are transmitted to its successor and the historian can trace the line of their transmitted effect as the biologist will recognise the origins and development of transmitted physical attributes.

It is true that the average Irishman was unlearned in history. That was the fault of the system of education imposed on him; a system that denied not only that Ireland had a history but even denied the very existence of Ireland as a country. The Board of National Education decreed that Irish children should sing:-

>"I thank the goodness and the grace
>That on my birth have smiled
>And made me in those Christian days
>A happy English child".

But was the average Irishman vastly different in this lack of knowledge from the average American or Briton? What does the average American know of Washington or Lincoln? He associates an axe with both but in one case it fells a cherry tree, in the other it splits rails. Yet the very sound of the names of either of those great men is an inspiration to Americans. What is the average Englishman's knowledge of Drake or Nelson, whose names are the fibre of English naval tradition? A game of bowls and *"Kiss me, Hardy"*. History for the average Irishman is not and cannot be in the tomes of the National Library nor in the manuscripts of the Irish Academy. He learns it from those with whom he associates, from their ideas and instincts. It is the warp and woof of his childhood memories, of fireside speech and comment, in his firsthand knowledge of the beliefs and activities of a past generation. And so I could understand and appreciate the viewpoint of William Casey and felt, too, as we parted that he had a clearer and more sympathetic appreciation of mine.

Again the oft repeated sudden awakening, *"The British are here"*, greeted me in the early morning. It was true enough but they weren't looking for me.

They were raiding into the Millstreet Battalion area. They passed, a dozen lorries, along the road in front of the house to join another party on the main road a mile away.

In the village I met Donal McSweeney, who was probably the most prominent member of Sinn Féin in the constituency. He and I discussed matters affecting Sinn Féin and those relating to the progress and success of the Republican Courts. Donal was in great measure a perfectionist. When he was reasonably satisfied, one could be sure that things were going well. We made arrangements for a meeting of the Sinn Féin Executive and for a sitting of the District Court, and then I left for Kiskeam.

We arrived at Kiskeam at dusk. Here we met a Volunteer, newly arrived, looking for us. The Tans had burned a house near Newmarket and had then gone on towards Kingwilliamstown which they had been heard to say they intended to finish. I felt that Kiskeam, the known centre of dissatisfaction, was also due for a lesson and decided that if there was any burning done it would be for a very definite reason. We had six rifles and half a dozen bombs which we got at Tureengarriffe. We took up a position on the cliff over the bridge looking into Kiskeam from Kingwilliamstown. It was a perfect position from the bomber's point of view. We could at least get two lorries before any real fight started. Here we waited for several hours. We left only when four Volunteers arrived from Kingwilliamstown to inform us that the Tans had gone towards Kerry. These men, Liam Moylan, David McAuliffe, Johnny Jones and Con Morley had been at Jones', Glencollins, when they heard the Tans were again burning houses. They rushed down to the village again with their rifles to find two more houses burning and the Tans departed. Coming back they heard that we were lying in ambush at Kiskeam, believed that we had information of another group of British and came on to join us.

Of those who were with me that night I have already mentioned Johnny Jones, quiet, dependable, whose sense of responsibility marched with his courage. Davy McAuliffe, also only a boy, was small, thin and delicate, yet his spirit overcame his physical deficiencies, his energy was inexhaustible and I always envied him his cool courage. Tom McNamara was not unlike those two in character, quiet, cool, imperturbable, easy to handle.

There were four others, however, who were different and a problem. These were Con Morley, Denis Galvin, Seán Healy and Liam Moylan. I called them the *"Three Musketeers"*, not that they had anything in common with the characters created by Dumas other than their daring and the fact that they were four in number. Liam had been recognised as a front line soldier since the night he accompanied Paddy McCarthy to Millstreet. The others were a hard bitten trio; experienced and capable fighting men who believed that soldiering should have its due accompaniment of relaxation and that pubs should not be out of bounds, nor pockets patriotically empty. They had fallen into disfavour with officers who had taken to heart too literally the phrase, *"Ireland sober is Ireland free"* and had graduated with many others of their like into a sort of Foreign Legion under my command.

They had a Hotspur's contempt for Staff Officers. If they did not invent the expression they were among the first to use the derisive term *"Spare General"* to indicate officers not attached to Combat Units. Two of them,

Morley and Galvin, were infantry men pure and simple; the third, Healy, was a natural mechanic and was put in charge of the first machine gun we captured. Liam was drawn into their company by youthful admiration of their exploits and by their devil-may-care attitude to life. He, too, was mechanically minded and our second captured gun fell to him. The four became the core of a machine gun section.

Others were associated with them as time went on but they maintained a distinction between themselves and all such others. No matter what close association the exigencies of battle brought about, their private lives were their own into which no other was admitted except on sufferance. They had a nose for battle wherever they were, and even though it was essential to use such men in many activities other than actual fighting they always turned up on the morning of a fight, were always ready to accept the brunt of any attack, to hold the last line of defence when a column had to retreat. The fights they were in have been, or will be, recorded by others. They were not concerned with the archives. They were not aware that they were making history. But history is better understood if one has a conception of the personalities of those who make it, will be better indicated by a few notes on their strayings from the narrow path of rectitude rather than by any panegyric on their courage or capacity.

A few weeks after the ambush at Tureengarriffe I heard that there was a good deal of local gossip about the car we had hidden in Caherbarnagh and that its hiding place had become a resort for sightseers, all interested in the car captured by the I.R.A. A party had come from Rathmore village on the previous Sunday and with so wide a knowledge of its whereabouts it was now only a matter of time until the British discovered it. One afternoon I sent off the Musketeers, two of whom could drive, to remove the car and bring it to a safe hiding place which I designated. I was busy all day and forgot about them but as I went to bed at midnight I remembered them and suddenly thought *"What if the police at Rathmore knew all about the car and were merely waiting until some Volunteers came to inspect or remove it?"* I got a bicycle at about 1 a.m. and started to cycle to Caherbarnagh. I got punctured on the way and had to trundle the bicycle the greater portion of the way to Cullen. At Cullen I knocked up the Bard who was familiar with all our goings and comings. He informed me that the boys had called in the evening and had left about 9 p.m. After almost an hour's delay he got me another bicycle and I made another start. It was now after three o'clock. I made very bad going, the night was dark, the road rough and muddy. I got several punctures and didn't get to Caherbarnagh until six. I knocked at Horan's and Andy opened the door. He was fully dressed and the kettle was singing on the fire. His welcome assured me that nothing had gone amiss.

I asked him if he knew anything about the car. *"I do, of course"*, he said, *"the boys are after carrying it with them to the wedding"*. *"To the wedding?"* I asked. *"At the Cathedral at Killarney"*, he said. I swore to high heaven. Here was a car, the description of which was in every barracks, a car in size, power and colour standing out from the ruck of cars like a sore thumb. And these lunatics had driven it into Killarney. *"Do you mean to tell me"*, I said, *"that they drove the car to a wedding at the Cathedral?"* *"They did"*, he said, *"and what's more, they took the bride and bridesmaid with them. The car that was to take them broke down on the road and the boys, sooner than disappoint the girl, drove her to town".*

Truly the age of chivalry was not dead but I swore that if these Knights Errant lived they'd hear from me. And they did live. They drove the car right through a town alive with British military, Tans and R.I.C., parked it at the Cathedral gates and headed the wedding procession on its way back through the town again. There is a special providence watching over fools and children.

I did not want to see them again until my temper cooled and they carefully avoided contact with me for several days. In the meantime Con O'Leary of Kerry 2 Brigade came to see me. He had planned an ambush and wanted my help to carry it out. My arrangements were such that I could not agree to his proposal. I did not, however, like to refuse and went over his plans with him so as to ascertain his needs and see if I could find a method of being of assistance. It struck me on going into the matter that the forces at his disposal were adequate and that with the addition of a machine gun team he'd be able to deal with any eventualities. I asked him to stay over for the night and sent for the Musketeers. They came in the morning exhaling righteousness at every pore. The senior man started to report. I snapped at him *"I don't need a report. You're to get out a machine gun and go with Commandant O'Leary and I'll be at no damn loss if I never see you again".*

They left disgruntled and came back in an hour ready to move. Yet not quite ready. Machine guns were so valuable that every effort to prevent their recapture by the British had to be made and all precaution thereto taken. The two men who served the gun were each armed with two forty five revolvers. The rifleman whose job was to protect the gun had each one revolver. It so happened that a revolver, the property of one of the gunners, had been sent away for repairs and he asked for one to replace it. I handed him one without comment and they departed. A newspaper report a few days later informed me that the ambush had been successfully carried out. The machine gun party duly reported back and the past was forgotten.

A few days later a Volunteer from the Brigade area where they had been came to me looking for his revolver. I didn't understand what he was talking about. Then he told me that he had seen them equipped with two revolvers each, didn't see why they needed two revolvers and bargained with and bought one from them. The arrangement was that the gun was to be delivered when the fight was over, but when he looked for the fulfilment of the bargain the boys were gone and his money with them. Now I knew that a Volunteer would do anything to get possession of a gun. I knew also that any of my men would not think, under any circumstances, of parting with his gun. I, therefore, had grave doubts of the truth of his story. I sent for the Musketeers. They came and I questioned them. They denied point blank that they had sold the gun. Getting on my right side they asked, *"Did I believe for a moment that they would sell a gun?"* I roughly ordered the unfortunate man out of my sight. He left disconsolate.

Years after I heard the truth of the matter. They were dead broke after the wedding and ensuing celebrations. My attitude towards them was such that they dared not ask for any money. They planned, therefore, to sell the gun believing that in the excitement and division of the spoils, to which they had no claim, after the fight that they could slip away unnoticed. They managed to do so and did not cry halt until well inside their own Brigade area. Four hours later they changed the fiver in Kingwilliamstown and, as they said, had four pints by the throat in Klondike's pub drinking to the health of the farmer who provided the cash.

## XIV

### [Outrage In Knocknagree / Drishanebeg ambush]

The members of the Battalion A.S.U. who had been away for a few days' rest were now back again and full of disappointment because of their absence from Tureengarriffe. An attack on Newmarket Military Post was my King Charles Head.* I thought of and tried to plan for it at all times. Now again I set about making preparations for it. I and other Volunteers went into Newmarket and watched the movements of Black and Tans and soldiers. Con Moylan and Jack O'Connell couldn't see everything and I did not want to be entirely dependent on their observations. One night I slipped up the New Street in the darkness. When I reached Denis Murphy's house I saw the patrol approaching from the Cross. I was going to run back and enter an archway not far from me but first I pushed Murphy's door, it opened and I stepped into the shop, which was in darkness. There was a murmur of voices in the kitchen and then just as the patrol passed there was an unearthly yell from upstairs and a patter of bare feet. The patrol halted and then a child's voice from the top of the stairs yelled: *"Daddy, come up here and tell Jackie to keep his cold bottom off my neck"*. I sniggered in the darkness. *"Kids"* said a soldier and the patrol moved on. I waited 'till it returned, noted its numbers and disposition and then joined my comrades, Davy McAuliffe and Liam Moylan, who had, respectively, been watching the Police and Military Barracks.

I felt after a few days of such observation that we had sufficient information as to troop and police movements; then one night I called home to see my mother. She and my sisters had been subject to a good deal of annoyance from the military. The doors had been periodically kicked in and the house ransacked. All my books had disappeared as a result. She and I talked together in the shop. I asked her if she had had any recent raids and she confessed that for several weeks things had been quiet except for the day after Tureengarriffe

---

* [*King Charles Head*: Charles I was beheaded and a character in Dickens' *David Copperfield* was gripped by a compulsion to mention the fact—"Mr. Dick had been for upwards of ten years endeavouring to keep King Charles the First out of his Memorial; but he had been constantly getting into it." J.L.]

ambush when raiding Auxiliaries had taken over the town. Just then I heard the footsteps on the road outside. Since curfew was being rigidly imposed I knew whose they were. I suggested she should go upstairs and ascertain if all was clear as I intended departing. My real reason was that I didn't want her present when the fight which I believed to be imminent started. I moved to the back of the shop and looked through the glass door leading to the room behind. There were two soldiers in the room. One, an officer, whose head was within a foot of my revolver, was talking to my sister. The other, a sergeant, was near the outer door engaged in animated laughing conversation with a Miss Baby O'Mahony who was that night staying in the house. I stood still as a statue until, after a few minutes, they both left. The door was shut and both girls collapsed into the nearest chairs. They both knew where I was, they expected shooting and yet they smiled and calmly talked themselves and me out of a most difficult situation. I stood without movement outside the house for five minutes and then reasonably assured that the coast was clear headed for the west.

British raiding parties were very active in Kerry just across the Blackwater that week. Buttevant was headquarters for all British troops operating in Kerry. Those raids were apparently conducted by troops moving from Killarney to Tralee to Buttevant or vice versa. In either case they did not seem to return to their particular base for several days after every raid. Sunday seemed often to be the day for such return. I determined to try my luck on the following Sunday, February 6th. On Saturday I went over the road and selected a position about three miles east of Kingwilliamstown. That night I crossed the fields to a house where I intended to stay and sleep. Part of my way was along a pathway used by children attending Foilagoling school. When I arrived at my destination I had a meal and then prepared for bed. As I slipped off my belt I missed a Mills bomb which was attached to it when I started. I immediately concluded that it had dropped off as I crossed one or other of the fences on my route. I thought of the pathway I had traversed and of the fact that some children might find the bomb, with tragic results. I set out and retraced my steps. In the early hours of the morning I found it beside a fence along which the children travelled. I breathed a prayer of thanks for my luck.

Sunday was a beautiful summer-like day. We got into position beside the road in the early morning and waited. About 3.30 p.m. a message came from Kingwilliamstown that the military had passed through the village but instead of coming direct for Buttevant through Newmarket they had continued south to Knocknagree. On top of our disappointment came a tragic story that night. The raiding party had apparently divided forces somewhere in Kerry. One half had come through Kingwilliamstown, the other half had travelled through Gneeveguilla to Knocknagree. In a field beside Knocknagree village a hurling match was in progress between a number of small boys. These little lads had no anticipation of danger and stood in groups about the playing pitch to watch the approaching lorries. Two bursts of machine gun fire directed towards them was the first indication they had of any danger. Some of the boys rushed southwards, the others lay on the fields and beside the fences. The British soldiers advanced, pouring volley after volley on the fleeing boys and on the playing pitch. When the firing ceased the boys on the playing pitch were rounded up. It was then found that Michael J. Kelleher, aged seventeen, had been shot through the head; Michael Herlihy, aged thirteen, was shot through the thigh and Donal Herlihy, his brother, was shot through the lung. The Herlihy boys recovered. As I write, one of them is the Rev. D. J. Herlihy, D.D., L.S.S., All Hallows, Dublin, the other the Rev. M. J. Herlihy, C.C., Tralee, Co. Kerry. The body of young Kelleher was taken to Rathmore R.I.C. Barrack. The R.I.C. Sergeant there refused to be associated with the dirty work of the military. The military then returned to Knocknagree and handed over the body to the boy's father.

The official report as published in the *Irish Independent*, February 8th, 1921, said: *"A military patrol saw a body of armed civilians in a field near Knocknagree. Fire was opened and replied to, resulting in the death of one youth and the wounding of two others"*. How can one comment on this except to quote: *"Now I find report a very liar"*.*

The Parliamentary Constituency covered the greater part of the western half of the Brigade area. My pioneer work for Sinn Féin had made me familiar with men in every parish throughout the constituency. I thus had ready-made contacts with men in other battalion areas; this I might not have had if others were concerned only with the military side of the movement. The result was, of course, closer co-operation between all five battalions west of the Blackwater. Cullen Company in the seventh battalion worked in very close co-operation with me. D. T. O'Riordan, the Company Captain, and Donal McSweeney of the Sinn Féin Executive were men with whom I found it necessary to discuss matters now and again. I arrived in Cullen two days after the Knocknagree tragedy and was told by O'Riordan that the seventh battalion A.S.U. was in position waiting a British party travelling by rail from Buttevant to Kerry. As I walked down the village street I heard what I believed to be intermittent rifle fire. *"The fight is on"*, I said to O'Riordan. He laughed and said, *"The Tans in Millstreet have also been deceived by those explosions. That's an oil engine at Drishane Convent"*. The fight was not to come off until two days later. This was the manner of it and the facts leading to its success.

In the Summer of 1920 the railwaymen refused to handle trains on which armed British soldiers travelled. Lately, however, armed troops were again using the railways. I.R.A. observers had noticed some of these parties travelling past Millstreet between Buttevant and Tralee. A watch was kept and reports came back that all these soldiers were unarmed. Further investigation showed that all these apparently unarmed troops carried rifles when they entered and left the train, however they disposed of them during the journey. A Volunteer entering the train at Buttevant discovered that the military party on board had their rifles stowed beneath the seats and wrapped in greatcoats on the racks. It was decided to lay an ambush one mile east of Millstreet Station at a point where high embankment made it possible for riflemen lying on each side of the track to have a clear field of fire without danger to each other. The question of stopping the train in the desired position was then

---

* [From *The Taming Of The Shrew*. J.L.]

discussed. It would have been possible to derail the train but this idea, as it might involve a serious crash and injury to the civilians travelling, was rejected. Then the idea of assembling the I.R.A. at Millstreet Station for the purpose of rushing any train carrying military was discussed. This, too, was turned down on the grounds that the probable wait of several days for the opportune moment would tend to gossip or discovery and militate against success.

The plan eventually decided on was to post several Volunteers armed with revolvers at Millstreet Station. These were to watch the trains until one carrying British military arrived. They were then—as the train left the station—to jump on the footplate and force the driver to bring the train to a halt in line with the position where the I.R.A. waited. After a fruitless wait of over a week at Millstreet, a more elaborate plan was evolved. Another waiting party was stationed at Rathcoole Station between Millstreet and Banteer. Trains did not halt here except when passengers notified their intention of alighting. But a Volunteer was also assigned to Banteer Station. He was, each evening, to purchase a ticket to Rathcoole, to move through the train, discover if any British military were travelling and then, alighting at Rathcoole, to give his comrades their agreed signal.

After some days waiting, on February 11th the long awaited signal was given in Rathcoole and as the train steamed out the waiting party jumped on the footplate and issued their orders to the engine driver. Doubtless, in view of the general attitude of the railwaymen to the British, he was nothing loath to obey orders. The column was in position as the train approached. The two weeks nightly wait had made them tense and anxious. Suddenly a long whistle from the engine, the prearranged signal, shrilled through the air. A lamp was placed on the permanent way and the train, with a noisy protest, slowed to a halt. It had run through the ambush position but the I.R.A., running swiftly, cast lighted oil torches into the cutting beside it, thus thoroughly illuminating the carriages and showing where the British were situated. The sudden halt had alarmed the Tommies and when a call to surrender was made to them they opened fire. Then the column fired as the British tumbled out of and under the train. The fight could have only one conclusion. While the cover beneath the train was reasonably good, the light of the flaring torches showed up the position of each man and the I.R.A. had the advantage of the darkness. Ten minutes from the time of the train's arrival the I.R.A. ceased fire and again called to the British to surrender; fourteen soldiers came out from under the train; another lay dead on the permanent way.

Almost coincident with the surrender, a man in British uniform rushed up the slope of the cutting and in spite of warning to halt came forward to the muzzle of Jer Long's rifle. A nervous man might have shot him, but Long, afterwards a Column Leader, was an exceptionally cool and experienced Volunteer. He contented himself with pushing the climber down the slope again. It transpired that he was a Munster Fusilier, due for demobilisation and on the way to his base at Tralee. Afterwards we heard he joined a column in Kerry. Of this I have no definite knowledge but there was a strange sequel to this incident.

One of the men in the column that night was Michael O'Riordan of

Millstreet. He was Company Captain in the town. After Easter Week 1916, he and his father had been interned in Frongoch and he was the eldest of three brothers who served with the Active Service Unit from its inception to the end.

Many years after Michael was on holiday in Ballybunion. The air of Ballybunion is most bracing and while tremendous seas roll in on the strand the bathing is safe and most pleasurable except under certain conditions. Michael, a poor enough swimmer, unthinkingly swam far out and with a turning tide was unable to return. As he was giving himself up for lost, two swimmers churned their way to him and after a struggle helped him back to shore. One of them proved to be the Munster Fusilier who had climbed the railway slope that night at Drishanebeg.

The A.S.U., starting the fight with eight rifles, marched away with twenty-three and with their ammunition reserve increased by one thousand rounds. Patience to wait in secret, careful planning, meticulous attention to detail are elements of success here as elsewhere and the main credit for this success might go to the Battalion staff; C. J. Meany, Jerh. Crowley, Jerh. Long, Con Meany and to the local Company Captain, Michael Riordan. Con Meany, afterwards T.D. for North Cork, is the only one of those men living.

*Go maire sé. Agus Dia libh, a laochra Gaedheal atá imighthe.*\*

## XV

## [The Bower / Clonbanin Ambush / British Military Leadership]

Con O'Leary, Adjutant of Kerry No. 2 Brigade, came again to see me at the end of February. Con had brains and had a soldierly thrust and determination. He had information of the fact that there were regular movements of the British between Killarney and Rathmore. Subsequent to the attack on Rathmore Barracks in 1920 the R.I.C. had been strongly reinforced by Black and Tans and the lorries travelling from Killarney brought them supplies and pay. He was anxious to attack one of these parties and as they varied in strength he wanted my co-operation to ensure success. We were still getting ready for an attack on Newmarket Barracks but as I knew that the Barracks would not disappear I very gladly accepted the offer made to me.

We arrived in Kerry on the last day of the month and on March 1st got into position at the Bower, which is about midway between Killarney and Rathmore. Its name is deceptive; it is a cold, bare and windswept glen. The country here is, particularly in winter, rather desolate, with none of the scenic beauty for

---

\* ["May he live long. And God be with you, Irish warriors gone before". Translated by Pat Muldowney. J.L.]

which the south and west of the county is famous. When we arrived, the Kerrymen were in possession and while arms were few there were men in plenty. All the local companies turned up, some with shotguns, most of them completely unarmed. We lay in position all day without result. Still another day passed and still nothing happened. On the morning of the third day we discovered the reason why the British had not come our way. General Strickland, who was G.O.C. of the British forces in Munster, was on an inspection tour in Kerry. We read the details of his tour when somebody arrived with a newspaper. He had rounded up the people of Tralee and given them a minatory talk, informing them, among other things, that there were armed men with Cork accents hanging round the borders of the county and threatening dire consequences for Kerry if anyone gave aid or comfort to any of these people. He seemed to be fairly well informed of our movements. A little later we were informed that a large party of British was approaching along a by-road to our rear. This necessitated the re-arrangement of our position. Just as this had been done a solitary motor coming from the east drove into the Glen. It might be merely the leading unit of a number of British cars. I gave an order to the men to withhold their fire and as it came well into the ambush position jumped out on the road and halted the driver. He pulled up swiftly and we advanced on the car with rifles at the ready. There were four men in it, two of them American journalists. Another was a photographer, the fourth a hired driver. I asked them to give me their word that they would not mention the fact of meeting us to anybody. They assured me of their absolute neutrality and gave that word. They certainly kept it.

Four days we waited and without profit. On Friday evening the likelihood of our position becoming known to the British was fairly clear. I spoke to Denis Galvin, asked him to take three companions, to go back to County Cork and to select an ambush position on the main road west of Banteer. I also instructed him to get in touch with the Millstreet Battalion so that we might have the co-operation of their riflemen and of the companies whose areas adjoined the selected position. I gave him further instructions about the movements of the A.S.U. and the preparation of billets for them. Galvin left with his companions and after dark we moved to Ummeraboy in the parish of Knocknagree. Jack Mahony was the keyman here. He was an earnest and capable worker and I knew that billets would be ready and that horses in good condition would be available to us for transport on the following morning. At midnight Galvin reported back to me at Ummeraboy. The position chosen was at Clonbanin and all other arrangements had been made. We left at 3 a.m. for Clonbanin and the latest comers were in position before 6 a.m. It was a beautiful calm morning, we had an unusually strong force, riflemen from Charleville, Newmarket and Millstreet, as well as the riflemen from Kerry who had come with us. We also had one of the Hotchkiss guns captured at Mallow and half a dozen road mines. Commandant P. O'Brien had put the troops into position while I arranged for the laying of the mines. When I had finished he took me round to each section. In our tour we had the leader of the section with us so that each man should have a clear idea of the plan of attack. We made it quite clear that General Strickland and his party were the objects of our attack and we intended to ignore every other opportunity for attack offered no matter how tempting the offer proved to be. It was well that we were so insistent on this matter as later events proved.

While on this tour of the position a messenger arrived from the Brigade O/C. in search of me. A meeting of the Brigade Council had been called while we were in Kerry and due to the secrecy of our movements the Brigade Despatch Riders had been unable to get in touch with me. The first men he met were the Musketeers. He asked for me and was told I'd be arriving immediately. In the course of conversation he mentioned that the Brigade O/C. was in a towering rage with me. He had had no report from me for more than a week. A Brigade Council meeting had been called and all those entitled to be present were at Brigade Headquarters for several days awaiting the arrival of Commandant O'Brien and myself. The pre-occupation of the Brigade O/C. with written reports was too much for men who had been constantly hunted and harried for several months. They suggested with, I'm afraid, an insubordinatory lack of respect for the Brigade O/C. that if he was so fond of reading and had no other business in hands he might concern himself with the reading of the newspapers of the past few months and they recommended particularly and with a prophetic instinct that he should pay particular attention to the newspapers of the following Monday. I came along, dismissed the messenger with a brief explanatory note and returned to my examination of the position.

As we passed through Mark Shaughnessy's farmyard, Mark, pulling on his coat, hailed me from the door, asking with much profanity and a wealth of adjectives what I thought I was, waking the countryside at that hour of the morning. I knew Mark's form and wasn't unduly worried by his mock abuse. He invited us indoors and produced a bottle of whiskey. Most of those present were non-drinkers. I and a few others joined him in a drink. As I left I said: *"Mark, you ought to give us that bottle of whiskey; we have a long day before us"*. *"You may go to the devil"*, he said *"I'll be alone here this evening when you're gone and the British are after arriving. If I haven't a drop of whiskey here to give them they'll burn my house down"*. And sure enough, the bottle from which we got the drink in the morning was finished by some British officers that same evening. It was now seven o'clock and there was nothing to do again but to wait. I walked along the line on the northern side until I came to where the men from Charleville lay. They showed me the newspaper of the day before. It carried the story of the murder in his own home by Black and Tans of Seán O'Brien, the Chairman of Charleville District Council. Another good friend of theirs and mine had gone and I knew by their grim looks that if the opportunity was given them that day a heavy penalty would be exacted.

At 10 o'clock we got word from the Signallers that the British were coming. I had a good view of the road leading from the west and turned my glasses on it. The road was empty. I sent a messenger swiftly to the nearest signaller. Yes, the British were coming from the east. On they came, three wire-covered lorries, one man playing an accordion, the others singing. Poor devils, they little knew how close to disaster they were. What a horrible thing is war. Here were men against whom we had no personal hatred. Yet, because of the unwisdom of a statesmanship that refuses to recognise right except when it is backed by force, a single shot fired by accident, or by a nervous or excited youngster meant swift dissolution for all of them. Yet that shot was not fired. It was a magnificent test of I.R.A. discipline; discipline on the part of men who had waited a week, lying in a wet ditch for such an opportunity as now presented itself. The lorries travelled away to the west, went over the crest of the hill, disappeared. Until then there was silence. But now a murmur of excited speech broke out in every group. Men were questioning the wisdom of the order given. What if we got no second chance? I confess that I, too, began to have doubts. Commandant O'Brien and I walked along the road, at the cross roads there was an oldish man breaking stones. He made various sarcastic comments about playboys with guns who wouldn't fight when they got the opportunity. If our prediction was wrong, any shred of reputation we had was lost.

Again we went back to our positions. Again the weary wait began. Noon came, one o'clock and two; still no sign from the west. It looked hopeless. At 2.15 p.m. an excited signaller came with the news. This time they were coming from the west. The signallers on the hill behind us had seen them. They were not yet in view from the position in which I stood. I focused the glasses on the hill crest. In a few moments the first lorry appeared, then two other vehicles, next came an armoured car, behind that again three more lorries. They were spaced at such intervals as to cover a half mile of the road. We had expected this and had spaced our section and the road mines accordingly. I watched the coming of the armoured car. The mine in the centre of the ambush position was destined for it. As it passed over the mine I pressed the switch on the battery. I got a shock that almost knocked me over. It had short circuited. But all the others were watching too and at once a burst of rifle fire rang out. The leading lorry was ditched. And now we had a slice of luck; Liam Moylan with his Hotchkiss gun had concentrated on the armoured car and one lucky shot had got through the slit in front wounding the driver. The armoured car, too, was ditched. The British dived for cover. Apart from the advantage of surprise which we had, they were now in as good a position as we were, and then began the long duel that ended only at dusk. We suffered one great disadvantage. Lack of ammunition and thus the impossibility of rifle practice militated against good marksmanship. Had we had twenty good marksmen that day the fight would have been shorter and complete success would probably have crowned our efforts. In numbers we were about equal, but in armament we had no answer to the heavy Maxim that roared continuously from the armoured car. Maurice O'Brien of Charleville, with a section from that battalion, made several attempts to drive in the British right flank. I tried the same manoeuvre on the left. The armoured car commanded the whole position. Nothing could live on the road and we were lucky to be able again to take cover unscathed. Under cover of their machine guns, the British tried the same outflanking tactics, but they, too, were unable to advance under our fire.

I crossed to the south side, accompanied by the section with which I had tried to drive in the west flank of the British position, where the Kerrymen and the Millstreet A.S.U. were in position. These Volunteers on the south side could not lie on the roadside fence as they would have been directly in the line of fire from the north. For this reason they had to take up a position about two hundred yards from the road on a sharp rise of ground. A deep ditch and several houses gave the British a first class cover against attack from this side and they had a fine field of fire against the I.R.A. position. Yet we were able to keep them pinned in this position. The fight started about 2.30 p.m. It seemed to me that it had been in progress less than an hour when I looked at my watch. It was 5.30 p.m. My worry then was British reinforcements. Kanturk and Newmarket, where there were strong garrisons, were but a few miles distant. Buttevant, the main British garrison, only twenty five miles away. The sound of firing could be heard (it actually was heard) in Newmarket and Kanturk. The reinforcements were overdue. Con Meany and Tom McEllistrim took a section over to cover the road from the east. The fight went on and still no reinforcements arrived. I heard afterwards that a lorry with troops left Newmarket, and, hitting a fence, overturned a mile from the town. The soldiers in Kanturk, in no way anxious to participate in the brawl, dug themselves into the various public houses in the town and were with difficulty collected. It was not until darkness was falling that the reinforcements arrived and when they came, they came in strength. Talk about the taxicabs of the Marne, the line of lorries was like the parked cars in O'Connell Street. As darkness fell we moved away. Millstreet and Kerry troops to the west. Those from Charleville and Newmarket retired north to Kiskeam.

As I and my 5th Battalion Section crossed the fields at Dernagree we saw in our rear a large group of men whom we took to be those of our comrades who had been fighting on the northern side of the ambush. We slowed down to wait for them but as they reached the boundary fence of the field in which we were they opened fire. It was then we realised that the reinforced British party was hard on our heels. Luckily dusk had fallen and we were in extended order: there were no casualties. The British did not pursue us further. We then fell in with a few Volunteers of the local company. They informed us that a British General had been killed. While we had waited for General Strickland and believed he was among the party, yet we discounted the story but later got information of its truth. The officer was General Cummins who had been in charge of the British troops in Buttevant and Ballyvonaire. He and several members of his staff had been killed; what the other British casualties were we never discovered. We spent the night in Kiskeam and lay low there on the following day.

At night Commandant O'Brien and I set out for Nadd where the postponed Brigade Council meeting was to be held on the following day. We first went to Clonbanin and got in touch with members of the local company. With their aid we recovered the mines that had failed us on the previous day. The British had either overlooked or been chary of touching them. In the morning we arrived at the meeting place to find the Brigade O/C. immersed in the newspaper account of our exploits of the previous Saturday. The group that gathered round the table that morning to discuss plans and operations were in a happy mood. Immediately the meeting ended I left for Lisgriffin. Men of the Kanturk Battalion were lying in ambush for a police patrol at Father Murphy's Bridge near Banteer. I was advised, therefore, to cross the Blackwater at Roskeen Bridge. It was my intention to destroy a bridge on the direct road from Buttevant to Kanturk. I went to the house of Tom Frawley, the Company

Captain, where I had a meal and waited until dusk to start the demolition job. We had no explosives but at dark we tackled it with picks, wedges and bars. It was a harder job than I had expected but at 2 a.m. the breach was quite a satisfactory one. As the work proceeded we got word that the ambush at Father Murphy's bridge had been successful. The R.I.C. and Tan patrol had been attacked and disarmed.

Many times since then I have considered with amazement the response which the human body is capable of making when the demand is made by an unwearied spirit. I was not physically robust, for months I had had no more than a few hours sleep nightly. During the few recent weeks even these short hours had been cut in half, yet immediately the work was done I cycled to Dromagh, about fifteen miles distant.

One is always struck when reading the biographies of successful soldiers with their capacity for work. This characteristic of unceasing effort, of untiring energy on the part of his subject runs through the whole story of Henderson's *Stonewall Jackson*. Crozier's *Brass Hat In No Man's Land* is a bare unboastful record of attention to detail, or resolute vigour. Guedella's *The Duke* tells the tale of patient plodding tenacity. I have not as yet read any book on Montgomery or Rommel but the day to day newspaper reports on the North Africa campaign do emphasise that pre-eminently among the qualities of these great soldiers was the outstanding one of capacity for continuous, vigorous and resolute effort.

It would be insanely ridiculous to make any comparison between the skirmishes in which we were engaged and the great battles of the recent war, but the same quality—capacity for untiring vigorous effort—was everywhere possessed by the local leaders of the I.R.A. and this was the basis of any success they achieved.

Strangely enough, British military leadership in Ireland was not noted for its possession of this quality. Perhaps it was because of the, to them, insignificance of the fighting. For whatever reason, they never developed a soldierly aggressiveness. Their substitute for it was the undisciplined Black and Tans and Auxiliary, the attack on property and on the civilian population. The same lassitude and lethargy of military leadership was apparent in the American War of Independence; Howe, Burgoyne, Cornwallis, from Bunker Hill to Yorktown, displayed the same unreadiness and indecisiveness. Valley Forge, the fierce testing place of a victorious American army, could have been the graveyard of American hopes had there been in Philadelphia in the bitter winter of 1777-8 a British General who was something other than a Knight on carpet considerations*. There was only one real answer to the I.R.A. tactic, that was to substitute for the concentration of large bodies in camps and barracks and their intermittent raids and rounds up, and for the smaller groups in the "*concentration camp*" outposts, groups of well-trained disciplined, well-armed men living off the country as Active Service Units did, constantly seeking battle from the Active Service Units, and capable of taking the same risks and enduring the same discomforts as these did. One hundred such men, with their better military training, superior armament and experienced leadership, in each battalion area would not have absorbed one fourth of the British

---

[* *carpet considerations*: a preference for the lounge, rather than the battlefield. J.L.]

army of occupation in Ireland and would in a month have made it impossible for the I.R.A. to exist as it did. Of course, such commandos are not easily created, fighting men of the type necessary, sufficiently self-reliant to be capable of individual action, are few and far between; the average Englishman was war weary and disillusioned; Britain had many pre-occupations other than Ireland, but even when all this is considered, French, Macready and Strickland were no more to be commended for their work in Ireland than were Burgoyne, Howe and Cornwallis for their achievements in America. But even had the British adopted the commando system and had successfully dealt with the I.R.A., that was not necessarily the end. Determined, earnest men, familiar with the face of the Grim Reaper, would have devised alternative methods of embarrassment for Britain. And while the dice would be always heavily loaded against them, Imperial strategy never succeeded in manipulating these with skilful unerring hand.

I travelled along a tangle of rough bye-roads till I reached Dromcummer. Here I halted beside the main road while a string of British lorries went by towards the west. It must then have been 4 a.m. I wondered at the night activity. I knew it boded ill for somebody but had no premonition of its import. Cautiously I cycled in the wake of the lorries, got into the fields when I crossed the Allua and carefully examined the cross roads at Ballymaquirk before I ventured on to the road again.

At Dromagh I met Maurice Clancy, Captain of Derrygallon Company. My appointment with Maurice was for 2 a.m. and it was now three hours later. I had thought to be finished at midnight in Lisgriffin. Maurice had heard but had not seen the lorries. He had dismissed his men at four o'clock on my failure to turn up and had waited for me to make a new arrangement about the work we proposed to do. We parted and I went south towards Rathcoole, called to the house of a friend there and found in possession three members of the Kanturk Battalion who had been at the Brigade Council meeting of the day before. They had news of a British round-up at Nadd but had no details. I told them of the train of lorries I'd seen a few hours previously. We knew then that the news they had was in all probability correct.

# XVI

## [The Blackwater English / Raid On Nadd / A Traitor]

The River Blackwater, forming portion of the boundary between Cork and Kerry, rises in the Kerry Hills a few miles west of Kingwilliamstown. It passes for the first dozen miles of its course through bare bleak bogland. This district is called the Ceathramha Riabhach. But from Banteer to Youghal it flows through a rich and fertile valley, past deep grasslands, shadowy woods and rugged mountains. The gentle, murderous poet, Spenser, sang of its beauty. Sir Walter Raleigh, by some process of law or royal dictate, became the possessor of a huge slice of it at Youghal, was dispossessed by the craftier adventurer, Boyle, the first Earl of Cork, who came to Ireland with twenty pounds in his pocket, and sent on his way to the Tower of London and his death. Boyle afterwards clashed with Stafford and Stafford suffered the same fate as Raleigh. The valley and all the rich bottom lands were in possession of the Anglo-Irish:—

> "Upton, Evans, Bevan, Bassett is Blair,
> Burton, Beecher, Wheeler, Farren is Phair,
> Turner, Fielding, Reeves is Waller is Dean
> *Cromaill is a bhuidhean, sin scaoileadh is scaipeadh ar a dtréad".*

I quote from a list given in four verses of his poem, *"A fhile chirt ghéir "*, by Eoghan Ruadh Ó Súilleabháin, of English families who were rewarded with Irish lands for their services in quelling the native Irish. The gallows, the Barbados, Virginia or Connacht cleared the majority of the mere Irish from their lands. But in spite of every effort to complete the dissolution of the race, some of them succeeded in clinging to their native hills and among the bogs and stony places from Mullaghareirc in the north to Derrynasaggart and the Boggeraghs in the south the dispossessed Irish dug in, spread and strengthened. Hunted like wild beasts, later despised as serfs, later still hated because they refused to accept the status of serfdom. Again I quote Eoghan Ruadh, who lived among them and knew them:

> *"Ní h-é an bochtanas is measa liom*
> *Ná bheith síos go deo*
> *Acht an tarcuisne a leanann é*
> *Ná leigeasfadh na leomhain".*

> ["It is not the poverty that I cannot endure
> Nor being the underdog all the time
> But the insult (arrogance) that accompanies it
> That even the lions (warriors of old) could not cure."]**

Poverty, hardship and suffering they could endure but the denial of their manhood, that was insupportable. In these mountain lands and among these people there was always support for those who stood for the dispossessed Irish nation, a long tradition of wrong and resistance thereto. Here it was that we found shelter and a place of retreat when hard pressed.

In those early days of March 1921, Brigade Headquarters were established here at Nadd—*Neadh an Ioláir*—one thousand feet up on the slope of the Boggeragh, surrounded by rugged hills and glens, inhabited by a loyal people, at a point where five Battalion areas converged. It was an ideal place for its purpose. The nature of the terrain facilitated the placing of outposts and made difficult the unseen approach of any enemy. A few men from the Mallow and Kanturk Battalions were attached to Brigade H.Q. These, with

---

* [See full poem and translation at Annex 1. J.L.]
** [Translated by Pat Muldowney. J.L.]

the local company, took their turns on outpost duty. In the dark of the morning of the 9th of March an excited Volunteer rushed to the houses where the members of the Brigade Staff were sleeping and awakened them and all the Volunteers off duty with the report that the British were surrounding the district. Hard on his report came another of machine gun and rifle fire. The British, appearing, were fired on by the outposts, took cover and themselves opened fire. As they carefully advanced under cover, the Volunteers retreated, still keeping up their fire. As a result of this delaying action, the Brigade Staff got away with all their material, as did the great majority of the Volunteers. Three men were killed and a number wounded. Their comrades succeeded in getting the wounded away across the hills. The British attempt, while it resulted in the deaths of good men, might be counted a failure inasmuch as they met a sturdy defence and were deprived of the prey of which they were certain of capture. Their lack of success was due to the failure of one party of troops to arrive in time. While I was engaged on the Buttevant-Kanturk road a party of Volunteers of the Mallow Battalion were digging a trench, wide and deep, on the Mallow-Banteer road. The armoured car leading the lorries loaded with troops and advancing on Nadd skidded into this trench and was overturned. By the time the British had decided that their efforts to haul it on to the road were useless and had filled in the trench to enable the lorries to cross, several hours had been lost. The party that had arrived on time advanced at the appointed hour and before all exits from the hills were blocked, the I.R.A., familiar with all the mountain paths, got clear away. The British had planned wisely and had been well informed. How had they got the information on which their plans were based? There was a man, whom I had known for a long time though I had never spoken to him, whose name was Shields. He had served in the British army for some short period. He was a big, clumsy and uncouth individual, a blackguard, given to drink and with a cast in his eye which gave him such a sinister appearance that, if there is anything in the theories of Lombroso, marked him as a criminal type. I had always disliked and distrusted this fellow and got a distinct shock when I heard he had been recruited into the Kanturk Battalion. I recounted the rumour to some of my friends and they, knowing the fellow's character, refused to believe the story. It passed from my mind.

On the 8th March, Martin McGrath, a Kanturk Volunteer, who was not at that time a suspect by the R.I.C., was in Kanturk on Volunteer business. McGrath was a Wexford man who had been attached to the Volunteers in his native county. He came on transfer from his own company to Kanturk where he had about 1918 secured a post as an Irish teacher. McGrath's father had been an R.I.C. sergeant and stationed in Kanturk was a policeman who had served with him, a Kerry man and native Irish speaker. Because McGrath was the son of a man he had known and because McGrath was also a fluent speaker of Irish they had spoken in Irish to each other on many occasions since McGrath's arrival. On this particular night the old policeman, seeing McGrath, beckoned him down a side street, informed him that Shields was in the R.I.C. Barrack where he had arrived at dusk and where he had been since in conversation with the officer in charge of the British troops in the district. McGrath immediately departed for Nadd, which he had left only a few hours before. He passed his information to his immediate superior and asked to be permitted to talk to the Brigade O/C. His request was refused and his information considered of little moment. Neglect to inquire into the character of a man who turned out to be a traitor, lack of intelligence to understand the vital nature of the information, or careless neglect in making it known, were responsible for the deaths of three men and might have resulted in the complete disruption of the Brigade. Luckily we escaped this major disaster.

## XVII

## [Clonfert Bridge / Death Of Charlie O'Reilly / Barley Hill]

I cycled to Knockacluggin, Mick Sullivan's home, calling on my way to Jack Mahony of Ummeraboy and to Jim Riordan of Knockavoreen. Before we went to Kerry Jack and I had arranged to build a dug-out in a bog adjoining his farm. We realised that as the pressure became greater we'd have occasion now and again for a complete disappearance and for such purpose settled on this project. We discovered a large boghole with a gravel subsoil which did not retain water and had set about building an underground chamber here with a subterranean exit into a similar hole at a distance. Charlie O'Reilly was in charge and engaged in the work with him were a few specially selected and trustworthy men. It was our proposal, subsequently carried out, to build another dug-out, the existence of which the local public would be aware, in a less remote place by way of a cover to our real intentions. Here I found the men busily engaged in the work and for the remainder of the week I took part in the work.

On Saturday night we took a party to Newmarket in an attempt to smash Clonfert Bridge, half a mile from the town. We had no explosives and again had to depend on sledges, bars, etc. I had little hope of smashing the bridge but believed that the ringing sound of the sledge on steel in the stillness of the night would induce the police and military to investigate. With this end in view, I placed half a dozen riflemen, all I had, in positions close to and covering the military and police barrack. Until early morning the hammering went on and from my position outside the police barrack I could hear the constant crash of the sledge ringing through the night like an alarm bell. Lights appeared in the barrack and men moved about inside. We waited, alert and tense, but the police decided that a masterly inactivity was to be their policy, and, while the lights remained on, there was no further movement. The military acted in the same manner as the police. At daybreak we returned to Knockacluggin.

We needed certain tools for the work of roofing and propping our dug-out.

I had arranged with Con Moylan during the night for the collection of these for me. Mick and I took a car to Newmarket for them. As we left, Charlie O'Reilly decided to accompany us. He had a bad cold and he wanted to get something for it from the chemist. We left our car a mile from the town and in single file we walked in. We moved most carefully. I felt, and even said to the others, that if I were in charge of the British troops I'd lay an ambush at both bridges that night in expectation of an I.R.A. return to complete the work of demolition. I also mentioned that if I had the Active Service Unit at my immediate disposal I would lay an ambush in anticipation of this movement. We got in without meeting a soul, collected the tools, waited while my uncle returned from the chemist with O'Reilly's bottle and set off again. Con Moylan came with us. We halted at the bridge and while the others went forward to harness the horse I finished my conversation with Con.

As I arrived at Horgan's of Coolagh where we had left the car I met the others coming out on the road. We checked the tools, found one missing and decided we had left it on the bridge. O'Reilly and I were on the road. Mick was in the car and said *"I'll go for it"*. As he started off, O'Reilly stepped into the car and I followed slowly down the road. Half way to the bridge I heard the crash of rifle fire; bullets whistled past me and rocketed off the road beside me. I dived for the fence and pulled my gun. My anticipation was too correct. The British had laid an ambush and had arrived almost simultaneously with Sullivan and O'Reilly. There was another volley, then a scattered fire and I heard the horse galloping on the road below making for home by his usual route. I crept across the road and over the fence, across a field and on to the Rockchapel road, across this and into the fields again. I had little hope that my comrades had escaped but there might be some chance that they might have been wounded and had got away somewhere and needed my help.

It was bitter cold as I crawled through the sodden field, revolver in hand and seeing a British soldier in every swaying bush. I got to the bridge and could hear the tramp of the troops as they marched back to the town. I waited, examining the roadway and fences outside. Finally I came out on the road and searched for any traces of my friends. Not a sign anywhere. Along the Rockchapel road I went three quarters of a mile, as far as Jerry Doody's cottage. Jerry was a friend and a loyal man but the house was in darkness. It was two a.m. and I did not like to disturb at that hour, and in the circumstances of the time, a household where there were small children. The darkness was deceptive. While I stood outside O'Reilly was inside suffering agonies from two bullet wounds, one through the liver. Jerry had crossed the river and was at that time making his roundabout way through the fields for the doctor. This man was Dr. Algie Verling, who had been a British officer and had served all through the war in France. He was not noticeably a supporter of ours but was a good friend and O'Reilly, when sending for him, knew that no risk would deter him from coming.

I decided to search along the Kingwilliamstown road. I returned to the bridge and again my weary quest of the roadsides began. A mile from the bridge I found what I took to be the first clue to the whereabouts of my comrades, a saw in the middle of the road where it had fallen from the car. Further on I found a hammer and at intervals for the next few miles I picked up one of the various tools we had brought from Newmarket. I began to hope that all was well. I felt the boys would have known that I could take care of myself and getting out of the ambush had galloped hell for leather for home.

Probably about 5 a.m. I reached Mick Sullivan's home. I went to the bedrooms where O'Reilly, Mick and I had slept on the previous day. The rooms were empty and the rifles which had stood by the bedsides had gone. I sat on the bedside to think. I concluded that the boys had escaped, had at some time arrived home and not finding me had taken their rifles and gone to look for me. I found somebody shaking me and looked up to find Mick Sullivan. In sheer weariness I had dropped off to sleep. Mick had spent the night after his escape from the ambush in search of O'Reilly and of me. He had been over the same ground as I had covered but at different times and had finally decided that he could only get news of us by coming home. He was relieved to see me and had no explanation of the absence of the rifles.

That explanation was not long in coming. Johnnie Jones and Liam Moylan arrived. They had been sleeping in the house of the man to whom the horse belonged which we had driven to Newmarket. They had been awakened in the early hours of the morning when the horse trotted into the farmer's yard and came to a halt at the door; being unable to account for his return they searched for us at Sullivan's. Not finding us there they feared the worst, took the rifles and set out for Newmarket in search of us and of news of us. They had heard that O'Reilly had been wounded. Later we heard that he was in his own home guarded by British soldiers. He died the following day. His funeral was the occasion of a great demonstration of force and intimidation on the part of the British. But in spite of this its dimensions proved where the sympathies of the people lay and their respect for the dead soldier.

A soldier's sorrow for the death of a comrade is neither insincere nor evanescent; but in war death is a clear possibility; in our circumstances it seemed to be an inevitability. O'Reilly's death and that of the men who had died that week in Nadd did not affect the routine of our existence. There was work to be done and we did it. This lack of concern with disaster, this refusal to consider the odds or to count the cost was the attribute in men which had the greatest effect in maintaining morale. It was rooted in a grim idea among all the fighting men that they were dead men, and you can't kill a dead man or modify his opinions. These men, my friends, with whom I had been closely associated, whose lives had been ended by British bullets, had no thought of surrender, no belief that they would live through to the end. One by one they had passed on, the next day it might be our turn, some day and soon it surely would be. We had developed a philosophy about it. One might say we were in a trap of our own making; from which there was no escape and from which we had no desire to escape. The ambush at the bridge gave me an idea. I decided to destroy Barley Hill Bridge, two miles north of Newmarket, and lay an ambush there.

The number of attacks we had made up to that time, or indeed succeeded in making up to the end, bore no relation to the number of attempts made to organise such attacks. A dozen times plans were made, ambushes arranged. Men endured an endless weary wait in all weathers without success. It showed how closely we had pinned the British to their bases and outposts.

But we could not see it thus. Activity to us meant one thing—clash of arms with the British—and no matter how we were occupied the days that passed by without such a clash were regarded as wasted days. It would have been foolish to have believed that the British living in such close contiguity to us could have been wholly without information in regard to our movements. The people in the towns who chose to ignore them soon found themselves deprived of their freedom. The wiser ones, or those wiser in their generation, found a working compromise. The British could not be wholly insulated. They were bound to get some information and their deductions were not always faulty.

It was, therefore, necessary for me to move with the utmost caution. I got thirty riflemen together at Kiskeam, got the Newmarket Company Captain to mobilise his company for drills every night during the week and on the evening before the day on which I proposed to move into the ambush position I sent for him and gave him orders to demolish the bridge at Barley Hill that night. After dark the riflemen and I left Kiskeam, marching to the west, getting out of sight of the village we took to the fields and travelled almost entirely cross country till we reached the Newmarket-Meelin road half a mile south of Meelin. We continued in single file along the road from Meelin to Barley Hill. We moved cautiously, with scouts well ahead. This precaution was taken for fear that a sudden appearance on our part might be taken to mean the arrival of a British party and a consequent interruption of the work of demolition.

When we got within half a mile of the bridge we halted, lay against the fences and listened for the sound of pick or sledge. All was silence. We sent forward two scouts. These disappeared into the fields and we waited their report. They were back in twenty minutes. Half the bridge was down, picks, sledges and shovels were thrown on the road and the fence was lined with discarded overcoats. They had either been surprised or had taken alarm. We moved carefully forward, examined roads and fences on both sides of the bridge, finally came out on the road beside the bridge. Sure enough, half the bridge was down and the road was strewn with the instruments of demolition. These boys had left hurriedly. We gathered up the tools and waited. While waiting, I noticed two men sling their rifles and, stooping in the shelter of the fence, make a careful examination of the discarded overcoats. Satisfied apparently with the examination they divested themselves of the coats they were wearing and from the fence appropriated two which, I assume, they felt better suited to their condition. I made no protest. I felt now that there had been a panic dispersal as a result of a false alarm and hoped that the loss of the coats might be a lesson to their owners on the evil consequences of panic action.

The Company Captain, Jeremiah Sheahan, though he had been unable to control his men, did not himself lose his head. He had moved away with the others but returned again and finally, discovering that it was his own comrades who had arrived, made known his whereabouts. There was no hope of getting again together those who had departed. We tackled it ourselves for an hour, made a more satisfactory job of the demolition and, gathering the tools, departed.

We had already selected the houses in which the men were to sleep for a few hours. Arriving at the first of these we knocked and called and failed to get admission. Finally, we opened a window, one man slipped through and opened the door, we trooped in. The occupants of the house couldn't help knowing we were there and still no one appeared, yet I then felt sure, and still am certain, that the owner of the house had good reason to give us welcome. We found a workman sleeping in an outhouse. He made a fire and we put the kettle on. If we were not welcome to a bed we were going to eat. In a short time all present were making a hearty meal on ham and eggs. It was not worth while to seek a bed. We adjourned to a house near by where we knew we'd be sure of a welcome and here we gathered round the fire waiting for the dawn.

My wait was to be longer. I became violently ill. I had never recovered from my illness of the year before and, while I was able to endure any kind of hardship, I still had to be circumspect about my food. Meat I could not digest and the little amount of ham I had eaten acted on me as if I had taken deadly poison. My stomach felt as if some demon surgeon was operating on it with a red hot blunt scalpel. My head ached violently and cold sweat oozed from every pore. I was put to bed, where I lay helplessly. I had scarcely enough strength to speak yet I forced myself to discuss the proposed ambush with Mick Sullivan. He was quite as familiar with the ambush position as I was. He listened to and approved of my plans. As he left with the others to take up their positions my last instruction to him was to send for me at once when he had word of the arrival of the British and under no circumstances to leave his position until after dark.

All day long I lay in pain waiting for the sound of rifles that never rang out. At dark Mick Sullivan arrived with doleful countenance. They had waited until dusk was about to fall and then had retired. When they had almost reached the house wherein I was a Volunteer on a bicycle overtook them with the news that, almost coincident with their departure, a party of British soldiers had arrived, examined the damaged bridge and returned to Newmarket. It was too late to pursue them, another chance was lost. I was horribly disappointed, but so bitter were the looks of discomfiture on the faces of the others that I refrained from pointing out that my orders had not been carried out. The reason for the premature retirement was the belief (justifiable) that the British would not permit themselves to be caught away from their barracks as darkness fell. Their non-arrival as the dusk began to fall seemed to prove that they would not on that day venture out. For a week we haunted the roads round Newmarket, slipped into the town at night but no opportunity for attack was given us. We might have sniped the military and police posts but felt this to be a waste of ammunition leading only to indiscriminate fire from these posts to the danger of civilian lives. I moved back to Kiskeam to make a final trial of the gun with which we hoped to blow in the steel shutters of the R.I.C. Barracks.

The gun was housed in a barn. We trundled it out and got it into position. The powder was tamped in place and a newspaper was rammed home. The bore was rough and jagged, eaten by the rust of years, this must have caused the accident. As I placed the iron projectile in the mouth of the gun there was an explosion. The piece of iron was torn from my hand. I was blinded with smoke. My hands were numb and as I looked down I found my left hand covered with blood and gobbets of flesh hanging from it. That, for me, completed the day's experiment. The hand was tied up somehow and I drove into Boherbue to Dr. O'Riordan. He stripped off the bandage, took one look at the hand and produced a bottle of whiskey. He gave me a stiff drink by way of anaesthetic and then proceeded to operate. He was at that time practically retired from practice but the job he did was as perfect as any of the most eminent surgeon. He could not replace the missing tissue but otherwise the work was perfect. A glass of whiskey, however, does not produce a sufficient condition of insensibility to pain and when the operation was over I was weak and exhausted. But though the result of such an accident would in peace time conditions have meant a month in hospital to me, now, invalidism had to be ignored. I was due for a meeting on the morrow with the Brigade O/C. near Millstreet. The First Southern Division was to be formed.

# XVIII

## [Division Formed / Clonmult / Headford / Horse Riding / De Valera / A Cromwellian Gun]

Though the terms, Company, Battalion, Brigade and Division were used to describe the different units of the Irish Republican Army, yet the basis of organisation was entirely different to that of a regular army. These terms did not denote numerical strength or units designed to a specialised service. The basis of organisation was the parish; in every parish a Company was formed. The Battalion area was a grouping of parishes delimited by natural boundaries or some traditional cohesiveness. Cork County was originally one Brigade area, later still it was divided into five Brigade areas. As I have already intimated, each Brigade was self sufficient, depending on its own resources and free from any except a general direction from Headquarters. My only memory of association with or direction from G.H.Q. in the months from November, 1920 to April, 1921 was the constant appeal, relayed to me by the Brigade O.C., to take the pressure off Dublin. We knew how terrible that pressure was and I think the record will show that we did not fail in our efforts to ease it. But while the system of organisation was the only one possible, it had certain weaknesses that were considered possible of elimination.

The Brigade area was sacrosanct. Intrusion, within its limits, was resented by both Brigade Staffs and fighting units. This resentment was in part based on the feeling that such intrusion reflected on the capacity and forcefulness of those who suffered this intrusion, in part that it created dangers that would not be anticipated, and in part again because it disrupted plans or operations to which long preparation and careful thought had been devolved. Yet good opportunities presenting themselves were often pursued without regard for territorial susceptibilities.

One such intrusion I recall, because its result might be said to be its justification and because the resentment of it at the time was deep and lasting.

In November 1920, Cork No. 1 Brigade believed, as a result of close continued observation, that there was a golden opportunity for inflicting a smashing defeat on the British. The work was carefully planned, the preparation was careful and well considered. We were asked to send certain reinforcements and on the appointed day a selected party, with two machine guns, travelled by arrangement into Cork No. 1 area. They arrived back next day. The action had to be called off because the successful Kilmichael ambush, of which Cork No. 1 Brigade had no intimation, had taken place on the same ground almost as the proposed action was to be attempted.

At Clonmult a small party of I.R.A. was surrounded by a British Column. They fought until their ammunition was exhausted and until a number was killed and wounded. Most of those who surrendered were afterwards executed. It was a very grave disaster. The story current at the time, and the truth of which I have no proof, was that another I.R.A. column was within sound of the guns and made no attempt to discover what the cause of the shooting was. The ambush at Headford, Co. Kerry, where the I.R.A. leader, D. J. Allman, was killed, might have been entirely successful with the co-operation of North Cork troops who were based at the time only a few miles across the border and who would only have been too glad of an opportunity to participate in the fight.

For these reasons I welcomed the formation of the Division, believing that the goodwill between Brigades and their understanding of and respect for each other could be hammered into a closer co-operation effort. Opportunities were lost because of the lack of anything other than goodwill co-operation between Brigades; results in different Brigades were unequal and slackness anywhere militated against effectiveness everywhere. The idea of creating Divisions was a natural growth fostered by conditions. It would, we hoped, result in a more close knit organisation and now we were to take steps to put it into effect.

The cold of winter was gone, the sun shone with a comforting warmth, the scent of the furze blossom was heavy in the air, there was a lazy drift of smoke over Claragh as I travelled south from Cullen to Kippagh where the meeting was to be held. Here Paddy McCarthy's body had lain the previous November, and here now were gathered I.R.A. leaders from all the Cork, Kerry, Waterford and West Limerick Brigades. Some were old friends and associates of long standing, others were strangers known to me only by reputation. Seán Hegarty, O.C. Cork No. 1 Brigade, I hadn't seen for several years. He was now bearded, with a homespun trousers and blue coat, the whole ensemble roofed in a bowler hat. He looked like an old time music hall artist; a stranger seeing him would not be surprised if he broke into song. He was, however, no comedian but a serious man of keen intellect. If he had a sense of humour it was of that sardonic and devastating type peculiar to Cork. I had heard so much of Tom Barry and of his high reputation as a leader of troops in action that I was anxious to see him. Here he was; like Ernie O'Malley, he looked a soldier and didn't care a damn who knew it. He was slight and erect, his smart coat, riding breeches and gaiters giving an impression of uniform. Later as he sat across the table from me I watched him. His face was that of an intelligent, earnest, determined and intolerant man, one whose mind was closed to all issues other than that with which he was concerned. I don't think his appearance belied his character. A few weeks before he had had at Crossbarry a great success against the British.

Other Cork men were:

Florry O'Donoghue, Adjutant, Cork No. 1 Brigade, shrewd, brainy; Liam Deasy, Cork No. 3. West Waterford was represented by Pax Whelan; West Limerick by Garrett McAuliffe, newly appointed Brigade O.C. on the death of Seán Finn; from Kerry came Humphrey Murphy. Liam Lynch was accompanied by George Power, his six foot frame dwarfed by Power's appalling inches. Ernie O'Malley represented G.H.Q. and was to preside at the meeting.

It had been determined by G.H.Q. to appoint Liam Lynch as Divisional O.C. The meeting was called for the purpose of having formal assent from the Brigades to the proposal to arrange the appointment of a Divisional Staff and to discuss the methods whereby the greatest profit could be secured under the new dispensation.

The meeting opened with the reading of a communication from G.H.Q. At that time those who wrote such communications at G.H.Q. seemed to have as bedside book and Bible a copy of General Lettow Vorbeck's story of the war in East Africa.* From this and *Infantry Training, 1914*, I assume came the inexplicable military periods and inapplicable military proposals which this communication contained and which roused the ire of men of long fighting experience and terse speech.

I was reminded of the Brigade meeting of 1917 when Tom Hales attacked Tomás MacCurtain and Terry MacSwiney. Seán Hegarty, distrustful of G.H.Q., master of invective, tore the communication and its authors to ribbons. Tom Barry added his quota and others chimed in, glad of an opportunity of expressing an opinion of a G.H.Q. which had been swift to criticise and slow to appreciate difficulty or to express appreciation of effort. Oratory and flowing periods are out of place when men of set purpose and deadly intent are being addressed. Most of us sat back and enjoyed the fun, knowing that the storm would blow itself out.

Lynch tried to pour oil on the troubled waters. Eventually we got down to business and the appointment of a Divisional Staff and the necessary readjustments in the various Brigades. In a discussion of tactics I was very much impressed by contributions of the men from Cork 3. It indicated experience

---

* [*Lettow Vorbeck*: General Paul von Lettow Vorbeck, commanding a small force of Germans and Africans, conducted a successful resistance to a British attempt, from 1914 go 1918, to conquer German East Africa with a much larger Army. In 1920 he published *Meine Erinnerungen aus Ostafrika*. It was published in English translation the same year—*My Reminiscences Of East Africa*. J.L.]

and thought and was in step with the views that I had developed as a result of my own experiences.

Ned Murphy of Mallow Battalion was absorbed into this Division and I also lost one of my best men, Con Moylan. I was the victim of what is, I suppose, the practice of the *"Brass Hats"* of every army. They gather unto themselves the best men discoverable in all units.

Seadna went up the slopes of Claragh in despair and descended in content. I reversed the process. I ascended in good form and was starting down the slope for home much disgruntled at the loss of the man on whom I depended so much. The new Divisional O.C. called me. He was delighted with his new post and expressed that delight to me. He had an amiable boyish touch of vanity which did not detract from his earnestness and determination. *"You'll take over the Brigade"*, he said. I was not prepared for this. A Brigade O.C. has to concentrate on staff work and cannot personally concern himself with the clash of arms. It seemed to me that life as a Staff Officer would be intolerably dull for one of my experiences. It seemed to me that George Power of Fermoy should be appointed. He was Deputy Brigade Commandant. He had done his work well and was the obvious choice for the vacant post. I had no desire for a change that would take me out of the fighting line and relegate me almost entirely to staff work and organisation. I made my objections known but they were overruled. The Divisional O.C. told me he had discussed the matter with George Power, who was anxious that I, older and more experienced, should take command. This attitude of Power was in keeping with the whole attitude of the I.R.A. Men did not seek rank or position. Each man had a job to do. He did that with all his might, careless as to whom the credit went. Power modestly believed that I was more fitted for the post (with which view I disagreed) and stepped aside to permit me to occupy it. From that day and during the remainder of the short period I was to command the Brigade he gave me the fullest co-operation and support in everything I did.

I was in one sense pleased with my promotion. I had, for a long time, been pressing on the Brigade O.C. the necessity there was for a re-organisation of certain Battalions. Blame was to be apportioned for, among other things, the disaster at Nadd. I proposed to apportion it and to take other steps to make the Brigade a more efficient fighting unit. While I did not propose to proceed without deliberation, I felt I had sufficient facts to justify the action I proposed to take. I had, however, to attend to the readjustment of my own Battalion before attending to other matters. My Battalion Vice Commandant was Paddy Murphy of Tullylease. He was a pioneer in the movement, a quiet, earnest and effective worker. He was physically big and powerful but an accident in Belfast Jail in 1918, when he almost bled to death as a result of a severed artery, had deprived him of much of his vitality. The post was an important one, needed a man of thrust, energy and determination. I selected Seán Nunan. I have already described Seán Nunan's character. I want again to say that I have known no better man. I put Jim Riordan of Kiskeam into Seán's vacant post of Quartermaster. My headquarters had been at his house in Knockavoreen for almost half the time during the previous year. He was all the time at my beck and call and being quite familiar with the work of the

Battalion was an eminently suitable selection.

Seán Nunan and I spent a few days together at Geoffrey Sullivan's of Knockilla, where we discussed Battalion organisation. Paddy Geoffrey Sullivan had a few good horses and very often had provided transport for us. We came out into the farmyard one morning and found Paddy engaged in the training of a colt. We stopped to watch the proceedings and then I said, *"Paddy, I've always wanted to learn to ride a horse and never had the opportunity"*. *"Now is your time"*, said Paddy, handing over the long rein to a workman. He went into the stable and appeared leading a big chestnut. He put a saddle on the animal and said *"Up you go"*.

My idea of learning horsemanship was to secure for the purpose a smaller animal which the years had deprived of any ambition for undue effort and I was rather taken aback at the power, size and rolling eye of my proposed mount. Well, I had brought it on myself. I was hoisted into the saddle. The chestnut proved to be a not ungraceful ballet dancer. I was perched insecurely at a height which seemed to me to be about ten feet off the ground. Paddy led the animal out of the yard across the road and into a field. He then flicked the horse with his whip and away we went across the field. As I lifted into the air and came back with a thud on the saddle the exclamation that left my lips was a compound of fervent prayer and lurid profanity. When the hooves hit the ground each time I floated in a beautiful parabolic curve on the horse's neck; as they left it again I clashed with the saddle so hard that I thought I'd finish with my backbone protruding through my scalp. A low bank divided the field in which I was from the next field. My mount faced it, hit it beautifully with his hind feet, sailed over and continued his lunatic career. The next fence was high and topped by a thick growth of thorn. We pounded towards it. In midfield it dawned on me that if I pulled hard on the rein the beast might forego his intention to murder me. I did so; he swung round in a wide curve and faced back for the fence we had crossed. He and I repeated our previous performances and as he landed he broke into a trot which was for me a more excruciating experience than his gallop. At the end of the field where my audience waited in a gale of laughter he halted and my heart dropped back into place.

Paddy, choking with merriment, congratulated me on my success turned the horse round again for another trial. While the jarring of my backbone had not decreased, I had now much more confidence in my mount. I assume he realised, as I did, that I was a damn fool and decided to take care of me. Each further trip made me more confident but after an hour I felt it was time to call it a day. I dismounted, tried to walk and failed. Every muscle in my body ached. In the football field I have been knocked down and walked on by heavier men. I have taken knee, fist and elbow when the referee was more interested in the game than in the manner of its playing but never have I had such a complete battering as on that April day I trusted myself to the tender mercies of Paddy Sullivan. Those who join the Army School of Equitation need to be in good physical trim.

The Divisional Commandant on his way to Kerry called on me. He informed me that some of the politicians were becoming more and more uneasy about the outcome of our revolutionary effort, that, as a result, President de Valera was anxious to see for himself what conditions were outside Dublin and proposed to spend a month with the Active Service Unit in my Brigade. I was pleased, naturally, that my Brigade was the one selected and determined that our work and organisation should be such as to counter-balance in the President's mind the effects of any of the political *nervenkrieg*.\* But I was also worried; worried about my responsibility for the safety of the man whose personality was such a potent force, who was regarded as the spearpoint of the movement; whom the Irish people held in such esteem; who was loved and honoured everywhere among them. Further, while I was confident that the Brigade was effective there were limits beyond which its efforts were futile and the results of guerrilla tactics were uncertain and uneven. I was fearful that the opportunities for the fighting the President wished to see would not be in adequate measure afforded us.

The Senior Officers were informed of the projected visit. The pick of the fighting men everywhere were got together and Michael O'Connell of Lombardstown, now Brigade Quartermaster, went to Dublin to make arrangements. Here he met Seán O'Connell, who was a member of Collins's Staff, and after a discussion of the matter arrived home with the information that the President, uniformed as a railway guard, was to arrive on a particular train two days later. We moved into position in the early morning of the specified date. Trains passed to and fro all day but our visitor did not arrive. On the following day, as we were moving into position, I had a message from the Divisional Commandant to withdraw the men and come to see him. He was again at Lombardstown. He then informed me that the visit was cancelled. In our discussion I discovered that de Valera had been seriously worried as a result of listening to the views of various defeatists, had actually arranged for Michael Collins to go to the United States so that if the premonitions of evil had any basis at least one of the leaders would escape the trap and live to re-organise the Republican Movement. I found out afterwards that this last moment decision to cancel his visit to North Cork and Collins's visit to America was made because the first tentative approaches for a settlement had come from the British.

The Divisional O.C. had made arrangements to visit the Kerry Brigades and on his way there I accompanied him as far as Kingwilliamstown on the county border. Here I handed him over to Humphrey Murphy, Kerry 2 Brigade O.C.

During his visit there the Kerrymen provided for his inspection another gun of Cromwellian vintage. A demonstration of its effectiveness was arranged. It was loaded and fired—the target being a derelict house. The range was a short one but at the first trial the projectile hit the ground half way between the gun and the house after ploughing a deep furrow in the field ricocheted and sailed over the target. The muzzle was slightly elevated for the next trial. If this gun had survived it would have been the subject of close

---

\* [*nervenkrieg*: literally "nerve war" in German. Psychological warfare, perhaps. J.L.]

study by anti-aircraft gunners, for when the projectile left the barrel the second time, instead of hitting the target, as after the correction it should have done, it soared almost vertically into the air and landed at a point not twenty feet from where it started. Lynch suggested it should be sent into my Brigade for examination and a further trial. It arrived. If ever inanimate objects embody an evil spirit then the dull rusty metal of this gun was the armour of a most formidable one.

Victor Hugo in *'93* devotes ten brilliant pages to the description of a gun which had broken its moorings on a ship at sea\*. If the stories told of this Kerry gun by the men of the 2nd Battalion were collected they'd fill ten volumes. It was a lump of metal ten feet long, fifteen inches in diameter, tapering to nine. It smashed the cars on to which it was loaded, lamed the horses that drew it, crushed fingers and toes. It slipped off a cart, rolling madly downhill in erratic circles, transforming, in their effort to avoid it, a column of marching men into a mad riot of dancing dervishes; smashed through a gate, came to rest so deep in a slimy ditch that nothing of it appeared but the little lump of metal round the touch hole which stared up from the slime like an eye, glaring in gleeful malice at those who had retreated madly from its onslaught and were now engaged in recovering it from its slimy bed. Ernie O'Malley in his book *On Another Man's Wound* described its catastrophic and unregretted end. He does not record his sardonic comment as he looked at the widely scattered metal of its disintegrated remains— *"Proverbs of the I.R.A. No. 1 "Never put all your powder into one gun"*. We let it go at that.

# XIX

## [The Great Round-up And Escape / Taaffe's Further Adventures]

The Brass Hats of the Division who had come to see the experiment with the gun had moved off. I went, too, into the Millstreet Battalion area. My arrival was unexpected and I had to share a bed with *"Big Con"* Meany and Paddy Healy.

Nervous tension was probably the cause of my being a light sleeper and the reason why once awakened I was wholly awake at once, there was no period of semi-consciousness. This, and the fact that the men between whom I slept each weighed sixteen stone and thus rendered my position far from comfortable, was the reason that a few hours later I was alert at once on hearing the sound of footsteps in the yard and immediately after a soft warning tap at the house door. Then somebody came into the kitchen. Doors were never closed in the houses where we were guests so that men on guard could have swift access to us if the need arose. I slipped out of bed and into

---

\* [*"93"*: a novel of the French Revolution set in the year 1793. J.L.]

my clothes. I was already half dressed when the intruder reached my door and called to me. He told me the news. There were three fires alight on the surrounding hills. The first one visible had been far to the east, then another had sprung to life a few miles west of the first one. As he came into the yard a third still nearer had blazed up. It was apparent that the big raid, the imminence of which enemy activity during the past few weeks had given us warning, was under way and as I got out of the house accompanied by the other Volunteers a few moments later it was clear that the orders had been misunderstood or disobeyed or else the raid was a much bigger affair than we had bargained for. Fire blazed on the hilltops, not only to the east, but north, south and west also. Preparations had been made for many weeks to give adequate warning of the raid. Combustible materials of many kinds had been ready on the hilltops. Company Captains and Intelligence Officers everywhere had been given detailed instructions, very clearly instructed against false alarms. Even then it was possible that some highly strung individual might have gone off at half cock and there was no reason for hasty action on our part, roads were everywhere trenched or blocked in some fashion, making impossible any speedy advance of motor transport; the nearest strong garrisons were ten miles distant and infantry do not travel with the speed of light.

There was one danger. It was an exceptionally dry summer, the fields everywhere were as hard as the roads. Rivers were low and streams only a trickle. Good drivers could carry lorries over places in which in normal years they would have sunk to the wheel hubs. Actually, this did happen and had our preparations been less adequate might have proved disastrous for us.

The men of the local Company began to gather, a few with rifles, others with shotguns, the rest, alas, unarmed. Men of the A.S.U. arrived in pairs. Two men were allotted to each townland so that everyone might be warned. Later events proved that the whole Brigade area was alert that night. I went indoors.

I spread a map on the table and lighted a candle. I have heard men, who apparently know little of the countryside and less of military action, sneer at the use of maps by the I.R.A., by those who had a complete knowledge of the district in which they lived. Let me assure those that in the experience of a man who cut down his impedimenta to the barest minimum, maps are a most important essential in the soldier's equipment. One may have a most perfect knowledge of terrain but the lines of the map bring swiftly to the mind matters of important detail that the memory is too apt to overlook and in time of need for swift decision any device that permits one to concentrate on the main problem is to be highly regarded. The use of the map was neither imitation nor pretence. It was a real necessity.

At any rate, my examination of the map helped me to my decision. There was an opening to the north towards a mountainy district where, if the odds proved too great, it would be hard to find us. Here we had driven in several police barracks. The only forces that could successfully intercept us were a Brigade of British military garrisoned thirty miles to the west and they were unlikely to have smooth going. But it was essential to cross an open country intersected by many roads if we were to reach the district where cover could be found and our retreat continued in one of several directions. The A.S.U. fell in, with them was every Volunteer known to be wanted or likely to be wanted by the British; the others were to scatter and disappear. But first I must have a man on the spot who would bring me information of enemy activity. His appearance had to be such as would arouse no suspicion, yet he should be shrewd, absolutely reliable and have a good knowledge of the whole Brigade area.

The Dispatch Rider volunteered. As I said, he was short and looked much younger than his actual age. He went into the house and returned barefoot, his coat discarded and an old jersey substituted for it. His trousers were changed for a short pants, both articles the property of a school going son of the farmer in whose house we were. He did not look more than fourteen. I was satisfied with his appearance and his capacity to handle the job. The Volunteers disappeared. The augmented Active Service Unit marched off into the night, Indian file, well extended, and as the dawn broke reached their destination. We lay until the forenoon in a deep glen with the heather high above us and with hidden outposts placed at the strategic points. Children passed to school on the road above us. Farm carts rattled on their way to the Creamery. It was as yet too early for news. Then the creamery carts began to return. It was noticeable that the drivers were the older men. The younger men had gone to ground.

We waited and at last came a man we knew. The Company Captain of the district from which we had started stepped out on the road to talk to him. Had he seen the British or had he any news. He had. The roads were black with soldiers and police. They were searching everywhere, firing on anyone who failed to halt when called upon. Three men had already been shot, one an old man working in the fields. No, they didn't seem to be coming our way, they were working back towards the east. It looked like reliable news but we still decided to wait. We asked our friend to round up some provender for us and told him how many men lay hidden in the heather. In an hour the food arrived; home-made bread in huge buttered slices, jars of tea; bowls, mugs and cups as drinking materials brought by women and young girls driving donkey carts; leaving their jars and baskets at a gap in the roadside fence and departing, apparently incurious, but I have no doubt eaten with curiosity as to the identity of those they served.

We lay all day in the sun drenched heather, the hum of innumerable bees a lullaby in our ears. Smokers were restless without their tobacco. But most of us had long arrears of sleep to make up and took advantage of the opportunity. An aeroplane zoomed over us, turned in a great circle and came back, emphasising the need there was for refraining from any action that might betray our position. For this reason, too, I had issued a warning against a second visit by the food suppliers. We dined with Duke Humphrey*. At last darkness fell, the local Volunteers slipped in among us; we divided into parties and went off to eat a prodigious meal in the surrounding houses.

We should have reliable news now at any time. As I finished my meal the news came. The farmer whose house I had left in the early morning brought it.

---

* [*dined with Duke Humphrey*: went without a meal. J.L.]

The family had gone back to bed when we left and arose a little later than usual to milk cows and tackle the endless tasks which farm economy imposes on its bondsmen. The despatch rider busied himself with the others as if he had no concern with any matters other than the work of the farm. The farmer realised that news could come only with the arrival of the British, all else was rumour and unreliable. And rumours came thick and fast and always conflicting, except at one point. There was general agreement in the reports of calamitous happenings. The famous Calamity Jane's name was Burke. Therefore, she was probably Irish and one of a long-tailed family, none of whom other than herself emigrated to South Dakota. The day's disaster was in every morning face.

At noon the first line of British appeared from the north. It was apparent that the road running east and west, and which lay two miles south of the district in which I now was, formed part of the perimeter of the round-up. Along this and all other roads utilised labour had been conscripted to fill in trenches and to clear barricades thus permitting the full use of motor transport. Armoured cars cruised to and fro. Road intersections were held, all civilian movements brought to a stop. Soldiers in extended order moved across fields, beat the fences and searched farm buildings closely. It looked as if nothing could escape the search. In the afternoon they arrived to my headquarters of the day before. Here the search was more thorough than elsewhere, the questioning more intense. The British knew they were in an area of resistance but beyond that had no definite knowledge.

The despatch rider proved to be a mine of information for them. He foolishly blurted out confirmation of everything they already knew; was voluble about everything that they couldn't help discovering, guided them to all the houses and was entirely helpful. They were delighted with him. Here was a boy, not too intelligent indeed, but willing to be of assistance if possible and maybe at some point capable of giving really valuable news.

It was clear from the information brought that the area encircled was about one hundred square miles. The troops engaged were estimated to number six thousand. They had come from all parts of the compass and had not returned to Barracks but were camping in the open: the area now encircled was about fifty square miles.

The *"Informer"* had departed with the British troops. I moved back to my old Headquarters that night and before dawn was in position on a hilltop with a wide view of the valley as the morning mist arose. It spread before me like the checker board of Tipperary seen from the slope of Knockmealdown. Round it mile after mile were ranged the tents of the British, the nearest to me a half mile distant. It was truly a vast demonstration of force, a determined attempt to purge the wickedness of the mere Irish, and somewhere in the midst of it was my incorrigible practical joker putting on his act for the delectation of the British.

During the day there was more definite news. The beacons had carried the alarm in time. When the trap was sprung the quarry had departed. It was true that three men had been killed; true also that a number of men were being held for examination but no matter how close the search was now to be the operation was a huge failure. Again the Phantom Army had disappeared into the ground. The operation was completed, that night the Tommies packed up. The lorries and armoured cars departed. The countryside returned to what the people had now come to accept as normal. But with the soldiers had departed five truck loads of prisoners. It looked, therefore, as if we had been too optimistic, that the British had been better informed and more successful than we thought possible.

We need not have been alarmed. With the morning came my man, still clad in his juvenile habiliments. He was entirely cocky and self-satisfied. He had been everywhere with the British and had been treated royally by them. I asked about the prisoners. *"Oh, them"*, he said, *"They'll be all right. My father is arrested too"*. *"How did he come to get arrested?"*, I asked. *"I told the Tommies that he was Chief Intelligence Officer of the district"*. *"Why the devil did you do that to the poor old man?"*, I said. *"Well"*, he replied, *"my father was always boasting about how good an Irishman he was and I wanted to give him an opportunity to prove it. All the other fellows in the district are gone off with him to Cork"*.

I found this to be correct. As a result of information supplied by Taaffe, all whom he could reach of those who had no association with the I.R.A. were removed by the British. A few days later the hoax was discovered and all the dangerous prisoners returned to their homes.

The general information he brought me of the numbers of troops engaged, their nature and equipment, the different bases from which they had started was valuable in the remaining months before the Truce of July 11th.

## XX

## [Rathmore Ambush / Irish Cuisine / Farm Life]

The tour of inspection in the Millstreet area concluded. I went to Liscarroll. Here at O'Donnells of Aughrim I spent several days with Paddy O'Brien and Séamus Brislane. I was familiar with this Battalion area. There was no need for the urging of activity here. The leadership was sound and energetic; the morale of the men high, and I left the area convinced that no demand made on the Battalion would lack its adequate answer.

A record of routine effort such as this is, for the purposes of arousing general interest, about as effective as the Report of the Banking Commission. But such effort is the solid foundation on which continued success is to be built; the bastion which absorbs the shock of defeat; the centre on which hard pressed troops rally; where they find the antidote to discouragement and the incentive to combat.

As a result of the discussions, organisation was strengthened; forceful men replaced those of a less sure conviction, knowledge was acquired and shared. While there was no disagreement on purpose, no avoidance of effort, no shrinking from demand; yet sometimes these talks verged on the acrimonious. Strong men held opinions strongly and the local view at times obscured for them the broader national one; the immediate success overshadowed the long-term interest. The views of the complacent were easily overborne or set aside; the man of force and initiative was often less easily convinced of the wisdom of strategy and of the undesirability of action which he proposed to take.

It was my intention to tackle the Kanturk Battalion next. The men in this Battalion were earnest and in no way lacking in soldierly qualities, but the direction lacked fire, drive and initiative. It was my intention to make that change of leadership which I had been for some time urging on my predecessor.

Man proposes. On my way I got word of a successful ambush at Rathmore carried out by the men of the 5th Battalion in co-operation with men from Kerry 2 Brigade. Raids and reprisals were the aftermath of all ambushes. I decided that my presence in the 5th Battalion area would serve an immediate purpose and that Kanturk could wait. I found the men of the 5th Battalion in happy mood. Half a dozen men on the Active Service Unit waiting list had been armed with new rifles as a result of the ambush and the desire for fight in every Company was more urgent than ever. Béaslaí's statement that Southern Officers informed Michael Collins about this time that they could not continue this fight owing to shortage of arms and ammunition had no basis in fact.* The morale and aggressiveness displayed by the Fifth Battalion was typical of every Brigade in Cork, Kerry and Limerick with which I was at this time familiar.

The balance of victory and defeat is ever swaying. The house where I had the discussion with the Staff of the 3rd Battalion was the scene a few days later of one of the tragic happenings which we had come to regard as routine. Paddy O'Brien, his brother, Dan, and Jack Regan were at breakfast there when the house was surrounded by British troops. Jack Regan was riddled with bullets; Dan O'Brien was captured, to be executed a week later; and the other man, who seemed to have a charmed life, Paddy O'Brien, shot his way through the British troops and escaped amidst a hail of bullets.

But if Paddy O'Brien was indestructible I was not. Ill health had reduced me to a shadow, and now I had a note from the Divisional O.C. saying that G.H.Q. had made provision for my admission to a Dublin hospital and urging me to make arrangements to go there. I decided to reject the offer. I felt that my retirement from active effort for any reason would be misunderstood and would have a bad effect on my comrades. That retirement was now due and it came about in swift and ruthless fashion. I had never quite recovered from the illness I contracted in 1918, the return of which had kept me out of action in the early months of 1920. Now it was again to return to plague me. The conditions under which I lived imposed on my original disability resulted in

---

* [*Béaslaí's statement*: see *Michael Collins And The Making Of A New Ireland* by Piaras Béaslai, 1926, Volume 2, p250. J.L.]

my stomach refusing food and a constant issue of blood from ulcers. I was in sad case.

Good cooking is a factor in physical comfort, tends to the maintenance of good health and surely helps towards tranquillity of mind. In my *"Rambles in Eireann"* it had been my good luck at times to have my needs supplied by those who understood the art, but it has also been my misfortune to suffer at the hands of those whose real vocation was research chemistry. The consistency with which these latter could transmute good class beef into better class shoe leather; their capacity for changing fresh vegetables into synthetic rubber showed that their vocation lay in the laboratory rather than in the kitchen.

When I say that living conditions in the rural Ireland of 1920 were poor, I must not be regarded as one who makes complaint of the welcome given to the I.R.A. by the Irish people in their homes. That view would be entirely wrong. We were made truly welcome, anything the people had was given to us; they felt that we were entitled to the best that was in their power to give. We were truly grateful and in the years that have gone by since we have not forgotten the kindness and generosity shown to us by them. But having said so much, it is in no spirit of ungrateful criticism that I repeat that the standard of living in rural Ireland was unbelievably low.

Food was coarse and in general not well cooked. The facilities for cooking were primitive. A fire on the hearth, a large pot hanging on the crane and a bastable were the basis of equipment. Any graduate of Cathal Brugha Street forced to work under these conditions would have retired from culinary effort. Furnishings in general were inadequate, of poor design and craftsmanship. Houses were damp, airless, inconvenient; outhouses entirely unsuitable to their purpose. The evil system of land tenure under which the country had so long suffered had left its foul mark on the economics of the nation. Money that in a normal country would be put back in the land, into the purchase of badly needed amenities, was, where it existed, hoarded away in banks to be utilised outside the country as the capital of Industry and Commerce for the enrichment of other nations. The effects of any great national evil reach into the future and, because of tradition and experience, the Irish farmer could envisage no real security for his family only in his bank deposit, wrung with hardship from his land and gathered in an unjustifiable self denial; discomfort and wearisome effort.

Work under reasonable conditions, with adequate equipment, can be a pleasure. But it seemed to me that the never ending labour with the modest equipment in the Irish farm kitchens had retained our womenfolk in a condition of serfdom. Farmers and their womenfolk engage in a laborious occupation but there comes sometimes the day's end. But for the farmer's wife, and particularly for the female farm servant, there was no respite. From the dawn's early light to the sunlight's last gleaming she was still unflaggingly engaged. And fatheaded economists talk about the causes of emigration! It amazed me to see a slight young girl lift a huge pot of boiling potatoes from the fire and lug it into the farmyard to feed pigs and poultry. The carrying of these awkwardly shaped pots, weighing over fifty pounds, necessitated a posture that surely wrenched every organ in the body out of its proper alignment, with evil effects in after years. There should have been no need for such strenuous effort, for such continuous labour. Nowadays, when State recognition of the need for farm improvement is an accepted thing, it is high time to lighten this burden of effort that had borne so heavily and so long on the mothers of the race, whose lot on Irish farms is cast in any but pleasant places.

## XXI

## [Capture / Imprisonment / Trial]

G.H.Q. decided to issue a general order to all Brigades for an attack everywhere on the British on the 14th May, 1921. The order was doubtless the outcome of political exigencies which must on occasion over-ride military considerations. From a military point of view it was not well conceived. Opportunities may be grasped. It is seldom possible to create them. It may be said that the result of the order did not produce any more effective activity on that day that would distinguish it from other days. Our difficulties had been augmented by the fact that a Battalion of the Gloucester Regiment had come to Kanturk early in April, had cleared out the occupants of the old Union Workhouse and installed themselves therein. This new force proceeded to make things much more interesting for us and always moved in such large bodies that it would be madness for us to think of attacking them. I lay one sunny afternoon on a hillside watching a column of troops pass by on their way to Kerry. The column consisted of twenty-five lorries and two armoured cars. They proceeded slowly, stopping to search roadside farmhouses and to make excursions into the fields to search the farmhouses at some distance from the road. They held up and questioned everybody they met and after several hours passed out of my sight. They were proceeding at a rate of not greater than one mile an hour.

By some mishap, the order for action arrived only on the afternoon of May 14th. I went into Newmarket with about twenty men on that night and remained there till morning. There was no movement of British troops, R.I.C. or Tans. All these stuck closely to their barracks. The only activity open to us was the sniping of these posts and this did not seem wise to me as it would only lead to indiscriminate fire from the posts and would possibly involve the death or wounding of a number of civilians. We left the town as the day broke and returned to Kiskeam.

The Brigade O.C. of the West Limerick Brigade, Seán Finn, was killed in action a few months before and I had arranged with the new Brigade O.C. to visit West Limerick to co-operate with him in certain activities he had planned. It seemed to me an appropriate time to carry out my promises and arrangements were made on Sunday evening to move into West Limerick. We were to travel out of our own district in small parties and to meet at Taur where transport would be provided to take us to Mount Collins. With a few others I started in the evening from Knockavoreen and had proceeded only about four miles when I was overtaken by a cyclist who informed me that some officers from Kerry had arrived in Knockavoreen in search of me and that as there was no exact knowledge of my whereabouts Volunteers had cycled in different directions in search of me. I returned to Knockavoreen, arriving there about midnight, had a discussion with the Kerrymen, and as it was too late then to start on my journey to West Limerick I went to bed.

I was awakened about 3 a.m. and informed that the British had passed through Boherbue, four miles away, and that there was every likelihood of a raid. I got out of bed, went into the yard where half a dozen others were collected. They expressed the opinion that the British were much closer and suggested that we should move off to the West at once. I decided that it was a good idea. In view of the fact that the Active Service Unit had left the district, the usual care in regard to sentries and signals had not been taken and it was quite possible we might have been taken unawares. We went out on the roadway and at the yard gate we met a Volunteer who informed us he believed we were surrounded. Fifty yards away, in the passage leading to the next house, he had heard the rattle of rifle butts which led him to believe that the British had arrived. I ordered those who were with me to get inside the fence on the north side of the road and decided to investigate. If the British were here the sooner we knew it the better and the only way of finding out was for one man to walk into the trap, if a trap it was. This at least would give the others a chance to get away.

I walked down the dark passage about 20 yards and then heard a shout, *"Halt, hands up"*. I halted and put up my hands and was then instructed to come forward. I advanced one step forward, turned swiftly, ran a few steps and dropped on the ground. A volley rang out over my head. I jumped to my feet and got round a corner of a fence before the second volley came. The volley was sufficient signal to my comrades to get away swiftly which they did, and luckily they got out of the ring before it was finally closed. I ran towards the east. I was again fired at and doubled back and went to the north. Here again I drew fire. Finally I went towards the west. The ring had closed and the air seemed to be alive with bullets as I appeared. Escape was hopeless. I crawled back again into cover and got on top of a fence between furze bushes. As the day broke brightly I could see everywhere around me khaki clad figures of the British soldiers. It was *Nunc Dimittus* for me. I lay down and fell asleep. Possibly an hour later I was dragged from the fence by the British soldiers and brought into the yard which I had left a few hours before. Here a number of troops were drawn up. Among them was a group of civilians whom they had picked up in the various houses. Most of these were local farmers and workers. A few were Volunteers but none of these was prominent and none was likely to be known for his activities to the R.I.C.

An Officer sat at a table in the yard. Beside him stood an R.I.C. man. This man recognised me and gave to the British Officer a history of my activities. The British Officer questioned me and while he was questioning me I was busy reading the list of names which lay before him on the table. He seemed to have the name of every member of the Active Service Unit and also had the names of some of the prominent under-cover men, at which I was surprised. When the questioning was over I was taken away by a party of British soldiers to be held under guard until the completion of the raid. These men were tremendously interested in their prisoner but my memory now of their main concern was their anxiety to know what the pay of the I.R.A. was.

I and the others were then marched away several miles until we came to a road trench. Here the lorries were waiting. The soldiers waiting by the lorries were also interested in me. The comment of one of them was intelligent. *"He looks like an adjectival Gerry"*. I was handcuffed, taken to Kanturk and lodged in a cell there. Small as my wrists were, the handcuffs were still smaller and as I lay all day in my cell I suffered a good deal of pain from my swollen arms. In the evening as the guard was changed the Orderly Officer visited me. He was a small man, wearing the ribbons of the M.C. and Bar. He and I had a conversation for fifteen minutes and then he ordered one of the soldiers who was with him to get a new pair of handcuffs. These were much more comfortable and were attached by a chain about a foot long which gave me a limited opportunity of using my hands. I thanked him and expressed some surprise at his kindness, to which he stated *"I am British"*. The term British did not in my experience connote any form of chivalry or fair play and at that time I could not realise that it could mean those things to anybody. However, there are some British who do play the game.

The following day I was brought before the Colonel of the Regiment in his office. As I waited outside the office, I noticed a large gong on which the Arms of the Regiment were engraved. On the top was the word *"Egypt"* and in the centre the figures 1798. When I went into the office I found two men in civilian dress. One, an older man, was the Colonel. The other was a younger man whom I found out afterwards was Adjutant of the Battalion. This man had a Webley revolver in his hands. Why he needed this weapon to protect himself and the Colonel from a handcuffed prisoner in the midst of his enemies was beyond my understanding. The Colonel told me he wanted to get some information about the reasons for the trouble in Ireland. I asked him what good the supply of such information would do me. He replied that it would do me no good, that I was going to be shot anyway. He said he was really anxious to know something of the reason for Ireland's rebellious attitude. I said that, of course, if he proposed to discuss the matter on that basis I was quite willing. He put a number of questions to me to which I replied. Our question and answer developed into a discussion on British and Irish history.

Finally, he said, *"I am not anxious to remain here in Ireland. I want to go back home"*. I said, *"I am most anxious that you should do so and possibly the whole reason for our attitude is to ensure that every English soldier and official in Ireland should go back to England and cease interfering with matters in this country"*. *"Your chief difficulty"*, he stated, *"in this country is that you are living in the past. You take no cognisance of modern conditions. You think that the world has not progressed since the days of Wolfe Tone and Emmett and still think in the terms in which those men thought"*. I changed the conversation. *"By the way"*, I said, *"as I was coming into the office I saw outside a gong with the word 'Egypt' on top and the date '1798' in the centre. What does that signify?"* *"Oh"*, he said *"that commemorates a great battle which this regiment fought in Egypt in 1798. Surrounded there, our men fought back to back till the finish. You will notice"*, he said, *"That there is a badge both in front and back of the caps worn by the men of this regiment. We are not known as the Gloucesters but as the 'Fore and Afts'.* *"I understand"*, I said. *"I assume"*, I continued, *"that Regimental tradition is a great force".* *"Undoubtedly"*, he said. *"And British Regiments"*, I said *"must remember 1798 and Irishmen must forget it".* *"I am afraid"*, he said, *"we haven't shot you soon enough".*

I was then taken back to my cell and handed over to a party of soldiers from Buttevant. My handcuffs were removed and a new set supplied. The sadist who locked these on me took care to dig away a portion of the flesh of my wrist as he snapped on the handcuffs. I was then tied hand and foot with a rope, thrown into a lorry. A huge convoy of lorries waited outside the barracks to convey me to Buttevant. On arriving at Buttevant I was thrown out of the lorry on to the barrack yard and lay there for an hour watching a cricket match that was in progress on the ground. Used to the hurling game, I thought that cricket, which I saw for the first time, was dull and, though I have seen a few cricket matches since, I have never enjoyed it only when it is associated by Dickens with the oratory of Dingley Dell [sic]*.

When the stumps were drawn the General in charge of the troops, whose predecessor I had killed four months before, and who had been watching the match, came along and ordered that the rope which bound me should be removed. This was done. The Sergeant who removed it hung it across his shoulders and then with a file of soldiers marched me to the Provost Marshal's quarters. As we approached this building we were met by the Provost Sergeant who asked, *"Who is this so-and-so"?* The Sergeant in charge of the party replied, *"This is General Moylan"*. The Provost Sergeant drew back his fist and said, *"Did he bring his batman?"* I was ragged, unshaven, bloody, and the association of a batman with such a tramplike individual as I was tickled my sense of humour. I laughed. The Provost Sergeant dropped his arm and said *"Blimey"* and the blow he intended for me was not struck.

I was immediately put into a small cell and a few moments later had a visit from two Corporals who gave me a sound drubbing. These were men of the East Lancashire Regiment and, strangely, the name of one of the Corporals I found to be Reilly.

I was left in the cell all day and was not further attacked. At night the Brigade Intelligence Officer paid me a visit, talked to me and questioned me for several hours. I don't think he succeeded in getting any information from me as a result of our conversation but he was so assured of my immediate death he must have felt it was quite safe for him to let me have all the knowledge he had gathered about my Brigade and much of this information was to prove very valuable in the months to come. I feel it right to state that he used no violence, intimidation or threat.

---

* [*Dingley Dell*: see *Pickwick Papers* by Charles Dickens. J.L.]

The following day I was taken to Cork and lodged in the Detention Barracks. All the prisoners were locked up. The place was quite silent. There was a chill air of certain death about the whole place. Here it was that the first man executed in the South, Con Murphy of my Brigade, was executed and here it was that the last man shot in he South during that period, Dan O'Brien, also of my Brigade, was executed on the day of my capture. A Scotch Sergeant, a kindly fellow, took me over from the East Lancs. As in all hotels, there was a visitors' book to which he led me. I signed my name in the book under that of my comrade, Dan O'Brien. The Sergeant asked if I knew him. I said that he was my comrade. I had seen Dan O'Brien in action and I knew his character. I knew, too, that he would have faced a fiercer death than that before the British firing party without flinching. The Sergeant casually said, *"Well, you will follow him in the morning"*. I was in no doubt about it. *"However"*, he said, *"soldiers, like everyone else, must die. Maybe you would like to have a bath before I lock you up"*. I was delighted at the opportunity of getting rid of the mud of the previous few days. I was then locked in my cell, the cell from which all the others had marched out to die. The Chaplain came and heard my Confession. Then I went to bed and slept.

When a man who has lived as I had live[d], had been inspired with the ideals such as inspired me, had faced disillusion every day over a prolonged period, it is easy to die. There was never any heroism in my action. My attitude was quite matter of fact. My time had come and there was no more to be said. I felt sure that that is the attitude of all men in my circumstances.

The following morning I was awakened not, to my surprise, to face the firing party but to parade with all the other prisoners. For two days this continued. This made all the difference to me. It was easy to die, it was harder to wait for death. On the third day I demanded an interview with the Sergeant Major. Getting it, I asked to see my Solicitor. He said, *"You don't need a Solicitor, you are going to be shot"*. I said I was fully aware of the fact but said that I was fully entitled to see a Solicitor so as to dispose of my private property. My private property at that time consisted of the clothes I stood up in but he was not to know that. Apparently he consulted his superior officers and that evening I was brought to an office where there was a Notary Public. I had to make a certain statement before him, the terms of which I don't remember, and then I was informed that Mr. Barry Galvin, Solicitor, of Cork City, would be brought to see me. I protested. I said, *"I don't want to see Mr. Barry Galvin. The man I want to see is my own Solicitor, Mr Barry Sullivan of Mallow"*.

I was very anxious to meet Barry Sullivan. He was a brilliant young lawyer who, from the very start of the Republican Courts, had been most helpful to us. He had been Solicitor in the case of the Mallow railwaymen who had been murdered by the Black and Tans and whose dependants sought compensation from the British through the Courts. He was at that time engaged in the case of a number of men, prisoners in the Detention Barracks, who were charged with having participated in the attack on Mallow Barracks. He was, in my opinion, the first man in Ireland who conceived the idea of challenging the legality of the Military Courts and had unsuccessfully sought the co-operation of a number of Barristers in his efforts to prove them illegal.

He was eventually successful in getting the co-operation of Albert Wood, K.C., who entered determinedly into the fight and was, at that time, in Cork City engaged in the case of Harold, Barter and the others who were charged with the attack on Mallow Military Barracks.

My desire to meet Barry Sullivan was not rooted in any hope to save my own life but I wanted a reliable man to whom I could pass the information I had got from the Intelligence Officer in Buttevant and whom I could inform of the whereabouts of certain documents and arms and ammunition which I had secreted. After some discussion it was agreed that Mr. Barry Sullivan would be permitted to see me and the following day he came. I swiftly gave him all the information I had for conveyance to my comrades outside and when I was finished he asked me *"What about your own case?"* I said, *"I have no case, they intend to shoot me and it is waste of time to do anything about it. It is certain that I am to be shot and I may as well go down with colours flying rather than in any way recognise the legal authority of the British"*. He then told me that Albert Wood was in Cork in connection with the case of Harold, that Wood was much interested in my case and was most anxious to see me. I agreed to see Wood. A discussion with anybody was at least an ease to the monotony of my days inside the prison.

The following day I was called again to the office where I had a conversation with Barry Sullivan. There were three men in the office. One was Barry Sullivan, the other a tall, good-looking man, whom I knew immediately. His name was Burke. He was a Barrister and a son of the Recorder who lived at Banteer. A year before I had got him out of bed to get the keys of his car which I needed for the removal of the mails at Banteer. He did not know me. I made no reference to our previous meeting. The third man present was, to my unsophisticated seeming, a typical Englishman, beautifully dressed and groomed, and with an accent which seemed to me then to be the quintessence of Oxford. This was Albert Wood.

Wood proceeded to discuss my case with me and again I pointed out the fact that I didn't have a case and there was no use in taking any legal proceedings. Our discussions went on for over an hour. Wood referred to the case of Wolfe Tone and that of John Allen, who had recently been executed in Cork prison.

He then said something that amused me. He said that in six weeks time all the fighting would be over. I knew the determination of my comrades outside and I believed the I.R.A. would be annihilated before surrendering and I could not conceive of the British as being willing to pack up and leave Ireland. I did not believe that the I.R.A. were going to win. I knew their weakness numerically and from the point of view of armament and I knew the power of Britain and, if I had any conception at that time about the activities with which I had been connected, it was that they formed part of an age long war of attrition which could not be immediately successful but which sometime, near or distant, would eventuate an Irish liberty. I felt that there would never again be acquiescence to British Rule in Ireland.

Wood insisted that negotiations were going on and that a Truce was imminent. He said it was very important for many reasons that my case should be defended. It might mean eventually the saving of lives of other men engaged in activities similar to mine. Finally I said that if I am ordered by the I.R.A. Headquarters to defend my case I shall obey orders, but, I said, I must absolutely be permitted to refuse to recognise the British Court. Wood said immediately, *"If we meet your conditions, will you guarantee to say nothing in Court other than the fact that you refuse to recognise the Court?"* I agreed and we parted on that note.

A few days later I was brought up for trial. To my seeming, there could be no ending but one to the trial. I was not interested. As I walked across the yard to the room where the Court was held I had no fears and no regrets but I was young and it seemed to me that the sky was never so blue or the trees never so beautifully green as they were on that May morn and it seemed to me a pity to depart so young from all this earthly beauty. The Court was composed of three Officers. I assume that it was in order to emphasise the fact that it was a Court of Justice that there was a loaded revolver in front of the Chairman on the bench. The gallery was crowded with a number of curious onlookers—all British Officers—and soldiers stood round the chair where I sat with drawn revolvers. The lawyers arrived and the charge was read out to me. As agreed, my statement was a simple refusal to recognise the Court and then the argument started. I had no understanding of the points at issue nor was I greatly concerned, nor was I discomfited in any way when Wood took up his brief and, followed by the others, left the Court. I felt that was how it was going to finish anyhow. The various witnesses were examined and the Court adjourned. I was taken back to my cell.

A few days later I was again brought before the Court. On this occasion my stay there was short. The President of the Court, in summing up the evidence, referred to my chivalrous treatment of prisoners and said that, in view of my attitude towards these prisoners, instead of sentencing me to death I would receive fifteen years' penal servitude.

This talk about chivalrous treatment of prisoners was meaningless. No British prisoner falling into the hands of the I.R.A. anywhere was ill-treated. Irishmen with arms in their hands captured by the British were always executed. The British soldiers so captured had always been freed. The real reason was, in my opinion, that, as Wood had pointed out, a Truce was imminent. I had been a few weeks before elected a member of the Dáil and the execution of a member of the Irish Parliament at a time when discussions between that Parliament and the British Parliament were in the offing would have created difficulties not easily overcome.

# XXII
## [Cork Detention Barracks / Spike Island]

After the decision in my case was promulgated I was detained in Cork for several weeks. In the Detention Barracks there was the most rigid discipline and the British troops were always nervous and on the alert. So much so that on a number of occasions the sentries fired at their own comrades and one British soldier was killed by a sentry. The whole place was spotlessly clean. The result, of course, of adequate staff and long experience in organisation. I visited the same Barrack in 1922 when Free State soldiers were imprisoned there. Conditions seemed to be chaotic and I have heard from Republicans who were in Limerick prison in the same year of the vile insanitary conditions under which the prisoners lived. It is quite possible that the horrors of concentration camps, of which we hear so much, are often due to lack of real experience in running them and lack of adequate staff to discipline and control both the prisoners and their keepers.

We were released from our cells twice daily, in the forenoon and afternoon. Half of this period of freedom was spent in marching round the prison yard. During the other half we congregated in a large shed where we had permission to smoke. Each smoker had his tobacco in a bag to which his name and number were attached and these bags were handed out and collected daily by the Prison Warders. We were not allowed newspapers and we were not supposed to have any news of the outside world. Nevertheless, the constant influx of prisoners kept us in touch with happenings outside. One afternoon as we sat or walked about the shed, talking in groups, a British Officer and a party of soldiers appeared. In his hand he had a list and from the list he called the names of nine or ten prisoners. As each man stepped forward he was handed an envelope and returned to his place. The envelopes were opened, read and passed round. Each contained a note in almost identical terms:

```
"To..........................

The Court have passed a sentence of death
    upon you.
The Court have made no recommendation to mercy.
You should clearly understand:—
(1) that the finding or findings and sentence
    are not valid until confirmed by the proper
    authority.
(2) that the authority having power to confirm
    the finding or findings and sentence may
    withhold confirmation of the finding or
    findings;
    or may withhold confirmation of the sentence;
```

>             or may mitigate, commute, or remit the
>             sentence;
>             or may send the finding or findings and
>             sentence back to the Court for revision.
>     If you do not clearly understand the foregoing,
>     you should request to see an officer, who will
>     fully explain the matter to you.
>
>     7th. February, 1921
>             Date._____Colonel President,
>                                          Military Court".

    The note having been read by everyone present, the prisoners looked at each other and then everybody started to laugh. Maybe it was because of the meticulous care taken by the British, as exemplified in the last sentence, our risibilities were stirred. Perhaps there might have been a slight touch of hysteria but the laughter seemed to me at that time to ring true and loud and joyful. It was the answer of the unbreakable spirit of the people to the worst their enemy can do.

    After a few weeks I was awakened one morning at 3 a.m. and paraded with a number of others on the ground floor of the prison. The place was full of British soldiers, some with rifles on which bayonets were fixed, others with drawn revolvers. The Officer in charge of the party was busy checking on a list the names of the prisoners as they paraded. We were handcuffed, marched into the yard and loaded on lorries and driven through the silent streets of Cork to the quayside. Here we went aboard a boat. We were all long-term prisoners. None of us knew our destination. I believed at that time that the end of our journey would be Dartmoor. A few hours later we landed at Spike. We recognised our whereabouts as we came out of the hold of the boat because across the water from us we saw the town of Cobh. We were quickly marched up the pathway from the pier to the prison, which was called Fort Westmoreland. The yard was full of prisoners full of curiosity about the new arrivals.

    The prison in Spike was run on an entirely different system to that of the Cork Detention Barracks. Here the prisoners were controlled by their own Officers and no prisoner accepted an order from the British that did not come to him from his own Commandant. We were swiftly seated round a table in one of the huts and breakfast was given us by our new comrades. After the prison fare of preceding weeks the breakfast we now got seemed to us to be magnificent. I can still remember how delicious the first mug of real tea was after the bitter cocoa of the Detention Barracks. The man in charge of the arrangements was big and athletic. His general air of soldierly neatness and his spotless white shirt impressed me who was sartorially in very bad shape. This was Con Conroy, who had been an Intelligence Officer with Cork No.I Brigade, who was now serving a fifteen years' sentence, who was later to be transferred to Kilkenny Prison from where he tunnelled his way to freedom, and who was to become and remain my very good friend and comrade.

There were two prison camps in Spike. The one I was in held about 300 sentenced prisoners and in the other camp there were about 2,000 internees. There was very little interference with the prisoners in our camp and, apart from general rules imposed by the British, the camp was entirely run by the prisoners themselves. The hardship of one rule imposed by the British I did not realise. I was a non-smoker and I was entirely at a loss to understand the privilege that was being conferred on me when one prisoner, with a quarter inch of cigarette impaled on a pin, offered me a pull. The rule imposed a ban on smoking or the possession of tobacco.

The prison had different effects on different men. Some prowled about like caged beasts, chafing against their captivity. Others accepted it with placidity. We had a daily visit from a medical officer. After a few days I went to see this doctor. My wounded hand was still troubling me. I was anxious to get something done about it. The doctor spoke to me most contemptuously and offered me a pill. A few days later another prisoner, Seán Hayes, who was T.D. for West Cork, asked the doctor for some treatment for his eyes which were bothering him. The doctor, with the same contempt he had shown me, advised him to rub his fasting spit in his eyes. Con Conroy was Hospital Orderly. The doctor made some remark about Hayes to Conroy and Conroy said, *"That man is an M.P."*. The doctor was taken aback and said, *"My God, is he?"*. *"Yes"*, replied Conroy, *"and so is the man who came to see you with the wounded hand"*. *"You mean that ragged chap who was here a few days ago"*, said the doctor. *"Yes"*, said Conroy. The doctor immediately sent for me and asked to see my hand. I told him that I had no further intention of availing myself of his service. *"Well"*, he said, *"when you were here a few days ago I didn't know you were an M.P."*. I informed him that there was at one time a person called Hippocrates and that if he did not feel it his duty to treat the wound of a prisoner because he was a prisoner he should not propose to treat the wound of the same prisoner because he was an M.P.

This man, although he had long service with the British Army, came originally from Youghal. We never saw him in camp again. He was replaced by a younger man who had just returned from India and who did not concern himself with the prisoners' political views but treated each man as the need arose with the utmost consideration.

My capture at least had the virtue of ending all uncertainty for me and my illness did not bear heavily on me while in the Detention Barracks. Now suddenly I collapsed and was removed to the hospital cell. Conroy was in charge here and to his administrations I believe I owe the fact of my recovery. I was a week in bed when he took me out one day and I lay in the sun at the foot of the wall surrounding the camp. As Conroy and I chatted here we saw a soldier in full kit passing back and forth along the top of the wall which I believe was four or five feet wide. The weather was exceptionally hot and this boy was weighted down with tin helmet, rifle and heavy overcoat. Conroy informed me that the soldier was undergoing punishment drill for some offence. We could see as he passed the sweat pouring off him and his tongue now and again licking his lips as if he suffered from thirst. Conroy and I spoke to each other. Then Conroy went to the hospital cell where I had a few oranges. Conroy secured these and, watching his opportunity, dropped them on top of the wall. The soldier stooped and grabbed them as he passed and bit furiously into each one. As he passed again he dropped a packet of woodbines to us. This was the greatest gift that could have fallen into the yard at Spike Island and this was the beginning of a friendship between ourselves and this particular soldier, which had an interesting outcome.

The rule against smoking did not affect me. I was a non-smoker but the hunger for tobacco seemed to overshadow every other concern in the minds of the prisoners. Somebody sent me a parcel one day in which there were a few pounds of butter. I asked the Hospital Orderly, a rather innocent young Englishman, if he would like a pound of butter. He was delighted. There was, apparently, no butter ration issued to the British troops. They got margarine. A few days later I gave him a cake which somebody sent me and I asked him if there was any possibility of him getting some cigarettes from the Internment Camp. He arrived that afternoon with linen for the hospital cell. The linen consisted of a pillow case packed full of cigarettes with a few towels laid on top. In the weather news we often hear of a deep depression over Ireland. The dark cloud that floated over Spike Island that afternoon was not caused by any weather conditions but by the smoke arising from the cigarettes in the mouths of 300 prisoners. Everybody smoked. Some, like myself, for the first time. From that [day] forward the internees supplied us from their own store and after constant raids and punishment the rule against smoking went into abeyance.

The quality of the food served was often very poor. Contractors to prisons and those with whom they do business seemed to have very little scruples. Many complaints were made among the prisoners as to the quality of the food. Conroy got in touch with his soldier friend and got him to take a letter to be posted in Cobh on his next day's leave. This note was sent to a friend of his and gave the facts in relation to the quality of food being supplied to the prisoners. This information was conveyed to the officers of the Cork No. 1 Brigade. Inside a week there was a noticeable improvement in the quality of the food that arrived.

The prisoners' only bugbear in Spike Island was a Sergeant Major of the Welsh Fusiliers who had served many years in India and who seemed to think that he could treat Irishmen in the same manner as he had treated the Indians. His language was vile and he tried to create heavy work around the Island in which to engage prisoners whom, for one reason or another, he disliked. Prisoners were not unwilling to work. Moving outside within sight of the sea, the passing boats, and the mainland, was a relief from the monotony of the prison yard but they resented being engaged in the arduous labour which it seemed to be the wish of the Sergeant Major to impose on them. His abusive language, too, was bitterly resented. Conroy and I conceived a cure. We knew his wife and mother-in-law lived in Cobh and that he paid constant visits to his home there. We wrote him a letter threatening dire penalties for his wife and mother-in-law in the event of a continuance of his attitudes towards the prisoners and signed the letter "I.R.A." and gave it to our soldier friend who posted it in Cobh. A few days later the men were paraded. The Sergeant Major, red faced and grave, gave a lecture to the assembled prisoners on the evil that would befall them if anything happened to his wife and mother-in-law. The prisoners were amazed. None of them had ever heard of the existence of these ladies and were at a loss to account for the fumings of the Sergeant Major. Conroy and I had much difficulty to keep from laughing outright. Finally, the Sergeant Major saw me smiling and picked on me. I told him that, of course, none of us knew what he was talking about. He produced the letter and I proceeded to sympathise with him. I pointed out that he had done everything he could to make life unpleasant for the prisoners of the island. The only method whereby he could safely continue his career was by completely cutting off all communications with the mainland. I said,

"Even your own soldiers talk about your unjustifiable attitude to the prisoners. It is well known on the mainland what the attitude is. As a prisoner", I said, "I cannot offer you any advice but if I could do so I would suggest that if you have any concern for your wife and mother-in-law you should immediately mend your ways on the island and treat these men as soldiers and prisoners of war. Otherwise I am afraid you are merely asking for trouble".

He fumed again and swore again but behind all his bullying and bluff the fellow was a poltroon.

From that day forward things began to get easier. News from outside was eagerly sought by the prisoners. Letters were allowed but they were subject to a strict censorship. But occasionally a newspaper found its way to us from the Internees' Camp and now and again a new prisoner was added to our ranks. My anxiety was centred in North Cork. I knew my comrades so well as to realise there would be no cessation of activity. At last news came; a successful ambush of Auxiliaries—part of the new force that had been drafted into the area almost coincident with my capture and that was encamped round a big house west of Millstreet, at the foot of Clara*. The newspaper headlines were large and the account was reassuring. The boys were still in the ring. The organisation that had first come together under arms in 1916 had developed strength; had gathered experience; had achieved a fierce fighting quality that refused to allow the initiative to be taken from it. Everywhere there was activity. The youngest Company Captain in the Brigade, Leo Skinner, was wounded in a fight near Mitchelstown. The long planned co-operation with West Limerick bore fruit in a fight with the Tans at Abbeyfeale. But as usual the biggest fish got away. Every gun, every ounce of explosive and every fighting man in North Cork and West Limerick were mobilised for a fight near Abbeyfeale round which district the British were constantly moving in large raiding parties called by them *"sweeping operations"*. Careful observation indicated the certainty of their being engaged. For a week the I.R.A. buried themselves in a selected position without seeing hair or hide of their enemy.

At noon on July 11th they came out on the road. Half an hour later the party for which they had been waiting passed through their ranks on their way to barracks. The Truce had come.

---

[* The Rathcoole Ambush, 16th June 1921, where at least 12 Auxiliaries were killed. J.L.]

# XXIII

## [The Truce]

The prison building in Spike comprised about twenty apartments, each housing from fifteen to twenty prisoners. The attached yard was about eighty yards long by thirty yards wide, rather inadequate exercise ground for over three hundred men. We marched to Mass on Sundays and in groups to the shower baths on Saturdays. The internees attended Mass at the same time as the sentenced prisoners and in spite of the vigilance of the many guards, newspapers, tobacco and cigarettes were passed by the internees to their less privileged comrades. The cease fire brought hopes of less stringent prison conditions. A few days after July 11th we were marched down to the sea and permitted to bathe. (The bathing place was securely enclosed by barbed wire). This privilege was regarded by the prisoners as a prelude to a general easement of conditions. They were the more deceived. We went back to the ordinary routine again.

My release and that of Seán Hayes came in the early days of August. We were members of the Dáil, which was to meet on August 16th.

I arrived in Cork and was taken to Mrs. Martin's where I met Seán Hegarty, Michael Leahy and Dominic Sullivan of the Brigade Staff. Seán looked at me sourly and made a few uncomplimentary remarks on my appearance. He generally greeted his friends with obloquy. It was his way of expressing his genuine welcome, which he emphasised by immediately purchasing a suit of clothes for me. Jim Gray drove me to Divisional Headquarters where Liam Lynch waited to drive me home. It seemed an age since we had met though scarcely two months had passed and we talked far into the night of plans and hopes for the future. I returned to work next day.

With the coming of the Truce, conditions for the I.R.A. were of an entirely different nature but were no less a searching test of the characters of men. Courage, determination, capacity for continuous effort, willingness to sacrifice were the necessary attributes of soldiers engaged in the type of war which they had served. There was now to be a period of relaxation, when the discipline which physical danger imposes had disappeared and when men had to face the more subtle danger of a fleeting flattery and adulation. For a few weeks there was a certain joyous abandon, this was the natural reaction from the strain and tension of the previous years, but with the real fighting men this phase passed quickly. For many dour men it never existed. They realised that nothing was settled and that the Truce might be at best a breathing space. Training Camps were re-established and the lessons learned from the experience of 1920-21 formed matter for study additional to the previous routine of such camps. Workshops and foundries were further developed and every effort was made to produce munitions of war. Trained mechanics and machines not previously obtainable were put to work and since men met more easily ideas and information were more swiftly disseminated. It is true to say that from the Truce to the Treaty those who were the backbone of the I.R.A. worked more strenuously than ever. And there was reason in this. Word was passed round from Headquarters in Dublin that the Truce might break at any moment, that the negotiations with London could not succeed and that the fight would have to be continued, would be harder and more bitter than before. Knowing that we could not beat the British militarily, we did not believe that a Truce could come; believing that there could be no diminution of the Irish demand, we could not believe in its continuance.

Nevertheless, there was a demoralisation. Round every organisation, no matter how closely compact, there is a nebulous edge composed of men who are in it but not of it. They have no clear convictions; yet, while avoiding serious issues, court a certain limelight and convince the uninitiated that they are deeply involved in all activities, cognisant of all secrets. The Truce gave these fellows an opportunity for posing as war hardened soldiers. In public houses, at dance halls, on the road in *"commandeered"* motor cars, they pushed the ordinary decent civilian aside and earned for the I.R.A. a reputation for bullying, insobriety and dishonesty that sapped public confidence. More than this, they were an evil influence on young, generous, adventurous boys who, knowing of I.R.A. achievements, sought, too, an opportunity of proving themselves. It was impossible to deal adequately with these people. All of them had been enrolled in the Volunteers. Some of them, because of the original elective method of appointment, were officers of reasonably high rank. And the reason why this evil could not be controlled was that of the men who bore the brunt of the fighting some were closely engaged in training camp, foundry or workshop and many others, now feeling that their living off the country was no longer justifiable, had gone back to their farms or to whatever occupation they could find. They were the nation's army. They had been warned of the probable need for them to take up arms again in the national defence at any moment, yet the nation made not the least effort to provide for them. People talk rubbish about the degeneration of the I.R.A. as a result of hero worship. The air of hero worship is foul and flatulent to soldiers who have been denied the substance of living.

Was the Army forgotten in the pre-occupation of the political leaders with the negotiations with England? Was this forgetfulness an error or was it of deliberate purpose? Did Sinn Féin and the politicians believe that political effort had forced the truce and that the same method could conclude the negotiations satisfactorily? At a meeting of the Dáil on the 25th January, 1921, Liam Mellows said—*"Were it not for the Volunteer Movement they could not talk of Ireland abroad, and if it were not for the Volunteers they could give up any idea of a Republic"*. No man who knew anything of the matter could have said other. Any man who spoke of the Irish Republican Movement and did not include under the terms both Sinn Féin and the Volunteers, their inter-locking activities and their co-ordinated effort, had failed to grasp its real significance, composition and purpose. The men of the I.R.A. had served the nation without pay or reward. Their duty done, they would have been content to return to their civilian occupations.

The majority of these men returned to civilian life after the civil war under far greater conditions of difficulty, and who can say with truth that any of them proved to be poor citizens?

But they were told to hold themselves in readiness for a resumption of the fighting at any moment; that the truce was tactics and the negotiations a pretence, yet not a shadow of provision was made to enable them to live. Was it any wonder that the fire of the Army died down, that the organisation's strength, in spite of its valiant efforts, waned and that when the Pro-Treaty Government set about recruiting a new Army the men who had borne the brunt of the fighting felt themselves betrayed.

While I was in prison a new arrangement had been made, or rather the evolution of a problem of control created by circumstances had been recognised—the Brigade was divided and two Brigades formed. The Eastern half of the area became that of Cork 2 Brigade, the Western half that of Cork No. 4. George Power and Paddy O'Brien were the respective Commandants. The Divisional O.C. now placed me in charge of Cork No. 4 and P. O'Brien as my deputy. The fact that changes and demotions of this sort could be made without disruption or the creation of a sense of grievance displays the entirely unselfish purpose of all the men concerned. Yet I was in great measure to be only nominally in command of the Brigade. Membership of the Dáil entailed my being in Dublin part of almost every week and the main burden of organisation and direction was carried by the Deputy Commandant. In his efforts he had, of course, the invaluable aid and counsel of Seán Nunan, of Mick Sullivan, now a Staff Captain, of a capable Adjutant, Eugene McCarthy, and an able and energetic Quartermaster, Michael O'Connell. All these men believed, as I believed, as we were led to believe, that a resumption of hostilities was inevitable; sought to train, equip and recruit men and instil into them that earnest, aggressive spirit with which they themselves were imbued.

In these early days of August we had a visit from Richard Mulcahy, Chief of Staff. I had not seen him since 1917, when he was in North Cork as a Gaelic League organiser. There was no change in his appearance other than the fact that he was better dressed. He stressed for us the need of organisation and training and the practical certainty of our being called upon again to fight. Theretofore the ambit of my activities was narrow—the Brigade and contiguous areas. My contacts were limited to men whose thoughts and efforts were directed to the same purpose. Now I was to become an actor in a minor part on a larger stage. I was to meet, for my benefit, those whose views on many matters differed to mine, to meet also those whose irreconcilable Republicanism presaged the impossibility of the avoidance of further conflict and who were later to welcome the Treaty as the fulfilment of all our aims, the guerdon worthy of all the sacrifices made.

There was a huge enthusiastic crowd in and round the Mansion House on the day the Dáil met and an atmosphere of confidence and victory. So far we had accomplished our purpose. We had over the greater part of Ireland made British Government impossible. The King's writ ran only as far as British bayonets reached. What was to be the outcome? I confess that to me the speeches and discussions were meaningless. My education was elementary, my reading mainly technical. My political experience non-existent. These were deficiencies that might and have, I hope, been in some measure remedied. The real reason for my lack of concern was my belief that the Government and Army Headquarters were determined to accept no offer for settlement that did not ensure the fulfilment of our aims; that such offer was not likely to be made was expected, and that the alternative was a continuance of the fight. To anyone with a background different to mine, to men who have grown up since 1921, my outlook and attitude may be difficult of understanding or belief. But soldiers on active service, whose lives are hourly imperilled, who see the roll of dead comrades grow longer, have no concern for the future. I had none. I was bound in honour to the wheel of my past activities, and believed that the political manoeuvres were a propagandist effort to create a background for future fighting activities. I chatted in the hallway with Liam Mellows. An expression of his emphasised my views—*"Many more of us will die before an Irish Republic is recognised"*. I overheard Arthur Griffith speaking of de Valera to a few friends. *"He seems to know by instinct what it has taken me years of thought and political experience to discover"*. Collins was there, big, handsome, in high spirits, a centre of attraction. Ah me! How short a space they were to be with us! How bitter and searing were to be the circumstances resulting from their deaths! That is another story, a sad story; a difficult story to tell for one who called both Mellows and Collins friend, who held them both in high esteem, to whom their deaths were an agony and by whom their memory is revered. It is a story of failure and disruption, of bitterness and antagonism; from it may be learned the method of eliminating these evils and avoiding them in future. It were probably best told by one who played an active if minor part in those days of Ireland's Gethsemane, by *one "who does not despair of the old land yet, her peace her glory and her liberty"*\*. It shall be my endeavour at a future date to tell that story.

SIGNED: (Seán Moylan)

WITNESSED: (C. Saurin) LT. COL.

Date: 6-5-53

BUREAU OF MILITARY HISTORY 1913-21
BURO STAIRE MILEATA 1913-21
No. W.S. 838

---

[\* Thomas Francis Meagher, *Speech From The Dock*, 1848. J.L.]

# Annex 1

## O Keen, True Poet
(A poem against the foreigners)

O keen, true poet who reads the ancient authors
Who readily settles every hard, difficult question
Tell me truly, in your opinion,
How long will the Irish be under the oppression of the foreigners?

It is not false predictions or examining ancient authors
Nor the coming of brave, swift, nimble warriors
That will scatter the foreigners out of Ireland
But the power of the Son of God and he truly suppressing them.

Gibson, Brown, Townsend, Gibbs, Tonson and Gore,
Dixon, Knowles, Boulton and Bullen and Bowen,
Wrixon, Southwell, Moulton, Miller and Dore,
Jail and imprisonment and want on those of their race that live.

Southwell, Steelman, Stephens, Stannard and Swain,
Furnell, Fleetwood, Reever, Chapman and Lane,
Every baldy, beetle-black, foreign villain of their seed
Trounced, beaten, stretched (out in death) in the conflict of bullets.

Lysaght, Leader, Clayton, Compton and Coote,
Ivers, Damer, Bateman, Bagwell and Brooks,
Ryder, Taylor, Maynard, Marrick and Moore,
May we see the boors defeated by the brave breed of Cashel.

Upton, Evans, Bevan, Basset and Blair,
Burton, Beecher, Wheeler, Farran and Phair,
Turner, Fielding, Reeves, and Waller and Deane,
Cromwell and his crowd—defeat and rout on their kind.

O Jesus, O Good God, and O Father of the Lamb,
Who sees us in shackles and bound fast
O protective King of heaven, answer my lay,
Scatter and expel this mob from our midst.

*Eoghan Ruadh Ó Súilleabháin*

(Translated by Pat Muldowney.
The original is on the facing page)

## A FILE CIRT GÉIN

A File cirt géir do léigeas na sean-ugdair
  Is tapa do réideas gac daor-ceist docamlac
Aitris-se féin go léir go baramlac ——
An fada beid Gaedil fá géar-smact allmarac?  4

Ní reacaireact bréag ná féacaint sean-ugdar
Ná taisteal na laoc mear éadtrom fras-lúctmar
Do scaipeas as Éirinn Éilge allmaraig
Act fearta Mic Dé agus é dá gceart-múcad.  8

Gibson, Brown, Townsend, Gibbs, Tonson is Gore,
Dixon, Knowles, Boulton, is Bullen is Bowen,
Wrixon, Southwell, Moulton, Miller is Dore
Glas is gobann is lom ar a maireann dá bpór.  12

Southwell, Steelman, Stephens, Stannard is Swain,
Furnell, Fleetwood, Reever, Chapman is Lane,
Gac crocaire coimteac cior-dub ceanann dá bpréim
Trascarta claoidte sinte i gcaismirt na bpléar.  16

Lysaght, Leader, Clayton, Compton is Coote,
Ivers, Damer, Bateman, Bagwell is Brooks,
Ryder, Taylor, Maynard, Marrick is Moore,
Is go bfaiceam-na traocta ag trén-tsliocht Caisil na
  búir.  20

Upton, Evans, Bevan, Bassett is Blair,
Burton, Beecher, Wheeler, Farren is Phair,
Turner, Fielding, Reeves is Waller is Deane
Cromaill 's a buidean, sin scaoilead is scaipead ar a
  dtréad.  24

A Íosa, a Dia aoibinn, is a Atair an Uain,
Do cionn sinn i gcuibreac 's i gceangal go cruaid
A Rí neime dionta, freagair mo duain ——
Scaoil agus díbir an graitin seo uainn.  28

# Annex 2

[This is a version of a popular song of the time on the capture of General Lucas]

## "Where did General Lucas go? "

### Air: "Where the Blarney Roses grow".

'Twas over in Rathcormac near the town of sweet Fermoy
They captured General Lucas and away with him did fly;
They said, "You are our prisoner, and this you've got to know
You can't do Greenwood's dirty work where the Blarney Roses grow".

*Chorus:*

Can anybody tell me where did General Lucas go?
He may be down in Mitchelstown or over in Mallow,
He's somewhere in the County Cork, but this I want to know,
Can anybody tell me where did General Lucas go?

'Twas on a Sunday morning out a-fishing he did go
And when he had his fishing done he was caught by You Know Who!
They said "You'll have to come with us, or else down you will go,
For that's the way we'll treat you where the Blarney Roses grow."

*Chorus.*

"There's good men down in Galway and the same in County Clare,
But the likes of those young Cork men you won't find anywhere;
They treated me so kindly, and if they'd only let me go
I'd promise to stop reprisals where the Blarney Roses grow."

*Chorus.*

Now to conclude and finish, I hope it won't be long
Till we see old Ireland free again and the R.I.C. men gone,
And when they free our prisoners and tell them they may go
We'll do the same for Lucas where the Blarney Roses grow.

*Chorus.*

(Anonymous)

# Annex 3

## [Seán Moylan's contributions to Debates in the Second Dáil]

### [Debate on the Treaty, 22 December 1921]

**MR. SEÁN MOYLAN:** I am not very anxious to speak on this question which is before the House. The question, to my mind, is approval or disapproval of this Treaty, and I have been here more than a week listening to speeches on various subjects, from Relativity to Revelations, and I don't think that the Irish Republican Government have got much further with the work of the Irish Republic during this week.

It has been said here that there are two sides in the House, and the Minister of Finance [Michael Collins] has referred to the Coalition. Well, I think that there are three sides now, and I'm the third. I don't belong to the Coalition. I am a Republican. I don't flatter myself that, even though I am the third side, that I am the hypotenuse; but as far as the fighting men of the South are concerned, I think that I am. I was trying to keep to what I believe was the point. I have been asked the reasons for my views on the question. My reasons are well known. But I have been asked several times outside this House to give the reason for my opinions. Well I have reasons, and the only reason why I decline to give these reasons is because I am of a peaceful disposition and I dislike argument.

It has been said here during the week that the members of the Delegation are in the dock. That is not so. These men went to London with a formidable task before them. They did the best they could for Ireland. They brought us a document signed for our approval. They recommend that document to us. That is a manly attitude and requires no justification before this House or before the country. In giving you my views—and I will try to be very brief—I will ask you to accept them as I have accepted the work of the Delegation, as the views of men who wish to do the best they can for Ireland. I start with the assumption that every member of this Dáil has sufficient intelligence to know when a Treaty is not a Treaty, when an oath is not an oath.

To my mind it can't be said with truth that Britain has entered this pact with perfect good faith. My idea is that it is the old question of England's practised politicians throwing dust in the eyes of our too trustful representatives. Our watchword has been the extermination of British power in Ireland. It was the gospel preached by the Minister of Finance. How long is the heresy—since when has he then shed sentiment? This Treaty is a sham. Take the wrapping from it and what do you find? A weapon fashioned, not to exterminate, but to consolidate British interests in Ireland. Apply one simple test. As we stand here to-day in Dublin we have driven the British garrison into the sea out of what was once the inviolable Pale. We rule the land by the force of our own laws, our own judicature, our own executive. We're independent—we are a Republic. Approve of this Treaty, and you re-establish and re-entrench the forces and traditions of the Pale behind the new frontier—the frontier of Northern Ireland. And you abandon your own people in the North in the same loathsome way, for it is—if they believe what they say, that we are a murder gang—it is a loathsome way that they have abandoned their people in the South.

The Minister of Finance has said that the departure of the British is a proof, the chief proof needed, that we have recovered our freedom, and that we have satisfied our national aspirations. He also said that the terms of peace secured this result. The Minister for Foreign Affairs [Arthur Griffith] said that the plenipotentiaries brought back the evacuation of Ireland by the British troops. That is what the ambassadors have committed themselves to. The enemy forces depart from the North Wall and Dún Laoghaire, but they disembark on the Lagan and the Foyle. By virtue of the option given to the Northern Parliament it is left open to the British Crown to keep up its army establishment, to supply with funds its supporters; and at the moment England has turned the corner economically to re-establish itself over Ireland.

There is the old Irish proverb—beware of *dranntán madra nú gáire Sasanach*—the snarling of a dog or the smile of an Englishman. Beware of the Greeks even when they come with gifts. We are having a Christmas gift of freedom. This is the time when children get dolls and wooden horses. Has it struck any of those who are going to vote for this Treaty that this gift of freedom is a wooden horse ready at any moment to vomit forth armed forces of the tyrant? We are told that the Treaty gives us immense powers internally and externally, and we are told if we reject the Treaty that we are challenging the British Empire to war—mortal combat. We have a Republic, and because we are seeking to retain it and maintain it, we are told that we are challenging the British Empire to mortal combat.

Before I give any further reason—the reason I have said I am a third party—one of the principal reasons—there are men here voting for the Treaty who have been talking about the army just as if the army was what the British called it, a murder gang. The army, as an army even, is as well entitled to its opinions as any member of An Dáil, and the scandalous way the army has been talked about here in this assembly is a thing I would not put up with anyway. I have tried to appeal to you, not from sentiment, and I have not threatened you with war. In taking up that stand in the Dáil, in appealing to common sense, I have followed my chief, Deputy Mulcahy [Dick Mulcahy, Chief of Staff of the I.RA]—I was awfully pleased with the way he handled the situation.

Some of you here have been talking about going into the Empire with heads up, and Deputy Etchingham spoke of marching into the Empire with hands up; and now what I say is this: 'Hands off the Republic', and am I to be told this is a declaration of war on England? No English statesman will take it so. It is a definition of our rights, and Lloyd George if he wants war will have to declare war. If he is giving us freedom he can do so without declaring war. All we ask of Lloyd George is to allow us to carry on.

There is just one point more. It is this. As I said we have been fighting for the extermination of the British interests in Ireland. We are told we have it. I don't believe we have it. If there is a war of extermination waged on us, that war will also exterminate British interests in Ireland; because if they want a war of extermination on us, I may not see it finished, but by God, no loyalist in North Cork will see its finish, and it is about time somebody told Lloyd George that. The terms of reference must be interpreted in their broadest, and not in their narrowest, sense. For our Republic we are offered

        an Oath of Allegiance;
        a Governor-General;

a new Pale;
an army entrenched on our flank;
independence, internal independence;
the Treaty to preserve and consolidate British interests in our midst.

*The House adjourned at 1.30 p.m., to 3.30 p.m. On resuming, the chair was taken by THE DEPUTY SPEAKER [MR. BRIAN O'HIGGINS] at 3.40.*

## [Department of Defence, 28 April 1922]

**MR. SEÁN MOYLAN:** Several Republican members have dealt, I think, sufficiently well with the national viewpoint of the report of the Minister for Defence [Dick Mulcahy]. It may seem a small thing for me to take up a personal matter on the report of the Minister for Defence. I am not as quick on the draw as I would like to be but I am a gunman. During the war, the British enemy called me the leader of a murder gang. My hands are free from murder. The Minister for Defence, in his report, yesterday called me the leader of a robber gang. I am as free from the crime of robbery as I am free from the crime of murder.

I do not rise in any spirit of hostility to the Minister for Defence. I have always thought him to be a friend of mine. When we were fighting for the Republic, he knows I served him faithfully. And I still serve the Republic faithfully. We, unfortunate plain soldiers, not being used to legal quibbles and legal methods of speaking, were easily gulled by the politicians here in the Dáil. Everywhere we were told that the Truce was a breathing space to give us a chance to organise to carry on the fight for the Republic. And we did organise. We took men away from their employments. We drilled them and trained and armed them and got them ready to fight. And they were ready to fight. Those men have been out of employment, without a smoke, ill-shod, badly clad and—we are not all Pusseyfooters—in want of a drink too. That is the fault of the men who told us that the Truce was a breathing space.

We were guaranteed payment for those men, funds for the maintenance of those men. We did not get it. I have always seized every opportunity I could get to try and get comforts for my men—to clothe them, to put shoes on them, and to feed them. In February last, I issued an order in my area, seeing that no other action was taken by the Dáil, that the dog tax in the area should be paid to me. During the war, my word went in North Cork. In spite of any terms that would be applied to me to-day, my word goes there yet. I robbed nineteen Post Offices around Kanturk. In one particular village, I put up a notice on Friday evening that I would come to the parish on Sunday to collect the dog tax. I did, and I collected £47, and the people willingly paid me. Then I called to the local Post Office and I collected licences for two dogs that had been paid by two people who were up against us during the war and who are up against us yet. That is the extent of my robbery. I am not ashamed of it and, if the necessity arises again, I will carry out the same action, because I can say that, in doing things like this, I am standing up for and defending the Republic.

# [Debate on the National Situation—
# Army Officers' Deputation, 3 May 1922]

MR. SEÁN MOYLAN: I was a member of the Conference from which this statement has come. I was the only army officer there who did not sign it. Every thinking Republican views with horror the possibility of strife between comrades. To myself, personally, the idea of fighting the men who fought with me is particularly abhorrent and I was willing to explore every avenue to peace. It was for that purpose I went to the Conference. I went there and said to the other side that one of my great failings was that I found it difficult to believe evil of anybody and they all the time said they are as good Republicans as we are. I am willing to meet any man who is a Republican, because a Republican can only work for the Republic. Rightly or wrongly, I took up the Truce as an opportunity of making preparation to carry on the fight for the Republic. I am not a politician. I am simply a soldier of the Republic. I will remain a soldier of the Republic and I will serve no other Government but a Republican Government; but I am very anxious to accept, if possible, an assurance that the Treaty can be made a step to the Republic, that the Constitution, when drafted, will prove that this assurance is correct. I and the men I represent will anxiously await that. But in the light of the knowledge I have at present, and in the highest interests of the country as I conceive them, the men who are Republicans, like myself cannot agree, much as we want peace, with the document that has been presented here. We must stand by, or act to preserve the Republic.

# Annex 4

## [A Poetic exchange with a Blueshirt—Ned Buckley of Knocknagree]

### Seán Moylan
**(Written on his leaving Kiskeam for Dublin in 1944)**
by *Ned Buckley*

*Mo Bhrón*, he now has left Kiskeam
Although it shall go down in fame
Through being coupled with his name:
Seán Moylan

His station high and duties wide
Compel him henceforth to reside
Where Liffey mingles with the tide:
Seán Moylan

When there was no law but his will
In town or hamlet, dale or hill,
His rule was just—they speak it still:
Seán Moylan

In days of hate and cruelty,
And darksome deeds and vengeance free,
Bright shone his rugged chivalry:
Seán Moylan

What follower of his would dare
To treat a wounded foe unfair
If only he himself were there
Seán Moylan

He was the terror and the bane
Of those who would insult the slain
Or filch their purse, or watch, or chain:
Seán Moylan

And British officers so grim
E'en at the cost of life or limb
Would surrender to none but him:
Seán Moylan


Seek not his help by bribes or notes
Of former aid or future votes,
He'll say: *"Put that beneath your coats"*:
Seán Moylan


But be you black or be you blue
And meet him, as a man should do,
With a fair case— he'll see you through:
Seán Moylan


Once leader of guerrilla bands
Their life and freedom in his hands
He's now our Minister for Lands:
Seán Moylan


But whether chased like hunted game
Or on the topmost rung of fame,
To rich or poor, he's still the same:
Seán Moylan


And when I heard he'd left Kiskeam
My thoughts were like a whirling stream
But soon I settled to my theme:
Seán Moylan

# Reply to Ned Buckley
## by Seán Moylan

Kind words by Tennyson are praised
But your effusion leaves me dazed
I'm pleased, of course, but still amazed,
Ned Buckley

A man should fifty years be dust
Before his friends should have the crust
To say of him that he was just,
Ned Buckley

And just men seven times a day
Fall, I pursue my stumbling way
Quite conscious of my feet of clay,
Ned Buckley

And so I pray at each dawn's light
Lord! Guide me on my way aright
Through shadowed way, o'er dizzy height,
Ned Buckley

Lord! to the lowly in their need
Let me be kind in word and deed
Consider them no lesser breed,
Ned Buckley

Let me not seek renown or fame
Contented only that my name
In some child's heart has staked a claim,
Ned Buckley

For what is fame? Blown thistledown!
Evanescent is all renown
Time's sickle sweeps away each crown,
Ned Buckley

The only memory of the Chief.
Parnell, is now the ivy leaf
Forgotten is a nation's grief,
Ned Buckley

The farmer following the plough
Does he remember Redmond? How
Are all *his* efforts honoured now,
Ned Buckley?


Through Maryboro's bars apine
A prisoner saw the stars ashine
Dim grows the memory of O'Brien,
Ned Buckley


Who by Blackwater's tortuous tide
Lifts up his head in manly pride
Remembering how Dan Allman died,
Ned Buckley?


Tara is now a verdant lawn
The Monks from Clonmacnoise are gone
The Lee flows softly by Gougane,
Ned Buckley


Then mine no mighty pillarstone
No meed of praise, no bugle blown
When I am gathered to my own,
Ned Buckley


But mayhaps when the Rosary
Is said at night in Knocknagree
Someone will then remember me,
Ned Buckley


*Envoi*

Prince, when again you wield the magic blade
That shining bifurcated strip of steel
Excalibur surpassing; When arrayed
In golden armour, casque to spurréd heel
The lists you enter, Knightly Merryman,
Spare me the Columns of *The Kerryman*

# In Knocknagree
## by Seán Moylan

In Knocknagree there is a crowd
And politicians talking loud
Who the interrupter proud?
Ned Buckley

Who is that sterling democrat
Who has some brain beneath his hat
And always has his answer pat?
Ned Buckley

Bootless for Meaney 'tis to talk
Far better he should take a walk
Who is the man who will him balk?
Ned Buckley

Moylan is trying the same old game,
His speech is halting, poor and lame,
Who'll send him flying back to Kiskeam?
Ned Buckley

For Paddy Corney 'twas no use
To try to win by sheer abuse;
Who showed him he was but a goose?
Ned Buckley

Paddy the Master's tongue a-clack
Made fierce attempts to answer back
Who put the Ace upon his Jack?
Ned Buckley

No contest now as in those days,
No word of censure or of praise,
Except we find them in your lays
Ned Buckley

Envoi

Prince, when we fought elections long ago
When hasty word was followed by swift blow
When in the fourteen pubs did our fights end
And erstwhile foe became a trusted friend
'Twas for free speech which we must still maintain
Otherwise politics is all in vain.
And let me say, just between you and me
I, too, enjoyed those days in Knocknagree.

# Annex 5

## IRISH AMERICA

[Talk to a Fianna Fail-sponsored meeting at the
Mansion House. Dublin, 12 February 1946]

G.K. Chesterton says in *What I Saw In America*, that
> "A lecturer to American audiences can hardly be in the mood of a sightseer. It is rather the audience that is sight seeing; even if it is seeing a rather melancholy sight. Some say that people come to see the lecturer rather than to hear him; in which case it seems rather a pity that he should disturb and distress their minds with a lecture."

And in these days of limited patience when, before we leave here, the Senate may be again abolished or the Atlantic Charter rewritten it behoves a lecturer to remember that there are only two classes of people, the quick and the dead. And I am reminded of a story told of the great American humorist, Mark Twain. The story is that he attended a Thanksgiving sermon in Boston and, when the preacher had been under way for ten minutes, took five-dollar bills from his pocket as his contribution to the collection. At intervals, as the preacher progressed, Twain returned a dollar bill to his pocket and when, at the end of a two-hour exhortation, the collection plate was passed round put five cents in the plate. The long continued wind of the preacher's eloquence had completely dried the well-springs of his charity. We make no collection, but there is, at least for me, a moral in the story of Mark Twain.

Speaking in Dublin of Irish America it is correct procedure to start from Ireland; an island, not merely surrounded by the sea but cut off from the world by an antagonistic news control. *"They built a paper wall around Ireland; on the inside of it they wrote what they wished the Irish people to believe, on its outside they wrote what they wished the world to believe about Ireland."* Arthur Griffith, of whose words mine are a reasonable paraphrase, pointed directly to the machine of wise and deliberate contrivance which was so effectively used to create a world misunderstanding of Ireland's position, her claim to liberty and nationhood. The effect on the Irish people and on those of our race in America has been to create in their minds an unbelieving attitude towards any statement of the actual facts of which they have not had personal experience and knowledge.

The truth of G. K. Chesterton's expression that, *"in regard to propaganda nothing fails like success"*, is nowhere so completely borne out as in the incredulous attitude of the Irish people towards self satisfied claims to virtuous conduct or intention on the part of a foreign government, or towards vilifying charges made by one nation against another. As a people we have been immunised to propaganda.

The Minister for Education has lectured here on *"The place of history in education"*, and he and those who spoke with him stressed the need of the citizen for historical knowledge, for a critical attitude towards history and for a cold acceptance of its proven facts. Anyone interested in politics, anyone striving to do his part as a good citizen must try to inform himself as fully as possible of the history of his own country. The greater his desire to serve, the greater, too, must be the area of his historical knowledge, and his interest must be further directed towards a knowledge of general history, with particular reference to the history of those countries with which the story of his own nation is interlocked; with the development of which his own race has been closely associated; by whose future his own nation's future may be affected.

The proximity of these two islands here in the northern seas, their close, long and rugged association, a literature which has been for centuries, in great measure common to both, has given to our people a reasonably clear knowledge of the development of England's history, mind and personality. But because of distance, because of the paper wall, because of outside control and influence, our knowledge of America and of the story of our race in that great country is intuitive rather than factual; emotional rather than intellectual. Nowadays with America only a few hours distance, it is wise for us to discover for ourselves a clearer knowledge of it; to discover for ourselves the unknown country that lies behind the silver screen of Hollywood; to trace through the fabric of that nation the thread of Irish character and outlook; to realise that American development stretches back, not merely to Puritan England, but is rooted in every rifted rock of our mountains and has drawn its sustenance from the fertile valleys of our every province.

I shall quote Chesterton again,

"And then I suddenly remembered that liberty was still in some sense enlightening the world; was a lamp for one sort of wanderer; a star for one sort of seafarer. To one persecuted people this land had really been an asylum. They had made it so much their home that the very colour of the country seemed to change with the infusion; as the bronze of the great Statue of Liberty took on the semblance of the Wearing of the Green."

A recent article in *Studies* on *The Ulster Scots In Colonial And Revolutionary America* says: *"The history of national stocks in America other than English has excited a good deal of filio-pietistic interest, but of scientific research and interpretation there is little to be found on this subject".* We shall not serve our purpose by making unsupported claims in regard to the participation of men of our race in the making of American history. Reputable historians will quote source documents and it is to these historians we must go. Bancroft, the American historian, says that, *"History is the high court of humanity where truth must be heard and judgment be pronounced".* But other American historians such as Henry Cabot Lodge and Madison Grant who argue that the Irish in America were an insignificant body before the great post-famine influx ignore Bancroft's dictum and try to prove, to use Abraham Lincoln's phrase, by telling the truth what they could not prove by telling the whole truth. Madison Grant in his book, *The Conquest Of A Continent,* informs us that,

"Until the late 1840's the Leinster Protestants and the Ulster Presbyterians were the only immigrants from Ireland to this country. The so-called Irish of the Revolution were Ulster Scots either from the Lowlands of Scotland or from the North of England, who came to the Colonies by way of the north of Ireland after having lived there for two or three generations. These Ulster Scots were reinforced by Protestant English, who emigrated from Leinster, and both were widely removed, both religiously and culturally, from the South Irish Catholics who did not come to this country in any numbers until the potato famine in Ireland in the 1840's drove them across the seas."

The truth of the Irish in America is that they were of insignificant numbers in 1770 in comparison with the numbers that arrived there after 1847. It is also true to say that the 2,500,000 white population of America in 1770 was insignificant in comparison with its population in 1840. And with regard to the statement that there is that lack of scientific research and interpretation which I have mentioned let us note that Michael O'Brien in his book, *George Washington's Association With The Irish,* lists a number of publications and says,

> "The labour of research is all cut and dried for the historical writer and from these sources any person seeking the truth can obtain information proving that thousands of Irish Catholics came to this country in the eighteenth century."

Michael O'Brien does not adduce his proofs from wishful thinking. He quotes his sources—the records of Wills and Deeds in all the colonies, the land grants, court records, lists of taxpayers and voters, colonial newspapers, town and country records, parish registers, the Military Rolls of the Colonial and Revolutionary Wars, the 1790 Census of the United States. Here are documents about the authenticity of which there can be no dispute and from them O'Brien has set out coldly and logically the true facts of the history of our people in the United States; facts which that offshoot of Knownothingism, *"The Scotch-Irish Society of America"* was founded in 1889 to obscure and deny.

Nordic was a pseudo-racial term very much in use in America a quarter of a century ago. It was applied to Northern Europeans, Norwegians, Danes, Swedes and Prussians, the blonde racial stocks from which, we are led to believe, were bred the Herrenvolk of England and America. It embodied the idea that Celt and Latin and Southern European were racially inferior and ignored the contribution made to civilisation by these peoples. It is interesting to recall that Matthew Arnold, lecturing to a New York audience some sixty years ago said,

> "You are fifty millions mainly sprung from German stock. It is true, I think, to say of the German stock that it has been a stock of the most moral races of men that the world has yet seen, with the soundest lawyers, the least violent passions, the fairest domestic and civil virtues."

Yet one of America's foremost writers, Herbert Agar, says in his latest book, *"In the first place the Germans have been from the beginning outside of one of the main streams of Western Civilisation, the influence of the Mediterranean World which has done so much to help the rest of us to suppress the inner barbarian."* If northern Europe was outside the main stream of western civilisation why does non-Catholic America take such pride in its Nordic forbears? The term Scotch-Irish is a hyphenated imposture. D.W. Brogan in *American Politics* says, *"All Protestant Irish are Scotch-Irish even though they bear names that would brand them, in any county in Ulster, as putative members of the Ancient Order of Hibernians"*. Finley Peter Dunne makes the correct comment on racial terms of this sort when he makes Mr. Dooley say *"I'm as pure an Anglo-Saxon as ever came out of Anglo-Saxony"*. The Dooleys are one of the most highly respected Anglo-Saxon families in Co. Roscommon.

The Scotch-Irish character was described at the first meeting of the Scotch-Irish Society thus,

"It required more than a thousand years to perfect the Scotch-Irish character. It is of a creation single from all races of mankind, and a creation not of one people, nor of one century, nor even five centuries. But a thousand years of mingled effort and sacrifice ending in the Siege of Derry were required to present to the world the perfect Scotch character."

The English writer, Mr. J.A. Spender, in his book *America Of Today* writes of the intelligence tests applied to enlisted men in the American Army in the 1914-1918 war. According to these tests devised in accordance with American standards he informs us *"that nineteen per cent of the Englishmen attested proved to be of superior intelligence while only thirteen per cent of the native Americans reached that standard"*. Truly the perfection of the Scotch-Irish character in America is surpassed only by the intellectual supremacy of the English in the United States.

The writer of this recent article in *Studies* says, *"place names scattered over Pennsylvania mark the trail of the Ulster Scots"*. If there is any virtue in place names a casual glance at the map of the United States and at a general index of American cities and towns provides the information that there are in the various States three Munsters, three Tipperarys, one Kerry, five Clares, nine Waterfords, three Limericks, two of these in the State of Pennsylvania. The name of Dublin appears in nine different States. There is a Cork in Georgia and one in Kentucky, a Wexford in Pennsylvania, a Galway in New York, a Tralee in West Virginia. There are fifteen towns named Murphy or Murphyville, and from Georgia to Wisconsin there are eighteen towns named Kelly. I find four Kildares, one Kilkenny, one Killarney, and even in far off Missouri one Kilmichael. A thorough examination would, I have no doubt, prove that there is not a county in Ireland nor a town of any note that has not given its name to some American county or city.

How has it come about that these indubitably Irish place and family names are scattered broadcast over the American Continent? I shall in my remarks mention the name of Logan, an ancient County Meath name, of Calhoun, the name of a Breffni Clan, of O'Shiel, anglicised Shields, a well known Irish family name and I shall set aside these and the greater part of the unquestionably Gaelic names listed by Father Woulfe in *Sloinnte Gael is Gall*, and shall select from the list twelve names as Irish as the rock whence they were hewn, and going to the existing records of the names of those who served in the

American Revolutionary Army I find there 682 soldiers named Kelly, 486 named Murphy, 320 Ryans, 314 McCarthys, 3 O'Connors, 279 O'Reillys, 258 O'Sullivans, 241 O'Dohertys, 240 O'Neills, 236 O'Briens, 220 Connollys, 214 Burkes, a total of 3,801. And in the record of commissioned officers are given 1,484 Irish names; 259 of these officers were born in Ireland. *"When American Independence was declared"*, said John Adams, *"one third of the people were for it ,one third against it, and one third passive and uncaring"*. And this statement of Adams is reinforced by Woodward in his new American History when he states that the American Revolutionary Army never exceeded 30,000 men; and yet twelve Irish families provided almost 4,000 of this 30,000 and, further, among the officers of this Army were fourteen hundred and eighty-four men with Irish names.

When we in Ireland think of the United States our minds envisage places like New York, Boston and Chicago, San Francisco and Philadelphia and seldom are we conscious of the fact that in 300 years men of our race have settled in every State of the Union, in districts little known to us at home, in territories whose names connote for us only the Red Indian or the lone prospector. Nine years before Owen Roe defeated the English at Benburb, John Burrage Martin, a County Galway man, possibly a relative of Humanity Dick Martin, arrived in Massachusetts. Daniel Gilpatrick, arriving in 1639, was one of the first settlers in Greenwich, Connecticut. Matthew Carey charged with treason because he wrote a pamphlet in defence of Irish Catholics escaped from Ireland to France, arrived in America in 1784 where he became a writer of note, a newspaper editor and pamphleteer. Charles Carroll of Maryland signed the Declaration of Independence. Thomas Fitzpatrick guided the first emigrant trains to California and Oregon. James Logan, scholar and scientist, arrived in Philadelphia in 1699. I quote these few examples from a list so extensive as to make one wonder at the temerity of those who deny the early arrival of men of our race on American soil.

Bryce in his *American Commonwealth* says that the Tammany Society was founded in 1789 by William Mooney as a social and charitable society. Irrespective of what may be said for or against Tammany in its later years the fact emerges that it was organised in 1789 by a man born in America of Irish parents and was proof of the early appearance of Irish people on the American scene. The prevalent view that Irishmen were responsible for the political corruption of Tammany, and that Tammany corrupted the whole body politic of America, is a view that I would like, if it were possible within the limits of this lecture, to discuss and which, I believe, I could refute. I shall, however, on this occasion devote very little time to the matter, except to say that under Aaron Burr, Tammany first got its strong political tinge. Even in 1817 it was concerned with the morals of New York City and issued an address deploring the spread of foreign games as the Gaelic Athletic Association does in our own time in Ireland. It deplored in the address the spread of the foreign game of billiards as leading to the moral downfall of the young men of the upper class in New York. Eventually the Tammany Society became wholly absorbed in politics and Samuel J. Tilden, a candidate for the presidency, made an attack on Tammany part of his election campaign. Bryce says, *"The leading part in the campaign against Tammany was played by Samuel J.*

*Tilden, Chairman of the Democratic Party of the State, afterwards Governor of the State and in 1876 candidate for the Federal Presidency against Mr. Hayes"*. For an elaboration of this statement of Bryce I go to the book on *Boss Tweed* by Denis Tilden Lynch, where he says that Tilden relied on

> "the untiring labour of Charles O'Connor. It was a masterstroke to enlist the services of the venerable O'Connor. No one could ascribe other than the highest motives to any act of the great jurisconsult. Tweed's adherents could call Foley a meddling reformer and Tilden a self-seeking politician but no one could question the motives of a greybeard, who came from honourable retirement to be of unselfish service to the people. Not alone for his legal attainments was O'Connor selected, but because of his antecedents. His father was Thomas O'Connor, a journalist friend of Thomas Addis Emmet, brother of the immortal Robert Emmet, late Attorney General of New York City, who was one of the Directorate of the United Irishmen. Because of O'Connor's high reputation and because of his antecedents he was selected as the most suitable instrument for an attack on political corruption in New York."

One of those who worked energetically for the Reform Party in New York at that time was Diarmuid O'Donovan Rossa.

In regard to the riots of 1863, Bryce says the Irish mob rose in New York City. By the Irish mob, Bryce, of course, means Tammany, and Tammany leaders were undoubtedly concerned in the stirring up of the riots. Confusing Tammany with the Irish in New York is bad history, and accusing all those associated with Tammany of being responsible for the riots shows a lack of enquiry. Lynch's book says that William D. Kennedy, the leader of Tammany, raised a regiment composed exclusively of members of the Tammany organisation, the 42nd New York Infantry, which made a distinguished record, participating in over 30 battles, losing 420 by deaths and 298 wounded and missing. Kennedy died early in the Civil War. James A. Kennedy, Chief of New York Police during the riots, and acting on his own initiative, the Governor and the Mayor of New York having scuttled for safety, set guards on the arsenals to prevent the mob from securing the arms of the State. Col. H.F. O'Brien, a Civil War veteran, home on leave in New York, in charge of 200 Policemen, smashed a mob of 2,000 at 34th Street. On the same night as Col. O'Brien proceeded home without escort he was got by the mob and kicked to death. So it does seem that if Boss Tweed and his satellites were responsible for the organisation of the riots and if a few unthinking or ignorant Irishmen participated in them, all responsible leadership was on the side of the Government and the preservation of law and order.

We must not be concerned with making jingoistic and unhistorical claims to any superhuman qualities in those of our race in America. We must be content to state the facts of history; to look for those facts where there can be no danger of bias in our favour; in American works of history where they are generally matters secondary to the main thesis of the historian. I find some such facts in *The Prairie Years*, Carl Sandberg's biography of Abraham Lincoln.

Six score and seventeen years ago Abraham Lincoln was born in a log cabin in Kentucky. In arranging this series of lectures it is altogether right and fitting that the lecture which deals, however inadequately, with a section of the American nation and its history should be given on a date so notable in that history. That great American President who carried, through the years of his office, the burden of America's bitter tragedy is for the common people of the world even more than George Washington, the symbol of America. This outstanding man who carried with him to his grave the unpretentiousness of the frontier; the edge of whose sympathy was never to be blunted by rancorous enmity; whose judgment was never warped by injustice suffered, is to us the symbol of that America which was a haven for our oppressed people; to which we looked for aid and sustenance and understanding in our dire needs and in our tragic difficulties.

Lincoln, too, in one facet of his character, might stand as a symbol of our own people. He clearly saw his objective—the preservation of the Union. Could he have seen into the future, seen, as a result of the Civil War, the betrayal by his party of many of the principles on which the American nation was founded, he would still, I believe, have regarded American Unity as the paramount issue. Our people in all the long years of their travail have never permitted themselves to be diverted from their objective, the liberty of this nation; and as nature and circumstance transferred them to the shores of the United States they carried with them that love of liberty and hatred of oppression which sustained them at Valley Forge, which carried them triumphant from the ditches at Lexington to the redoubts at Yorktown; which has made them in time of trouble a bulwark of American liberties; in time of peace a spearpoint of her progress.

Abraham Lincoln was born beneath the shadow of Muldraugh Hill in Kentucky. What nostalgic Irishman seeing the bare Kentucky Hill red in the sunset and the evening mists remembered a beloved Maoldearg in the homeland? Did he come from the valley between the Galtees and Cnocmaoldown or was he from Inishowen or the Rosses, the forbear of that boyhood friend of Lincoln's, Austin Gallaher, who when Lincoln was drowning in the flooded waters of Knob Creek hauled him to safety? What does Carl Sandberg, Lincoln's biographer, say of the environment of Lincoln's youth?

> "The name of Muldraugh Hill was a rich act in connotation, for it has whisperings of namelessly shrewd and beautiful wishes that the older and darker landscapes of Ireland breathe and there were eloquent Irish with blessings, maledictions, proverbs. The far off hills are green; It will be all the same after you're dead a hundred years."

Lincoln, with little opportunity for education, had as his first reading book *The Kentucky Preceptor*. Who was the publisher that had printed in this school-book beside the inaugural address of Thomas Jefferson, Robert Emmet's last speech, and what lessons of noble eloquence and patriotism did the young Lincoln imbibe from the impassioned oratory of the man who five years before Lincoln's birth died because he wished "*to exalt*" his country to the highest station in the world?

Lincoln, born on the frontier, was until his adult years unfamiliar with any occupation other than that of arduous and toilsome manual labour. Perhaps the very first opportunity he got of emancipating himself from drudgery was that given him by an Irishman, John Calhoun, the Surveyor of Sangamon County, a democrat and a supporter of Andrew Jackson, who interested him in mathematics and gave him employment as a surveyor. From Calhoun, too, he got his first lesson in political tolerance. Lincoln, opposed in politics to Calhoun, apparently took the view that the offer of the post entailed a change in his political opinions and accepted it only when assured that Calhoun had no desire to impose such a condition. (Let it be again noted that the Calhouns are an ancient Breffni clan.) As Lincoln's ambition moved him to further experience his next big opportunity for advancement came from another Irishman, Judge Stephen Logan (the Logans are a County Meath clan) with whom he went into partnership as a lawyer and from whom he learned law. This is the man of whom Lincoln spoke in the highest terms, expressing his ambition to be as good a lawyer as Stephen T. Logan. In his book, *Emancipator Of The Nation*, Frederick Trevor Hill says of Judge Logan: *"When he was thirty-two years of age, Ex-Judge Stephen Logan, who had signed the order for Lincoln's admission to the legal profession, offered him a partnership"*. It was a great opportunity that Logan offered to the struggling young attorney. But it had not come to Lincoln by luck. He had earned the chance. The Judge, who had retired from the bench in 1837, was unquestionably one of the leading lawyers, if not the leading lawyer, of Illinois at the date of the formation of the firm of Logan and Lincoln. He specialised in jury trials and his name appears more frequently than that of any other lawyer in the appeal records of his day. In fact, he represented one side or the other of almost every important litigation in Illinois. At this time, too, Lincoln expressed, according to Carl Sandberg, another ambition *"to be the De Witt Clinton of Illinois"* to achieve for his state what this constructive Irishman had done for New York in getting the Erie Canal built and in bringing about school improvements.

From the words of Robert Emmet, Lincoln, with his avid enquiring mind, learned the lesson of patriotism; from Calhoun he learned the lessons of political tolerance; from Stephen Logan he learned law, but he received another lesson, and again from an Irishman, James Shields, a lesson in cautious utterance. Some lady friends of Lincoln, annoyed by their failure to attract the attention of Shields, wrote insulting articles about him in a local newspaper and induced Lincoln to write another article about Shields, which was, to say the least, in very poor taste. The result of this was a challenge from Shields, accepted by Lincoln, who, as the challenged party, nominated the weapons as swords. Biographers fall into the error generally of making their subjects whales among minnows, and Carl Sandberg in recalling this affair does his best to impress on his readers the magnanimity of Lincoln. He does not, however, recount the fact of Lincoln's apology to Shields, nor does he advert to the fact that Shields was an experienced and expert fencer, nor that Lincoln had no familiarity with the use of the sword. The outcome of the averted duel was honourable to both parties, and, though differing in politics, Lincoln and Shields became fast friends. Shields afterwards had a distinguished career in the Mexican and Civil Wars. During a dark period of the Civil War, Lincoln sent for Shields to discuss the situation with the Cabinet in regard to the defence of Washington. So high was the opinion formed and retained by Lincoln of Shields! Shields is the only man in American politics who represented three different States in the American Senate.

Shields was not a professional soldier nor does he rank among the outstanding soldiers of the Civil War, and if you rank Lee, Stonewall Jackson and Joe Johnston as the three greatest generals of the South their opposite numbers in the North are Grant, Sherman and the Cavan born Phil Sheridan. Perhaps it was Sheridan's statement that discovered for Lincoln the real reason for the prolongation of the American Civil War. That famous statement which said *"the trouble with our Army is that our Generals instead of going into battle with the purpose of licking the other side are merely concerned to avoid a licking"*. Sheridan himself at no time during the Civil War showed any inferiority complex to any of his opponents.

Our experience; the books we read; the characters of the men we meet are all factors in the formation of our own characters. The great qualities which Lincoln possessed, his patriotism, his generosity, his courage, his statesmanlike caution and tolerance were built up at least in part by his association with Irishmen of the type whom I have mentioned. The part played by Irishmen in the making of American History in pioneer days, and in the Revolutionary and Civil Wars is easily discoverable by the student of American History. But even the most casual survey of the current American scene discloses to the eye the significance of Ireland's contribution to America's development, not merely in these epochal events but in every phase of thought and activity through which a nation progresses.

Interested as a politician in social conditions in America I read the Government Contracts Act which lays down the terms in regard to hours, wages and conditions for all workers employed on Government contracts. It is in essence a labour charter. I find this Act is called the Walsh-Healey Act. This significant piece of legislation carried as its title the Irish names of the men who sponsored it. Among American writers from Matthew Carey, the 18th century author, to Jack Conroy, the present day proletarian author, may be found many with Irish names and Irish origins, such as John Ross Brown, born in Ireland in 1821, U.S. Minister to China in 1868; Charles Halpin, who emigrated to U.S.A. in 1851, became a brigadier general in the United States Army and wrote humorously of the lighter side of war, and James Farrell of Chicago, whose literary work is directed towards concentrating public opinion on the evils of slumdom.

Among dramatists there is Eugene O'Neill. Among actors Irish-born John Drew, famous in his own right, more famous as the grandfather of the Barrymores. Among artists there is Augustus St. Gaudens, who did the Parnell statue, Edward McCartin and John Flanagan.

In the realm of science, W. F. Murphy is a Nobel Prize winner. Another Murphy, Mr. Justice Murphy, of the American Supreme Court, has come lately into the news. Recently, the Supreme Court of the United States refused to intervene in the trial of the Japanese General Homma, who was sentenced to be shot by an American Military Court at Manila in the Philippines; Justices Murphy and Rutledge dissented from the majority judgment. A summary of the written opinion of Justice Murphy was given in some of the English journals. He said that a trial of this kind must be conducted in the noble spirit of the Constitution, or else *"we abandon all pretence to justice, let the ages slip away and descend to the level of revengeful blood purges. Apparently, the die has been cast in favour of the latter course, but I for one shall have no part in it"*. Mr. Justice Murphy's name indicates his racial origin. It is well to remember, too, that an Irishman named Rutledge signed the American Declaration of Independence. The wise and weighty words of these two members of the highest court in America are unlikely to be without some effect on public opinion in their own country and elsewhere. And we can congratulate America and the civilised world that two of her most noted jurisconsults have in a mad world retained their sense of reason and justice and their wise conception of their high office. The son of a Fenian, Dr. John Kelly of Pittsfield, was Edison's right-hand man. His sister, Dr. Gertrude Kelly, is the only woman to whom a public monument has been erected in New York. In *Country Life,* 27/4/45, Lieut. Col. F. A. M. Webster has an article entitled, *Why Do U.S.A. Athletes Win?* He traces back American athletic supremacy to Michael Murphy, the first modern athletic coach, and to the Irish American Olympic champions, Flanagan, Walsh, Sheridan, the impetus of whose successes carried America to the forefront in athletic competitions.

In America the problem of the sharecropper tends to become one of the outstanding social and economic problems. The most effective attempt to help this unfortunate section of the American farming community was made by an organisation significantly called *"The Land League,"* whose newspaper was also significantly called *The Rebel Farmer.* The driving force of the Land League was Tom Hickey, who had been a member of the Sinn Fein organisation in this country. Its lawyer and advocate was Robert Nagle. The Commission on Industrial Relations which made such a searching inquiry into farming conditions in Texas and Oklahoma had as its chairman a man named Walsh. A social worker who had been most prominent in relief work for farm labour has been Thomas O'Mahony of the Knights of Columbus. Frederick Louis Allen in his book, *Since Yesterday,* says,

> "The leading newcomer to the ranks of Presidential intimate advisers was a young man named Tom Corcoran, an Irishman from Rhode Island. Corcoran's skill in bill drafting, his indefatigable energy, his devotion to the new deal and to a high ideal of public service endeared him to Roosevelt. There was real significance in the fact that during the campaign of 1936 Corcoran succeeded Raymond Moley as one of the chief Presidential speech drafters."

The significance of the fact to me is that when the brain trusters of Roosevelt's first term failed to make the theories, which looked perfect inside the walls of universities, effective as a solution for America's economic and political difficulties, the President had perforce to call in the services of a practical politician and the man that filled the gap naturally had to be an Irishman. In the book, *The Political Education Of Woodrow Wilson* I find the statement of the then President of the United States: that *"Martin P. Devlin had influenced him more than any other person"*. And it is a well-known fact in American Politics that Joseph Tumulty was not merely the President's secretary but his closest adviser and collaborator.

These facts are gleaned from various American publications in which the writers are not concerned with Irishmen or Irish American associations. They can be multiplied a hundred fold; and because they are unconscious testimony they compel belief much more powerfully than if they had been collated into a thesis in support of my contention, that men of our race have played no ignoble part in the development of these United States. To use a phrase from the Declaration of Independence, *"A decent respect for the opinions of mankind"*. prevents me from now making a wider survey of American conditions and of the reactions of Irishmen in the United States thereto. I shall have to draw swiftly to a conclusion.

While it is to be hoped that the spirit of adventure will never be extinguished in the hearts of Irishmen, let us hope that the need for mass emigration will never again arise for them and that, as we develop our own institutions and more and more those qualities which are the hallmark of free men, we shall be able to create conditions here that will give a full and satisfying life to the coming generations. We cannot, nor do we wish to, look forward to the recreation of an Irish enclave in America, but we may look forward to a clearer recognition of the ties of an ancient, honourable association. And we may confidently look forward to the efforts of men of Irish blood in America to maintain that association.

During the past recent years two men died in America who had given long, invaluable, unselfish service to this country. One of them was born in Ireland and became a wealthy man in America; yet the change in his financial status made no alteration in his love of Ireland or in his generous instincts. A wide and thoughtful reader, all his reading was directed towards devising methods of helping Ireland. A man of wide business and social contacts, all his intimates were those whose first concern was for Ireland. A good citizen, yet he struck no roots in America. His one desire—to mould the Irish people in America into a weapon of Irish National influence. For this there was a dire necessity. Without this we could not have reached to-day's position. The man who had all his life prepared himself unselfishly as for a special mission appeared at the psychological moment for us at the head of a great organisation in 1920. This was Joe McGarritty. Because of his association with the Rising of 1916, Joe McGarritty was the subject of much undercover antagonism in the years following 1916. Answering a vile charge made against the memory of Roger Casement, he said of himself

> "As to myself, no charge has been made against me. I therefore need no defence; but there is a contemptible inference made which might lead many well-meaning persons to believe that I was guilty of some crime. To this cowardly English propaganda I can only answer there were no Benedict Arnolds among the Irish. And while today thousands of Irishmen would prefer death to take up arms to fight for England, you will find none among them willing to sell the United States."

We cannot in the future hope that work of the type done by Joe McGarritty in America can be undertaken by Irish-born citizens of the United States.

The other man was an American removed by at least four generations from Ireland, a cultured and scholarly man who came to an understanding of Ireland's position by way of a study of Irish literature, who had the views he formed confirmed by the Rising of 1916 and later by his association with the Taoiseach. This was John T. Hughes of Boston. During all the years since 1916 down through the war period till his death he preached the cause of this country and the justification of its attitude, in places and societies where the attitude to Ireland was uncomprehending or antagonistic. His wide scholarship and compelling personality made him a powerful advocate everywhere for Ireland. He could quote the Declaration of Neutrality of 1795, the substance of Washington's Farewell Address of 1796, Wilson's Message of August, 1914, the words of Wilson in February, 1916, *"I call you to witness, my fellow country-men, that I have spent every thought and energy that has been vouchsafed me in order to keep this country out of war"*, and he would have read and quoted Wendell Wilkie's approval of Turkish neutrality—*"In spite of being young, and comparatively weak, and small, Turkey looked good to me. It looked good because it was quite clearly determined to defend its neutrality with every resource at its command"*—in support of the attitude of the Irish people and the policy of their government during the past six years.

As the years go on, as the tide of emigration ebbs, the number of foreign-born residents in the United States will continue to diminish. There will be no divided loyalties, and in the future it will be on enlightened Americans, like John T. Hughes, we must place our reliance for the cementing of an international friendship.

In matters of fundamental importance the motivating influence between nations is reciprocity. Where a nation has little to offer she has little to expect. It may be asked then what has a small nation like ours to offer in return for the friendship of the United States. If our country is to have a place in the world of tomorrow she cannot in competition with great world powers create that place for herself by material progress. While we must make full use of and develop all our material resources to their fullest extent and in the most enlightened fashion, we cannot hope to compete with great countries with whose natural manufacturing and commercial resources ours are by comparison non-existent. We cannot attain to any position of leadership except in the sphere of the intellect and spirit and our efforts for world recognition must be in that sphere.

We are often regarded as adepts at national propaganda and it is true to say that we have a certain gift for effective publicity, but I don't know if we recognise the fact that a nation's literature is its highest and most effective propaganda and is something we can no longer neglect. We have been and are still often charged with hatred of England. We hate those English evils that Dickens pilloried; we detest those English pretences that Thackeray portrayed; we abhor the pious impostures which Trollope laid bare, not because we regarded them as English, but because we recognised them as evil and because we saw their vicious results made manifest in our own country in an English-imposed poor law and judicial system, in the development of a slavish snobbery, in our knowledge of the history of tithe and rack-rent, of packed jury and corrupt judge.

But reading those masters of the literary craft did we not get an understanding, too, of the fact that there was in England a depressed and outlawed class, martyred at Tolpuddle, murdered at Peterloo, that there were in England, too, men of high courage and honourable resolve and did we not, like Bret Harte's miners, *"roam through English meadows"* and discover that there, too, lived a people like our own with whom we could live in friendly sympathy? We could understand that love of country, which the line, *"There is a corner of a foreign field that is forever England"* displays as well as that hateful imperialism embodied in the line, *"The lesser breeds without the law".* England's successful publicity has not been produced by Beaverbrook nor Northcliffe nor Colonel Repington and *The Morning Post*, but by the men who wrote out of a full heart of their belief in and affection for their own people and their own land.

I think that besides governmental representatives in America we should, as our unofficial representatives there, have some of our historians doing research work, seeking out the facts of American history and the truth of the impact of our people's character and effort on that history. We should have there some of our most prominent writers capable of giving us a clear conception of the current American scene, disabusing the American mind of the idea that Ireland is a plague-stricken country from which its people desire to flee at the first opportunity, informing them that instead it is a country like their own that loves freedom and forthrightness, generosity of service and idealism of purpose.

There is no higher manifestation of national character than national art. In this country we have some great artists. We should organise a series of art exhibitions in the great cities of the United States. We should not merely confine these exhibitions to the showing of our own works of art, but should show also the work of the great masters which are in the national possession to emphasise the fact that love of culture is no new concept in this country, but is rooted in the fibres of our being and history. The Rhodes Scholarships were created to foster an opinion educated to a recognition of England's greatness in university circles in America. Can we not create a system of exchange scholarships? There is an Anglo-American system of exchange professorships. Seldom do we hear of Irish professors in American universities. It cannot be beyond the bounds of possibility to create such a system. If Americans have any major need it is a psychological need for a historical background. The whole American race is rooted in foreign soils. Each American citizen desires to trace his background to a country with a past of honour and achievement and we have too long failed to cater for that desire in people of our race in the United States.

We know, as thoughtful Americans know, that a country is not to be judged by its resources or opportunities, but by the quality of its manhood; by the reaction of that manhood to danger; by its resource in difficulty ; its attitude to high ideals ; its energy in their defence and fulfillment. That matters of Irish concern have been matters of intense interest in America might be signified by the fact that two of the most effectively critical books on Irish Land Tenure, written in recent years, have been by two Americans, and I will quote for you the final words of a book on Ireland by an American writer, Redfern Mason:—

"Ireland is immortally rebel against everything that hinders her in the fulfillment of her destiny as a sovereign people. She will not entrust the steering of her bark to any hands but Irish hands. Weaklings may compromise; but no compromise will be binding on the conscience of the Irish people. The will of the race is against it.

"Left to her own counsels, Erin will tread the path of national development, eager to make life more beautiful, receptive of all that may profit her in the example of others, but ever clinging with a tenacious grip to the ideal of well-being which has come down to her from ancient days.

"The Gael is fighting for a fuller, a better life. The cause of Ireland is therefore the cause of humanity."

Admiring the prudence, courage and resource, energy and idealism of America, we are aware, also, that Irishmen have been endowed with these qualities in no minor measure and that history cannot deny that these qualities in Irishmen in America have borne rich fruit for America. Let us, therefore, strive to foster here and in America a mutual esteem, recognition and effort that will be our greatest and most effective contribution to world peace and progress among nations that are united by the ideals of a small nation whose lust for conquest—the conquest of evil—has always consumed her.

[*The Capuchin Annual*, 1946-7.]

# Annex 6
## INDEX OF WITNESS STATEMENTS TO BUREAU OF MILITARY HISTORY

### See Notes on page 189

|  |  |
|---|---|
| Abbey, Thomas | IRA member |
| Active Service Units Association | |
| Agnew, Arthur P. | Liverpool |
| Ahern, Jim | Cork |
| Ahern, Con | Cork |
| Ahern, Eamon | Cork |
| Ahern, John (Jack) | Kerry |
| Ahern, Patrick | Cork |
| Ahern, Robert C. | Cork |
| Aherne, Joseph | Cork |
| Aherne, Maurice | DMP |
| Air Corps | |
| Alexander, Nicholas | Dublin |
| Allan, Sean F. | Son of Fred (IRB) |
| Allen, John | Cork |
| Allen, Rev. Br. | Historian |
| Aloysius, OFM Cap., Rev. Fr. | Chaplain to 1916 Leaders |
| Anonymous GHQ IRA | Intelligence Papers |
| Archer, Liam | Dublin |
| Ashe, Miss Nora | Sister of Thomas |
| Aughney, Eilis | Cumann na mBan |
| Augustine, OFM Cap. Rev.Fr. | Friend of 1916 Leaders |
| Austin, John | Battle of Ashbourne observer |
| Aylward, Edward J. | Kilkenny |
| | |
| Babington, Seamus | Tipperary |
| Bailey, Andrew | Wexford |
| Bailey, Edward | Louth |
| Balfe, Richard | Dublin |
| Balfe, Edward | Wexford |
| Bank of Ireland | |
| Banks, Henry T. | Dublin |
| Barrett, Annie | Cork |
| Barrett, Cornelius | Millstreet, Cork |
| Barrett, James | Galway |
| Barrett, John | Cork |
| Barrett, Joseph | Clare |
| Barrett, Thomas | Galway reporter |
| Barrington, Gilbert | England (Self-Determination Lge.) |
| Barry, Lt. Col. Brendan | Defence Forces |
| Barry, Dr. Alice | Friend of IRA Leaders |
| Barry, James | Cork |
| Barry, Matthew | Meath |
| Barry, Mrs. Tom | Cork |
| Barry, Peadar | Down |
| Barry, Thomas | Cork, 1918-21 |
| Barry, Thomas | IRB 1895 |
| Barry, Thomas | 1916 |
| Barry, Tom | Cork |
| Barry, William | Cork |
| Barton, Miss Dulcibella | Sister of Robert |
| Barton, Robert C. | Treaty signatory |
| Baxter, Leo | Longford |
| Beagan, Patrick | Armagh |
| Beaslai, Piarais | GHQ |
| Beaumont, Sean | IRA IO |
| Beaumont, Mrs. Sean (nee Maureen McGavock) | |
| Begley, Florence | Cork |
| Berkeley, George F.H. | Volunteer Officer |
| Bermingham, Patrick J. | DMP |
| Berry, Patrick J. | Mountjoy Warder |
| Bevan, Seamus | Fianna |
| Bhrian, Maire Ni | Cork |
| Bloxam, Elizabeth | Cumann na mBan |
| Blythe, E. | Dail Eireann |
| Boland, Patrick | Offaly |
| Bolger, John C. | Intelligence HQ |
| Bolster, John | Cork |
| Booker, Joseph | Dublin/Scotland |
| Booth, Frank | Belfast |
| Bourke, Dr. F.S. | Dublin |
| Bourke, Ms. | Galway |
| Boyce, Mary | Dublin |
| Boylan, Peter | Meath |
| Boylan, Sean | Meath |
| Boyle, Edward | Down |
| Boyle, Philip | Donegal |
| Bracken, Peadar | Tullamore |
| Bradley, J.J. | Cork |
| Bradley, Luke | Meath |
| Brady, Bernard | Cavan |
| Brady, Christopher J. | Printer of Proclamation |
| Brady, Hugh | Leitrim |
| Brady, Lawrence | Laois |
| Brady, Liam A. | Derry |
| Brady, Mrs. Margaret (nee Sweeney) | Cumann na mBan |
| Brady, Thomas | Roscommon |
| Branniff, Daniel | IRB/Belfast |
| Bratton, Eugene | RIC Meath |
| Breen, Daniel | Tipperary |
| Breen, Sean | Wexford |

| | | | |
|---|---|---|---|
| Brehony, Tom | Sligo | Butler, Sean | Cork |
| Brennan, Edward | Laois | Byrne, Bernard C. | The Squad |
| Brennan, Frank J. | Tullamore, Offaly | Byrne, Christopher | Dublin |
| Brennan, Garrett | Kilkenny | Byrne, Christopher M. | Wicklow |
| Brennan, James | Kilkenny | Byrne, Daniel | Carlow |
| Brennan, John P. | Sligo | Byrne, Gerald (Garry) | IRB Dublin |
| Brennan, Joseph | British Officer, Dublin Castle | Byrne, James | Scotland IRB, IRA |
| | | Byrne, Joseph | The Squad |
| Brennan, Michael | E. Clare | Byrne, Sean | Dublin |
| Brennan, Patrick J. | Dublin | Byrne, Sean | Dublin |
| Brennan, Patrick | Wexford | Byrne, Tom | South Africa/Dublin |
| Brennan, Robert | Dail Eireann | Byrne, Vincent | The Squad |
| Brennan, Seamus | Offaly | | |
| Brennan, Sean | Dublin | Caffrey, John Anthony | Dublin |
| Brennan, Thomas | Waterford | Cahalane, John | Lyre, Cork |
| Brennan, Timothy | Offaly | Cahill, James | Cavan |
| Brennock, James | Cork | Cahill, Mrs. Bessie (nee Harrington) | Kerry |
| Breslin, Patrick | Donegal | | |
| Brew, Maurice | Cork | Caldwell, Patrick | Dublin |
| Briody, John P. | Longford | Callaghan, Leo | Cork |
| Broderick, Sean | Galway | Callanan, Patrick | Galway |
| Broderick-Nicholson, Mrs. Margaret (Peg) | Galway | Callender, Ignatius | Dublin |
| | | Calnan, Cornelius | Cork |
| Brosnan, Cornelius | Kerry | Cannon, Patrick J. | Mayo |
| Brouder, Sean | Limerick | Canton, Patrick | Cork |
| Brown, Walter | Fingal | Canty, Daniel | Cork |
| Browne, Charles | Cork | Carmody, Thomas | Kerry |
| Browne, Daniel | Cork | Carpenter, Walter | Irish Citizen Army |
| Browne, Peter | Kerry | Carragher, Thomas | Monaghan |
| Browne, Rev. Fr. Michael | Secretary to Archbishop of Dublin | Carrigan, James | Dublin |
| | | Carroll, Jeremiah | Cork |
| Browne, Right Rev. Mgnr. Patrick | Friend of Sean MacDermot | Carroll, John | Wexford |
| | | Carroll, Michael | Dublin |
| Broy, Eamon | Dublin I.O. | Carroll, Nicholas | Kilkenny |
| Brunswick, Sean | Dublin | Carton, Patrick | Wexford |
| Bryan, Dan | Dublin | Carty, Francis | Wexford |
| Buckley, Jerome | Cork | Carty, James M.A. | National Library |
| Buckley, Leo | Cork | Casey, Patrick J. | Down |
| Buckley, Tim | Clondrohid, Cork | Cash, Patrick | Tipperary |
| Buckley, William | Cork | Cashel, Alice M. | Galway |
| Bucknill, Sir Alfred | British Forces | Cashin, Seamus | Fianna |
| Bulfin, Eamon | Dublin | Cashman, Daniel | Cork |
| Bullaid, O.V.S. | CIE | Cashman, James | Cork |
| Burbage, Rev. Fr. T. | Sinn Fein | Cashman, Joseph | Cork |
| Burgess, Alfred | Brother of Cathal | Cassidy, Martin | Kilkenny |
| Burke, F. Dr. | see de Burca | Cassidy, Patrick | Garda/Mayo |
| Burke, Fergus | Dublin | Cathaldus, OFM, Rev. Fr. | Franciscan Historian |
| Burke, James J. | Dublin | Ceannt, Aine | Widow of Eamon |
| Burke, Lieutenant M. | see de Burca | Chambers, Martin | Clare |
| Burke, Michael J. | Cork | Chambers, Philip | Cork |
| Burke, Mrs. | Dublin | Chevasse, Mrs. Mairin | Cork |
| Burke, Patrick | Waterford | Childers, Mrs. Mary Alden | Widow of Erskine |
| Busby, James Allan | Cork | Chonnaill, Eilis Bean Ui (nee Ryan) | Cumann na mBan |
| Butler, Patrick | Cork | | |

| | | | |
|---|---|---|---|
| Christian, William | Dublin Fianna | Conroy, Major David J. | Clare/S. Africa |
| Clancy, Joseph | Clare | Conway, David | Limerick |
| Clancy, Mrs. Mary | Limerick | Conway, John (Dick) | Galway |
| Clarke, Dr. Josephine | | Conway, Michael | Limerick |
| (nee Stallard) | Cumann na mBan | Conway, Michael | Wexford |
| Clarke, James | Kerry | Conway, Seamus | Longford |
| Clarke, James | Tullamore, Offaly | Cope, Sir Alfred | Ass. Under-Sec. Ireland |
| Clarke, Kathleen | Widow of Tom | Cordial, Michael | Offaly |
| Cleary, Michael | Galway | Corkery, Dan | IRB, Cork |
| Cleary, Thomas | Waterford | Corkery, John | Cork |
| Clifford, Patrick | Cork | Corr, Elizabeth & Nell | Belfast |
| Clifford, Peter | Louth | Corr, Henry | Belfast |
| Clifford, Sean | Limerick | Corr, Sean | Tyrone |
| Coakley, Daniel | Cork, Bolomore | Corrigan, William P. | Dublin |
| Coakley, Patrick | Cork, Ballinagree | Cosgrove, William T. | Dail Eireann |
| Cody, Sean | Dublin | Cosgrove, John | Armagh |
| Coffey, Diarmuid | Sec. Nat. Volunteers | Coss, James | Cork |
| Cogan, Denis | Land Bank official | Costello, Eileen | London |
| Coghlan, Francis X. | Dublin | Costello, James | Kerry |
| Colbert, Elizabeth | Sister of Con | Costello, John D. | Galway |
| Coleman, Michael | Cork | Costello, Patrick | Limerick |
| Coleman, Patrick | Mayo | Costello, Thomas | Athlone |
| Colgan, Major Patrick | Kildare | Cotter, Charlie | Cork |
| Colley, Senator Harry | Dublin | Cotter, Dick | Cork |
| Collins, Con | Cork | Cotter, John Kieran | Not known |
| Collins, Denis | Cork | Cotter, Sean | Cork |
| Collins, TD, James | Limerick | Cotton, Alfred | Kerry |
| Collins, Maurice J. | IRB | Coughlan, James | Dublin |
| Collins, Michael | Limerick | Coughlan, Jerome | Cork |
| Collins, Mrs. Sean | Sister-in-law of Michael | Courtney, Michael | Cork |
| Collins, Patrick | Cork | Courtney, Thomas | Galway |
| Collins, Patrick | Dublin | Cowan, Capt. Peadar | Cavan |
| Collins, Richard | Cork | Cowley, Michael P. | Dublin |
| Collins, Sean | Brother of Michael | Cox, Capt. Gerry | Military History Soc. |
| Colivet, Michael | Limerick | Coy, Patrick | Galway |
| Colum, Mrs. Mary M. | Cumann na mBan | Coyle, Rev. Canon Eugene | Tyrone IRB |
| Comerford, Maire | Cumann na mBan | Craven, Thomas | Liverpool |
| Conaty, Charles | Meath | Crawley, T. | Roscommon |
| Condon, Lawrence | Cork | Crean, Diarmuid | Kerry |
| Condon, Timothy | Cork | Cremin, Michael | Dublin |
| Conlon, Martin | IRB | Cremin, Mrs, Mary A. | |
| Conlon, Mrs. Martin | Galway | (nee Sheehan) | London |
| Connaughton, Patrick | Galway | Crenegan, James | Fingal |
| Conneely, Martin | W. Connemara | Crimmins, John D. | Cork |
| Connell, Francis | Cavan | Crimmins, Timothy D. | Cork |
| Connelly, Seamus | Clare | Cronin, Cornelius | Cork |
| Connolly, Cornelius | Cork | Cronin, James | Kerry |
| Connolly, James B. | Amer. Ctte. For Relief | Cronin, Jeremiah | Limerick |
| Connolly, John T. | Fermanagh | Cronin, Jeremiah | Waterford |
| Connolly, Joseph | Belfast | Cronin, Michael J. | Cork |
| Connolly, Joseph | Offaly | Cronin, Patrick | Cork |
| Connolly, Matthew | Bro. of Sean, ICA | Cronin, Rev. Fr. J. M. | (Casement) |
| Connolly, Michael | Kilkenny | Cronin, Timothy J. | Cork |
| Connolly, Richard | IRB | | |

| | | | |
|---|---|---|---|
| Crothers, Christopher | Dublin | Davis, Francis | Longford |
| Crowe, Edmond | Tipperary | Davis, Comdt. Gerald M.B. | Westmeath |
| Crowe, Maurice | Tipperary | Davis, Matthew | Roscommon |
| Crowe, Patrick | Kerry | Davitt, Mr. Justice Cahir | Dail Courts Judge |
| Crowe, Tadgh | Tipperary | Dawson, Anthony | Donegal |
| Crowley, Denis | Cork | de Brun, Seosamh | Dublin |
| Crowley, James | Cork | de Burca, Aoife | Cumann na mBan |
| Crowley, Michael J. | Cork | de Burca, Dr. F. | Dublin IRB |
| Crowley, Patrick | Cork | de Burca, Lt. M. | Kerry |
| Crowley, TD, Tadgh | Limerick | de Lacey, Michael | Wexford |
| Crowley, William | Cork | de Roiste, Liam | Cork, see Roche |
| Culhane, Sean | Cork | de Valera, Eamon | |
| Culhane, Thomas | Cork | Deasy, Jeremiah | Bandon, Cork |
| Cullen, James | Wexford | Deasy, Liam | Cork |
| Cullinane, Charles | Cork | Deasy, Patrick J. | Cork |
| Cummins, Michael | Waterford | Deignan, Thomas | Sligo |
| Cummins, Peter | Wexford | Delaney, Col. James | Kilkenny |
| Cunningham, James W. | Glasgow | Delarue, Thomas | Cork |
| Cunningham, Mollie | Macroom | Dempsey, Michael | Civil Servant |
| Cunningham. Nora | Macroom | Dennehy, Dan | Kerry |
| Curran, Edward | Waterford | Dennehy, P.J. | Cork |
| Curran, Mrs. Lily | Dublin | Dennigan, Joseph F. | Longford |
| Curran, Michael | Waterford | Department of Defence | |
| Curran, Rt. Rev. Mon. M.J. | Irish College, Rome | Department of Education | |
| Curtin, Mortimer | Cork | Desborough, Albert | |
| Cusack, Dr. Brian A. | Dublin | George Fletcher | British Army |
| Cusack, Sean | Antrim | Desmond, Michael | Waterford |
| Czira, Mrs. Sidney | Sister of Grace | Desmond, William | Cork |
| Gifford/ Girlfriend/ widow of Joseph Mary | | Devine, Thomas | Dublin |
| Plunkett/ authoress 'John Brennan' | | Devitt, Patrick | Clare |
| | | Dillon, Mrs. Geraldine | Sister of J. M. Plunkett |
| Dalton, Charles | The Squad | Dineen, Michael | Cork |
| Dalton, Emmet | London/Dublin | Dineen, Timothy | Cork |
| Dalton, J.P. | Dublin | Dobbyn, Seamus | IRB |
| Dalton, Richard | Tipperary | Dockery, John J. | Sligo |
| Daly, Daniel | Cork | Dockery, Sean F. | Offaly |
| Daly, David | Westmeath | Doherty, Mrs. Bridget | Leitrim |
| Daly, Denis | London | Doherty, Bryan | Longford |
| Daly, Francis | Dublin | Doherty, Dominick | Derry |
| Daly, James | Kerry | Doherty, Michael | Donegal |
| Daly, James | Wexford | Doherty, Patrick | Leitrim |
| Daly, Jeremiah | Cork | Doherty, Mrs. Patrick | Cumann na mBan |
| Daly, Joseph | Clare | Doherty, P.H. | Donegal |
| Daly, Liam | London/Dublin | Dolan, Edward | Dublin |
| Daly, Madge | Limerick | Dolan, Joseph | The Squad |
| Daly, MD, Patrick G. | Liverpool | Donegan, Maurice | Cork |
| Daly, Robert | Cork/Dublin | Donneabhain, Diarmuid | Cork |
| Daly, Comdt. Seamus | IRB, Dublin | Donnellan, Thomas | Galway |
| Daly, Thomas | Cork | Donnelly, Charles | IRB/Dublin |
| Daly, Miss Una | Sec. to Mellows | Donnelly, Frank | Armagh |
| Daly, William D. | London | Donnelly, James E. | Dublin |
| Dargan, Thomas | Limerick | Donnelly, John | Dublin |
| Davern, TD, Michael | Tipperary | Donnelly, Nellie (nee Gifford) | Citizen Army |
| Davin, Jerome | Tipperary | Donnelly, Simon | Dublin |

| | | | |
|---|---|---|---|
| Donnelly, Stephen | Mayo | Dwyer, Thomas | Enniscorthy |
| Donnelly, Thomas | Monaghan | | |
| Donnchadha, Bean Domhaill Ui | | Early, Hugh | Liverpool |
| (nee Sheila Humphries) | Cumann na mBan | Egan, Patrick | Dublin |
| Donovan, Daniel | Cork | Eithne, Sister (Lawless) | Sec. to Collins |
| Donovan, Maurice | Cork | Ellis, Dr. Vincent | Doctor to IRA |
| Doody, Daniel | Limerick | Ennis, Daniel | Waterford |
| Doolan, Joseph | Dublin | Enright, Dr. James J. | Attended IRA men |
| Doorley, Michael | Carlow | Enright, Ned | Limerick |
| Dore, Eamon T. | Limerick | External Affairs, Dept. of | |
| Dore, James | Limerick | | |
| Dore, Mrs. Nora (nee Daly) | Cumann na mBan | Fahy, Mrs. Ann | Cumann na mBan |
| Dorr, James | Roscommon | Fahy, Anna | Dublin |
| Dowling, Thomas | Dublin | Fahy, Frank | Dublin |
| Downey, Kieran | Dublin | Fahy, John | Galway |
| Downey, Paddy | Private Historian | Fahy, Martin | Galway |
| Doyle, Gerald | Dublin | Fahy, Patrick | Galway |
| Doyle, James | Cork | Fahy, V. Rev. Wm. Th. | Galway |
| Doyle, James | Dublin | Fallon, Martin | Roscommon |
| Doyle, James | Dublin | Fanning, Mrs. Annie | Escape of L. Mellows |
| Doyle, V. Rev. James | Dublin | Fanning, John | Cork |
| Doyle, John | Dublin | Farrell, Christopher (Kit) | Dublin |
| Doyle, John J. | Dublin | Farrelly, Sean | Meath |
| Doyle, Michael | Kerry | Farrington, Annie | Dublin (Barry's Hotel) |
| Doyle, Patrick | Wexford | Fay, Mrs. Bridget (nee Diskin) | Dublin |
| Doyle, V. Rev. Patrick | Naas | Feehan, John | Western Division |
| Doyle, TD, Peadar S. | Dublin | Feeley, James | Roscommon |
| Doyle, Seamus | Dublin | Feeley, Michael J. | Cork |
| Doyle, Seamus | Wexford | Fehilly, Patrick | Cork |
| Doyle. Thomas | Wexford | Fennell, Eamon | Clare |
| Doyle, Thomas J. | Dublin | Finn, Martin | Dublin |
| Drohan, Frank | Tipperary | Finn, Seamus | Meath |
| Dryer, Dr. Albert T. | Australia | Finucane, Matthew | Kerry |
| Dublin Board of Assistance | | Fitzgerald, George | Dublin |
| Duffy, John | Roscommon | Fitzgerald, James | Dublin |
| Duffy, Luke | Roscommon | Fitzgerald, James | Kerry |
| Duffy, Patrick | Louth | Fitzgerald, J.E. | Dublin |
| Duffy, Thomas | Dublin | Fitzgerald, John | Cork |
| Duggan, George C. | Dublin | Fitzgerald, Maurice | Cork |
| Duggan, James | Tipperary | Fitzgerald, Maurice | Kerry |
| Duggan, James (Seamus Bawn) | Clare | Fitzgerald, Patrick P. | Kerry |
| Duggan, Peg | Cork | Fitzgerald, Phil | Tipperary |
| Duggan, Very Rev. | Secretary to | Fitzgerald, Seamus | Cork |
| Canon Thomas | Bishop of Cork | Fitzgerald, Theo | Dublin |
| Dunbar, Martin | Wexford | Fitzgibbon, Sean | Exec. of Volunteers |
| Dunlevy, Patrick | Galway | Fitzpatrick, Mrs. Maire | Wexford |
| Dunne, Eugene | Cork | Fitzpatrick, Michael | Carlow |
| Dunne, James | Kildare | Fitzpatrick, Michael | Tipperary |
| Dunphy, Patrick | Kilkenny | Fitzpatrick, Patrick | Wexford |
| Dwane, John J. | Defence Forces | Fitzpatrick, Sean | Tipperary |
| Dwyer, Denis | Cork | Fitzpatrick, Thomas | Belfast/Antrim |
| Dwyer, George J. | Dublin | Fitzsimons, Christopher | Dublin |
| Dwyer, John | Wexford | Flanagan, John | Clare |
| Dwyer, Tadgh | Tipperary | | |

| | | | | |
|---|---|---|---|---|
| Flanagan, Margaret R. (Marie Perolz) | ICA | Gibbons, Sean | | Mayo |
| Flannery, John | Connaught Rangers Mutiny | Gildea, Charles | | Sligo |
| | | Gilhooly, Joseph | | Dublin |
| | | Gilligan, Walter | | Civil Servant |
| Floinn, Padraig Ua | Tipperary | Ginnell. Mrs. Alice | | Widow of Laurence |
| Flood, James P. | Longford | Glancy, Sean | | Roscommon |
| Flood, Rev Br. John P. | Athlone | Glavin, Richard | | Kerry |
| Flood, Patrick | Court Clerk, Ballinamore | Gleeson, James | | Wexford |
| | | Gleeson, Joseph | | IRB |
| Flynn, Bartholomew | Westmeath | Gleeson, Michael | | Clare |
| Flynn, Con | Cork | Gleeson, Patrick | | Thurles |
| Flynn, Daniel | Newmarket, Cork | Glendon, Edward G. | | Tipperary |
| Flynn, Lawrence | Galway | Glynn, Patrick | | Galway |
| Flynn, Thomas | Belfast | Glynn, Ll.B, Patrick | | St. Vincent de Paul |
| Fogarty, Joseph | | Gogan, Liam S. | | Executive of Vols. |
| Fogarty, Michael (Con) | Galway | Gogarty, Mrs. V. | | Drogheda |
| Fogarty, M. Rev. Dr. Michael | Bishop of Kildare | Gogarty, Dr. Oliver St. John | | Author |
| Folan, Peter | Dublin | Gogarty, Patrick | | India Mutiny |
| Foley, James | Dublin | Golden, Bernard | | Dublin |
| Foley, Michael | Cork | Golden, Gerry | | Dublin |
| Foley, Mrs. Michael | Dublin | Golden, Thomas J. | | Cork |
| Foley, Stephen | Dublin, Cork | Good, Joseph | | London |
| Foley, William | Cork | Gough, Peter | | Dublin |
| Foran, James | Dublin | Goulden, J.R.W. | | Mayo |
| Forde, Dan | Cork | Govern, Michael | | Meath |
| Forde, Liam | Limerick | Grace, Martin | | Tipperary |
| Forde, Maurice | Cork | Grace, Michael | | Associate of Griffith |
| Forristal, William | Kilkenny | Grace, Seumas | | Dublin |
| Fox, Thomas | Belfast/Cavan | Grant, John | | Armagh |
| Fraher, James | Waterford | Gray, Comdt. Michael | | Laois |
| Frewen, Jeremiah | Tipperary | Greene, Arthur | | Louth |
| Fulham, James | Dublin | Greene, Peter | | Galway |
| Fullerton, Edward | Newry | Gribben, Hugh | | Down |
| Furlong, Joseph | Wexford | Griffith, Mrs. Maud | | Widow of Arthur |
| Furlong, Thomas | Kilkenny | Grogan, Edmond | | Tipperary |
| | | Gubbins, James A. | | Limerick |
| Galligan, Peter Paul | Wexford | Guiney, Daniel | | [Kiskeam] Cork |
| Galvin, Edward J. | National Army | | | |
| Galvin, Patrick | Cork | Hackett, Miss Florence | | Kilkenny |
| Garraghan, Comdt. Bernard | Longford | Hackett, James | | Cork |
| Garvey, John | Tyrone | Hackett, James E. | | IRB, Tyrone |
| Garvey, Laurence | Galway | Hackett, John | | Tipperary |
| Garvey, Patrick | Kerry | Hackett, Rose | | Ir. Citizen Army |
| Gaskin, Frank | Liverpool | Hales, Donal | | Cork (Bro. of Sean) |
| Gavan-Duffy, George | | Hales, Tom | | Cork (Bro. of Sean) |
| Gavan-Duffy, Louise | Dublin | Hales, William | | Cork (Bro. of Sean) |
| Gavan-Duffy, Margaret | Widow of George | Hall, David | | Meath |
| Gay, Thomas B. | Dublin | Hallahan, Thomas | | Waterford |
| Gaynar, Sean | Tipperary | Halley, Edward | | Kilkenny |
| Gayner, John | Dublin | Halpin, James | | Limerick |
| Gayner, Liam | Belfast | Halpin, Lt. Col. Th. | | Tipperary |
| Geary, Michael | Cork | Hamill, Thomas | | Louth |
| Gerrard, Capt. E. | Brit. Army Officer | Hamilton, Gerard | | Editor of *Lilliput* |

|  |  |
|---|---|
| Handley, Edward | Sgt. Brit. Army, 1916 (Acquisition of arms for ICA) |
| Hanley, William | Tipperary |
| Hanratty, John | ICA |
| Haran, John P. | Roscommon |
| Hardiman, Frank | Galway |
| Harding, Sean | Dail Eireann |
| Hargaden, Patrick J. | Leitrim |
| Harold, Owen | Cork |
| Harpur, Comdt. James | Dublin |
| Harrington, David | Cork |
| Harris, Patrick | Cork |
| Harris, TD, Tom | Kildare |
| Harte, Christopher | Dublin |
| Harte, James | Cork |
| Hartney, Michael | Limerick |
| Haskin, Robert C. (Rory) | Belfast |
| Haugh, Comdt. Liam | Clare |
| Haverty, James | Galway |
| Hawes, Joseph | Galway (participant in Mutiny of Connaught Rangers, India 1920) |
| Hayes, James | Laois/Offaly |
| Hayes, Michael M.A. | Dublin |
| Hayes, Dr. Richard | Dublin |
| Hayes, Comdt. Sean | Meath |
| Hayes, Ted | Cork |
| Healy, Cornelius | Cork |
| Healy, Daniel | Cork |
| Healy, Daniel | Kerry |
| Healy, Francis | Cork |
| Healy, Maurice | Ballinhassig, Cork |
| Healy, Michael | Galway |
| Healy, Sean | Midleton, Cork |
| Healy, Sean | Cork |
| Healy, Sean | Dublin |
| Hearne, Comdt. Patrick | Waterford |
| Hegarty, Daniel | Cork |
| Hegarty, Denis | Cork |
| Hegarty, Edward F. | Cork |
| Hegarty, Patrick | Sligo |
| Hehir, Hugh | IRB/Dublin |
| Henderson, Frank | Dublin |
| Henderson, Capt. Ruaidhri | Dublin |
| Hennessy, Jack | Cork |
| Hennessy, Michael | Limerick |
| Hennessy, Sean | Cork |
| Hennessy, Sean | Dublin |
| Hennessy, Timothy | Kilkenny |
| Henry, Michael | Mayo |
| Hensy, Comdt. M. | Tullamore |
| Herlihy, Tim | Cork |
| Heron, Mrs. Aine | Dublin |
| Heron, Archie | Dublin |
| Heron, Ina | Connolly's daughter |
| Heslin, Michael F. | Longford |
| Heuston, OP, M. Rev.Fr. John | Brother of Sean |
| Hevey, Thomas | Mayo |
| Hewitt, James | Tipperary |
| Hewson, George | FCS, Mayo |
| Hickey, James (Seumas) | Millstreet, Cork |
| Higgins, Michael | Galway |
| Higgins, Patrick J. | Cork |
| Higgins, Patrick | Cork |
| Hilliard, TD, Michael | Meath |
| Hobson, Bulmer | IRB |
| Hobson, Claire | Kilkenny |
| Hoey, P.V. | Monaghan |
| Hogan, John J. | Cork |
| Hogan, Patrick | Cork |
| Holland, Daniel | Cork |
| Holland, Robert | Dublin |
| Holland, Stephen | Cork |
| Holohan, Garry | Fianna |
| Holohan, James | Kilkenny |
| Hoolan, Liam | Tipperary |
| Horgan, Cornelius | Cork |
| Horgan, Edward | Cork |
| Horgan, John J. | Cork |
| Horgan, Maurice | Kerry |
| Hosty, John | Galway |
| Houlihan, James | Kerry |
| Houlihan, Patrick | Kerry |
| Houlihan, Timothy (Ted) | Kerry |
| Hourihane, Thomas | Cork |
| Houston, Denis | Donegal |
| Howlett, Thomas | Wexford |
| Howley, Peter | Galway |
| Howley, Thomas | Mayo |
| Hughes, Desmond N. | |
| Hughes, James F. | Dublin |
| Hughes, Mrs. Julia | Witness to arrest of Sheehy-Skeffington |
| Hunt, Comdt. Jim | Sligo |
| Hurley, George | Cork |
| Hurley, James | Cork |
| Hussey, Thomas | Galway |
| Hutchinson, H. Warren | Glasgow |
| Hyde, Dr. Douglas | |
| Hyland, Joseph | Dublin |
| Hynes, Frank | Galway & Cork |
| Hynes, James | Mullingar |
| Hynes, John | Carlow |
| Hynes, Michael | Galway |
| Hynes, Michael | Tipperary |
| Hynes, Thomas | Galway |
| Ibberson, Geoffrey | British Army |

| | |
|---|---|
| Ingoldsby, Augustine (Gus) | Cumann na nGael |
| IRA Officers' Personnel Records, 11.7.1921 | |
| Irvine, George | IRB |
| Irwin, Rev. James A.H. | USA & Canada |
| Irwin, John Joseph | Civil Servant |
| Ivers, Sean C. | Cork |
| Jackson, Valentine | IRB/Dublin |
| John Ambulance Brigade | |
| Johnson, Thomas | Labour Leader |
| Jones, John | Clare |
| Jones, John | Cork |
| Jones, Liam | Cork |
| Jordan, Stephen | Galway |
| Jordison, Ernest R. | BP Co. Ltd., Dublin |
| Joyce, Col. J.V. | Dublin |
| Kane, Padraig | Carlow |
| Kavanagh, Andrew | Wicklow |
| Kavanagh, James | Dail Eireann |
| Kavanagh, Matt J. | Wicklow |
| Kavanagh, Peter Paul | Dublin |
| Kavanagh, Seamus | Dublin |
| Kavanagh, Capt. Seamus | Dublin |
| Kavanagh, Sean | S. Kilkenny/Dublin |
| Keady, Mrs. Margaret | Dublin |
| Kealy, Martin | Kilkenny |
| Keane, Dan | Cork |
| Keane, Patrick | Tipperary |
| Keane, William | Waterford |
| Kearney, Cornelius | Limerick |
| Kearney, Hugh | Dundalk |
| Kearney, Dr. Joseph | Cork |
| Kearney, Comdt. Michael | Cork |
| Kearney, Patrick | Dublin |
| Kearney, Peter | Cork |
| Kearns, Daniel | Galway |
| Keating, James | Tipperary |
| Keating, Jeremiah | Cork |
| Keating, Mrs. Pauline | Dublin |
| Keaveney, NT, Andrew | IRB/Roscommon |
| Keegan, John J. | Dublin |
| Keegan, Patrick | Enniscorthy |
| Keely, Thomas | Galway |
| Kehoe, Michael J. | Irish Brigade, Germany, [Galway] |
| Kelleher, Cornelius | Cork |
| Kelleher, John | Cork |
| Kelleher, Capt. Matthew | Cork [Kilcorney] |
| Kelleher, Tom | Waterford |
| Kelliher, Edward J. | Dublin |
| Kelly, Daniel | Scotland/Donegal |
| Kelly, Daniel C. | Cork |
| Kelly, Edmund | Hibernian Rifles, |
| Kelly, John | Dublin |
| Kelly, Michael | Roscommon |
| Kelly, Patrick J. | Galway |
| Kelly, P.J. (Paddy) | Dublin |
| Kelly, Robert | Mayo |
| Kelly, S. | Newry |
| Kelly, Thomas | Dublin |
| Kelly, Thomas | Roscommon |
| Kelly, William J. | Tyrone |
| Kelly, Jnr., William J. | Dungannon |
| Kelly-Mor, Michael F. | Tyrone |
| Kenna, Mark | Fr. Griffin killing |
| Kennedy, Andrew | Kerry |
| Kennedy, James | Tipperary |
| Kennedy, Jeremiah | Thurles |
| Kennedy, Luke | Kerry |
| Kennedy, Miss Margaret | IRB |
| Kennedy, Patrick | Dublin |
| Kennedy, Sean | Dublin |
| Kennedy, Tadhg | Dublin |
| Kennedy-O'Byrne, Moira | Kerry |
| Kenny, James | see O'Byrne |
| Kenny, James | Dublin |
| Kenny, John | Dublin |
| Kenny, Joseph | Dublin |
| Kenny, Patrick | Dublin/Wicklow |
| Kenny, Seamus | Wexford |
| Kenny, Sean | Dublin |
| Kent, William | Cork |
| Keogh, Miss Margaret | Cork, bro. of Thomas |
| Keogh, Michael | Inghini na hEireann |
| Keogh, Sean | Cork |
| Keohane, Denis | Meath |
| Keohane, Timothy | Cork |
| Kerin, Patrick | Cork |
| Kerryman, The | Clare |
| Kerney, Leopold H. | Newspaper |
| Ketterick, Thomas | Irish Trade rep. Paris |
| Keyes, Ralph P. | Mayo |
| Keys, Stephen | Cork |
| Kidd-Davis, W. | Dublin |
| Kiely, George C. | Kilmashogue |
| Kiely, Jeremiah | Waterford |
| Kieran, Peter | Limerick |
| Kiernan, Patrick | Louth |
| Kiernan, Thomas | Longford |
| Kilbride, Bernard J. | Westmeath |
| Kilkenny, Eugene | Longford |
| Killeen, Joseph | Leitrim |
| Kilmartin, James | Wexford |
| Kilmartin, Michael | Tipperary |
| Kilroy, Gen. Michael | Clare |
| King, Frank | Western Division |
| | Fermoy RIC |

| | | | |
|---|---|---|---|
| King, John C. | W. Connemara | Looney, Patrick | Cork |
| King, Martin | ICA | Looney, Timothy (Tadhg) | Cork |
| King, Paddy | Galway | Lordan, Denis | Cork |
| King, William | Galway | Lorton, Harry | Irish Volunteers |
| Kingston, Samuel | Cork | Loughran, Eugene | Armagh |
| Kinnane, Patrick | Tipperary | Loughran, Patrick | Meath |
| Kinsella, Joseph | Dublin | Lucey, Mrs. Margaret | Cork, Cum. na mBan |
| Kinsella, Robert | Ferns | Lucey, Sean | Cork |
| Kirwan, Andrew | Waterford | Lucy, John J. | Cork |
| Kissane, Jane Miss | Dail Eireann | Luckie, Thomas | Armagh |
| Knighly, Michael | Dublin | Luddy, Patrick J. | Cork |
| Knightly, Robert | Kerry | Lynch, Diarmuid | IRB |
| | | Lynch, Eamon | Kerry |
| Laffan, Nicholas | Dublin | Lynch, Edward | Clare |
| Laithwaite, Sir Gilbert | Brit. Ambassador | Lynch, Fionan | Dublin |
| Lalor, James | IRB/Kilkenny | Lynch, TD, John (Jack) | Kerry |
| Lalor, Mrs. Molly Hyland | National Exec./ Cumann na mBan | Lynch, Michael | Fingal |
| | | Lynch, Michael F. | IRB/Cork |
| Langford, Riobard | Cork | Lynch, Patrick | Donegal |
| Langley, Liam | Dublin | Lynch, Patrick | Waterford |
| Lannin, William | Cork | Lynch, Patrick J. | Cork |
| Larkin, James TD | Son of Jim | Lynch, Sean | Cork |
| Laurence, ODC, Rev. Fr. | *re* Kevin Barry | Lynn, Dr. Kathleen | ICA |
| Lavelle, Mrs. Patricia | Dail Funds | Lynskey, William | Dublin |
| Lavin, Thomas | Roscommon | Lyons, Denis | Cork |
| Lavin, Rev. Fr. Th. J. | Re Dr. O'Dwyer, Bishop of Limerick | Lyons, George | IRB |
| | | Lyons, Patrick | Kerry |
| Lawless, Eitne Sister | Sec. to Collins | Lyons, Patrick | Mayo |
| Law Society of Ireland | | | |
| Lawless, Joseph | Fingal | McAleese, Daniel | Custom House civil servant |
| Lawless, Michael J. | Dublin | | |
| Lawson, Patrick | The Squad | McAlliffe, David | (Son Mac)Kerry |
| Leahy, Denis | Cork | McAllister, Capt. Bernard | Fingal |
| Leahy, James | Kilkenny | McAllister, Michael | Fingal |
| Leahy, James | Tipperary | McAnerney, John | Monaghan |
| Leahy, Michael | Cobh, Cork | Macardle, Dorothy | Writer |
| Leahy, Thomas | Dublin/ ICA | McArdle, T.J. | Civil Servant |
| Leavy, Sean | Roscommon | MacAuley, Charles J. | Prisoners Aid Assoc. |
| Leddy, Con | Cork | McBride, Maud Gonne | Dublin |
| Lee, Frank K. | London | McBrien, Harold | Sligo |
| Leech, Mrs. Mary | Galway | McCabe, Alec | IRB |
| Lenehan, John 'Jaco' | Kerry | McCabe, Felix | Donegal/ Ferm. |
| Lennon, Daniel | Dublin | McCabe, Kevin | IRB/Dublin |
| Lennon, Michael J. | Civil Servant | McCabe, Patrick | Mullingar |
| Lennon, Patrick | Westmeath | McCabe, Sean | National Army |
| Leonard, Joseph (Joe) | The Squad | McCabe, Wm. (Liam) | Kerry |
| Lillis, Thomas | Clare/Dublin | McCaffrey, James | Donegal |
| Linehan, William | Cork | McCann, Peadar | Cork |
| Liston, Daniel | Limerick | McCann, Peadar | Newry |
| Little, TD, Patrick J. | S. Africa & Argentine Rep. | McCann, Seamus | Derry |
| | | McCannon, Patrick | Sligo |
| Lochlainn, Cait Ni | Galway | McCartan, Patrick Dr. | IRB |
| Lonergan, Michael | Dublin | McCarthy, Cathleen Mrs. | (sister of Padraig O'Riain) |
| Looney, John (Jack) | Cork | | |

| | | | |
|---|---|---|---|
| McCarthy, Dan | Cork (Donoghmore) | McDunphy, Patrick | Dublin |
| McCarthy, Dan | Dublin | McElhaw, Jack | Armagh |
| McCarthy, Daniel | Cork (Lombardstown) | McElligott, Patrick J. | Kerry |
| McCarthy, Daniel | Cork (Rylane) | McElligott, T.J. | Sergeant RIC |
| McCarthy, James | Cork | McEllistrim, TD, Th. | Kerry |
| McCarthy, Lt.Col. John M. | Limerick | McElvogue, Arthur | Tyrone |
| McCarthy, Joseph | Wexford | MacEntee, Margaret | Wife of Sean |
| McCarthy, Justin A. | Limerick | MacEntee, Sean | Dail Eireann |
| McCarthy, Mrs. Maisie | | McGahey, John | Monaghan |
| McCarthy, Michael | Cork | McGaley, Jack | Tralee |
| McCarthy, Patrick | Cork | McGallogly, John | Glasgow/Dublin/ Manchester |
| McCarthy, Seamus | Cork | | |
| McCarthy, Tadhg | Cork | McGann, Art | Belfast |
| McCarthy, Thomas | Dublin | MacGarry, Maeve | Dublin |
| McCarthy, William | Cork | MacGarry, Milo | Dublin |
| McCarthy, William | Limerick | McGarry, Sean | IRB |
| McCarthy, William J. | Waterford | McGeehin, Mary | Cum. na mBan, London |
| MacCarvill, Mrs. Eileen | Dublin | McGill, John | Carlow |
| McCluskey, Sean | Dail official | McGinley, Bernard | Donegal |
| Mac Conaill, Prof. Mich. | Belfast | McGinley, Charles | Donegal |
| McConnell, J.J. | RIC DI | McGinley, Elizabeth | (nee Brennan) Griffith's Sec. |
| McConville, Sean | Armagh | | |
| McCorley, Roger | Antrim | McGinley, Dr. Joseph P. | Donegal |
| McCormack, Anthony | Westmeath | McGleenan, MP, Ch. | Armagh |
| McCormack, John | Clare | McGlynn, Thomas | Donegal |
| McCormack, John P. | Tuam | McGonnell, Comdt. John | Monaghan |
| McCormack, Michael | Westmeath | McGowan, Henry | Donegal |
| McCormack, Patrick | IRB | McGowan, Martin B. | Sligo |
| McCoy, John | Armagh | McGowan, Seamus | ICA |
| McCoy, Michael | Westmeath | McGowan, Tady | Sligo |
| McCrave, Thomas | Dundalk/Louth | McGrath, Edmond | Tipperary |
| McCrea, Patrick | Dublin | McGrath, Edward | Tipperary |
| McCullough, Denis | IRB | McGrath, Frank | Tipperary |
| McCullough, James | Armagh IRB | McGrath, Maurice A. | Tipperary |
| McDermott, Seamus | Cavan Town | McGrath, Miss M.A. | Tipperary |
| McDermott, Sorcha | London/Cum.na mBan | McGuill, Felim | Antrim |
| McDonagh, Francesca | Sister of Thomas | McGuill, James | Dundalk |
| McDonagh, John | Tipperary/Dublin | McGuinness, David | Belfast |
| McDonagh, Joseph | Dublin | McGuinness, Joseph | Dublin |
| McDonagh, T.S. | Clare | McGurl, Patrick | Meath |
| McDonnell, Andrew | Dublin | McHugh, Michael | Mayo |
| McDonnell, Lt.Col.Daniel | Dublin | McHugh, Patrick | Dundalk |
| McDonnell, Denis | Limerick | McInerney, Thomas | Galway |
| McDonnell, Kathleen | Wife of Volunteer organiser | McKay, Hugh | Donegal |
| | | McKenna, James | Monaghan |
| McDonnell, Col. Mich. | Dublin | McKenna, John | IRB/Monaghan |
| McDonnell, Peadar | Galway | McKenna, John | Kerry |
| McDonnell, Capt. Peter | Connemara | McKenna, Joseph H. | IRB/Monaghan |
| McDonnell, Vera | Dail Eireann | McKenna, Liam | *Irish Bulletin* |
| McDonough, Joseph | Dublin | McKenna, Patrick | IRB/Tyrone |
| McDowell, Cathal | Belfast | McKenna, Patrick | Kerry |
| McDowell, Mrs. Maeve Cavanagh | Waterford | McKenna, R.C. | National Army |
| | | McKenna, Seamus | Belfast |
| McDunphy, Michael | Director of BMH | McKeon, Capt. James | Longford/ |

| | | | |
|---|---|---|---|
| McKeon, Michael | Brother of Sean Longford | Maloney, James | Limerick |
| MacKeon, Gen. Sean | Longford | Manahan, Liam P. | Limerick |
| McLoughlin, Mary | Clan na nGael | Manning, John | Donoughmore |
| McLoughlin, Sean | Dublin | Manning, Michael | Galway |
| McLoughlin, Sean D. | Donegal | Mannion, Annie | Dublin |
| McMahon, Liam | Manchester | Mannion, Thomas | Galway |
| McMahon, Matthew | Kerry | Mannix, Patrick | DMP |
| McMahon, Michael | Clare | Mansfield, James | Waterford |
| McMahon, Lt.Gen.Peadar | Limerick | Mansfield, Michael J. | Waterford |
| McMahon, Rt. Rev. Mons. J.T. | Australia | Markey, Thomas | Fingal |
| McMahon, Seamus | Clare | Marron, Philip | Monaghan |
| McManus, S.T. | Longford | Martin, Mrs. Bridget (nee Foley) | Cork |
| McMeel, Patrick | Monoghan | Martin, Eamon | Fianna |
| McMonagle, Lt.Col.James | Donegal | Martin, Frank | Louth |
| McMullen, Liam | Ballycastle | Martin, Joseph | Meath |
| McNally, Henry | Tullamore/Offaly | Matthews, Sean | Waterford |
| McNally, Col. Thomas | Belfast | Meade, Maurice | Irish Brigade, Germany |
| McNamara, Rose | Cumann na mBan | Meade, Sean | Limerick |
| McNamara, Sean | Clare | Meagher, Th. Francis | Wexford |
| McNamara, Sean | IRB/Clare | Meagher, Thomas | Kilkenny |
| McNamara, Thomas | Clare | Meagher, William | Tipperary |
| McNamara, William | Clare | Meaney, Charles | Cork |
| McNeill*, Mrs. Agnes | (Widow of Eoin) | Meaney, Cornelius | Mushera Company, Cork |
| MacNeill, Maj. Gen. Hugo | Dublin | Mee, Jeremiah | Kerry |
| | | Meehan, Bernard | Sligo |
| McNeill, Josephine | (Widow of James) | Meehan, Patrick | Limerick |
| MacNeill, Col. Niall | Dublin | Meehan, Patrick | Meath |
| McNulty, Aileen | (Widow of Peadar) | Meldon, Thomas J. | Dublin |
| McQuaile, Charles S. | Dublin | Melinn, Joseph | Kerry |
| McQuillan, Francis | Dundalk | Mernin, Mrs. Lily | Dublin Castle |
| McShea, Thomas | Donegal | Merrigan, Paul | Tipperary |
| McSweeney, Daniel J. | Cork | Mhairtin, Brighid Bean Ui | see Martin |
| McSwiney, Eithne | Cork, sister of Terence | Mhic Giolla Padraic, Maire Bean | see Fitzgerald |
| McSwiney, Muriel | Cork, widow of Terence | | |
| McWhinney, Mrs. Linda | Cumann na mBan | Millar, Seamus | Laois |
| | | Mills, Patrick | Scotland |
| Mackey, Robert Owen FRCI DPH | Friend of Casement | Mitchell, Albert D. | re The O'Rahilly |
| | | Moane, Edward | Mayo |
| Mackin, John | Mullingar | Molloy, Brian | Galway |
| Madden, Denis F. | Waterford | Molloy, Dominick | IRA, Mayo |
| Maguire, Conor A | Dail Eireann Courts | Molloy, Mich. J. | (compositor of Proclamation) |
| Maguire, Edward | Cemeteries Ctte | | |
| Maguire, Comdt. Hugh | Cavan | Moloney, David | Limerick |
| Maguire, James | Mullingar | Moloney, James | Cork |
| Maguire, Patrick | Belfast | Moloney, John | Cork |
| Maguire, Patrick | Galway | Moloney, Kath. Barry | (sister of Kevin Barry) |
| Mahony, Patrick | Galway | Molony, Helena | Cumann na mBan |
| Mallin, Thomas | (Brother of Michael) | Monaghan, Brian | Donegal |
| Malone, Anthony | Clare | Monaghan, Denis | Donegal |
| Malone, Bridget (nee Walsh) | Galway | Monohan, Alf | IRB/Belfast |
| | | Monteith, Robert | Casement |
| Malone, Tomas ('Sean Forde') | Limerick | Mooney, Martin | Mayo |
| | | Moran, Christopher | Fingal |

| | | | |
|---|---|---|---|
| Moran, J. J. | S. Africa | Murphy, Michael | Cork |
| Moran, John | Mayo | Murphy, Michael | Kerry, valet to Vickers |
| Moran, Sean | Dublin | Murphy, Comdt. Mich. | Longford |
| Morgan, Joseph P. | Cork | Murphy, Very Rev. Canon Michael | Wexford |
| Moriarty, Maurice | Casement landing | | |
| Morkan, Eamon | Waterford | Murphy, Comdt. P.J. | Cork |
| Morkan, Phyllis | Dublin | Murphy, Very Rev. Canon Patrick | Wexford |
| Moroney, Sean | Clare | | |
| Morrissey, Gilbert | Galway | Murphy, Philip | Tipperary |
| Motherway, Michael | Cork | Murphy, Seamus | Dublin |
| Moylan, Sean | Cork | Murphy, Sean | Cork |
| Moylett, Patrick | Sinn Fein Courts | Murphy, Sean | Cork Volunteers |
| Moynihan, Manus | Kerry | Murphy, Stephen | ICA |
| Moynihan, Maurice | Official, Dail Eir. | Murphy, Thomas | Cork, Kilbarry |
| Moynihan, Thomas | Limerick | Murphy, William | S. Dublin Union |
| Moynihan, Timothy | Cork, Kiskeam | Murray, Fred | Cork |
| Mulcahy, Mary Josephine | Wife of Richard, Wexford | Murray, Capt. Henry S. | Dublin |
| | | Murray, J.J. | Armagh |
| Mulcahy, Patrick | Limerick | Murray, Joseph | Antrim |
| Mulcahy, Patrick A. Maj.Gen. | Clare | Murray, Joseph | Dublin |
| Mulcahy, Paul | Tipperary | Murray, Joseph | Garda Supt. Donegal |
| Mulcahy, Richard | C. of S. IRA, 1919-21 | | |
| | | Murray, Michael | Westmeath |
| Mulchinock, Denis | Cork | Murray, Patrick A. (Pa) | Cork |
| Mullane, Denny | Cork | Murray, Seamus | Dublin |
| Mullane, Michael | Cork | Murtagh, Dermot | Solicitor, Sec. Military History Soc. |
| Mullaly, Richard | Dublin | | |
| Mullen, Patrick J. | Dublin | | |
| Mullen, CC, Rev. Fr. E. J. | Donegal shooting | Myles, William | Tipperary |
| Mullins, William | Kerry | | |
| Mullooly, Patrick | Roscommon | Nagle, John | Tipperary |
| Mulvey, Paul J. | Leitrim | Napoli-McKenna, Mrs. Kathleen | Dail Eir. typist |
| Mulvihill, Daniel | Kerry | | |
| Mundow, Henry J. | Dun Laoghaire | National Library | Dublin |
| Murnane, Dr. John | re Monteith | Necy, Frank | Dundalk, journalist |
| Murnane, Sean | IRB Newmarket/ IRA Clare | Needham, Martin | Tipperary |
| | | Neligan, David | Agent in British police |
| Murphy, Con | Cork 24 | Neville, Edward (Ned) | Cork |
| Murphy, Denis | Cork | Neville, Frank | Cork |
| Murphy, Eileen Mrs. (nee Walsh) | Cumann na mBan | Neville, Laurence Morrough | Cork |
| Murphy, Fintan | Dublin | Nevin, Rev. Fr. Eugene | Easter 1916 |
| Murphy, Gregory | Dublin | Nevin, Michael | Sligo |
| Murphy, Lt.Col. Harry | Dublin | Newell, Martin | IRB/Galway |
| Murphy, James ('Spud') | Cork | Newell, Michael | Galway |
| Murphy, James | Cork | Newell, Th. Sweeney | Galway |
| Murphy, Jeremiah | Kanturk | Neylon, John J. (Tosser) | IRB/Clare |
| Murphy, Jeremiah | Macroom | Nicholls, Harry | Dublin |
| Murphy, John J. (Sean) | Dublin | Nohilly, Thomas | Galway |
| Murphy, John C. | Cork | Nolan, Bernard | Dublin |
| Murphy, Kevin | Cobh, Cork | Nolan, George | Dublin ASU |
| Murphy, Liam | Cork, IRB Centre | Nolan, James | Waterford |
| Murphy, Matthew | Cork, Kilmurray | Nolan, Nan | Carlow |
| Murphy, Matthew | Millstreet, Cork | Nolan, Nicholas | see O'Nuallain |

| | |
|---|---|
| Noonan, Denis | Cork |
| Noonan, Joseph | Clare |
| Noonan, Maurice | Cork |
| Norris, William | Cork |
| Nowlan, Alexander | Wexford |
| Noyk, Michael | Legal Advisor to IRA |
| Nugent, Laurence | Dublin |
| Nunan, Sean | Sec. to Dev in USA |
| | |
| O'Boyle, Manus | London/Belfast |
| O'Briain, Liam | Dublin |
| O'Brien, Mrs. Annie | Cumann na mBan |
| O'Brien, Denis | Cork (Rathduane) |
| O'Brien, Denis | Cork (Timoleague) |
| O'Brien, Denis | Cork (Ballinhassig) |
| O'Brien, Donnchadh | Wexford |
| O'Brien, Edmond | Cork |
| O'Brien, Edmond | Limerick |
| O'Brien, Elizabeth A. | Kerry |
| O'Brien, Henry, | Westmeath |
| O'Brien, John J. | Limerick |
| O'Brien, Laurence | Dublin |
| O'Brien, Liam | Compositor of Proclamation |
| O'Brien, Mary | see Ni Bhriain |
| O'Brien, Michael | Wexford |
| O'Brien, Nora Connolly | Daughter of Connolly |
| O'Brien, Comdt. Patrick | Cork |
| O'Brien, Patrick | Cork |
| O'Brien, Stephen | Cork |
| O'Brien, William | Lab. Leader/IRB |
| O'Broin, Leon | Secretary, Dept. Posts & Telegraphs |
| O'Broin, Padraig | ICA |
| O'Broin, Sean | Sec., Dept. of Agric. |
| O'Brolchain, Maire | Inghini na hEireann |
| O'Buachalla, Domhnall | Maynooth/last Governor General |
| O'Byrne, Maire Kennedy | Cum. na mBan |
| O'Byrne, SC, Joseph M. | Dublin |
| O'Byrne, Sean | Wexford |
| O'Callaghan, Mrs. Cait | Limerick |
| O'Callaghan, David | Castletownroche |
| O'Callaghan, Liam | Cork |
| O'Callaghan, Margaret (nee Peg Flanagan) | Cumann na mBan |
| O'Callaghan, Matthew | Cork |
| O'Caoimh, Padraig (Paudeen) | see O'Keeffe |
| O'Carroll, Jeremiah | Cork |
| O'Carroll, Joseph | ICA |
| O'Carroll, Liam | Dublin |
| O'Carroll, Michael | Kilkenny |
| O'Carroll, Patrick | Kildare |
| O'Carroll, Sean | Tipperary |
| O'Carroll, Thomas | Tipperary |
| O'Cathain, Padraig | see Kane |
| O'Ceallaigh, Padraig | see O'Kelly |
| O'Ciardubhain, Micheal | Wexford |
| O'Connell, Charles | Cork |
| O'Connell, Christopher | Cork, Eyeries |
| O'Connell, James | Cork |
| O'Connell, Jeremiah | Kerry |
| O'Connell, John (Jack) | Cork |
| O'Connell, John P. | Cork |
| O'Connell, Michael | Cork |
| O'Connell, Mortimer | Cork |
| O'Connell, Patrick | Limerick |
| O'Connell, Peter | Meath |
| O'Connell, Richard | Limerick |
| O'Connell, Sean | Cork |
| O'Conner Cox, Eamon | Irish Vols. 1915 |
| O'Connor, Thomas D. (Tommy) | USA |
| O'Connor, Eamon | IRB/Liverpool |
| O'Connor, Eamon | Kerry |
| O'Connor, Mrs. Fergus | Widow of Fergus |
| O'Connor, Frank | Westmeath |
| O'Connor, James J. | Wexford RIC |
| O'Connor, James | Dublin |
| O'Connor, John | Kerry |
| O'Connor, John (Blimey) | Kimmage |
| O'Connor, Joseph | Dublin |
| O'Connor, Mrs. Batt | Friend of Collins |
| O'Connor, Norbert | Brother of Rory |
| O'Connor, Padraig | Dublin |
| O'Connor, Patrick (Ninepence) | Dublin |
| O'Connor, Patrick | Kerry |
| O'Connor, Seamus | Founder of Vols. |
| O'Connor, Thomas | Kerry |
| O'Cuill, Michael | Cork |
| O'Cuill, Sean | Cork |
| O'Daly, Very Rev. Canon James | Tyrone IRB |
| O'Daly, Patrick | Dublin |
| O'Dea, Louis | Solicitor, Galway |
| O'Dea, Michael | Clare |
| O'Doherty, Felix | Cork |
| O'Doherty, Kitty | Kilkenny/Dublin |
| O'Doherty, Liam | Dublin |
| O'Donel, Miss Geraldine | Dublin |
| O'Donnell, Art | Clare |
| O'Donnell, Mrs. Bernard (nee Eitne Coyle) | Cumann na mBan |
| O'Donnell, Frank | Kerry |
| O'Donnell, Michael | Cork |

| | |
|---|---|
| O'Donnell, Patrick ('Kit') | Donegal |
| O'Donnell, Patrick | Galway |
| O'Donnell, Thomas J. | National Army |
| O'Donnell, William | Tipperary |
| O'Donoghue, Charles | Cork |
| O'Donoghue, Daithi | Dail Eireann |
| O'Donoghue, Florence | Cork |
| O'Donoghue, Humphrey | Cork, Cullen |
| O'Donoghue, Michael V. | Cork |
| O'Donoghue, Mrs. Sheila (nee Humphries) | Cumann na mBan |
| O'Donoghue, Patrick | Manchester |
| O'Donoghue, Paud | Cork |
| O'Donoghue, Very Rev. Thomas | Parish Priest, ICA/ Fianna |
| O'Donohue, Andrew | Clare |
| O'Donovan, Con | IRB/Dublin |
| O'Donovan, Daniel | Cork |
| O'Donovan, James L. | GHQ |
| O'Donovan, John | Journalist |
| O'Donovan, Mrs. Julia | Friend of Collins |
| O'Donovan, Kathleen | Sister of Harry Boland |
| O'Donovan, Thomas | Cork |
| O'Driscoll, Daniel | Cork |
| O'Driscoll, Denis J. | Tipperary |
| O'Driscoll, John | Cork |
| O'Driscoll, Michael | Cork |
| O'Driscoll, Patrick | Cork |
| O'Driscoll, Sean | Cork |
| O'Droighneain, Mich. | Galway |
| O'Dubhtaigh, Proinsias | see O'Duffy |
| O'Duffy, Francis | Enniskillen |
| O'Duffy, Liam | Donegal |
| O'Duffy, Sean M. | Dublin |
| O'Dwyer, Eamon | Tipperary |
| O'Dwyer, Liam | Cork |
| O'Dwyer, Nicholas | Dail Eireann |
| O'Dwyer, Patrick H | Tipperary |
| O'Dwyer*, Seamus | Cumann na nGael |
| O'Farrell, Seamus | Cum. na nGael, 1907 |
| O'Flaherty, Liam | Dublin (1916) |
| O'Flanagan, George | Dublin |
| O'Flanagan, Michael | Dublin |
| O'Flynn, James | Tipperary |
| O'Flynn, William | Tipperary |
| O'Glasain, Padraig | see Gleeson |
| O'Gorman, John | Donegal |
| O'Grady, Brian | Kerry |
| O'Grady, Charles J. | Fianna |
| O'Grady, Tom | IRB/Sligo |
| O'Hagan, Henry | Scotland |
| O'Halloran, Alphonsus J. | Limerick |
| O'Hannigan, Donal | Dublin / Dundalk |
| O'Hannigan, Donnchadh | Limerick |
| O'Hegarty, Patrick S | IRB London |
| O'Hegarty, Sean | Cork |
| O'Hegarty, Sean | Cork (Bro. of P.S.) |
| O'Higgins, Joseph | Louth |
| O'Higgins, Col. Th. | Officer, Def. Forces |
| O'Hora, William J. | Mayo |
| O'Keeffe, Christopher Joseph William | Cork |
| O'Keeffe, Daniel | Tipperary/Cork |
| O'Keeffe, Denis | Rathmore, Cork |
| O'Keeffe, Eugene | Cork, Enniskeane |
| O'Keeffe, Henry | Waterford |
| O'Keeffe, John (Jack) | Cork |
| O'Keeffe, John | Tipperary |
| O'Keeffe, TD, Patrick (Paudeen) | Sinn Fein General Secretary |
| O'Keeffe, Sean | Clare |
| O'Keeffe, Sean | Dublin |
| O'Keeffe, Tim | Cork |
| O'Keeffe, William T. | Mayo |
| O'Kelly, Fergus | Dublin |
| O'Kelly, J.J. (Sceilg) | Ed., Cath. Bulletin |
| O'Kelly, Mrs. K. (nee Murphy) | Belfast |
| O'Kelly, Prof. M.J. | Cork |
| O'Kelly, Mairead | Dublin |
| O'Kelly, Lt. Col. Mich. | Dublin |
| O'Kelly, Michael | Kildare |
| O'Kelly, Padraig | Dublin |
| O'Kelly, Dr. Seamus | Associate of Eoin MacNeill |
| O'Kelly, Sean | Limerick |
| O'Kelly, Sean T. | President |
| O'Leary, Diarmuid | Cork |
| O'Leary, Edward | Tipperary |
| O'Leary, Jeremiah J. (Diarmuid) | Director of Publicity, Sinn Fein |
| O'Leary, Liam | Wexford |
| O'Leary, Michael | Fianna |
| O'Leary, Michael | Liverpool |
| O'Leary, Mortimer | Pilot of German Arms Ship |
| O'Leary, Tadhg | Cork |
| O'Leary, Timothy | Kerry |
| O'Lochlainn, Colm | Dublin |
| O'Loughlin, Peter | Clare |
| O'Mahony, Mrs. Anna Hurley | Cork |
| O'Mahony, Con | Cork |
| O'Mahony, BL,KM, Eoin | Cork |
| O'Mahony, Henry | Cork |
| O'Mahony, James | Cork |
| O'Mahony, John | Cork |

| | | | |
|---|---|---|---|
| O'Mahony, Michael S. | Son in law of Peadar Bracken | O'Sullivan, Denis J. | Kerry |
| O'Mahony, Patrick C. | IRA, Dungarvan IRB | O'Sullivan, Dermot | Dublin |
| O'Mahony, Seamus | Cork | O'Sullivan, Diarmuid | IRB |
| O'Mahony, Thomas | Galway | O'Sullivan, Edward | Cork |
| O'Malley, Ernie | Writer | O'Sullivan, Edward | Kerry |
| O'Malley, John | Arms purchaser | O'Sullivan, Gearoid | Son of Adjutant General for IRA |
| O'Mara, Henry | Clare | O'Sullivan, James | Cork |
| O'Mara, Jack | Waterford | O'Sullivan, John | Cork |
| O'Mara, Mrs. M.A. | Widow of James | O'Sullivan, Michael J. | Killarney |
| O'Mara, Peadar | Dublin | O'Sullivan, Michael | Cork |
| O'Mara, Timothy | Killarney | O'Sullivan, Michael | Cork |
| O'Meara, Seumas | Athlone | O'Sullivan, Michael | Cork |
| O'Muineachain, Seumas | Son of doctor | O'Sullivan, Miss Mary | Secretary to Lord Mayor of Dublin |
| O'Mullane, Mrs Bridget | Cumann na mBan | | |
| O'Neill, Edward | Dublin | O'Sullivan, Patrick | Ballyvourney, Cork |
| O'Neill, Patrick | Kerry | O'Sullivan, Patrick | Brother of Joseph O'Sullivan shot for killing Wilson |
| O'Neill, Seamus | Tipperary | | |
| O'Neill, Sean | Dublin | | |
| O'Neill, Sean | Galway | O'Sullivan, Patrick | Skibbereen, Cork |
| O'Neill, William | Cork | O'Sullivan, Dr. Patrick | Cork |
| O'Nuallain, Nioclas | Dail Eireann | O'Sullivan, Seumas S. | Dublin |
| O'Rahilly, Miss Aine | Sister of The O'Rahilly | O'Sullivan, Col. Sean | ADC to 1948 President of Ireland |
| O'Regan, Con | Cork | | |
| O'Regan, Martin | Loughrea | O'Sullivan, Sean | Manchester/ Dublin IRB |
| O'Regan, Michael | Cork | | |
| O'Reilly, Miss Bridie | H Q | O'Sullivan, Tadhg | Cork |
| O'Reilly, Eily O'Hanrahan | Cumann na mBan | O'Sullivan, Ted | Cork |
| | | O'Sullivan, Timothy | Cork |
| O'Reilly, John J. | Wexford | O'Toole, James | Wexford |
| O'Reilly, Michael W. | Dublin | Oman, William | ICA |
| O'Reilly, Mrs. D. | *Connaught Tribune* | Ormond, James | Cork |
| O'Reilly, Patrick | Meath | Ormond, Patrick | West Waterford |
| O'Reilly, Samuel P. | New York | Osborne, Harry | Belfast |
| O'Reilly, Stephen J. | Dublin | | |
| O'Riain, Padraig | Fianna Eireann | Paul, Patrick J. | Waterford |
| O'Riordan, John | Kerry | Passes, British Military | Various |
| O'Riordan, Liam S. | Mayo | Pelican, Thomas | Kerry |
| O'Rourke, Joseph | IRB | Peppard, Thomas | Fingal |
| O'Rourke, Sean | Down | Perolz, Marie Mrs. (nee Flanagan) | ICA |
| O'Shaughnessy, Daniel F. | Limerick | | |
| O'Shea, James | ICA | Phibbs, Harry C. | Celtic Literary Soc. |
| O'Shea, Jeremiah | Cork | Phillips, Francis | Sinn Fein, Cashel |
| O'Shea, Joseph | Cork | Pierce, Michael | Kerry |
| O'Shea*, NT, Patrick | Kerry | Pinkman, Charles | Leitrim |
| O'Shea, Sean | Bought arms in Italy | Plunkett, Grace (nee Gifford) | Widow of J.M. |
| O'Shea, Sean | Dublin | Plunkett, John (Jack) | Brother of J.M. |
| O'Shea, Timothy | Limerick | Portley, Morgan | Limerick |
| O'Shiel, Kevin | Land Courts | Pounch, Seamus | Dublin |
| O'Sullivan, Christopher | Cork | Powell, William | Cork |
| O'Sullivan, Cornelius | Bandon | Power, Edmond | Waterford |
| O'Sullivan, D. | Brit. Civil Servant | Power, George | Cork |
| O'Sullivan, Daniel P. | Kerry | Power, James | Waterford |

| | | | |
|---|---|---|---|
| Power, Michael | Waterford | Roche, Thomas | Cork |
| Power, Patrick J. | Wexford | Roche, William | Cork |
| Prendergast, James | Waterford | Rock, Michael | Fingal |
| Prendergast, Sean | Dublin | Rogan, James | Armagh |
| Prendiville, Denis | Kerry | Rogan, Patrick L. | Wicklow |
| Price, Eamon (Bob) | Dublin | Ronan, Patrick | Wexford |
| Price, Sean | IRB/Dublin | Ronayne, John | Cork |
| Pugh, Thomas | Dublin | Rooney, Mrs. Catherine | Cumann na mBan |
| Purcell, Robert | ASU/Dublin | Rosney, Joseph | Kilcoole gun running |
| | | Rowan, James | Dublin |
| Quigley, James | Roscommon | Ruane, Sen. Sean T. | Mayo |
| Quilty, John J. | Limerick | Russell, Michael | Clare |
| Quinlan, Dr. Catherine | Associate of Sean McDermot | Russell, Richard | Cork |
| | | Ryan, Aine | Offaly (Cum. na mBan) |
| Quinn, James | Clare | Ryan, Daniel E. | Dublin |
| Quinn, John | Clare | Ryan, Daniel | Galway |
| Quinn, Patrick | Meath | Ryan, Desmond | Dublin |
| | | Ryan, Edward John | Tipperary |
| Rabbitte, Roger | Galway | Ryan, James | Clonmel |
| Ramsbottom, James | Laois | Ryan, James | Cork/Clonmel |
| Ramsbottom, Patrick J. | Laois | Ryan, Col. Jerry | Tipperary |
| Rankin, Patrick | Derry | Ryan, John ("Bishop") | Clare |
| Reader, Seamus | Scot. Brigade/IRA | Ryan, John C. | Cork |
| Reardon, William | Millstreet, Cork | Ryan, Mairin | Kerry |
| Redmond, Laurence | IRB/Enniscorthy | Ryan, Martin | Galway |
| Regan, Declan | Waterford | Ryan, Michael F. | Waterford |
| Regan, William C. | Cork | Ryan, Michael J. | Galway |
| Reidy, Amos | Limerick | Ryan, Michael Joseph | Longford |
| Reidy, Patrick | Clare | Ryan, Miss Molly | Dail Eireann |
| Reidy, Thomas | Cork | Ryan, Mrs. Bridget | Tipp. (Cum. na mBan) |
| Reidy, Thomas | Galway | Ryan, Mrs. Brigid (nee Brophy) | Carlow Cumann na mBan |
| Reilly, Bernard | (Casement) Kerry RIC | | |
| Reilly, James | Westmeath | Ryan, Patrick | Tipperary |
| Reilly, Michael | Galway | Ryan, Patrick | Waterford |
| Reynolds, Joseph | Fianna | Ryan, Thomas | Carlow |
| Reynolds, Mich. Francis | Longford | Ryan, Thomas | Tipperary |
| Reynolds, Molly | Dublin | | |
| Reynolds, Peter | Dublin | Saunders, Sean | Dublin |
| Rice, Vincent S.C. | Legal Advisor 1921 | Saurin, Lt. Col. Charles | Dublin |
| Ridgway, Dr. J.C. | British Officer 1916 | Saurin, Col. Frank | Dublin |
| Rigney, Mary | Cumann na mBan | Scally, Stephen | Roscommon |
| Riordan, John | Waterford | Scannell, John | Kerry |
| Riordan, Michael | Cork, Bandon | Scollan, James | Donegal/Ferman. |
| Riordan, Patrick | Kerry | Scollan, John J. | Dublin |
| Riordan, Patrick | Offaly | Scott, Sean | Tipperary |
| Riordan, Timothy | Cork | Scully, Sean (Bertie) | NT, Kerry |
| Riordon, James J. | Knockavorheen, Cork | Scully, Capt. Thomas | Dublin |
| Robbins, Frank | ICA/ITGWU | Seery, Edmund | Westmeath |
| Roberts, George Henry | Clare | Sexton, Laurence | Cork |
| Robinson, Seumas | Dublin | Sexton, Capt. Sean | Longford |
| Roche, James M. | Limerick | Sexton, Timothy | Cork |
| Roche, James | Limerick | Shalloe, Michael | Waterford |
| Roche, Liam (de Roiste) | Cork | Shalloo, Thomas | Clare |
| Roche, Moses | Waterford | Shanley, V. Rev. T. J. | USA |

| | | | |
|---|---|---|---|
| Sharkey, John | Tipperary | Sullivan, AM, KC, | 'Defended' |
| Sheehan, Patrick | Dail Official | Sergeant | Roger Casement |
| Sheehan, Patrick | Kerry | Sullivan, Capt. James | Castletownbere |
| Sheehan, Thomas | Tipperary | Sullivan, James | IRB/Monaghan |
| Sheehy, Michael | Cork | Sullivan, Mrs. T.M. | Daughter of Timothy |
| Sheehy, Comdt. Mich. | Limerick | | Healy |
| Sheerin, Michael | Derry, Tyrone, | Sweeney, Alphonsus | Dublin |
| | Donegal | Sweeney, Bernard | Leitrim |
| Shelly, Charles | Dublin | | |
| Sheridan, Liam | Member National | Tally, Albert | Tyrone |
| | Movement, 1901 | Tannam, Liam | Dublin |
| Sheridan, Comdt. Sean | Cavan | Teehan, Michael | Kerry |
| Sherry, Eugene | Monaghan | Thornton, Nora | Courier to Kerry |
| Shields, John | Tyrone | Thorton, Dr. Bridget | |
| Short, James | Armagh | (nee Lyons) | Cumann na mBan |
| Shouldice, John F. | Dublin | Thorton, Frank | Dublin |
| Simons, Frank | Roscommon | Thunder, Frank X. | Dublin civil servant |
| Siocfradha, Padraig | | Thunder, Joseph T. | Dublin civil servant |
| (An Seabhach) | Gaelic League | Tierney, Timothy, | Tipperary |
| Sisk, Edward | Cork | Timony, John | Mayo |
| Sister of Mercy | Dublin | Tobin, Edmund | Limerick |
| Skinner, Leo B. | Cork | Tobin, Liam | Director of Intelligence |
| Slater, Thomas | IRB/ Dublin | | under Collins |
| Slattery, Declan F. | Waterford | Tobin, Peter | Tipperary |
| Slattery, Col. James | The Squad | Tobin, Sean | Waterford |
| Slattery, Peadar Dr. | GPO | Togher, J. | Galway |
| Smart, Thomas | Dublin | Toibin, Micheal | |
| Smith, Eugene | Dublin | Tomney, James | IRB/Tyrone |
| Smith, Richard | Cork | Travers, John | Donegal/Ferman. |
| Smyth, James J. | Leitrim | Traynor, Oscar | Dublin |
| Smyth, James | IRB/Belfast | Treacy, Patrick | Galway |
| Smyth, Michael | Kildare | Treacy, Thomas | Kilkenny |
| Smyth, Nicholas | Tyrone | Tuite, Daniel | Dundalk |
| Smyth, Patrick | Dub. Workhouse | Tully, James | Dublin |
| Soughley, Michael T. | Sergeant DMP, | Tummon, Francis | Monaghan |
| | 1916 Executions | Tuohy, Thomas (Tomo) | Clare |
| Southwell, John | Newry/IRB | Twamley, John | Dublin |
| Spain, Con | Tipperary | Tweedy, Robert N. | Commission on |
| Spicer, George | Kerry | | Industrial Resources |
| Spillane, Michael | Kerry | Twomey, Edmond | Cork |
| Spollen, Jack | Westmeath | Twomey, Patrick P. | Cork |
| Stack, Michael J. | Limerick | Twomey, Tadhg | Cork |
| Stack, Mrs. Una | Cork | Tynan, W.A. | Laois |
| | (Widow of Austin) | | |
| Stafford, Jack | IRB/Dublin | | |
| Staines, Michael | Dublin | Veale, Michael A. | Waterford |
| Stanford, Joseph | Galway | Volunteer Membership Cards | |
| Stanley, Joseph | Publisher | | |
| Stapleton, Daniel J. | Kilkenny | Walker, Charles | Printer |
| Stapleton, Wm. James | Squad/Dublin | Walker, Michael | Dublin |
| Staunton, George | Galway | Wall, Charles | Limerick |
| Stephens, Edward M. | Nat. Land Bank | Wall, James | Kerry |
| Styles, John J. | Dublin | Wall, V. Rev. Canon Th. | Limerick |
| Sugrue, Patrick | see Siocfradha | Wallace, Thomas | Limerick |

| | | | |
|---|---|---|---|
| Walpole, R.H. (Harry) | Dublin | Whelan, J. | Waterford |
| Walsh, Dr. Thomas | Galway | Whelan, Patrick | Limerick |
| Walsh, Edmond J. | Kerry | Whelan, Patrick | Waterford |
| Walsh, Eugene | Cork | Whelan, Patrick J. | Cork |
| Walsh, J.J. | Cork | Whelan, Patrick J. | Waterford |
| Walsh, James | Cork | Whelan, Sean | Wexford |
| Walsh, James | Dublin | Whelan, William | Dublin |
| Walsh, John | Cork | White, Alfred | Fianna |
| Walsh, John | Kilkenny | White, Dr. Vincent | Mayor of Waterford |
| Walsh, John J. | Kerry | White, George | Dublin |
| Walsh, Laurence J. | Louth | Whittle, Nicholas | Waterford |
| Walsh, Liam | Portlaoise/Waterford | Wickham, James | Cork |
| Walsh, Martin | Wexford | Wickham, Mark | Cork |
| Walsh, Michael | Cork | Wilcox, Patrick | Cork |
| Walsh, Michael | Cork, Gaggin | Willis, Richard | Cork |
| Walsh, Michael | Kerry | Wilson, Thomas | Galway |
| Walsh, Mrs. Mary | Cork, Cum. na mBan | Wilson, Thomas | IRB/Belfast |
| Walsh, Patrick | Galway | Winters, John | Cork |
| Walsh, Patrick | Kerry | Woods, Mrs. Mary Flannery | Dublin |
| Walsh, Richard | Mayo | Woods, Peter | Monaghan |
| Walsh, Robert | Tipperary | Woods, Seumas | Belfast |
| Walsh, Sean | Mayo | Wordsworth, Mrs. A.K. | (niece of Alice Stopford Green) |
| Walsh, Thomas | Dublin | | |
| Walsh, William | Kerry | Wylie, QC, Hon. W.E. | British Prosecutor of 1916 leaders |
| Walshe, Sean E. | Tipperary | | |
| Ward, Patrick | Dublin | Wyse-Power, Judge Charles | Defended IRA |
| Ward, Rev. Brother | Drogheda | | |
| Warren, Timothy | Cork | Wyse-Power, Dr. Nancy | Cumann na mBan |
| Waters, Thomas P. | Belfast/Cork/Tipp. | | |
| Wedick, Michael | Dublin | Young, Edward | Cork |
| Weston, Charles | Dublin | Young, Thomas | Dublin |

## Notes

The names which appear above are essentially as they appeared in the original list of the Bureau of Military History before the files were opened to the public in March 2003. However, some of the names which were on the original list did not appear in the published list after the files were opened (and were omitted from the first edition of this book). These are:

| | |
|---|---|
| Breathnach, Micheál | IRB |
| Ergen, Rev. Fr. C.P. | |
| McDunphy, Patrick | Armagh |
| McGeehin, Sean | IRB |

Subsequently, further names disappeared from the Bureau list. We continue to list them as we do not know why they were dropped, but have indicated them with an asterisk.

When using the Index reasearchers should be aware that some entries may be listed in Irish and/or English. Furthermore, those consulting the Bureau list may not always find names in the correct alphabetical order.

# INDEX TO MOYLAN'S STATEMENT

Abeyfeale 141
Allen, John 135
Allen, Larkin & O'Brien 13,36
Allensbridge 65
Allman, D.J. 118
Allua 109
America 9,47, 108
*An t-Óglach* 17,75,84
*An t-Oileánach* 36
Ananias 43
Ardnageeha 95
Army School of Equitation 121
Aughrim 127
Aungier St. 46
Australia 9

'Bogtrotter' 92
'Brown, Master William' 14
Bagwell 146
Ballinahinch 13
Ballinamuck 13
Ballinguilla 84
Ballybunion 103
Ballydrocane 64
Ballylanders 53
Ballymaquirk 109
Ballyvonaire 107
Banteer 102, 107,109, 111,135
Barbados 110
Barley Hill 16
Barley Hill Bridge 112,115
Barry, David 16
Barry, Fr. 64
Barry, Kevin 69
Barry, Michael K. 87
Barry, Tom 118-9
Barter, Denis 135
Bassett 110
Bateman 146
Béaslaí, (Piaras) 128

Beckett, Martin 43
Beecher 110
Belfast prison 81
Bevan 110
Blackwater 100,109
Blair 110,146
Boer War 13
Boggeraghs 39,110
Boherbue 33,117,131
Bolster, Jack 62,84
Boulton 146
Bowen 146
Bower, The 103
Bowler, Fr. 56
Boyle, Richard 110
Breen, Dan 94
Breen, Seán 40
Brislane, Séamus 85, 89, 127
Brooks 146
Brown 146
Bruff 9
Budenny 47
Bullen 146
Bunker Hill 108
Burgoyne 108
Burke, Edmund 19
Burns, Robbie 20
Burton 110,146
Butler's *Lives Of The Saints* 11
Buttevant 64,80,89,93,100, 101,107,133,135
Byrne, Louis 47

Caherbarnagh 94, 97
'Calamity Jane' 126
Carleton 11
Carpenters' Union 46
Casement, Roger 16
Casey, William, J.P. 94-5
Castleisland 90
Castlemagner 65

Cathal Brugha St. 129
Catholic Defence Associations 12
Cavaliers 92
Cavan Election 37-8
Ceathramha Riabhach 109
Chapman 146
Charleville 63,104-5,107
Chuzzlewitt, Martin 23
Cicilia 47
Clancy, Maurice 109
Clancy, Paddy 52-7,109
Clara/Claragh 118,120,141
Clare Election 35
Clayton 146
Clausewitz 70
Clemenceau 48
Clonbanin 90,103-4, 107
Clonfert Bridge 112
Clonmult 117-8
Cobh 138,140
Colenso 13
Collins, Michael 71,89, 122,127,128,145
Compton 146
Condon, Lar 45,52
Conna 51
Connacht 110
Connolly, (James) 92
Conroy, Con 138-41
Constantinople 47
Cooking 129
Coolagh 113
Coote 146
Corbett, Dr. 64
Cork city, burning of 83
Cornwallis 108-9
Crimean War 12
Cronje 13
Cromwell 110
Cremona 67
Creggone 53
Croke, Archbishop 30

Crossbarry 119
Crowley, Jerh. 103
Crozier 30,108
Cruikshank 23
Cúchulainn 70
Cullen 95, 97
Cullen, Tom 55,101,118
Cummins, General 107
Curragh 47
Curtin, Denis B. 53
Curtin, Denis D. 88
Curtis, Professor 29
Cusack 15
Custume, Sergeant 70

Dail 77,82,143-4
Daly, John 35
Damer 146
Dartmoor 138
Davis, Thomas 35,37
Davitt 12,30,92
de Valera 35,117,122,145
De Wett 13
Dean 110,146
Deasy, Liam 119
Deebert/Dibirt 10
Delaney, Matt 35
Denikin 47
Dernagree 107
Derrygallon 109
Derrynasaggart 110
Deschanel 48
De Vere, Aubrey 70
Devoy, John 12
Dickens 11,133
'Dingley Dell' 133
Dixon 146
Doheny, Michael 92
Donegal 39-40
Doody, Jerry 112
Dooley, Mr.48
Dore 146
Dostoevsky 44
Downpatrick 13
Drake 95
Drishane Convent 101

Drishanebeg 99,103
Dromagh 108
Drominarigle 67-9,79,80
Dromina 85
Dromahane 13
Dromcummer 109
Drumcondra 94
Dublin Castle 30
Duffy, Charles Gavan 35
'Duke Humphrey' 125
Dumas, A. 96
Dunn, Captain 9
Dunquin 14
Dwyer, Michael 13

East Africa 119
East Lancashire
 Regiment 133
Easter Week
 10,18,37,48,83,103
Egypt 182-3
Emmett, Robert 10,132
Evans 146

*Fore & Afts* 133
Farren 110
Fenian Rising 9
Fenians 9-13,44,83,92-3
Fermoy 63
Fielding 110
Finn, Seán 119.130
Finucane, Con 79,91
Fitzgerlad, Lord Ed. 10
Fleetwood 146
Fleming 10
Flynn, Con 80,84-5
Foilagoling 100
Foran, Tom 46
'Ford, Seán' 53
Foxhound Concerts 14
Fr. Murphy's Bridge 107-8
Frawley, Tom 107
Freemount 66,81,86
French, Lord 47,109
Frongoch 103
Furnell 146

German Plot 19
'Grim Reaper' 109
G.A.A 19,30
Gaelic League 14,19,
 32,144
Gaffney, Joe 15
Gaffney, Nicholas 10
Galli-Curci, (Amelita) 27
Galvin, Barry 134
Galvin, Dan 14,60
Galvin, Denis 91,93,
 97,104
Galvin, Mrs. Nora 83
'Gamp, Sairey' 23
General Election, 1918. 39
Gethsemane 145
Gibbs 146
Gibson 146
Glashakinleen 14,83
Glen, The 104
Glenacurrane 84
Glencollins 87,90,96
Gloucester Regimt. 130,133
Glounakiel 32-3
Glounalougha 79
Gneeveguilla 84
Gore 146
Gray, Jim 142
Green family 10
Griffith 15,37,145
Guedella 108
Guiney, John 40

Hales, Tom 25,119
Harding, Chris 55
Harold (Owen) 135
Hayes, Seán 39,42
Headford 117-8
Healy, Paddy 123
Healy, Seán 84,91,97
Healy, Tim 12
Heffernan, Billy 35
Hegarty, Seán 25,118,142
Hempenstall 13
Herlihy, Donal 101
Herlihy, Michael 101

Herlihy, Rev. D.J. 101
Herlihy, Rev. M.J. 101
Herlihy, Tom 67, 91
Hitler 47
Hippocrates 139
Holmes, General 91,941
Horan's 94,97
Horatius 70
Horgan's of Coolagh 113
Hotchkiss gun 84,106,
Hotspur 96
Howe 108-9
Hugo, Victor 123
Humber car 88

*Irish Independent* 101
*'Ironsides'* 92
Influenza of 1918. 39
I.R.B 29
Irish Academy 95
Irish Guards 172
Irish Tourist Assoc. 16
Ivers 146

Jack the Ripper 43
Jackson Day Dinner 47
Jones, Johnny 87,90,91,96
Joubert 13
Kanturk 31,33,36,55, 64, 66,68,69,90,97,99, 109,111, 128,130,132
Keeffe, Joe 67
Kelleher, Michael J. 101
Kemalist Chamber of Deputies 47
Kenny, Michael 42
Keogh, John 13
Kickham, C.J. 11,92
Kiely, Tim 35,37
Kilbrin 64
Kilcorcoran 81-2
Kilgarvan 43
Kilkenny prison 138
Killala 13
Killarney 84,90,97,103
Killoseragh 86

Kilmallock 9,10,14,15, 93-4
Kilmichael 118
'King Charles Head' 99
Kingwilliamstown 84,87,90, 94,96,99,100,189,112,
Kippagh 118
Kiskeam 31,34,35,69, 81, 25,28,90,96,97,115, 116,120,130
Klondike's pub 49
Knockacluggin 112
Knockavoreen 112,120, 131
Knockilla 121
Knockmealdown 125
Knocknagoshel 36
Knocknagow 11
Knocknagree 99,104
Knowles 146

Ladysmith 13
Lalor 12,37,44
Land League 34
Landru 43
Lane 146
Leader 146
League of Nations 47
Leahy, Michael 142
Leary's Cross 84
Lecky 10
Leinster, Duke of 10
Leonard, Fr. 81
Lewis Gun 90
Limerick 84,89,93, 94,139,131,141
Limerick jail 9
Lincoln, Abraham 45
Linehan, Corney 68
Liscarroll 64, 127
Lisgriffin 107, 109
Listowel 94
Liverpool Ministry 28
Lloyd George 82,84

Lombardstown 121
Lombroso, (Cesare) 111
Long, Jerh. 102-3
Looney, Tadgh 62
Lovelace, Richard 41
Lucas, General 63
Lung, Kai 27
Lynch, Jack 55
Lynch, Liam 45,50,55,57, 119,123,142,
Lysaght 146

'Murphy, Mickeen' 14
MacCurtain, Tomás 25, 39,44,119,
Mackey, Captain 12
Macready, General 109
MacSwiney, Terence 25, 69,119
Mahony, Jack 104,112
Mafeking 13
Mallow 45,54,58,61-3,89, 110,111,120,134,135
Malone, Tom 53
Marne 107
Marrick 146
Marshalsea Lane 13
Martial Law  83
Martin, Mrs. 142
Marxists 19
Maxwell, Sir John 16
Maynard 146
McAuliffe, David 91,96
McAuliffe, Davy 98
McAuliffe, Garrett 119
McAuliffe, Michael 140
McCarthy of Creggone 53
McCarthy, Eugene 144
McCarthy, Paddy 51,60, 62,66,75,79,80,82,96,118
McCarthy, Tom 16
McEllistrim, Tom 107
McGrath, Martin 111
McLoughlin, John 40
McManus, T.B. 10

McNamara, Tom 90,91,96
McSweeney, Donal 96,101
Meagher 12
Meaney, 'Big Con' 103,107,123
Meaney, C.J. 103
Meelin 66,80,86,87,115
Meenkeragh 87
Mellows, Liam 28,143,145
Milford 10
Miller 146
Mills bomb 100
Millstreet 37,47,79,80-1, 96,101-107,117, 123, 141
Milroy, Seán 28
Mississippi Negro 10
Mitchel, John 11,12,37
Mitchelstown 141
Modder River 13
Moll Carthy's Bridge 73-4
Montgomery 108
Moore 146
Morley, Con 91,93,96-7
Morpheus 67
Morrissey, (volunteer) 64
Moulton 146
Mount Collins 131
Moylan, Con 82,84, 88,90, 112,120
Moylan, Liam 80,84,91,96,106,114
Moynihan killing 84
Mulcahy, Richard 144
Mullaghareirc 110
Munchausen 43
Munster Fusilier 102-3
Murphy, Con 90,134
Murphy, Dan Martin 32
Murphy, Denis 99
Murphy, Fintan 55
Murphy, Fr. John 13
Murphy, Humphrey 119,122
Murphy, John 87
Murphy, Ned 120

Murphy, Paddy 120
Murphy, William 51
*Nation, The* 10
*'Nunc Dimittus'* 131
Nadd 107-12
National Brotherhood of St. Patrick 10
National Library 95
Nelson 95
New Ross 17
Newmarket 9,13,16,33,3 7,47,51,54,64,66,80,82, 84-90,96,99,100,107, 112, 114-6,130
Noonan, Mr. 64
North Africa Campaign 108
Nunan, Seán 74,77,120,121,144

O'Brien, Dan 128,134
O'Brien, Maurice 106
O'Brien, Paddy 64,104- 7,127,128,144
O'Brien, R. Barry 29
O'Brien, Seán 105
O'Brien, William 12
O'Connell 12,29
O'Connell St. 107
O'Connell, Jack 56,64, 87,99
O'Connell, Michael 121, 144
O'Connell, Seán 122
O'Connor. Morris 28-9
O'Donoghue, Florry 118
O'Keeffe, Páidín 39,46,62
O'Leary, *'Pagan'* 12
O'Leary, Con 88,103
O'Leary, Jerh. 67
O'Leary, John 12,86
O'Leary, Stephen 10
O'Mahony, Miss Baby 100
O'Malley, Ernie 54,59,62- 7,79,119,123
O'Reilly, Charlie

40,50,82,112-4
O'Riordan Dr. 117
O'Riordan, D.T. 101
O'Riordan, Michael 102
O'Súilleabháin, Eoghan Ruadh 110
Oliver, Richard 10
Oom Paul 13
Ossa 44
Oxford 135

*'Peter the Painter'* 55
Paris Peace Conference 40,47
Parnell 16
Pearse 10
Peel, Sir Robert 28
Pélion 44
Phair 110
Philadelphia 108
Pickett, Patrick 9,11
'Pip' 11
Plunkett, Captain 30
Poland 18
Portmagee 50
Power, George 52,53, 119,120,144
'Prig, Betsy ' 23
Prince Eugene 67
Raleigh, Batt 10,11
Raleigh, Sir Walter 110
Rathcoole 102,109
Rathmore 90,97,101,103, 127
Redmond, John 12,16
Reever 146
Reeves 110
Regan, Jack 128
Republican Courts 17,21, 22,24,74-78,96
R.I.C. 27-30
Ring College 46
Riordan, Jim 112,120
Riordan, Michael 103
Roche, Larry 15
Rockchapel 31,32-4,88,112

Rommel 108
Roskeen 107
Ross Castle 90
Rossa, O'Donovan 37
Rostov 47
Russian Revolution 48
Ryder 146

*'Stonewall'* Jackson 108
Sadlier 13
San Francisco 10
Santander 48
Saul 71
Saurin, C. 145
Scartag 91
Schusnigg, Kurt von 47
Seadna 120
*'Seán na Cóta'* 14
Shannon 92
'Sharp, Becky' 11
Shaughnessy, Mark 105
Sheahan, Jeremiah 115
Sherman 48
Shields, (Dan) (informer) 111
Shinanagh 89,90
Sidney, Sir Philip 86
Sixmilebridge 87
Skinner, Leo 101
Smith, Colonel 94
Somerville, Michael 46
Southwell 146
South Dakota 126
Spain 48
Spenser 110
Spike Island 137-42
Stack, Austin 81
Stafford 110

Stannard 146
Steelman 146
Stephens, James 44
Strand St. 36
Strangeways 51,82
Strickland, General 104, 107,109
Sullivan, Barry 134-5
Sullivan, Dominic 142
Sullivan, Mick 96,112, 114,116,144
Sullivan, Paddy Geoffrey 121
Sullivan, Sergeant 94
Swain 146
Sweetman, Roger 82

*The Taming Of The Shrew* 101
*'Three Musketeers'* 96-8,109
*Times, The* 40
Taaffe 73,123
Tadgh Vic Flurry 61
Taylor 146
Texas 42
Thackeray 11
Tipperary 36,125
Tobin, Liam 55
Tonson 146
Townsend 146
Tralee 90, 100,102
Treacy, Seán 99
Treaty 142,144
Truce 142-44
Tullyease 80,86,120
Tureen 84
Tureengariffe 86,94,97,99

Turner 110,146
Twomey, Moss 58

Ulster Volunteers 15
Ummeraboy 104,112
United Irishmen 10
Unionist Club 38
Upton 110

Valencia 48
Valley Forge 108
Vaughan, Dan 90,91
Verling, Dr. Algie 49,112
Virginia 110
Vorbeck, Gen. Lettow 119
Voroshilov 47

Waller 110
Washington 95
Weller, Tony 61
Welsh Fusiliers 140
Wheeler 110
Whelan, Pax 19
White Russians 47
Wicklow 13
Wilde, Oscar 42,62
Willis, Dick 59,84
Wilson, Woodrow 47
Wolfe Tone 37,132,135
Wood, Albert, K.C. 135-6
Woodenbridge 16
Wormwood Scrubs 151
Wrixon 146

Yeats 60
Yorktown 108
Youghal 109
Young Irelanders 47

# Epilogue

"The intransigent who, when his country was invaded and overrun during the latest great war, took up arms against the invader and in secret, and in civilian guise, killed, burned and destroyed the forces and equipment of the invader is lauded as a hero—in Poland *tuigeann tú*—but here in Ireland every man who took up a gun, who, with the dice completely loaded against him, went out to fight for his country's liberty in the only fashion possible, was deemed a murderer by those who controlled all the organs of publicity."

When Sean Moylan wrote that paragraph half a century ago, he was describing the state of affairs that existed when, as a young man, he went to war against the British Army to give effect to the decision of the Irish electorate that Ireland should be an independent state. The independent state was brought into being, and he was a member of its Government when he wrote the Memoir reproduced in this book. Those who engaged in military action to give effect to the mandate of the 1918 General Election were not called murderers in the 1950s. They had won. Their cause had triumphed and they did not call themselves murderers. But half a century later they are again being called murderers.

Britain is the most historically conscious state in the world. It devotes great effort to clearing up—or cleaning up—the past as it moves along. It makes up the past to serve its purposes in the present. It employs thousands of professors, lecturers and writers to re-arrange the past and erase the black spots. And its television 'history' is propaganda, whether the form is documentary or fiction.

By virtue of its power of patronage, which is very much greater than that of the Irish state, Britain has secured the services of many academics in the Irish Universities, paid for by the Irish tax-payer, in the doing of this work.

The Republican Volunteers who challenged the right of the British Government to continue governing Ireland in disregard of the 1918 Election result are described as serial murderers in a book published by Oxford University in 1998, by Peter Hart *The IRA And Its Enemies: Violence And Community In Cork, 1916-1923* (The Clarendon Press at Oxford, 1998).

The British state left many of its institutions in place in Ireland when it was obliged to leave. Its financial institutions operated discreetly, behind the scenes, aiming to be effective without being noticed. Its ideological institutions—the chief of which were Trinity College and the *Irish Times*—also thought it prudent to keep a low profile for a while. But ideology operates differently from finance. It cannot function without being noticed because ideas are its subject matter, and it operates in the medium of thought. The mind must be disturbed and affronted in order to be changed. And the change in question requires a very great disturbance. People who were thought to have engaged in a praiseworthy and heroic struggle for democratic rights are now held to have been serial murderers, and even to have been engaged in a genocidal rampage.

Trinity College, an English University occupying an extensive area at the heart of Dublin and paid for largely by the Irish taxpayer, has the purpose of regaining the ground lost by England between 1918 and 1921. The first step is to misrepresent what was done between 1918 and 1921 both by British power in Ireland, and by the Irish electorate and those who engaged in military resistance to British power on behalf of the Irish electorate.

Some ancient Roman—Plutarch, perhaps—said that, while memory is essential to human existence, what is remembered need not be what actually happened, and that false memory is as good as true if it is believed to be true. The history department of Trinity College is engaged in an ambitious project to construct a false memory of the events of 1918-21 as a basis for a comprehensive alteration of conduct in the present.

I first became aware of this project when I came across a publication of the *Trinity History Workshop*. This was a collection of articles by a dozen Trinity students, edited by Professor David Fitzpatrick, *Revolution? Ireland 1917-1923*. It was published in 1990 with funding from the *Irish Times*, the Bank of Ireland and Trinity College. What caught my eye on glancing through it was the opening sentences in the article on *Ideas And The Volunteers* by Joost Augusteijn:

"To what extent were ideas important to the Volunteers in the War of Independence? Since ideas played a very limited part in the actual fighting, we will consider here what role they did play in people's reasons for joining the Volunteers" (p25).

What struck me was the mindlessness of what is said here, its detachment from the realities of life, its inability to imagine the situation in which people thought and acted in those years.

It seemed self-evident to me that ideas played a much greater part in the actual fighting than in the joining of the Volunteers. The country voted to be independent of England and its Empire. When England ignored the vote, it became obvious that what had been voted for could only be achieved by using force in the cause of the democracy to prevent England from continuing to govern by force. The individual had to decide whether to fight for what had been voted for or submit to the will of a superior force. This was an existential matter—a matter of temperament and character—rather than an intellectual matter to be decided by thought. But thought followed on the decision to fight.

The Irish electorate had never voted for independence before 1918. No Irish party had contested an election on an independence programme before 1918. The reason was not that there was no wish for independence in Ireland until 1918, but that the authoritarian British state, which was the world Superpower of the time, had made it clear to the Irish people that voting for independence would be futile. One of the great English Liberals had said that the Irish must remain part of the Empire, even though it was gall and wormwood to them.

The British state was an authoritarian state in Ireland, whatever may have been its nature in Britain. It did not attempt to conceal its authoritarian stance. It made its authoritarianism clear in order to overawe the Irish voters, and to deter them from voting for independence by making them understand that a vote for independence would be futile.

Irish independence could only be gained by defeating the British Empire in military conflict. And, since that seemed an impossible task, the Irish electorate resigned itself to seeking a measure of devolved government within the British state. The minority which could not resign itself to British subjugation made secret preparations for war.

The word 'democratic' is loosely used nowadays to describe the Home Rule movement, the physical force movement being branded as undemocratic. But it is a misuse of the idea of democracy to apply it to any of the political tendencies under the authoritarian state in Ireland. Ireland was governed by the will of an external power, which was a world Empire. That external power denied that the Irish electorate had a right of decision about Irish affairs. The Home Rule Party accepted this decree of the external power, and contented itself with seeking what it was *"constitutionally"* allowed to seek. And that submission to the authoritarian decree of the British state was no more democratic than the refusal of the Fenian movement to submit to it.

The real distinction between the Home Rule and Fenian movements is that the one was pacifist and the other was not. And a pacifist appeasement of authoritarian rule resting on military power is not self-evidently more virtuous than an attempt to resist it by the use of physical force.

When a democratic state was established in Ireland, Moylan was one of its outstanding democrats. But he was a soldier before he was a democrat. He was a soldier in order to become a democrat. By Britain's decree, the way to democracy lay through war.

The futility of Irish political life under the *"Constitutional movement"* is described in some of Canon Sheehan's novels. Moylan, who grew up under the influence of some old Fenians and yet was subject to the debilitating influence of the Constitutional parody of democracy, describes how the pervading sense of futility was dispelled:

"I accepted the view that the days of armed revolution were over, that the grip of England, England the rich, the powerful, the invincible, was too firmly fixed on Ireland ever to be broken in the field of battle. That concessions might be won by persuasion I believed, yet doubted; that the nation's freedom might be fought for I could not realise; war was a far off thing, of long ago or of distant country. It could not concern me and I was ashamedly glad. I owed no loyalty to England and was pleased and yet not pleased that my loyalty to Ireland would not be tested in combat for her rights. Perhaps I had lived too long with old men, beaten men, and had absorbed their philosophy, and so when 1913 came I found it difficult to realise that either the Irish or the Ulster Volunteers were in earnest. Yet I joined the Volunteers..."

—and then one thing led to another: the arming of the Ulster Loyalists for war against their Parliament, Britain's escape from civil war into war on Germany, Redmond's Woodenbridge speech making the Home Rule movement an active participant in Imperialist conquest, and the national response

in the form of the 1916 Rising.
And that brought an end to Moylan's life as a carpenter.

\*

The *Irish Times* has been busily 'problematising' the Rising in recent years—constructing it into an undemocratic event with a view to subverting the legitimacy of all that followed from it. Moylan treats democracy as having nothing to do with it:

"The faith of the few was rooted in a refusal to disbelieve. Irishmen, they could not accept the view that they were of a lesser breed, that their country was fated to remain a Province. Blindly, instinctively, they held to this refusal; out of it, because they were blindly, intuitively right, came light and guidance and strength to achieve. 1916 proved one thing—that Irishmen could fight and die for their country. It proved, too, that, the first breath-taking shock past, Irishmen's allegiance was still to their own land... The spell of national inanition was broken."

I spent twenty years trying to get the Six Counties incorporated into the democratic political structures of the British state, and I came to appreciate the accurate use, and non-use, of the word, democracy. It would not be appropriately used in connection with 1916 and Moylan does not use it.

The Rising was not a democratic event. But neither was it undemocratic. An undemocratic action is an action undertaken within a democratic situation which goes against the principles of democratic government. The situation within which the Rising was enacted was not a democratic situation. The Rising, therefore, was a non-democratic event enacted in a non-democratic situation. Democracy had nothing to do with it.

The *Irish Times* repeats a couple of hundred times a year that the 1916 Volunteers had no democratic mandate for what they did. That is an indisputable statement of fact.

But who did have a democratic mandate in 1916?

Government was being conducted on an electoral mandate which had run out of time. And the electoral mandate was in any case not a democratic one. The 1910 Election was held under an elite franchise, under which much less than half of the adult population was entitled to vote. That elite electoral mandate ran out in November 1915, but the Government decided to keep on governing without a mandate until the end of the World War which it had launched in August 1914.

And the Government which set aside the electoral process in 1915 was not the Government which had been elected in 1910. A change of Government was enacted in the Spring of 1915 without consulting the electorate.

Two General Elections were held in 1910, both resulting in deadlock between the British parties. The second Election was fought by the Liberal Party and the Irish Home Rule Party in alliance. The Liberal Party governed from 1910 to 1915 with a majority given to it by the 80 Home Rule MPs. The Home Rulers enabled it to enact a controversial Budget and to break the power of the House of Lords, and the Liberals in return brought in a Bill for

Irish devolution. The Unionist Opposition opposed the Irish Home Rule Bill in Parliament and in the country, and raised an Army—the Ulster Volunteer Force—to prevent its implementation when it became an Act in the Summer of 1914. (The House of Lords was allowed to impose a two-year delay on legislation and the two years would be up in 1914.) As Britain was apparently heading for civil war over the Home Rule Act, an opportunity of making war on Germany presented itself and was availed of. The Home Rulers declared support for the war at the outset. The Liberal Government, with the support of the Unionist Opposition, enacted the Home Rule Bill in September 1914 but immediately suspended the Home Rule Act for the duration of the war. The Liberal Government gave an equivocal undertaking to the Home Rulers that the Act would be implemented at the end of the war, and the Home Rulers thereupon became recruiting agents for the British Army.

The Unionist Party, which was supported by the core of the military establishment, was better fitted for waging war than the Liberal Party. In 1915 it forced its way into government—without an election—by threatening the Government with having to hold an election. A Coalition was formed in March, with the two most prominent leaders of the Ulster Rebellion of 1913-14 gaining senior Cabinet positions—Edward Carson becoming Attorney General and F.E. Smith becoming Solicitor General.

That change of Government meant that the Home Rule Act would lie stillborn on the Statute Book. The dependence of Asquith's Government on the Home Rule Party ended in substance with the declaration of war on Germany—the Unionists being more competent warmakers than the Liberals or Home Rulers—and it ended formally with the formation of the Coalition. And, with the Ulster Unionist leader taking a seat in the Cabinet, while the Home Rule leader continued to sit on the backbenches, the pro-Home Rule Government of 1911-1914 was cancelled and an anti-Home Rule Government took its place. Then in 1916 the Prime Minister who had *"put Home Rule on the Statute Book"* was ditched. A new Coalition was formed, with Lloyd George replacing Asquith and acting as a Liberal figurehead for a Government whose substance was Unionist. And the Liberal Party, which had been shocked by the formation of the 1915 Coalition, broke up under the impact of the sacking of Asquith. All of this, without an election, after the 1910 electoral mandate had run out!

So what sense is there in discussing the Easter Rising as if it was an arbitrary action committed in a democratic situation?

It was, in fact, an arbitrary action against an arbitrary Government.

England was content that Parliament should prolong its life beyond the period of its mandate. English society is geared for the combination of war and commerce. It is a militaristic society, and I know from direct experience of it as well as from historical knowledge that it is at its happiest when it is at war. It gave tacit consent to the suspension of elective government for the duration of the war. I would put it even stronger than that: It took it for granted that, when England was engaged in its primary business of fighting a war, secondary matters like elections would be set aside.

The Government which called the Election of December 1918 bore little resemblance to the Government formed on the basis of the Election held eight years earlier. The War Coalition, which had governed arbitrarily from 1916 to 1918, fought the 1918 Election as a Coalition. The English electorate returned it with a landslide majority, and all but wiped out the Liberal Party, which had governed from 1910 to 1914, but had dissented from the 1916 changes.

And the Irish electorate all but wiped out the Home Rule Party, which had sustained the Liberals in Government from 1910 to 1914.

But the Home Rulers and the Liberals were punished electorally for different things. The Liberals were punished for being insufficiently militaristic, and Lloyd George was rewarded for breaking the Liberal Party in order to free the Unionists to wage the war more stubbornly. The Home Rule Party was punished for an excessive and misguided militarism.

English society is profoundly militaristic, while Irish society is essentially pacifist. The militarism of English society was evident to me when I first saw a Remembrance Day celebration in Whitehall over forty years ago, and that first impression has been confirmed by everything I have seen and read since. And one of the things I find peculiar about the sophisticates of the revisionist movement is the simple-minded way they believe the most superficial layer of British propaganda which reverses the functional order of things—asserting that English society is peace-loving, while militarism is latent throughout Irish society.

The peace-loving stance of English society is no more than a proper pretence. It never seemed to me that it was seriously intended to deceive but, since it does sometimes deceive, it must be rated useful as well as proper. But, in essence, it is no more than Burke's *"decent drapery"* of virtue by means of which the necessary grossness of life is disguised by euphemism in polite conversation.

The English message is that it knows how to pick its wars and its allies so that it always ends up on the winning side. In the history of the English state since the Battle of the Boyne there has only been a single generation in which it did not make war—the Walpole generation in the second quarter of the 18th century. And, insofar as militaristic impulses survived the deadening influence of the Penal Laws in Ireland, they were cultivated and given an outlet by the British Army.

I think it is meaningful to distinguish between military activity engaged in for an immediate and clear defensive purpose and a generalised disposition towards killing people which seeks an outlet—and to apply the word militarism to the latter. The two things are different in kind and they require different names. And, when I say that English society is militaristic, I use the word in the latter sense.

The English state has had no occasion to engage in defensive military activity since its present regime was established in 1688. And 1688 itself was a strange event—in form a Dutch invasion, but an unresisted invasion which functioned as a *coup d'etat* which deposed a regime that was friendly towards France, and cleared the way for centuries of "balance-of-power" wars in Europe.

The Irish Army is a Defence Force. It provides no outlet for the militaristic impulse. But there have been signs in recent times that a frustrated militaristic spirit has grown up within it. It acted as if it was part of the British Army by participating in the funeral ceremonials of a British soldier killed in the fourth British invasion of Iraq in 2003, describing him as an *"Irish soldier"* merely because he happened to have been born in Ireland. I would have thought that a soldier takes his operative nationality from the state in whose military service he undertakes to kill.

The fact that English society is militaristic finds expression in only one piece of contemporary Irish writing that I know of. And it comes from a very surprising quarter, Myles Dungan, who celebrates Irish participation in British militarism:

> "In a society where military service was an integral part of the cultural landscape and where wars of one kind or another have been fought in each generation, the rush to 'join up' after the declaration of hostilities in 1914 was understandable. The armed forces have long been a 'proving ground' where men tested their courage and endurance, in a sense their very 'maleness'. The relatively small British Regular Army did not permit many to undergo such a rite of passage. Therefore the mass recruitment drive of late 1914 undertaken when it became clear that the war would not be over in a matter of weeks and could not be won by the British Expeditionary Force alone, afforded a unique opportunity for thousands of men to 'test their mettle' without the necessity of making the army or navy their career. But Ireland was not such a society. The country had no great military tradition of its own, and by the early 1900s most of its soldiers were merely adjuncts to the army of its near neighbour and coloniser."
> (p15, *They Shall Not Grow Old. Irish Soldiers In The Great War*, 1997.)

War is its own justification for the English. It is one of the main things that England does. The Irish had to be given special reasons to overcome their lack of the spirit of militarism. The reasons they were given appear absurd in retrospect, but in the overheated atmosphere of the Summer of 1914—when civil war in both Ireland and Britain appeared imminent—they were effective in recruiting members of the "respectable" classes into the British Army. When those special reasons were falsified by the actual conduct of the war, Redmond was found guilty of having presented a false bill of sale.

## Ideas And The Volunteers

Here is another notion produced by Professor Fitzpatrick's apprentices in the Trinity Workshop:

> "Most Irishmen opposed violence at home, especially at a time when many Irishmen were fighting for freedom in Europe. It is well known that this changed, although maybe not as rapidly and thoroughly as some have claimed. Particularly in garrison towns, Volunteers encountered a lot of hostility right through the War of Independence…
> "After the rising the people that had been in it and those that had been interned had reason enough to fight the British…" (Augusteijn, p31).

And he says that the natural resentment of internees "was fuelled by the idea that the executed leaders should not be allowed to have died in vain". When the internees were released, they set about reorganising the Volunteers. "A striking characteristic of the Volunteers, in several cases, was the absence of a father" (p33)—the fathers of Sean Treacy and Dan Breen were dead.

"During the Conscription crisis in April 1918 men flocked to the Volunteers again. This was mainly a form of protest and an expression of the fact that they did not want to join the British army. It was not evidence of a sudden willingness to fight. At this stage participation in the Volunteers did not imply fighting but it could add greatly to a man's local standing. When the threat of Conscription disappeared at the end of the War, the Volunteers were once again in a difficult position. There was some expectation that Home Rule would now come soon. There was also a fear among the Volunteers that England would come down hard on them now that its continental difficulties were over. Many started to waver... However, the actions of a small group and the English reaction to it were soon to change the pattern again.

"...The ambush at Soloheadbeg was intended to bring attention back to the military side of the struggle now that the political side had become so dominant after the elections. It created a public reaction similar to that in 1916. The most militant Volunteers came under attack from the police as well as from the population and even within the movement" (p35-6).

Nevertheless, the physical force movement gathered strength:

"Recruitment might follow the death of a brother or friend, maltreatment by the police, admiration for the fighters in the columns or a general feeling of outrage at the excesses of the Black and Tans".

This section of the Trinity Workshop is entitled, *Ideas And The Volunteers*, and the suggestion is that the Volunteers had no ideas—they just wanted to fight and the trouble caused by their fighting produced a widening circle of resentment against the authorities which were trying to suppress them:

"Many of those interviewed in Mayo and Tipperary either could not explain why they got involved or stated merely that they fought for Irish Freedom...

"The events of 1920 and 1921 made most people at least sympathetic to the Volunteers. In this period activists were even less inclined to reflect on their reasons for being in the movement" (p38-9).

And Professor Fitzpatrick himself says in a Preface that "the activists had fairly simple and commonplace notions of their nationality, and should not be regarded as an intellectual elite" (p7).

In this account of what happened, two distinct and dissimilar events are run together—the 1916 Rising and the War of Independence; an event which occurred between the two, which gave the second a fundamentally different character from the first, is barely mentioned, is unexplained, and has no influence attributed to it—the General Election of 1918; and the Irishmen who were "fighting for freedom in Europe", and by implication are held to have been motivated by "ideas", are contrasted with those who "stated merely that they fought for Irish Freedom", which was a "simple and commonplace notion" and not an idea at all.

The suggestion that those who joined the British Army were "fighting for freedom in Europe" is a simple-minded repetition of the British war propaganda which sits strangely amidst all this pretentious methodological display. And it is not even mentioned what freedom they were supposedly fighting for—the freedom of Europe or the freedom of Ireland. Did they go to war as a consequence of mature reflection on the nature of German autocracy, or Nietzscheanism, which were the bogeys of the moment in the war propaganda? Or were they fighting for Britain in Europe (and in the Middle East a few months later) because they understood that to be the price required by England for the concession of Irish 'freedom' in the form of Home Rule under British sovereignty as a component part of the Empire?

Augusteijn says nothing about the actual character of the British war on Germany, or the British war on Turkey which followed five months later, and he does not consider whether disillusionment about "fighting for freedom in Europe" began to set in at a certain point, influencing conduct in Ireland. I would have thought these were obvious questions to ask in the Workshop project. It does not seem possible to me that a mind engaged in such a project should not think about them. But I imagine that Professor Fitzpatrick set out tight guidelines for the task work, which prevented the apprentices from straying into the real world, and that Basil Fawlty's rule applied: Whatever you do, don't talk about the War!

## The Election

The General Election of 1918 is another unmentionable. The Election is, of course, connected with the war. The Conscription Crisis of 1918 was a watershed in Irish political life. It broke the morale of the Home Rule Party and prepared the ground for the Sinn Fein election victory. And the Conscription issue can only have been a crisis on such a massive scale because the War had gone sour on people.

The Home Rule Party supported the War as a fight for freedom. And the extension of the War to Turkey was hailed as a development towards universal liberation.

If Germany won, civilisation would perish. If Turkey was not defeated the Middle East would remain unfree.

Three and a quarter years after the British declaration of war, Germany was still undefeated. It had held out against the British and French offensives over the years, and in the Spring of 1918 it launched its own major offensive. The British Army reeled under the shock. Panic began to set in and British public life began to show some of the phenomena that appeared in Germany at the end of 1918 after America had won the war. Those were the circumstances in which the Government decided to apply Conscription in Ireland.

Surely, then, the Conscription crisis was a conflict between the Home Rule Party, which supported it as a measure that was necessary to the salvation of civilisation, and Sinn Fein, whose nationalist vision prevented it from seeing what was at stake?

It was in fact a united struggle of the Home Rule Party and Sinn Fein against the Government. And that signified a moral collapse of the Home Rule Party on the position it had adopted in August/September 1914. People who actually believed what they had been saying about the War for close on four years would not have behaved as the Home Rule leaders behaved in 1918.

It has become the academic fashion in recent decades to suggest that the Sinn Fein landslide victory in the 1918 Election was a kind of technical result, rather than a substantive one. For example:

"Although it won under half the total vote, the party nevertheless gained seventy-three seats to the Irish Parliamentary Party's dismal six and the twenty-six won by unionists... Sinn Fein set up an alternative parliament in Dublin... A kind of rebel government was formed" (*Armed Struggle: The History Of The IRA* by Richard English, Professor of Politics at Queen's University, Belfast; Macmillan, 2003, p15).

It is certainly a fact that Sinn Fein got less than half the vote. But the kind of fact it is can be best demonstrated with reference to another fact: In the 1921 Election Sinn Fein gained all the seats in the 26 Counties that were open to democratic contest even though it did not get a single vote.

If you came across the statement in one of these histories that Sinn Fein got all the seats without getting a single vote, you would suspect that something fishy was going on and you would inquire further. And that is why that statement is never made.

Sinn Fein got all the seats in the democratic constituencies in 1921 because no other party put up candidates. Four seats were reserved for an elite University electorate and Sinn Fein did not contest these. And so it took all the democratic seats without anybody voting for it.

What happened in 1918 was that it gained a quarter of the seats without a contest. The voters in the 25 constituencies where Sinn Fein support was strongest were deprived of the opportunity to vote for Sinn Fein.

The Home Rule Party, which had urged the people to participate actively in Britain's war on Germany and Turkey on the ground that Home Rule was on the Statute Book and would be implemented at the end of the War, was in moral collapse in December 1918. Home Rule was a dead letter in a Statute Book. The Unionist Party had taken over the Westminster Government in the course of the War. The War for idealistic purposes advertised in 1914 had turned out to be another Imperialist war. And the Home Rule Party itself had become an abstentionist party with regard to Westminster, having withdrawn from the House of Commons in protest against the decision to impose Conscription in Ireland.

In December 1918 Home Rule gave up the ghost in the following constituencies, leaving them uncontested to the independence party:

*Cork*: North, North-East, Mid, East, West, South and South-East.
*Kerry*: North, West, South and East.
*Tipperary*: North and Mid.
*Clare*: East and West.
*Cavan*: East and West

*Kilkenny,* North
*Limerick,* West
*Mayo,* South
*Galway,* East
*Roscommon,* North
*Carlow* County
*King's* County.

One Cork constituency was contested, the City. Sinn Fein took both City seats with huge majorities: 20,801 and 20,506 against the Home Rulers' 7,480 and 7,162 and the Unionists' 2,519 and 2,254.

The Home Rule position in Moylan's constituency (Cork, North) had fallen long before 1918. The Home Rulers lost it to an Independent Nationalist in the first of the 1910 General Elections and conceded it without a contest in the second 1910 Election, the Independent position having by then taken on organisational form as the All For Ireland League. And the AFIL took all but one of the Cork constituencies in December 1910.

Some of the most important books of Irish history remain unwritten. One is a history of the Great War from an Irish viewpoint. Another is a history of the 1918 Election, its causes, conduct and consequences. In the absence of Irish histories of these events, the British view is bound to take over in Ireland.

The British view of the Great War is still the same view that was blasted out in the war propaganda of 1914. What we are told in the official commentary accompanying the Remembrance Day militarism is that Britain defended its freedom in 1914-18 and in the course of doing so defended, or established, freedom in the world. And Remembrance Day, according to the official commentary, also commemorates 80 other British military actions in defence of freedom. Though they have been counted by the British Legion, those actions are not listed in the commentary. But, since no exceptions are made, the Black and Tan War is included. Remembrance Day is a blanket sanctification of British military action around the world since 1914.

The things done by the British state to strange peoples in faraway places weigh light on the casuistic British conscience. They are unproblematical because there is no pressing need to think about them. The Black and Tan War is different. It happened close to home. Officially, indeed, it happened *at home.* And it was waged, at the end of the Great War for the defence of democracy and the freedom of small nations, against a small nation which had voted, within the British electoral system, to establish its own independent government.

It was a war on the democratic presumptuousness of the Irish. Unlike other wars of its kind, it was not quite won, and the British state was not able to write the history of it. Dan Breen, Piaras Beaslai, Tom Barry, Pat Lynch, Florrie O Donoghue, Dorothy Macardle, Liam Deasy, Ernie O'Malley etc. had the writing of the history of it. And Britain is depicted in these histories much as Germany was depicted in British writing during and after the Great War. These Irish histories of the Anglo-Irish War circulated widely in England amongst the large Irish emigration that was intermarrying with the English, creating within English life a strong undercurrent of feeling that there was an evil streak in the make-up of the state.

English society is very much more self-righteous today than it was when I first experienced it in the mid-1950s. Although it was then only a decade out of the 2nd World War, and the revelation of the SS Extermination Camps might have entitled it to a degree of moral smugness, it was much less morally pretentious than it is today. Perhaps the reason was that it was still openly Imperialist then and it was understood that the conducting of an Empire involved the doing of dreadful things. Today its imperialism is oblique and devious and masquerades as something else.

It is now too good to be true, and truth has been sacrificed to goodness.

Nationalist Ireland fell into a condition of uncertainty about itself in the middle or late 1970s, and that is when England began to pour resources into the business of cleaning up—or falsifying—the history of its conduct in Ireland in 1918-1922.

I have never seen a history of the Malayan War—or the "Emergency", as it was officially called, so that war crimes might be committed with impunity—or the war in Kenya or the war in Cyprus. What was done to strange peoples in faraway places is not a source of unease. But the flow of English academic publications on Ireland has become a deluge. And the central purpose seems to be to marginalise the 1918 Election so that it scarcely impinges on the consciousness, and thus to represent the military conflict of 1919-21 as a mere continuation of the action taken to suppress the Rebellion in 1916.

There was no election contest in North Cork. The only contest was over the selection of a Sinn Fein candidate, but that was vigorously contested. Revisionist writers, who avert their eyes from the Election, try to make something favourable to the British cause out of the vigorous part played by the Volunteers in the selection of candidates. But that is a very un-British criticism. In the British system the methods used in the selection of candidates are for the political parties themselves to decide. The Americans, who have always been more democratic in their outlook than the English, decided in the 19th century that the selection of candidates by the political parties is hardly less important than the choice between the different parties finally made by the electorate in general, and they instituted the system of "primaries"—elections within each of the parties to choose candidates. But that system was not adopted by the British state, which came to a kind of democracy very late in the day, as a political price that had to be paid for military conscription.

Sinn Fein candidates were selected with perhaps a higher degree of active involvement by the electorate than was the case in Britain where the election was tightly run by the War Coalition, and deliberately held before the troops got home. The Volunteers were active in the electoral process, as they had every right to be. And, if it was the case that the 'extreme' element was to the fore amongst the Volunteers because the 'moderates' in leadership positions had been arrested and locked up by the Government in the 'German Plot' crack-down, the Government had nobody to blame but itself.

There being no election in North Cork, Moylan went electioneering to Donegal—where Sinn Fein took three of four seats, the Home Ruler taking East Donegal.

Moylan makes nothing of the fact that the Government ignored the Election result. He was not shocked by this. He took it for granted that voting for independence would not bring independence. He knew something of the history of the British state in Ireland and therefore did not expect that it would relinquish power to a mere vote.

Moylan and his colleagues did not believe that the British state stood in a democratic relationship with the Irish electorate, and they simply took it in their stride when the British state acted in accordance with their understanding of it. But that doesn't mean that there was no Election, or that the Irish electorate did not give a democratic mandate for independence.

Moylan and his colleagues did not go into moral shock, and wring their hands in anguish and call to high Heaven in protest, when the State which had just won a four-year War for democracy and the rights of small nations ignored the democratically expressed will of the Irish nation. If they had done that, Britain would have got away with over-ruling the Election. It was because they went to war that Britain made a substantial compromise with the will of the electorate three years later.

The fact that democracy had nothing to do with it on the British side does not mean that democracy was not at issue. Nor does the fact that Moylan, with his well-grounded scepticism about Britain's democratic posturing, makes no great fuss about the election, justify the revisionist historians in brushing it aside.

In Peter Hart's book about Co. Cork in 1916-23, the 1918 General Election does not appear at all as a distinct event, only being mentioned incidentally without giving the result. (And the 1921 Election is not even listed in Hart's Index.)

Here are the incidental mentions:

"…the *Irish Times* reported that: 'the enthusiasm of the young element has reached such a point as to cause family friction in many households. Some refuse to help their fathers on the land unless they exact a promise to support Mr. McGuinness [the Sinn Fein candidate] while daughters decline to pursue their domestic duties without laying similar toll'.

"These reports of intimidation of fathers by their children continued unabated through to the general election of December 1918. As for the latter event (when, for the first time, 'boys' could vote alongside their parents), one breathless account had it that 'young people (egged on by the curates!) ran it and actually, in many cases, locked the old people into their homes so that they might not be able to attend the booths'." (p166.)

The first reference in this passage is to the Longford by-election of 1917, held before the democratisation of the electoral franchise. It is part of Hart's technique to run together the post-1916 by-elections and the General Election. (He makes no reference to the fact that the mandate of the 1910 Election ran out in 1915.) Hart says:

"The elections of 1917 and 1918 provided the other great proving ground for activists. Scores of Cork Volunteers… travelled to constituencies all over Ireland to immerse themselves in the work of the movement. Each campaign was a miniature revolution, galvanizing local units and fusing the disparate militants into a single force. These were formative experiences for many future guerillas, away from homes and jobs—often for the first time—and surrounded by fellow republicans. Sean Moylan was 'deeply influenced' by his work in Donegal" (p253).

No explanation is given, that I can see, of why Cork Volunteers travelled all over the country for the Election—that Republican opinion was so dominant in Cork that Unionists and Home Rulers put up no candidates.

The elections, says Hart, "provided the other great proving ground for activists". *"Other"* besides what?

"The first of the 'Sinn Fein universities' were Richmond barracks and Frongoch Camp, where captured rebels and hundreds of their suspected accomplices were gathered after the 1916 rising. For the first time, isolated provincial republicans who had endured hostility and derision ('Here comes the Kaiser and his country boys') and whose most rebellious act had been to wear a tricoloured tie to Easter mass, found themselves thrown together with battle-hardened republican fighters. They were dangerous—and important—after all.

"The next identifiable cohort of guerillas came out of the British crackdown and subsequent hunger strikes of early 1920" (p252).

And "the elections of 1917 and 1918" provided the other proving ground.

Internment, hunger-strikes and a General Election were proving grounds for the development of guerillas!

But the guerillas, who were not yet guerillas, won the General Election. Since they won the Election, why did they go on to become guerillas and wage war against the Government? Because the Government decided to carry on governing after losing the election.

When Conor Cruise O'Brien flipped over, changing from a fairly aggressive nationalist to an extreme anti-nationalist, he put up the argument that the Republicans in 1919-20 gained popular support by small-scale actions against the British Government which provoked Government reprisals which aggravated people who had not been involved in the provocations, etc., and thus the people were Republicanised. Great democrat that he is, he failed to notice that the people had voted Republican *before* the guerilla actions began.

Hart's incidental comments on the 1918 Election appear in a chapter entitled *Guerillas*. There is also a chapter on *Volunteers*. There is no chapter on *Politics* or on *Elections*.

Professor Fitzpatrick's Trinity Workshop is equally coy about the Election. But it offers this thought, which would have been relevant to a chapter on the election if there had been one:

"In the environment of political struggle that had dominated Ireland since the 1880s, most Catholics grew up with the notion that Ireland was a separate nation. This idea became a 'fact of life', particularly for children growing up in this atmosphere… Some people developed this notion into a willingness to fight" (p25: this is from Augusteijn's chapter on *Ideas And*

*The Volunteers).*

But a willingness to vote came before the willingness to fight. If the voting had been effective, there would have been no fighting. And the greater tenacity and purposefulness of the fighting in 1919-1921, as compared with all military efforts since the Jacobite War of 1690, is attributable to the fact that it came after voting.

The *"notion that Ireland was a separate nation"* was generally held amongst the populace long before the 1880s. When O'Connell assembled the people by the hundred thousand at "monster meetings" around the country, the only question was what was to be done about it. Only the regime of despotism by which the Penal Laws were enforced had prevented such expressions of nationality during the century preceding O'Connell's campaign. The notion that the Irish were English—or that vacuous thing, British—never caught hold of the Irish. They might perhaps have been British as Jacobites, but the Jacobite monarchy was the only form of the British state with which they ever felt a sense of affinity. After the Battle of the Boyne there was nothing for them to be but Irish, and the only object of the new British regime—Williamite, Hanoverian, Windsor—was to keep them from giving expression to their will in the political sphere.

Home Rule was never chosen in preference to independence. Irish independence was categorically ruled off the agenda of political possibility by the British state. The Irish were given to understand that the infinite resources of the Empire would be brought to bear on them and would bring them back to order if they broke loose. Home Rule was on the extreme margin of what was allowable— even that was doubtful—so the Irish voted for Home Rule.

What happened at the 1918 Election was not that the Irish electorate changed its mind about what it wanted, but that it decided to vote for what it wanted rather than for the substitute which it had been intimidated into accepting.

It did this at a moment when the Home Rule substitute had been reduced to a dead letter on the Statute Book; when the grandiloquent propaganda about democracy and the rights of small nations, with which the British state had deafened the world for four years had devalued all the intimidatory restraints with which the state had confined the Irish electorate within Imperial parameters; and when the unexpected stresses of the war on Germany had obliged the state to introduce universal adult male franchise and substantial female franchise for the post-war election.

And so the Irish voted for independence in the first democratic election held in the United Kingdom. And the democracy proved to be a sham as far as the British state in Ireland was concerned. And the Irish were given the choice of slinking away from the decision they had taken, or giving effect to the decision of the ballot by use of the bullet.

## The War

Can a democracy be in rebellion against lawfully constituted authority? Is there, in the democratic era, some source of lawful authority beyond the will of the democracy, which is entitled to over-rule the decision of the democracy in the matter of forming the Government?

The Irish democracy elected Sinn Fein to establish an independent Irish Government. On the strength of this mandate, the Sinn Fein MPs called all the MPs elected in Ireland to assemble in an Irish Parliament in Dublin in January

1919. The small minority of Unionists and Redmondites did not respond to the call. They went to Westminster instead and placed themselves under allegiance to the sovereignty of the Crown. The MPs who assembled in Dublin adopted a Declaration of Independence in accordance with their election mandate, and appointed an Irish Government.

Professor Henry Patterson, in a history of the IRA called *The Politics Of Illusion* (London, 1997), describes this Irish Parliament as "the illegal Dail" (p20).

Professor Patterson, like many of his colleagues in the 'revisionist' academic culture, was once a fundamentalist Marxist and is now a fundamentalist Unionist. He is an adviser to the Ulster Unionist leader, David Trimble.

The Sinn Fein MPs did not go to Westminster and swear allegiance to the Crown. If they had done so, they would have been in clear breach of their election mandate. Because they did not do so they were not, in British law, legal representatives of their constituencies.

Professor Patterson does not indicate how those who were elected on an independence programme might have acted lawfully—within British law—to give effect to their mandate. In fact there was no way it could have been done. The elected Sinn Feiners could only have made themselves legal representatives under British law by swearing allegiance to the Crown in the process of taking their seats at Westminster, thereby pledging themselves to be bound by whatever decision Westminster made about the governing of Ireland. And the landslide majority gained by the triumphalist War Coalition (which was predominantly Unionist/Tory in composition) made it a certainty that Irish independence stood no more chance in the 1919 Parliament than Repeal had done in the Parliaments of O'Connell's time.

There was a fundamental conflict between law and democracy which could not be resolved legally or democratically because British state power did not operate democratically, and was not representative, and British law did not recognise democracy as its source.

Revisionist writers make great play with the fact that the 1916 Rising was not enacted in accordance with a democratic mandate—ignoring the fact that the electoral basis of government was in suspension from December 1915 to December 1918. But they make nothing of the democratic election which preceded the War of Independence.

The ethos of democracy has, however, influenced them enough to prevent them from saying straight out that in 1918 the Irish democracy went into unlawful rebellion and had to be curbed.

But that is what the Unionist press in Belfast said.

Given the pre-democratic ethos in which the British state was constructed, and that this ethos survived formal democratisation, the only way the will of the Irish electorate could be implemented was by direct action in breach of British law. This was done by establishing an Irish state apparatus under the authority of the Dail. Local Government bodies dissociated themselves from the Castle administration and operated under the Dail ministries. The Local Government Elections of 1920 confirmed the mandate of the 1918 General Election. And military action was conducted against the coercive apparatus of the British administration.

Britain decided not to apply in Ireland (or indeed anywhere else in its

Empire) the slogans about democracy and the rights of small nations that it used for recruiting in its Great War. That is why there was an Anglo-Irish War.

The Anglo side of that War is unproblematic. War is a normal activity of the British state. But it was a thoroughly abnormal activity in Ireland. The Irish, in 1919, had not made war on their own behalf for two centuries and a quarter.

What happened in Wexford in 1798 was a kind of wild upsurge, brought about by intense provocation, which was easily contained by the militaristic British state. In the West, a French invading force used the Irish as cannonfodder. In Antrim and Down the Presbyterian United Irish had made elaborate preparations for a war but called it off at the eleventh hour. In 1848 there was a brief flash of spirit with little force in it. In 1916 a small group of exceptional individuals placed themselves in a fortress-situation in the centre of Dublin and resisted a siege for a week. What was done between 1919 and 1921 was different in kind from all of these.

We are told by the Trinity History Workshop that:

"Irish rural society was imbued with a sense of warfare, which became a real experience for the guerilla generation" (Article on *The Guerilla Mind* by E. Davis).

No evidence is given in support of this statement. It is the kind of thing that is said nowadays and taken to be axiomatic. Charles Townsend said it and he set the fashion in these things.

I would say that the "sense of warfare" was all but broken in Irish society for two centuries by the draconian pacification that followed the Williamite conquest. In the 18th century the military spirit was drained off into the Irish Brigades in France and Austria. In the late 18th and 19th centuries there was extensive Irish recruitment into the British Army, but that too seemed to reinforce the helpless pacifism of the Irish at home. When O'Connell, who was not otherwise a pacifist, said that Irish freedom was not worth the shedding of a drop of blood, that statement might be understood as expressing the actual condition of Irish society. As a moral stance it was disputed by the Young Irelanders and repudiated by the Fenians. But the helplessness of the Irish during what is euphemistically called the Famine shows that, though morally deplorable, it was the case that the Irish would passively endure whatever was done to them by the English at the level of politics.

The last war before 1919 was the Jacobite War. It was the last war in which Irish society at large was engaged. It was the last sustained military effort in Ireland by the Irish.

Moylan mentions Sergeant Custume. That is sufficient reason to give Aubrey de Vere's poem, which was once generally known but has been forgotten in the revisionist era for no good reason. It is a virtual certainty that Moylan knew it. His range of literary reference is very much de Vere's range. Two generations later I grew up in the same area in a culture that was still very similar. I have noticed in recent times that 'Jacobite' has become a term of dismissal, especially in circles that used to call themselves "official Republican" but have become so Imperialist in outlook that they are best known by the nickname they were given in Belfast thirty years ago— Stickies. Jacobite culture is one of the best things in the Irish national tradition, and the last one that comprehensively embraced Protestant and Catholic.

## "The Bridge Of Athlone"
### Or, How They Broke Down The Bridge

"Does any man dream that a Gael can fear?—
    Of a thousand deeds let him learn but one!
The Shannon swept onwards, broad and clear,
    Between the leaguers and broad Athlone.

'Break down the bridge!'—Six warriors rushed
    Through the storm of shot and the storm of shell:
With late, but certain, victory flushed
    The grim Dutch gunners eyed them well.

They wrenched at the planks 'mid a hail of fire:
    They fell in death, their work half done:
The bridge stood fast; and nigh and nigher
    The foe swarmed darkly, densely on.

'O who for Erin will strike a stroke?
    Who hurl yon planks where the waters roar?'
Six warriors forth from their comrades broke,
    And flung them upon that bridge once more.

Again at the rocking planks they dashed;
    And four dropped dead; and two remained:
The huge beams groaned, and the arch down-crashed;—
    Two stalwart swimmers the margin gained.

St. Ruth in his stirrup stood up, and cried,
    'I have seen no deed like that in France!'
With a toss of his head Sarsfield replied,
    'They had luck, the dogs! 'Twas a merry chance!'

O many a year upon Shannon's side
    They sang upon moor and they sang upon heath
Of the twain that breasted that raging tide,
    And the ten that shook bloody hands with Death!"

When Ireland did not slink away from its General Election vote under British intimidation, it had the problem of learning how to fight a war. And what it did between 1919 and 1921 was unprecedented, not only in the history of Ireland since the Williamite conquest, but in the history of modern imperialism.

    The Boer War was not a precedent, because the guerilla phase of that War came after two years of regular warfare between the Armies of the Boer Republic and the British Empire. The Boers were battle-hardened when, at the destruction of their states, they resorted to guerilla methods.

Moylan refers to Lettow-Vorbeck's memoirs, but makes little of them. Certain of the Republican leaders read them in the absence of anything more relevant to their situation. General Paul von Lettow-Vorbeck resisted the British conquest of German East Africa between 1914 and 1918. With a small force of 1,000 Germans and 10,000 Africans, and, cut off from Germany by the British navy, he not only kept his army in being against the larger and better supplied British forces, but actually extended the area under his control. This was perhaps an inspiration to Republican leaders in very general terms, but it is hard to see how they could have gained any particular knowledge from him about the conduct of operations. His Army was the Army of an established state, and it continued to operate as a regular Army on its own ground even when cut off from its state.

The Volunteers who became the IRA had to think how to develop and sustain a war in a militaristic police-state, with world-wide resources, whose agencies honeycombed the country. And, in order to do this, they thought a lot more intensively and effectively than Professor Fitzpatrick's apprentices did when they came up with the notion that ideas played little part on the Irish side in the War of Independence.

Peter Hart was one of those apprentices in 1990, before going on to produce his own master-work on Co. Cork. His contribution to the Trinity Workshop is *Youth Culture And The Cork IRA*, in which he reveals that "the real revolution" was not the effort made by the nation to make good its democratic will against the will and the power of the Imperial state, but was a revolt of the young men against the older men. Young men "formed a sort of underclass without power or authority". They "were reared almost solely by their mothers", from whom they learned their nationalism. And they were urged to rebellion by their mothers and sisters.

The best sense I can make of his argument is as follows. The youth culture of rural Ireland was deferential to the authority of male elders. But, "Traditional youth culture also contained or accepted an element of ritualised rebellion which allowed for a temporary reversal of roles" (p15). On certain occasions, the young men might wear masks and engage in rowdy activity against their elders. "When this mask was assumed by the Straw Boys and their ilk, it was in most senses playful, and the symbols were rendered routine and drained of meaning. As they moved along the continuum ["the continuum" is not explained, B.C.], however, these symbols and rituals acquired political content and became radicalised by confrontation: they became meaningful. In these new contests, they had the power to either mobilise or marginalise the people against whom them were directed" (p17). And then the whole community began to act behind the mask of anonymity of the Straw Boys, and to do things they would not otherwise have done.

"The family resemblance between the IRA operations and the actions of the Straw Boys is close and clear: the same use of masks or blackened or painted faces, often the same 'queer clothes', the same-sized gangs of young bachelors acting anonymously under a 'Captain', the same pseudo-military posturing, the same nocturnal raiding of houses and petty intimidation... The Volunteers evoked the same type of responses as the Straw Boys. Some people welcomed them, others only grudgingly complied with their demands, and a few refused them... The revolution turned the reversal of roles implicit in festival rituals into a political reality".

So the Irish revolution was a Strawing that got out of hand and set the British Empire unravelling!

I have not made a study of Straw Boys, but I remember them. They were still active in Slieve Luacra when I was young. I have a clear memory of a strawing at a wedding in Lamanagh. (In those times it was still usual for wedding celebrations to be held at home.) At a certain point in the festivities a group of young men dressed in straw and with straw helmets covering their faces came in and enlivened the proceedings even more. They sent the newly married couple off to bed with bawdy remarks of encouragement, and then continued their encouragement outside the window. And the following morning, with the marriage thus launched into a good start, the couple went off on honeymoon.

The strawing was an element in a stable way of life. I do not recall any expression of disapproval of it in the townlands with which I was familiar. But I can see that a distaste for strawing was likely to develop amongst elements of the community which were moulding themselves to the refinement of the anti-sexual culture of English Puritanism that was incorporated into the modernising Catholicism of Cardinal Cullen.

*

There is much talk of a martyr complex in connection with the IRA. There is much more evidence of it with regard to the British Army. When I first read a detailed account of the first day in the Battle of the Somme, what it put me in mind of was the Gadarene Swine who were possessed by demons who led them to destruction over the edge of a cliff. They died *en masse*, collectively, in a mindless, futile slow walk into machine-gun fire.

The IRA had no cannonfodder. It acted in the form of small voluntary associations of individuals. Each man was motivated to do what he did on each particular occasion, whereas the man who enlisted in the British Army gave up all right of decision. The survival of each individual was a high priority for each Volunteer in the IRA because survival was itself a kind of victory. In Kitchener's Army you walked into machine-gun fire as part of a herd, or your company officer shot you if you refused to go.

## The "Civil War"

The War of Independence was maintained until the Summer of 1921. The British Government then agreed to a Truce without preconditions so that negotiations could be held. That was the first act in the unravelling of the British Empire. It implicitly acknowledged that the power in Ireland, on which the Black and Tans and the Auxiliaries had been let loose, was a legitimate power.

The plenipotentiaries sent to negotiate in London allowed themselves to be intimidated into signing an Agreement under which Britain would recognise a kind of self-government in Ireland, with certain reservations. But it was a condition that this Irish Government would be conducted as part of the British Empire under the sovereignty of the Crown.

Collins and his colleagues signed the Treaty under pressure of a very short ultimatum from the British Government. If they did not sign within hours, Britain would return to military action. They signed without consulting De Valera, who was head of the Government of the Republic.

De Valera had been on the moderate wing of the Republican movement since 1919. The terms of the Treaty did not meet his moderate requirements.

The essential difference between Collins and De Valera, as far as I could discover, was that Collins signed an Agreement with the intention of breaking it as the opportunity arose, while De Valera wanted an Agreement which would be a settlement.

Collins failed to carry the Army in support of the Agreement which he had signed under duress. The greater part of the Army considered itself bound by its Oath to the Republic and would not walk away from that Oath and take another one which conflicted with it.

De Valera was held responsible by the Treatyites for the "Civil War" which followed because he would not support the Treaty. That view of the matter is ill-founded. De Valera was very much on the political side of the Republican administration of 1919-21. Collins was the Army man—and the Republican intransigent until he signed the Treaty. De Valera did not have the influence to determine how the Army would behave. But he estimated that not enough had been got by Collins in the Treaty to carry the Army in support of it. That proved to be the case, despite Collins's hyper-activity during the six months following the Dail vote accepting the Treaty by a very small majority.

A curious thing now emerges in 'revisionist' history. The Dail whose democratic legitimacy is denied between January 1919 and December 1921, when it was united in supporting Republican Government, suddenly has democratic legitimacy conferred upon it when, under duress, it votes for the Treaty by a small majority.

Everything that was done in Irish politics from December 1921 to 1922 was done under duress—under threat of *"immediate and terrible war"*. The understanding was that the British threat was to adopt in Ireland the methods by which it had won the Boer War twenty years earlier—the sweeping up of the populace of whole regions into Concentration Camps and the establishment of tight control over the country by means of a system of Blockhouses: a thing advocated by Spenser, the poet, three centuries earlier in *A View Of The Present State Of Ireland*.

An Election was held in 1922, and again British intimidation gained a majority for the Treaty: And our modern historians, who treat the 1918 Election as being of no account, hail the 1922 Election as the beginning of Irish democracy.

I cannot see how an election held under threat of war by the British Army, if the people voted the wrong way, can be held to be a free election. Indeed, we are always told nowadays (with regard to the Balkans or Zimbabwe, for instance) that an election in which the electors vote under any kind of duress is not a democratic election.

As for the war of 1922-23, I cannot see how it was a Civil War at all. A civil war is a war within a state to determine what the state is to be. That is what the

English Civil War of the 1640s was, and what the American Civil War of the 1860s was, and the Spanish Civil War of the 1930s. The Royalists and Puritans, like the Yanks and the Confederates, were free agents with disagreements that they could not resolve in any way short of war.

The parties to the Irish 'Civil War' were in agreement about what the state should be. What they disagreed about was whether to submit to a British ultimatum, made under threat of war, that it must be something different.

Collins's intention was to break the Treaty after accumulating a certain amount of power by apparently submitting to it. After his death, many of his colleagues abandoned his project and became Imperialists. What De Valera did in the thirties amounted to implementing Collins's project. He brought about in the 1930s what he had advocated n 1921.

Moylan took up an anti-Treaty position in 1921-22 and never came to think he had been wrong to do so. When he engaged in his good-humoured poetic exchange with Ned Buckley, Treatyite poet of Knocknagree, the Treaty had been undone.

I was at Ned Buckley's pub in Knocknagree a number of times in the late forties and heard him reciting his poems. And the state we were living in was not Kevin O'Higgins's fragment of the Empire. It was the independent state established in substance by De Valera in the 1930s, and formally proclaimed to be a Republic by the Treatyites who had adapted back to Republican ways.

Moylan's Dail speech on the Treaty has been reproduced in this book. His undertaking to exterminate the Loyalists in North Cork was an appropriate response to Lloyd George's threat to apply to Ireland the methods by which the Boers had been defeated.

There is another speech which he made. I quote it here because of the use made of it by Peter Hart. It was made at a meeting in Kanturk and was reported in the *Cork Examiner* of 3rd April, 1922. According to this report, he spoke of bringing the Ulster Unionists in on a stretcher if need be. Although I spent twenty years trying to do something very different in Belfast, I cannot pretend to be horrified by this. That is precisely what was done by the North to the South in the American Civil War, which is usually held up as one of the great events in the history of democracy.

Peter Hart has the following entry in the Index to *The IRA And Its Enemies*: "Moylan, Sean ...anti-Protestant declaration". When you look up the page numbers indicated, you find a quote from Moylan's Dail speech in the treaty Debate: "if there is a war of extermination on us... by God, no loyalist in North Cork will see its finish: (p288 in Hart; the full speech is reproduced above).

This can only be taken to be an anti-Protestant declaration by taking "Protestant" and "Loyalist" to mean the same. And objection can only be taken to the statement if Loyalists are accorded an exceptional political status, a kind of Ascendancy status in the democratic era, which relieves them of all obligation to abide by the will of the democracy amongst which they live.

A Loyalist was somebody who continued to give allegiance to the British state after the Irish democracy had determined to establish an independent Irish state. When the British Government threatened immediate and terrible war if the Dail and the electorate did not return under British sovereignty, Moylan said that, in the event of Britain launching the threatened war, he would make war in similar manner on any in his Brigade area who gave allegiance to the British state in defiance of the Irish democracy. And I just cannot see what was objectionable in that statement.

I am only too well acquainted with the Loyalist mentality. I spent over twenty years close to it in Belfast trying to coax it into democratic ways. I tried to lure it into the democratic politics of the *British* state, and failed. In order to understand it, I traced its development over a number of centuries. I know, for example, that in 1886 even Loyalists of a radical Liberal background took their stand against the *First Home Rule Bill* (providing for devolution within the United Kingdom) on the ground that the Protestants in Ireland were a people superior to others, with superior rights, and that it would be against nature if they were to be subordinated to the common Irish, even in a local government set-up. I had been hoping to find that they had based their opposition to the Home Rule Bill on other grounds, but that is what I found.

The same mentality was still there in 1918-19. The election result was seen as an act of rebellion by the electorate. One Unionist paper even described it as a declaration of war. And all supported the military dictatorship of 1919-21, by which the British Government attempted to break the will of the rebellious democracy and return it to due subordination to the master race.

Hart gives a second "anti-Protestant" quotation from Moylan:

"In an ominous speech given several weeks before the massacre [an alleged massacre of Protestants in West Cork], Sean Moylan, the North Cork Brigade commander and T.D. declared that 'they would give a call to the fine fat Unionists with fine fat cows. The domestic enemy was the most dangerous and they would have to start fighting him now" (p288).

Hart gives the reference for this as the *Cork Weekly Examiner* of 8th April 1922. I have been unable to see a copy of the *Weekly*, but the passage quoted by Hart is in the report of the daily *Cork Examiner* for 3rd April:

"Mr. Sean Moylan, T.D., who was greeted with enthusiasm, said he did not believe in talk or meetings. The people never expected talk from him—what they wanted was action, and that he had tried to give them. He was annoyed with talk about the Treaty, and talk about threats of war. About eighteen months ago he happened to adjudicate in a Court, and had occasion to bind to the peace a volunteer. Later, when they were going into action, the same volunteer came to him and said: 'What will I do—I'm bound to the Peace?' (laughter). The people talked now as if they were all bound to the peace. Continuing, he said he had spoken his views on the Treaty in Dublin, and he stood by what he said there. He said there that he was a Republican—he was a Republican, and if he followed anything it was the Republican ideal (cheers). He was not a party politician, and he was not a follower of Arthur Griffith or of De Valera—he was a Republican, and a whole-hog Republican (cheers). They were told in Dublin that there was no Republican in the North Cork Brigade, and that it had gone Free-State. "We have one or two defaulters", said Mr. Moylan, 'but we managed to carry on during the war without them, and we can carry on without them yet'. There would be no Free State army in the country round there. Dick Mulcahy said that the Irish Republican Army would remain an Irish Republican Army, but he went back on his word, for he was making every attempt to produce a Free State Army from the Republican Army, and was using every omadhaun [fool, Ed.] to help him to do so. People said it was Griffith and Collins that won the war; Padraig O'Keeffe said it was some old woman that boiled a couple of eggs that won the war; but he told them that it was the plain fighting man that won the war, and they would win again. If the people stood by them they would get good value for their money. There were some people who did not stand by them the last time, and they would not be forgotten on the next occasion. They would not bother about Padraig O'Keeffe's old woman so much, but they would give a call to the fine fat Unionists with fine fat cows. The domestic enemy was the most dangerous, and they would have to start fighting him now. He was not absolutely convinced that all the members of the Republican Party wanted to smash the Treaty—he believed a lot of them would take it with modifications. He would not take it; his policy was to smash the Treaty, smash the Provisional Government, throw the Treaty men out of office, and carry on the Republic they had fought for (cheers). These Pro-Treaty men were not doing Ireland's work. They were doing England's work. They heard talk about bringing in Ulster, but, declared Mr. Moylan: 'I'd bring in Ulster on a shutter, and that's the proper way to bring her in'. One idea they (Republicans) should get rid of was that the Free State people were honest— for they were not. No Free State would ever function in North Cork— elections or no elections. He was not speaking for the Army, but he was speaking for a Brigade of it, and let Beggar's Bush take that. They had fought for a Republic, and let them stick to it and keep it (cheers).

"The proceedings ended. Prior to and after the meeting the Kiskeam Brass Band and the Rockchapel Fife and Drum Band paraded the town and played selections of music."

Again, Moylan makes no mention of Protestants. And, as it is well known that he was on good relations with Protestants in his area who were not Loyalists, there are no grounds for suggesting that he meant Protestants when he said Unionists.

The term *Fifth Column* had not yet been invented in 1922. It dates from the Spanish Civil War about fifteen years later, and describes elements in a locality who refuse allegiance to the democratic Republic and are biding their time, holding themselves ready, at an opportune moment, to act with the military forces which are intent on destroying the Republic.

There can be little doubt that, if the Treaty ultimatum had been rejected by either the Dail or the electorate, and Lloyd George had unleashed his threatened war, there would have been Fifth Column elements here and there eager to cooperate.

## The All For Ireland League

Moylan grew up in an area in which, during his youth, there had been political turmoil and development of a kind which made it very unlikely that he would have had an anti-Protestant disposition. In 1910 this development culminated in the displacement of the Home Rule Party from the Parliamentary seats in all but one of the constituencies in Co. Cork. The political force that arose and displaced the Redmondites was the All-For-Ireland League, inspired by Canon Sheehan, with D.D. Sheehan as chief organiser and

William O'Brien as the leader.

The Home Rule Party was opposed by the new political force on three major issues—land purchase by tenant farmers; the intrusion of a Catholic ascendancy element into Home Rule politics; and the hard alignment of the Home Rule Party with the British Liberal Party, which led through the operation of party political conflict within Britain to the hostility of the other party to any concession to Irish national sentiment.

One of the components of the AFIL was the Land And Labour Association, founded in Kanturk in the 1890s.

In British terms, the concept of *"Land and Labour"* makes no sense— Land and Labour exist at the expense of each other. The British attitude to the rural population is exemplified by a conflict which erupted in a conversation between the British Prime Minister, Blair, and the French President, Chirac, early in 2003. Blair criticised Chirac for insisting on EU policies which preserve large numbers of *paysans inutiles*. (He prides himself on speaking French.)

I grew up as a member of a landless family in a community of these *paysans inutiles*, or useless peasants! Thirty years before I was born those *paysans inutiles* rebelled against the Home Rule Party for dragging its heels on the issue of liquidating landlordism, and for breaking with the Parnell tradition by involving a Catholic secret society, the Ancient Order of Hibernians, in the structure of the Party, thus making it a mirror image of the Unionist Party with its Orange Order component.

The matter was thrashed out at public meetings around the County, and the Home Rule Party lost all its seats except one in which it fielded a Protestant candidate. And the Home Rulers did not even contest North Cork in the second of the 1910 Elections.

In his supposedly in-depth investigation of public life in County Cork, Peter Hart skates around that exceptional development which undermined the Home Rule Party in Cork long before 1918, or 1916, or 1914.

I published a brief and inaccurate account of the AFIL development as a pamphlet twenty years ago (1984). I was then preoccupied with Belfast politics, and doing my best to make out a democratic case for the Ulster Unionists in the hope of bringing them to democratic modes of thought. Around 1990 I gave up that project as hopeless, and had time to go into the AFIL phenomenon in greater depth in a book published by *Aubane* a few years ago.

I would have thought that the inaccuracies in the 1984 pamphlet made it suitable for positive use by Hart, and I can only account for his treatment of it by assuming that he did not want to know about the AFIL, because it was incompatible with the stereotype which he set out to impose on his subject.

I wrote that "The AFIL stood down in 1918 so that Sinn Fein might have a clear run against the Irish Party… Over the following years the AFIL strongholds were the areas where the war of independence was chiefly fought."

Hart commented: "A detailed evaluation of the links between AFIL, Sinn Fein and the IRA is impossible at this point as very little is known about O'Brienite membership or support. However, to say, as Brendan Clifford does, that 'the AFIL strongholds were the areas where the war of independence was chiefly fought' is clearly untrue" (p205). And he proceeds to demonstrate that it is "untrue" by saying that there was more Republican military activity in East Cork, which the Redmondites had held in 1910, than in North Cork.

I meant that the War of Independence was mainly fought in the general area where the AFIL had flourished, and I don't think anything else could reasonably be taken from what I wrote. I made no comparison between the different regions of Co. Cork. (I didn't even give the election results.) The comparison was between the general AFIL area (Cork, Kerry, Limerick) and the rest of the country, which had remained staunchly Redmondite in that pre-War era.

It is, of course, true that the transition from the AFIL/Redmondite dispute of 1910 to the Sinn Fein unity of 1918 is not known about in detail. That is because the professional historians—and the historians of the revisionist era most of all—have chosen to delete the history of the land purchase dispute, and all that followed from it in general politics in Cork and thereabouts, from the official record.

One of the longest quotes in Hart's book is from Frank O'Connor's autobiographical short story, written in the 1940s, *The Cornet Player Who Betrayed Ireland*:

"I don't profess to remember what we inhabitants of Blarney Lane were patriotic about: all I remember is that we were very patriotic, that our main principles were something called 'Conciliation and Consent', and that our great national leader, William O'Brien, once referred to us as 'The Old Guard'. Myself and other kids of the Old Guard used to parade the street with tin cans and toy trumpets, singing 'We'll hang Johnnie Redmond on a sour apple tree'.

"Unfortunately, our neighbourhood was bounded to the south by a long ugly street leading up to the cathedral, and the lanes off it were infested with the most wretched specimens who took the Redmondite side for whatever could be got from it in the way of drink" etc.

This is the story of a child whose father had played in a British military band and was now playing in a Cork band with political associations. The Nationalist split brought two bands into being. The father of the narrator, whose chief interest was in the band rather than its political association, was in the wrong band for such political convictions as he had—or else he defected to the wrong band—I forget which. And that was how he "betrayed Ireland".

The thing is written in the same way, as far as I remember, in O'Connor's straight autobiography, *An Only Child*. He was a child of seven at the time of the AFIL/Home Rule split. It would seem that he remembered that conflict as something incomprehensible and never afterwards bothered to find out about it. And I suppose that's fair enough for a writer of fiction for the international market.

(As for the fiction, I was very disappointed with it, apart from a rather charming "civil war" story, *Soirée Chez Une Belle Jeune Fille*, and the story called *Peasants*, in which he displays an unexpected insight into the actual relationship of priests and people out in the country.)

But it is another thing when a historian whose book is published in the name of Lord Clarendon does that sort of thing. In the mood established by his extract from the story, Hart dismisses "the mysteries of Conciliation and Home Rule".

There was nothing mysterious about that conflict. A perfectly intelligible political position was established in it by the *paysans inutiles*. And, though it might have been largely forgotten in the rush of great events from 1914 onwards, there can be little doubt that social culture was influenced by it.

Neither Jack Lane nor myself had any specific knowledge of the AFIL when, having done our best to defend West Belfast against the pogrom of August 1969, we went strongly against the trend of nationalist Ireland of that time by insisting that a radically different approach to the Ulster Protestants must be adopted. We discovered later that what we attempted was in line with what had been attempted by the AFIL in 1910.

(I find I am cited on another page by Hart. He says: "This place, roughly corresponding to the Gaelic heartland Sliabh Luacra was home to the largest concentration of Irish speakers in the county". I am given as the authority for this fact. But, far from saying the Slieve Luacra was Irish speaking, I have said in numerous publications that what is distinctive about it is that it made itself English speaking through a voluntary effort in the early 19th century and transferred much of its culture from Gaelic to English.)

## Conclusion

> "...men like Tom Barry and Sean Moylan were essentially maverick figures" (Michael Hopkinson, *The Irish War Of Independence*, Gill & Macmillan 2002).

Were Barry and Moylan alike? Barry was a British soldier who helped to conquer Mesopotamia for the Empire. He became a soldier in order to be a soldier. He came home, was caught by the politics of nationality, and offered his services as a professional to the amateurs of West Cork, and brought irregular warfare to the brink of positional war of movement at Crossbarry. From 1922 to the end of his life he remained a soldier without a war to fight. War was his vocation.

Moylan was a carpenter obliged by circumstances to take up warfare. If Britain had made a settlement on De Valera's terms in 1921 he would in all probability have returned to carpentry. (Liam Deasy, in Mid-Cork, went back to his trade after the civil war, and spent forty years as a builder before writing his memoirs.) In 1922 he was active in the attempt to avert a Treaty split in the IRA. After the triumph of the Treatyites, he became involved in an effort to forge the anti-Treaty position into a political party. He was a member of the Fianna Fail Government which undid the treaty arrangements in the 1930s. And he was one of those who gave a strong Labour orientation to Fianna Fail.

I grew up knowing that we were his relatives, but I am weak on the specifics of family relationships. We were related through my father's mother, who was a Culloty from Glencollins. He was possibly my father's first and second cousin. At any rate, we were close enough relations for it to be thought that my father might be an avenue of influence to him.

My father was easy-going and unambitious, like myself—what some people would call a ne'er-do-well. He was a bit of a handyman who could suddenly have a notion to do something that had not been done before, and he would set about doing it, which isn't really the way to make money.

My parents eloped and went to live in a rented room in a three-roomed house in Gneeves at the end of a long bohereen, which was a rather unusual thing then. I was born in that rented room. When I was about four, my father, along with uncles on both sides, built a bungalow on a small plot at the beginning of the bohereen. And, when Moylan was Education Minister, a farmer, whose son or daughter—usually a daughter—was about to sit for the Leaving Certificate, would ask to have a private word with my father. And my father would have to explain to him that he had no great influence with Moylan, and that in any case Moylan was one of your sea-green incorruptibles. (Carlyle's phrases were not unknown in Slieve Luacra.)

Many years later I investigated the history of the abolition of the Theatre in Cromwellian England, and I came across a pamphlet on the evils of democracy by an anti-Puritan playwright of the Restoration, Abraham Cowley. Cowley, arguing from classical precedent, maintained that democracies debased the politicians, who had to curry favour with everyone and promise them everything. In those days, republicanism and democracy were thought to be incompatible—republicanism in general being understood as independence of spirit. And it may be that in these days the same thing is very often the case again. But, when I was reading Cowley, I thought of Moylan, the abrasive democrat who curried favour with nobody. He was a thorough republican democrat.

**Brendan Clifford**<br>June 2003

# Postscript To Second Edition

Moylan concludes his War of Independence Memoir with an undertaking to write the story of his part in what is called the Civil War. His Independence Memoir is dated 6th May 1953. Fianna Fail was out of office from 1954 to 1957. It would be surprising if he had not availed of those years as an opportunity to tell the story of the 'Civil War' from his viewpoint. It is a story that badly needs telling, as he knew very well. If he wrote it, there is no trace of it on the public record. It remains therefore a story that has not been *told*.

It is natural that there should be private sensitivities about the publication of authentic 'Civil War' materials. We are, in effect, still in the first generation after the 'Civil War', and, in a society where community is not yet extinct, personal matters of the previous generation still count. But, if the authentic story is not told, a false story will certainly be told.

Indeed, the false story *is being told*. The British state has undertaken to write the history of Ireland between 1914 and 1922 in a way that is advantageous to itself. A brochure issued by Oxford University Press in 2002 openly proclaims: *The Re-writing Of Irish History.*

I grew up, without schooling, on the novels of Canon Sheehan (and Goethe and Dostoevsky—the mind of 'rural Ireland', in its sociable townlands in those backward times, was more European than the mind of the Celtic Tiger is in these modern times) and the poems of Ned Buckley (and Byron and Shelley). The Canon Sheehan novel that was most appreciated (for reasons that I did not then appreciate) was *Glenanaar*. It is many years since I read it. Its theme as I recall it was that political conduct is in great part a product of circumstances. It is not an eternal quality which passes down by heredity through the generations regardless of the situation.

Ned Buckley was a Blueshirt poet. He was both a Blueshirt and a poet. He was sometimes a poet of the Blueshirts. But he was also a poet of the community, and was recognised as such by political enemies, of which Moylan was one. The poetic exchange between Buckley and Moylan (in which Moylan's verses struck me as more elegant) must have been a political event in its time.

I knew nothing of these things when, around the age of ten, I was taken to Knocknagree by Dan Garret of Lamanagh to meet Ned Buckley. One of those occasions had been arranged by Dan to show Ned off to a very intellectual English cousin of my mother's, Nora Godsil. Ned declaimed his verses in the porch of a shop close by his pub, overlooking what was then the Fair Field. This was shortly after the end of the World War, when travel between Ireland and Britain was opened up again. Nora Godsil, who was a teacher or lecturer, then took to spending the entire Summer away from suburban London. Slieve Luacra conversation was addictive.

I took little interest in politics until very many years later. I only knew what everybody knew and made a point of knowing. The first political event that forced itself on my attention was a Blueshirt meeting that was scheduled for Boherbue but was prevented from being held. There was a buzz in the air one Sunday morning around the Chapel, where political meetings were held. A great confrontation was anticipated. But it would seem that the Blueshirts called off their meeting or demonstration in the face of preparations being made to prevent it.

That must have happened near the beginning of the World War.

\*

*A propos* the World War: Moylan clearly had a good conscience about Irish neutrality in it. And in my view he had good reason to have a good conscience.

Jeremy Paxman, the English television showman who has a holiday home in Ireland, writes, mockingly, that the Second World War was called *"The Emergency"* in Ireland. It wasn't. It was called the World War. The *"Emergency"* was the state of readiness in Ireland to resist either Britain or Germany if it tried to extend the war into the 26 Counties, Britain being the more likely invader. I remember seeing armoured cars on manoeuvres west of Boherbue. And signposts were taken down. My uncle, John O'Connor of Gneeves (who was invariably known as Jack Con Horan, because there were so many O'Connors about) kept the Lamanagh Cross signposts under his bed.

Ireland was in a state of Emergency in preparation to cope with an invasion. The suggestion of some recent Irish historians that it was in denial about the existence of the World War is absurd. So is the line by a British war poet about Ireland being the *"neutral island in the heart of man"*. Republican Ireland—and the War made nationalist Ireland Republican again—knew that there was a war on, and knew that this war was a very complex business, far removed from the black-and-white affair of British war propaganda.

Although I was very young I read the papers during the last year or two of the War. (I had picked up reading before going to school from a neighbour, Danny Kane, who was about two years older than me, and lived in a mud house with a thatched roof; and whose grandmother could not be broken of her taste for gruel and passed it on to me.)

And I heard the War discussed then and during the years immediately afterwards in forges and cobblers' shops and rambling houses. And, when I went to London in my early twenties, I was surprised by the badly-informed simple-mindedness that passed for knowledge of the War there. It was sheer mythology; a made-up story.

The World War was launched by Britain as a balance-of-power war against Germany. The German/Polish border dispute was the means used to bring about the War. Poland was encouraged to be intransigent in its determination to hold onto the German city of Danzig. The Poles thought they had a military alliance with Britain and France, but in September 1939 they were left to fight alone. While deserting the Poles, Britain declared war on Germany, but it was a *"Phoney War"*. From September 1939 to May

1940 a British Army squatted in France on a war footing but not engaging in battle. During this period Britain made active preparations for war with Russia in Finland. Russia demanded a piece of Finland to strengthen its Baltic defences, and offered Russian territory to Finland in exchange. When Finland refused the deal, Russia invaded. Britain declared this Russian action to be a crime against civilisation, expelled Russia from the League of Nations, and began preparations to send an army to Finland. But the Finns settled with the Russians before the British Army could be dispatched. And then Germany met the declarations of war on it by striking at the British and French Armies on its frontier and breaking them.

Britain had played the leading part in this bizarre sequence of events. The French, having been led to disaster by Britain, made a settlement with Germany in June 1940. They had declared war on Germany and lost. With the French Army broken and a German Army in occupation of France, the only alternative to a settlement that was available to the French regime was terrorist action against the occupying force—such as the Iraqi regime only resorted to in 2003 when denied the possibility of a settlement.

Hitler, who was a great admirer of the British Empire, allowed a substantial remnant of the defeated British Army to be brought home from Dunkirk. He positively wanted the British Empire to be preserved. He made no attempt to invade Britain during the months when it was highly vulnerable, and did not begin bombing British cities until Churchill launched a senseless bombing raid on Berlin.

In June 1940 Britain resumed the Phoney War stance of the earlier period. It denounced the French for making a settlement, but it made no attempt to carry the war to Germany itself. The only rational purpose in this Phoney War was to keep Germany on an active war footing in the hope that the war would spread. This policy bore fruit in the volatile situation in eastern Europe in June 1941 when Germany and Finland launched an invasion of the Soviet Union. From that moment on, the substance of the war in Europe was the conflict between Nazism and Bolshevism.

From June 1941 to June 1944, the *"cause of civilisation"* came to depend on the triumph of Bolshevism. A year and a half earlier, when Britain was getting ready to make war on Russia in alliance with the Finns, the enemy of civilisation was Bolshevism. But civilisation came to depend on the triumph of Bolshevism when Germany in alliance with Finland attacked the Soviet Union.

From June 1941 to June 1944 Britain was a minor ally of Russia, and the mainstream British media functioned in many respects as an extension of the Soviet propaganda system.

Britain had no taste for serious fighting in the War it had brought about. It resisted both Russian demands and American urgings to open a Second Front in France in 1942 and 1943. It did so in 1944 because it was evident after the Battle of Kursk that the Red Army was going to roll up the German Army, and that any further delay was likely to see Stalin replacing Hitler at Calais.

Britain supposedly went to war to liberate Poland, having allowed it to be conquered without firing a shot in support of it, despite Treaty obligations. Poland was liberated from Germany by the Red Army in 1944. Until the final surrender of Germany in 1945 the Soviet presence in Poland was presented in the British media as liberation. After that point, it began to be presented as subjugation and oppression.

Churchill regarded Bolshevism as the fundamental enemy of the civilisation that Britain stood for, and in 1927 he went to Rome to praise Mussolini as the saviour of civilisation. After 1945 he reasserted the view that Bolshevism was the fundamental enemy. The *"anti-fascist war"*—the war against the saviour of civilisation in alliance with the fundamental enemy of civilisation—was the accidental product of bungling foreign policy.

Field Marshal Alanbrooke, who was Churchill's military adviser in the later stages of the war on Germany, revealed in his Diaries that Churchill expressed the wish to use nuclear weapons on Russia after Russia had defeated Germany. But Britain did no have any at that point. And, when it got them, Churchill was out of office and the Soviet Union had itself acquired the nuclear deterrent.

Britain, the Superpower of the 1920s and 1930s, brought about a World War and bungled its conduct of the war to such a degree that in the course of it the fundamental enemy became the dominant power of Europe. That was the crowning achievement of the British Empire.

The Cold War of 1945-1990 was a continuation of the Second World War. It remained a Cold War because the enemy—the Ally which defeated Germany—had nuclear weapons. When the Soviet regime collapsed in 1991, Bolshevism was authoritatively described in British governing circles as having been a great criminal conspiracy during its entire existence. No dissent from that view was audibly expressed anywhere within the spectrum of British politics.

Moylan had a good conscience about Irish neutrality in that utterly unprincipled War. And I can see no good reason why he should have had a bad conscience about it.

(In the War mythology developed long after the event, the British decision to go to war is presented as having had something to do with saving the Jews. It hadn't. The Jewish issue did not figure in the British decision to start a war on Germany, and it was not given prominence even in the later stages of the war, when the Polish underground presented Churchill with evidence about the extermination camps. Anti-Semitism was very widespread in Europe. In the 1920s and 1930s the new states in Eastern Europe had been strongly anti-Semitic without any prompting from Hitler. The British and American authorities judged that it would not be advantageous to the war effort to make too much of what Hitler was doing to the Jews.

Britain did not go to war to save the Jews. But the Jews were a casualty of the way Britain went to war. The German Government had no plans before the war to exterminate the Jews. The extermination of the Jews was extemporised in the hinterland of the fearsome war with Russia, in which the death of hundreds of thousands was a commonplace event.)

\*

Irish neutrality in this World War, whose complexity was better understood on all sides in Ireland than in Britain (where narrow blinkers of self-righteousness are always worn on such occasions), had a unifying effect. No public figure, Treatyite or anti-Treatyite, apart from James Dillon, wanted to put Ireland at the disposal of Britain for war purposes. And Churchill's agent, Elizabeth Bowen, considered Dillon to be a Fascist.

Ireland could not have gone to war on its own account. It was not allowed to have an Army under the terms of the Treaty, only a minimally-armed Defence Force. And, when De Valera broke the Treaty, Britain ensured that he could not acquire major armaments. Britain's demand that Ireland should enter the war as an ally meant only that it should place itself at Britain's disposal as a naval base and an air base.

The Civil War division melted away between 1939 and 1945 in the face of a common determination that Ireland should not be used as cannonfodder in another of Britain's wars, and that an invasion of Ireland, by whichever side, should be met with a people's war of the kind that was fought in 1919-21. And, shortly after the War, Civil War enemies (General MacEoin, Piaras Beaslai, Florrie O'Donoghue, Tom Barry and Oscar Traynor) got together to publish a joint account of the War of Independence—a significant book which has been relegated to oblivion in this 'revisionist' era, but which Aubane intends to republish

Some of the people I knew well in the townlands west of Boherbue were Blueshirts and others were Republicans. I did not know this at the time. I found it out much later when I found the Blueshirt magazine in a Library.

The only echo of the Civil War on a personal level that I can recall had to do with a wedding, in 1945 or 1946 as far as I can judge, between a cousin of my mother's and a cousin of Michael Collins. The reception was held in the Hi B in Mallow. The sociable meeting of the two sides had an edge of political excitement to it. And, after the wedding, there was the saga of an overcoat. Somebody on the other side was given a lift to the reception by somebody on our side and left an overcoat in the car. For weeks afterwards negotiations went on about the return of the overcoat. As I recall, they were long-drawn-out and functioned as a kind of evocation and marginalisation of Civil War feelings

A couple of years after the World War the first Coalition Government was formed. John A. Costello, the former Treatyite, was Taoiseach. Sean MacBride, IRA Chief of Staff in the 1930s, who was too Republican to join Fianna Fail, was Foreign Minister. I don't think that that combination would have been possible but for the common front presented by Treatyites and anti-Treatyites to British demands during the War.

In 1948 the State was declared to be a Republic. De Valera had made the state an actual republic, repealing the Oath of Allegiance to Britain, issuing passports without reference to the King, and conducting an independent foreign policy at the most testing moment. When questioned on the matter, he said that the state corresponded with the meaning of *"republic"* given in the dictionary. The *"dictionary republic"* was ridiculed in some quarters, but Dev was content to give the state the substantial character of a republic, and then let inessential matters be. He did not make the gesture of formally taking Ireland out of the British Commonwealth. He simply ignored the British Commonwealth, and let the British authorities make what they would of the fact that Ireland ceased to play any part in Commonwealth affairs.

(The deliberate ambiguity in which De Valera left the formal relationship between Ireland and the Commonwealth was of assistance to the Indian National Congress in its negotiations with the British Government after 1945. The Indians (who had been considerably influenced by Sinn Fein around 1920) could cite Ireland as a precedent and ask why they could not follow Ireland's good example—which was of course a very bad example from the British viewpoint, but one which they had difficulty explaining away. When Dev got his first break from office after fifteen years he made a world tour, and his first port of call was India, where he was feted.)

In recent years it has been argued that, because Dev did not make the formal gesture of declaring that Ireland had withdrawn from the Commonwealth, it would be in accordance with his policy if Ireland now rejoined the Commonwealth. But that is false reasoning. The direction of movement under Dev was away from Empire and Commonwealth. He established actual independence in a dangerous situation, and avoided provocative gestures because the situation was dangerous. Rejoining the Commonwealth would signify a change of direction, a U-turn back towards the Empire. And the Empire is not dead. The Imperial aspiration has been reviving strongly in Britain in recent years. It is inhibited only by weakness, and it hopes to grow stronger. The propaganda barrage directed at the land de-colonisation movement in Zimbabwe would have been a preliminary to direct action if Britain had been stronger, or if the major African States had been less stubborn in their refusal to go along with British policy.

The 'land settlement' made by Cecil Rhodes in Rhodesia (Zimbabwe) a hundred years ago is comparable with the land settlement made three hundred years ago in Ireland under the Williamite conquest (known as the Penal Laws). It took the Irish two hundred years to undo the Williamite settlement, and they were slandered the whole time while doing it.

It is evident that Zimbabwe is still Rhodesia to a very influential section of British political opinion, and that the colonial stratum of great landowners established by Cecil Rhodes is equated with 'civilisation'. The *"white man's burden"* has not yet been laid down. A voluntary Irish return to the Commonwealth would, in these circumstances, be certain to add support to the Imperial revival.

Fine Gael's formal declaration that the state was a republic added nothing to the substantively republican character of the state. And its withdrawal of Ireland from the British Empire and Commonwealth did not reduce Irish participation in that institution, because it had already ceased to participate.

It was nevertheless a significant event. While what it abolished was only the empty semblance of an Irish relationship with the British Empire and Commonwealth, that was not nothing. The British Foreign Office has a talent for making political use of mere semblances. The Treaty party deprived it of the last semblance of Irish participation in its Empire. And the fact that it was the Treaty party that did it was the most significant thing about it.

I recall that the event was celebrated across the board in North Cork—a three-seat constituency which elected a TD from each of the three parties—Anti-Treatyite, Treatyite, and Labour. On reflection I can only think that the event aroused such enthusiasm, despite the fact that it changed nothing in the substantive character of the state, because it was understood to be the end of the 'Civil War' insofar as matters of substance were concerned. The Treatyites had gone full circle and returned to their initial position—the position of Collins in 1922, which they had lost in 1924.

De Valera had established the *"dictionary republic"*, the republic of accomplished fact. And he had discarded the Constitution that Britain had imposed, under a hollow pretence of 'negotiation', in 1922. He proposed a new Constitution in 1937, to be enacted by referendum. The Treatyite party had campaigned vigorously against the 1937 Constitution. But now in 1948 it put the cap on the 'dictionary republic', simply taking the 1937 Constitution for granted in doing so.

I gave a talk on the Civil War at a meeting in Newmarket about ten years ago. The packed meeting engaged in a vigorous discussion following my talk. I was informed that this was the first public meeting on the subject ever held in Newmarket. I would possibly have refused to speak on the subject if I had known that beforehand. On the other hand, possibly not. I had spent twenty years in a dangerous situation taking a contentious stand. Coming from a close involvement in Belfast politics, I was out of touch with the tendency of things in the Republic. And so I blurted out what I had to say, without regard for sensitivities, as I was accustomed to do in the North. I gathered that the organisers of the meeting were on tenterhooks and would not have been surprised if it had collapsed into disorder. Nothing like that happened. There was a long, intense discussion, from which I learned at least as much as the audience.

The gist of what I said was that the Civil War division was not a class division (as the strong Marxist tendency of 'Official' Republicanism maintained) or a conflict between secularists and the clergy (despite the excommunications). It was fought because of the Oath of Allegiance, which was not a trivial thing to people who felt themselves in honour bound. And the outcome of the Civil War, after the shooting had stopped, was that the new state acquired a functional two-party system very early in its existence.

My long involvement with Six County affairs had made me acutely aware of the crucial importance of political parties to a system of representative government based on a democratic electoral franchise.

My position in the North was that it had never been democratically governed because it had always been governed outside the party-political system of the state. In 1969-70, along with Jack Lane, I had argued at meetings in Dublin, Cork and Limerick that the Ulster Protestant community would not give way under pressure (which was then the general expectation), but would hit back hard, and that 'normal' political conduct could not come about in the North until the normal political structures of either the British state or the Irish became operative in it. (I debated this matter with Eoghan Harris thirty years ago at a meeting in Limerick organised by the late Jim Kemmy. Harris denounced me as an Imperialist—and then went on to become one in earnest himself.)

Having been dealing for 20 years with a situation in which there was no party system, properly so-called, I saw the party-system that emerged from the Civil War as something which placed the Irish state amongst the advanced democracies. The typical post-colonial situation is that there is one great all-embracing national party. Unity in this single national party is a necessary means of achieving independence. At the moment of independence the new state is a one-party state in fact, even if the existence of other parties is not prohibited.

The Imperial Power tries to split the national independence movement. If it succeeds, it does not concede independence. If it fails, and is obliged to concede independence, the result is that the new state is governed by the all-embracing national party which forged the unity of the populace and has unrivalled prestige as the party which obliged the Imperial Power to let go. The Imperial Power, which bears the actual responsibility for this state of affairs, then condemns the newly-independent state as undemocratic because it is in fact a one-party state. And the external pressure applied by the former Imperial master tends to perpetuate the one-party arrangement which had been a pre-requisite for the achievement of independence. The development of a multi-party system then becomes highly problematical.

The Irish State was proclaimed by the attempted *coup d'etat* of 1916. It was founded as a functioning administration in 1919 on the basis of the overwhelming democratic mandate of the 1918 General Election. The actions of the 1919 Dail, and of the Republican Army which came into being to uphold Dail government against the British Government which tried to carry on governing in defiance of the election result, were ratified by the Local Government elections of 1920 and the General Election of 1921.

The Dail was a *de facto* one-party Parliament from 1919 to 1922, being boycotted by the small Ulster Unionist minority and the minuscule Redmondite remnant. Britain suffered its second crushing electoral defeat in Irish politics in 1921 (its catspaws in the 26 Counties abandoning the democratic constituencies and retreating to the elite University franchise). If, in the London negotiations of late 1921, it had conceded independence to the 26 Counties in which its supporters had not even contested a seat, *de facto* one-party government would have continued. It is probable that Sinn Fein would have held indisputable dominance for a generation, and the emergence of a viable alternative party capable of winning an election would have been problematical. (As I write Kenya has had its first change of government. The national party which gained independence two generations ago has lost an election for the first time. An Opposition capable of winning an election has eventually materialised, and claims that its victory marks the beginning of Kenyan democracy. That is nonsense, though perhaps an understandable form of nonsense. The cause of long-term government by a single party in Kenya, as in many other countries, lies in the way that the Imperial Power exercised control.)

When Jack Lane asked me to write a postscript on the Civil War for the second edition of this book, I thought I should check that certain statements I had made on the basis of memory were true. The outstanding one was the assertion that in the 1921 Election Sinn Fein gained all of the democratic representation without a single person voting for it. I knew that was the case, but felt I should make absolutely certain, and also make the statement credible to the reader by giving an authoritative reference for it.

In Britain there is a standard multi-volume reference work on elections, F.W.S. Craig's *British Parliamentary Election Results*. An Irish counterpart was published by the Royal Irish Academy in 1978: *Parliamentary Election Results In Ireland, 1801-1922*. I found a copy of it in a Library, flicked to where the 1921 results should be, and found that they weren't there. The last General Election dealt with was 1918, though By-election results were continued up to 1922.

Could it be that I had simply imagined, not only the result of the 1921 Election, but even the fact that there had been an Election in 1921? Was it true, after all, what Professor Roy Foster said in his Oxford University book, *The Irish Story*, that we just invented suitable stories and pretended (without even knowing that we were pretending) that they were historical facts?

Fortunately I was able to gain access to a microfilm of the London *Times* for 1921. It confirmed that it is those who omit to mention the 1921 Election who are *"making it up"*. Here is the *Times* report:

"The elections to the Southern Parliament have taken place without the slightest disturbance. In every case except one—namely County Donegal, where there were six Sinn Fein candidates and one Unionist candidate for six seats—the returns for the whole Southern Parliament were unopposed. At the last moment, however, the Unionist candidate withdrew. The result is a sweeping victory for Sinn Fein and a virtually unanimous repudiation of the Government of Ireland Act.

"Four member—Messrs. Thrift, Alton and Fitzgibbon, and Sir James Craig M.D.—were returned this morning for Dublin University. Their ideal is a united Ireland, but they are prepared to employ the present Act as a stepping stone to better things. With these four exceptions Sinn Fein secured today the return of some 120 out of the total membership of 128 in the Southern Parliament. The nomination for the National University will be held to-morrow, when it is certain that four Sinn Feiners will be returned" (14 May, 1921. 'Dublin University', of course, is Trinity College.)

The re-writing of Irish history of the 1918-22 period, in line with the present day requirements of the British state, that is being fostered by Oxford University, was given concentrated expression in a long letter in the *Irish Times* on 24th September 2003. It denies that the War of Independence was fought to give effect to the democratic electoral mandate of 1918, and it denies by implication that it was a War at all, suggesting that it was only a kind of banditry: "...the gunmen were working to their own bloodthirsty agenda:, and they engaged in "assassination". (The word *"assassination"* is used as a term of disparagement here, which is a rather old-fashioned usage for our very 'modernist' revisionists, seeing that assassination has been made a normal mode of action by the Israeli Government in dealing with the 'terrorism' of the Palestinians, whose country is being taken from them, and that the American and British Governments launched their war on Iraq with what they frankly described as an assassination attempt.)

The *Irish Times* writer comments on the General Election:

> "Whatever the mandate of 1918 was, it was not for further violence. Those who voted were not asked for, and did not give, approval for a war. Those who started the assassinations of policemen in 1919 were a tiny self-appointed group".

It is true that Sinn Fein did not ask the electors to vote for war in 1918. It asked them to vote for independence, which they did. I know of no instance anywhere in the world where a decision to go to war was put to the vote of the electorate. By normal democratic reckoning the categorical refusal of the British Government to contemplate Irish independence, even though the Irish electorate had voted for it, was an effective mandate for disabling the structures of the British state in Ireland by whatever means were appropriate to the task. And unfortunately the British attitude made warfare the only appropriate method.

The writer continues: "It [the 1918 Election] was certainly the expression of a majority wish for a 32-county state outside the United Kingdom and a hope that this claim could be pursued at the Peace Conference in Paris. But the major obstacle to the fulfilment of this wish was the resistance of Protestant Ulster."

In fact , Irish independence, in whole or in part, was ruled out of the question by the British Government.

By December 1921, when the Treaty split occurred, Britain had already partitioned the country and set up a Northern Ireland Government in the Six Counties. Partition was not the issue in the Treaty debate. The issue was the subordination of the 26 Counties to the sovereignty of the Crown. Moylan's strong speech against the Treaty was a response to the speech of General Mulcahy immediately preceding describing the dreadful things that would follow if the Dail rejected the British ultimatum. Moylan was prepared to face the British onslaught. When he spoke of applying strong measures against Unionists who acted with the British Government in a war of extermination, he was not referring to Ulster Unionists in the Six Counties.

What was at issue between Ireland and Britain in December 1921 and in the first half of 1922 was not the complicated situation in the Six Counties. What was at issue was whether the 26 County region, where Sinn Fein held every Parliamentary seat outside Trinity College, should have republican government in defiance of Britain or should submit to Crown sovereignty under the threat of all-out British war.

The single party form of government in nationalist Ireland existed for about three years (1919-22). It gave way to a multi-party structure as an accidental by-product of the 'Civil War' (1922-23). A functional Opposition was in being by 1926 and came within a whisker of forming a Government in 1927. (And it would have been much better for the future prospects of the Treaty party if it had gone out of office in 1927, because it was its conduct as a Government in 1927-32 that undermined it to such an extent that it has never since won an election, or been the largest party.)

The fact that the Irish party structure is an accidental product of the 'Civil War' is held in some quarters to de-legitimise it. The idea that only political parties based on class, or the ideology of class, are authentic, is not soundly based. The very system itself (of representative government by alternating parties) was an accidental product of the long English Civil War and its longer aftermath. (A resumption of the Civil War which began in 1641 was barely averted in 1714. It flared up again in 1745, and if Bonnie Prince Charlie had been bolder and had marched on London there would probably have been another change of regime—and in 2003 we all know what regime change can lead to.)

The replacement of the Whig/Liberal Party by the Labour Party did not result from the systematic rise of class politics. It was an accidental consequence of the self-destruction of the Liberal Party under the stresses of the Great War which it launched in 1914. There has been only one period when the Labour Party governed as a Socialist Party (1945-51), and there are strong signs that the present Labour leadership hankers to return to the Liberal fold, which had been its natural habitat until the Liberal Party broke up.

The American party system is likewise a product of the Civil War. The Democrats are the party of the Confederate secession—the defeated party in the War.

The British and American party systems are the longest-established, the most durable, and the most powerful. It is therefore hardly reasonable to regard the Irish party system as unauthentic on the grounds that it is the accidental product of Civil War. It is, like the British and American systems, a structure thrown up by actual events of historic importance, and it is therefore appropriate to the situation in which it exists.

The British purpose in manipulating the Irish into a Civil War was, of course, not to give the new state a multi-party structure. Its purpose was to weaken the Irish State. It would undoubtedly have been better if a united Sinn Fein party had continued in being during the 1920s and 1930s, whatever difficulties this might have put in the way of the development of an alternative party capable of governing. But it is not a slight thing that, having been manipulated into a Civil War by Britain, we forged a party-system from the war.

It is true that our party system is somewhat lop-sided. That is due to the fact that Michael Collins's successors lost sight of his purpose in signing the treaty and became an Empire party under the guidance of Kevin O'Higgins.

(Jack Lane suggests that the Blueshirt movement brought Michael Collins back on the agenda of the Treaty party, and was the beginning of its return to Republican ways under pressure of the Fianna Fail victories in 1932 and 1933. That strikes me as a sound idea. The process was completed by the neutrality consensus in the Second World War, which prepared Fine Gael for its Republican declaration of 1948.)

Moylan was an active participant in the life of the state for thirty-six years after the moment at which his War of Independence memoir ends. He was both an observant and a reflective person. I am a product of the same general culture that produced him, and I grew up in that culture at a time when he had become a major figure in it. I have set out the sense which events between 1921 and 1948 make to me. I would guess that they made much the same kind of sense to Moylan. But that is something that cannot be known unless he continued his Memoir, and unless the continuation is found and published.

**Brendan Clifford**
*September 2003*

## Pamphlets from the Aubane Historical Society:

* **St. John's Well,** *by Mary O'Brien*
* **Canon Sheehan: A Turbulent Priest,** *by B. Clifford*
* **Local Evidence to the Devon Commission,** *by Jack Lane*
* **The Life and Death of Mikie Dineen** *by Jack Lane*
* **Aubane School and its Roll Books** *by Jack Lane*
* **Kilmichael: the false surrender.** A discussion *by Peter Hart, Padraig O'Cuanacháin, D. R. O'Connor Lysaght, Dr Brian Murphy and Meda Ryan* with "Why the ballot was followed by the bullet" *by Jack Lane and Brendan Clifford.*
* **Evidence to the Parnell Commission** *by Jeremiah Hegarty, Canon Griffin and Dr Tanner MP*
* **Notes on the history of Millstreet** *by Canon Michael Costello and Pádraig O'Maidín*
* **A Millstreet Medley** *by various authors with rediscovered material by Canon Sheehan and Eoghan Ruadh O'Súilleabháin*
* **Millstreet—"the cockpit of Ireland"** *by various authors*
* **Aubane versus Oxford—a response to Professor Roy Foster and Bernard O'Donoghue** *by various authors*
* **Millstreet—a "considerable town"** *by various authors*
- **A Millstreet Miscellany** *by various authors*
- **The 'Boys' of the Millstreet Battalion Area**—Some personal accounts of the War of Independence *by veterans of the Battalion*

Orders to: Noreen Kelleher
Aubane Historical Society
Aubane
Millstreet, Co. Cork
(Tel: 029 70 360)